Different Beasts

Different Beasts

Humans and Animals in Spinoza and the Zhuangzi

SONYA N. ÖZBEY

OXFORD
UNIVERSITY PRESS

Oxford University Press is a department of the University of Oxford. It furthers
the University's objective of excellence in research, scholarship, and education
by publishing worldwide. Oxford is a registered trade mark of Oxford University
Press in the UK and certain other countries.

Published in the United States of America by Oxford University Press
198 Madison Avenue, New York, NY 10016, United States of America.

© Oxford University Press 2024

All rights reserved. No part of this publication may be reproduced, stored in
a retrieval system, or transmitted, in any form or by any means, without the
prior permission in writing of Oxford University Press, or as expressly permitted
by law, by license, or under terms agreed with the appropriate reproduction
rights organization. Inquiries concerning reproduction outside the scope of the
above should be sent to the Rights Department, Oxford University Press, at the
address above.

You must not circulate this work in any other form
and you must impose this same condition on any acquirer.

Library of Congress Cataloging-in-Publication Data
Names: Ozbey, Sonya Nihan, author.
Title: Different beasts : humans and animals in Spinoza
and the Zhuangzi / Sonya N. Özbey.
Description: New York, NY, United States of America :
Oxford University Press, [2024] |
Identifiers: LCCN 2023028394 (print) | LCCN 2023028395 (ebook) |
ISBN 9780197686386 (hardback) | ISBN 9780197686393 (epub) | ISBN 9780197686416
Subjects: LCSH: Spinoza, Benedictus de, 1632–1677. | Zhuangzi. |
Philosophical anthropology. | Human beings.
Classification: LCC BD450 .O888 2024 (print) | LCC BD450 (ebook) |
DDC 128—dc23/eng/20231027
LC record available at https://lccn.loc.gov/2023028394
LC ebook record available at https://lccn.loc.gov/2023028395

DOI: 10.1093/oso/9780197686386.001.0001

Printed by Integrated Books International, United States of America

Contents

Acknowledgments ix
List of Abbreviations xiii

Introduction: Cross-Cultural Philosophy and Critical Animality
Studies 1
  A. Intersectional Critiques of Dualistic Thinking 2
  B. Seeking a Savior in "Monistic" Philosophies 5
  C. Why Compare? Critical Mimesis and New Areas of Inquiry 10
  D. Roadmap 15

PART I. READING SPINOZA WITH THE *ZHUANGZI*: CONVERSATIONS AND TOOLKITS

1. Contexts and Means for Interpreting the *Zhuangzi* 21
  1.1 Inching Out of Animality: Early Chinese Recipes for Power and
     Teachings for Humanity 23
  1.2 Loitering Idly with Zhuangzi's Big but "Useless" Words 32

2. Contexts and Means for Interpreting Spinoza 46
  2.1 Lifting Up and Placing Down the Man into the Machine-
     World: Contested Routes to Knowledge and Salvation 48
  2.2 Seeking True Philosophy, in the Proper Order, with Spinoza 56

Conclusion: Strange Companions—Thinking about Animals with
Spinoza and the *Zhuangzi* 69
  A. Form, Context, and Function 70
  B. Hermeneutical Challenges and Opportunities 75

PART II. PORTRAYALS OF HUMAN DISTINCTIVENESS

3. Rich in Complexity: Human Distinctiveness in Spinoza 81
  3.1 "That Eternal and Infinite Being We Call God, or Nature" 82
  3.2 Eliminating the Anthropomorphic God and the Theomorphic Man 84
  3.3 What Distinguishes a Man from an Ass 88
  3.4 A Ladder of Complexity: From Worm to Man 94

4. Pinnacles of Versatility: Human Distinctiveness in the *Zhuangzi*   99
    4.1 The Ten Thousand Things under Heaven   101
    4.2 Dethroning the Heart   103
    4.3 Finding the Pivot of all *Daos*   109
    4.4 What Distinguishes People from Turtles and Fish   112

Conclusion: Admiring and Humbling Humanity   118
    A. Like a Worm, Like a Tree   118
    B. Finding Empowerment in a Univocal versus Polyvocal World   121
    C. Certainty with a Bias, Humility without an Agenda   123

PART III. ANIMAL AFFECTS: CURIOSITY VERSUS THREAT

5. Zhuangzi and the Happy Fish: Animal Affects in the *Zhuangzi*   131
    5.1 Wandering with the Fish, Zhuangzi, and Huizi   132
    5.2 Effective and Affective Communication in the *Zhuangzi*   139
    5.3 Bonding through Banter and Laughter   149

6. Spinoza's Serpentine Worries: Animal Affects in Spinoza   156
    6.1 Making Use of Beasts as We Please   157
    6.2 Choosing Eve over the Serpent   161
    6.3 On Misanthropic Melancholy and Fraternal Cheer   167

Conclusion: Affects, Solidarity, and Power   173
    A. The Cementing and Loosening of Human Bonds   173
    B. The Power to Include and Exclude   179

PART IV. THE ORDERLY AND THE CHAOTIC

7. From Nature's Order to Civil Order: Onto-Political Formations in Spinoza   187
    7.1 Individuation and Identity in an Orderly World   188
    7.2 Uniting as One Mind and Body   193
    7.3 Big Fish Eat Small Fish   199

8. Unmanaging the Personal and the Political Body in the *Zhuangzi*   205
    8.1 From Unity to Fragmentation: Undermining the Heart of the Personal and Political Body   206
    8.2 Transforming into a Rat's Liver or a Butterfly's Dream   210
    8.3 Muddying the Waters: Reimagining Hundun and Antiquity   216

Conclusion: The State of the World: The Topsy-Turvy and
    the Ship-Shape   227
    A. Tales of Identity and Disintegration   228
    B. In the Absence of Civil Order   231

PART V. HUMANS' ANIMALITY: TEXTUAL
TRACES AND ABSENCES

9. Rethinking Animal Imagery in the *Zhuangzi*   239
    9.1 The *Zhuangzi* on Distant Lands, Humble Professions,
         and Unruly Minds   241
    9.2 Women in the *Zhuangzi*   255

10. Animalized Others in Spinoza's "Imagination"   262
    10.1 On "Turks" and Common People   263
    10.2 On Women, the Infantile, and the Sub-rational   268

Conclusion: Our Kind   279
    A. Those "We" Uplift or Leave Behind   279
    B. The Limits of What "We" Can Imagine "Us" to Be   282

Epilogue: Looking at There and Then to Reflect on Here and Now   287

References   293
Index   309

Acknowledgments

It is a well-known joke that academics publishing their first monographs have the longest list of acknowledgments. One likely reason for this pattern is that the publication of the first book requires navigating an intimidating, as well as greatly consequential, intellectual and emotional territory. My long list of acknowledgments reflects the abundance of sources of goodwill and generosity that helped me navigate this process.

As a student of early Chinese thought, I shall start with the roots. Had I not met Franklin Perkins in graduate school, I would not even have the opportunity to be in this field. Aside from introducing me to a new and rich world of ideas and voices, he has imparted in me a determined attitude to recognize and own my arguments. Another important force in my graduate training was Brook Ziporyn, whose catching zest for big questions and openness to spirited conversations helped sustain the life of this mind when I was overwhelmed with all the different learning curves I have had to climb. I also owe special thanks to Richard A. Lee Jr., whose disagreements with me on Spinoza taught me how to carefully craft my arguments, word by word, so that they can hopefully hold some sway, if not wield persuasive force. He used to joke that the graduate school only grants one a learner's permit. I disagree only because it does not do justice to the fact that these men went above and beyond to encourage me in pursuing my own research intuitions and interpretive approaches. For that I will forever be thankful to them.

As we link with different networks of ideas and practices, our questions, approaches, and methods shift, expand, and mold to a different reality. A turning point for this monograph was my virtual book manuscript workshop, which was held at the University of Michigan in March 2020—when we all thought the world might be coming to an end. The internal and external readers, Erica Fox Brindley, Miranda Brown, Yitzhak Y. Melamed, Michael Nylan, and Tad Schmaltz, compelled and encouraged me rethink and recast the structure, purposes, and even the arguments of the project. I owe every one of these scholars a tremendous amount of gratitude. Conversations with them allowed me to have an honest conversation with myself about my intended audience, the stakes of the comparison, and my own biases. Their rigorous and copious feedback, which they conscientiously delivered during a time of global uncertainty, made me realize what makes not simply successful academics but true citizens of the world of ideas: they show up for others.

It takes a strong person to ask for help when needed. Miranda Brown continually volunteered to offer help especially when I was not strong enough to ask for it. Tad Schmaltz was always available for advice and support, even when he was chairing a department during the first chaotic years of the pandemic. Sarah Buss and Christi Merrill came forward to share their thoughtful feedback about the project at key moments. Donald S. Lopez Jr. offered invaluable guidance with super-human speed about the framing of the project and its publication. S. E. Kile generously shared his book proposal with me when I was preparing to approach publishers. Bill Baxter, Christian de Pee and Reginald Jackson offered not only intellectual support but also moral encouragement during difficult moments. Alexus McLeod readily shared his manuscript with me, months before its publication, before he had even met me. Mercedes Valmisa, Aaron Stalnaker, and Michael Ing offered timely support and advice about the publication process when I was wavering, which helped pull me through to the other side.

On the other side of the process, during the preparation of the book for publication, my acquisition editor, Lucy Randall, expertly and efficiently guided the initial and critical stages of the process, when she was due to give birth soon. Lauralee Yeary offered her guidance for part of the review process, when Lucy was on maternity leave. Christopher Ahn offered his meticulous copy-editing and formatting services, which was greatly appreciated during a process when planning and accuracy are key. Brent Matheny, Jeremy Toynbee, Stuart Allison, and Patterson Lamb offered their dedicated and timely support throughout the production process, which was pivotal in ensuring a smooth workflow during a critical period. I owe all these individuals my deepest appreciation for their intellectual labor and expertise.

While working on this project, I was inspired and enriched by a community of scholars whose paths crossed with mine thanks to the workshop series: *Zhuangzi* Beyond the Inner Chapters. I owe thanks to each one of these *Zhuangzi* lovers for sharing their expertise and often times laughter: Youngsun Back, Erica Fox Brindley, Scott Cook, Steven Coutinho, Mark Csikszentmihalyi, Wim De Reu, Michael Dufresne, Chris Fraser, Joanna (Asia) Guzowska, Esther Sunkyung Klein, Jing Liu, David McCraw,

Hans-Georg Moeller, So Jeong Park, Franklin Perkins, Hagop Sarkissian, Stephen Walker, John Williams, Brook Ziporyn, and Tobias Zürn.

The life of the mind needs both material and immaterial support to fare well. I owe special acknowledgment to the Lieberthal-Rogel Center for Chinese Studies for housing the Tang Junyi Postdoctoral Fellowship, a position made possible by the great Donald Munro, which brought me to Michigan. The Lieberthal-Rogel Center has continually supported my research at its different stages as I transitioned from a postdoctoral fellow to an assistant professor at the Department of Asian Languages and Cultures and the Department of Philosophy.

No academic unit can function without the resourcefulness of its administrative workforce, which you are regularly reminded of when you have affiliations with three different academic units. For their dedicated and generous help, I owe thanks to the directors, chairs, and staff of my academic homes: Elizabeth Anderson, Shelley Anzalone, Judith Beck, Erin Brightwell, Benjamin Brose, Kelly Campbell, Mary Gallagher, Nikki Gastineau, Susan Juster, Kim Larrow, Donald S. Lopez Jr., Ann Chih Lin, Markus Nornes, Youngju Ryu, Ena Schlorff, Tad Schmaltz, Carol Stepanchuk, and Patrice Whitney. I am privileged and proud to call the Department of Asian Languages and Cultures, the Department of Philosophy, and the Lieberthal-Rogel Center for Chinese Studies my intellectual homes for all the support they have provided me over the years.

Above all else, I owe a debt of gratitude and heartfelt thanks to my mother, Elif Özbey, who, like many women, has had to live a life of sacrifice, to Gulis Zengin for her lifelong camaraderie, for Dilek Hüseyinzadegan for her allyship, and to my partner and better half, Yanay Israeli, for being my rock and joy.

List of Abbreviations

Works by Spinoza

CM	*Cogitata Metaphysica* (*Metaphysical Thoughts*)
E	*Ethics* (*Ethica*)
Ep	*The Letters* (*Epistolae*)
KV	*Short Treatise on God, Man, and His Well-Being* (*Korte Verhandeling Van God, De Mensch En Deszelfs Welstand*)
Principles	*The Principles of René Descartes' Philosophy* (*Renati Descartes Principia Philosophiae*)
TIE	*Treatise on the Emendation of the Intellect* (*Tractatus de Intellectus Emendatione*)
TP	*Political Treatise* (*Tractatus Politicus*)
TTP	*Theologico-Political Treatise* (*Tractatus Theologico-Politicus*)

References to the *Ethics* (E) will follow Curley's abbreviations

Roman numeral:	part
ax	axiom
app	appendix
c	corollary
def	definition
d	demonstration
ex	explanation
L	lemma
p	proposition
prol	prolegomenon
post	postulate
pref	preface
s	scholium

Notes

References to the CM, TP, and TTP denote the chapter number and the paragraph (e.g., 1.3). References to the TIE cite section numbers from the Curley translation.

Quotations of Spinoza's works are from the following translations, with occasional modifications:

E, TIE   *The Collected Works of Spinoza*, vol.1, trans. Edwin Curley (Princeton, NJ: Princeton University Press, 1985)
Ep., KV, TP   *Spinoza: Complete Works*, ed. Michael L. Morgan, trans. Samuel Shirley (Indianapolis, IN: Hackett, 2002)
Principles   *The Principles of Cartesian Philosophy*, trans. Samuel Shirley (Indianapolis, IN: Hackett, 1961)
TTP   *Theological-Political Treatise,* trans. Michael Silverthorne and Jonathan Israel (Cambridge: Cambridge University Press, 2007).

Citations to the *Zhuangzi* 莊子 are by chapter and page number in GUO Qingfan 郭慶藩, *Zhuangzi* Jishi 莊子集釋 (Collected explanations of the *Zhuangzi*) (Beijing 北京: Zhonghua Shuju 中華書局, 2012).

When translating passages from the *Zhuangzi*, I consulted the following translations: Brook Ziporyn, *Zhuangzi: The Complete Writings* (Indianapolis, IN: Hackett, 2020); Burton Watson, *The Complete Works of Zhuangzi* (New York: Columbia University Press, 2013); and Victor H. Mair, *Wandering on the Way: Early Taoist Tales and Parables of Chuang Tzu.* (Honolulu: University of Hawai'i Press, 2000).

Introduction
Cross-Cultural Philosophy and Critical Animality Studies

Different Beasts explores conceptions of humanity and animality as they emerge in the writings of Spinoza and the *Zhuangzi*. The project thus brings together works from distant and different pasts to bear on the debates regarding the human-animal binary in its many constructions. It also investigates what is at stake in the formation of responsible comparison—one that is sufficiently fine-grained and contextually grounded—to allow different articulations of the human-animal binary to come forth, each asserting its own logic and indebtedness to an intellectual habitus.

The multifaceted aims of this book mirror its multiple target audiences: scholars and students of classical Chinese philosophy and literature, early modern European philosophy, comparative philosophy and literature, and critical animality studies—also sometimes referred to as critical human-animal studies.[1]

The issue of animality has been taken up by many scholars for a variety of purposes ranging from highlighting the uniqueness of human experience (mostly formulated in terms of their rational, linguistic, and/or political capacities) to raising the possibility of shared cognitive and affective capacities among human and nonhuman animals (the gist of which is captured by Jeremy Bentham's famous question: "Can they suffer?").

The past few decades have witnessed a new interest in the "question of the animal" as part of two recent developments within the humanities. One is the rise of ecocritical studies, which addresses the relations between humans and nonhuman nature. The other is the still growing interest in the question of

---

[1] These two terms—"critical human-animal studies (HAS)" and "critical animal (or animality) studies"—are sometimes used interchangeably because of the simple fact that many of our conceptions of animality are intertwined with the human-animal boundary. Hence, as DeMello puts it, the "exploration of the spaces that animals occupy in human social or cultural worlds" necessarily tackles various conceptions of humanity as well. Margo DeMello, *Animals and Society: An Introduction to Human-Animal Studies* (New York: Columbia University Press, 2012), 4.

difference and otherness, where "the animal" serves as the limit case for "otherness" and is revealed to be the founding trope for gendered, raced, abled, and classed distinctions within humans. The latter critical approach rests on the view that the human-animal binary has historically served two closely intertwined functions. First, it has provided a vantage point from which humans have perceived themselves. Second, it has served as a social marker of identity through which humans have declared who is more or less human among themselves.[2]

This project looks at animality and animals as they are represented and imagined in Spinoza's corpus and in the *Zhuangzi*.[3] Since the ways in which animals and animality are imagined have never been completely separate from how humans are imagined, this book is also about different constructions of human identity, different views of the limits of human knowledge, and different perspectives on the nature and significance of human togetherness.

There is, of course, a history behind carrying out philosophical reflections on the human-animal binary as well as a complicated legacy to confront when it comes to deploying so-called heterodox texts (defined from a certain Euro-American vantage point) to contest this binary. The entangled dimensions of this project reflect the entangled histories of these sites of inquiry.

A. Intersectional Critiques of Dualistic Thinking

Addressing the metaphysical foundations of various oppressive practices is a critical tool that has been adopted across intersectional political movements. Young and Fanon have addressed the ways the mind-body binary has informed the ridicule and exploitation of gendered and raced others that are associated less with reason and more with the body and its allegedly "natural" determinations.[4] Butler has exposed how the sex-gender binary is founded

---

[2] For a well-known attempt to map a wide variety of social distinctions within humans onto the distinction between human and nonhuman animals, see Kari Weil, *Thinking Animals: Why Animal Studies Now?* (New York: Columbia University Press, 2012).

[3] Here I am adopting Bogg's usage of the term "animality," which refers to the qualities associated with animals and "operates on a spectrum where 'the animal' [in its own right] is one position." Colleen Glenney Boggs, *Animalia Americana: Animal Representations and Biopolitical Subjectivity* (New York: Columbia University Press, 2013), 8. This study addresses representations of "real" animals as well as discourses of animality with an eye toward the intersections between the two.

[4] See Iris Marion Young, *Justice and the Politics of Difference* (Princeton, NJ: Princeton University Press, 2011), 122–155. Frantz Fanon, *Black Skin, White Masks*, rev. ed., trans. Richard Philcox (New York: Grove Press, 2008), 142–156.

on an untenable nature-culture dichotomy.⁵ Irigaray has scrutinized the gendered nature of the binaries that are foundational to the Western epistemic and psychoanalytic enterprise, such as the speaking subject-silent object, conscious-unconscious, and light-dark.⁶ The divide between the human and the animal has recently garnered attention in relation to these argumentative paradigms, especially after Derrida's and Agamben's insistence that the human-animal binary has historically functioned as the unspoken basis upon which *all* theories of social difference have been constructed.⁷

It is not difficult to see how the human-animal binary has fed into the free-slave, white-people of color, and male-female binaries in cultures associated with European modernity. Apart from the similarities between the systems of oppression used to control the bodies and products of animals and human communities that are deemed inferior, these devalued communities have also either been symbolically associated with animals (such as women being called "cow," "bitch," "sow," and "fox" in the English-speaking world) or have literally been seen as closer to animals (e.g., the nineteenth-century view that black Africans are the missing link between humans and apes). It is no surprise that the human-animal binary has garnered so much attention as a pivotal topic in discussions of difference, otherness, and exclusion.

Certainly, the difficult task of contesting the validity and limits of the boundaries surrounding "humanity" entails various battles unfolding across different platforms. For the humble work of history of philosophy, the task involves critically examining, rather than presupposing, entrenched patterns of thinking that inform discussions regarding who counts as "human." To

---

⁵ Judith Butler, *Gender Trouble: Feminism and the Subversion of Identity* (New York: Routledge, 2006), 10–12. Butler also explores the connection between the mind-body dichotomy and the male-female dichotomy (16–17) and between the mind-body dichotomy and the gender-sex dichotomy (176).

⁶ See Luce Irigaray, *Speculum of the Other Woman*, trans. Gillian Gill (Ithaca, NY: Cornell University Press, 1985).

⁷ See Jacques Derrida, *The Animal That Therefore I Am*, ed. Marie-Louise Mallet, trans. David Wills (New York: Fordham University Press, 2008). Also, see Giorgio Agamben, *The Open: Man and Animal* (Stanford, CA: Stanford University Press, 2004). For recent works on critical animal studies that discuss the intersectionality of oppression *à la* Derrida and Agamben, see Adam Weitzenfeld and Melanie Joy, "An Overview of Anthropocentrism, Humanism, and Speciesism," in *Defining Critical Animal Studies: An Intersectional Social Justice Approach for Liberation*, ed. Anthony J. Nocella II, John Sorenson, Kim Socha, and Atsuko Matsuoka (New York: Peter Lang, 2014), 3–27. Also see Cary Wolfe, *Animal Rites: American Culture, the Discourse of Species, and Posthumanist Theory* (Chicago: University of Chicago Press, 2003). For a criticism of Derridean animal studies for discrediting, while sometimes also appropriating, ecofeminist works (some of which had preceded Derrida's famous 2002 work by some forty years), see Carol J. Adams and Lori Gruen, "Groundwork," in *Ecofeminism: Feminist Intersections with Other Animals and the Earth*, ed. Carol J. Adams and Lori Gruen (New York: Bloomsbury, 2014), 30–32.

this end, many scholars have also turned their attention to the fundamental metaphysical premises of the "Western" intellectual tradition, construed as drawing from either the so-called Greco-Roman or Judeo-Islamo-Christian traditions of thought (or a combination of the two).[8]

Regardless of how the "Western" intellectual tradition is imagined and to what origins its problematic approaches are traced, there is a general consensus that dualistic thinking (particularly mind-body dualism) and essentialist formulations of difference have informed various modes of conceptual oppression and marginalization in one way or another. Criticisms of dualism, and even of Descartes himself (who is blamed for all the sins of modernity), are now so commonplace that they have even made their way into punk songs such as Propagandhi's "Nailing Descartes to the Wall/(Liquid) Meat Is Still Murder."

It is difficult to deny that certain oppressive practices in Europe, and in countries whose histories are strongly connected to Europe via immigration or colonialism, were indeed abetted by prevalent metaphysical views. It is more difficult to argue, however, that these practices transpired *because* the dominant discourses in the West were dualistic. In fact, as Tad Schmaltz observes, European intellectual history also has well-known examples like Poulain de la Barre (1647–1725), who offered Cartesian arguments for gender equality (including the catchy slogan "the mind has no sex").[9] This point is important to remember given how often genealogical critiques of what are labeled "Western" modes of thought are accompanied by an ardent

---

[8] Lynn White, in his very influential essay "The Historical Roots of Our Ecologic Crisis," separates the Greco-Roman tradition from Judeo-Christian orthodoxy and blames the latter for destroying pagan animism, which, he argues, has contributed to humans' indifference to the fate of natural objects. Thirty years later, Baird Callicott named Greco-Roman, Judeo-Christian, and Islamic textual traditions as equally important sources for problematic environmental practices in the West and emphasized points of overlap among all these traditions, such as soul-body dualism and various articulations of anthropomorphism. A terminological approach similar to Callicott's is also taken up by Derrida, who, in his *The Animal that Therefore I Am*, opts for the label "Greco-Judeo-Christiano-Islamic" tradition to describe Western philosophical paradigms. See Lynn White, "The Historical Roots of Our Ecologic Crisis," *Science*, New Series, 155, no. 3767 (March 1967): 1203–1207; J. Baird Callicott, *Earth's Insights: A Multicultural Survey of Ecological Ethics from the Mediterranean Basin to the Australian Outback* (Berkeley: University of California Press, 1997), 14–36; and Jacques Derrida, *The Animal that Therefore I Am*, 55. No matter which cluster of traditions one chooses to censure for all the ills of modernity, the misleading broadness of the label "Judeo-Christian," let alone "Judeo-Islamo-Christian," is difficult to overlook. For a historical examination and critique of the label "Judeo-Christian," see Yitzhak Y. Melamed, "Spinoza's 'Atheism': God and Nature in the Ethics and the TTP," in *Spinoza: Reason, Religion, Politics: The Relation Between the Ethics and the Tractatus Theologico-Politicus*, ed. Daniel Garber (Oxford: Oxford University Press, forthcoming).

[9] See Tad M. Schmaltz, *Early Modern Cartesianisms: Dutch and French Constructions* (New York: Oxford University Press, 2017), 104–107.

search for non-binary ontologies that are expected to effortlessly open up new and liberatory lines of thought.

B. Seeking a Savior in "Monistic" Philosophies

In the quest to dislocate dominant paradigms of thinking, inspiration has sometimes been sought in figures and texts that are considered to be devoid of both dualism and transcendence. It is against the backdrop of this co-construction of two contrasting images—Western philosophical orthodoxy on the one hand, and everything that falls outside of it on the other[10]—that works considered as being outside of the Western philosophical canon have gained popularity. A prevailing hope has been that these works could inspire new paradigms for thinking about humanity, animality, and human-world relations. Among these works are classical texts from Asian intellectual traditions and the writings of one rogue offspring of the European philosophical tradition: Benedict de Spinoza.[11]

Spinoza's recent posthumous rebirth is impressive both for the diverse attention that his philosophy has attracted and for the motivations behind the attempts to appropriate it. Deleuze and Guattari drew inspiration from Spinoza's philosophy some forty years ago when they developed a new ontological vocabulary that emphasized relationality over taxonomic affiliations,

---

[10] For a critique of comparative philosophy's long-standing "East-West" focus, which is also complicit in the further marginalization of Latin American and African philosophies, see Gabriel Soldatenko, "A Contribution toward the Decolonization of Philosophy: Asserting the Coloniality of Power in the Study of Non-Western Philosophical Traditions," *Comparative and Continental Philosophy* 7, no. 2 (December 2015): 138–156. David Kim traces comparative philosophy's fixation on an "East-West" dialogue to the "long-standing reign of the Hegelian world-historical hierarchy in which it is believed that only the expressions of Asian civilizations begin to approach those of Europe." See David Kim, "What Is Asian American Philosophy?," in *Philosophy in Multiple Voices*, ed. George Yancy (Lanham, MD: Rowman and Littlefield, 2007), 222–224. Similar broad-stroke comparisons have a long history in the field of sinology as well. For an examination of early twentieth-century debates on whether "Chinese thought" exhibited a different logical structure than that found in Europe, see Miranda Brown, "Neither 'Primitives' nor 'Others,' but Somehow Not Quite Like Us: The Fortunes of Psychic Unity and Essentialism in Chinese Studies," *Journal of the Economic and Social History of the Orient* 49, no. 2 (2006): 219–252.

[11] Throughout this study I will be using Spinoza's Latinized name. As Melamed points out, there is no trace of evidence that Spinoza ever used his given Hebrew name in his adult life and that the now-ubiquitous gesture of referring to him as Baruch Spinoza is part of the larger attempts to tailor Spinoza's image to fit our politically correct version of his philosophy. See Yitzhak Y. Melamed, "Charitable Interpretations and the Political Domestication of Spinoza, or, Benedict in the Land of the Secular Imagination," in *Philosophy and Its History: Aims and Methods in the Study of Early Modern Philosophy*, ed. Mogens Laerke, Justin E. H. Smith, and Eric Schliesser (Oxford University Press, 2013), 265.

which translated into a radical blurring of the boundaries between the human and the animal.[12] Spinoza's philosophy has also been utilized in the field of affect studies, which challenges the reason-affect dichotomy that has often been intertwined with human-animal and male-female dichotomies.[13] Finally, deep ecologists have found inspiration in Spinoza, whose philosophy, they argue, can help us formulate a new notion of an "ecological self" that "identifies" not only with other humans but also with other ecosystems. Deep ecologists and many other scholars of environmental philosophy have made use of Asian philosophical traditions as well, including various strands of Daoist, Confucian, and Buddhist textual traditions.[14]

What these diverse fields of study find inspiring in Spinoza's philosophy and Asian "wisdom literatures" is their alleged metaphysical outlook, which is broadly—and perhaps too readily—labeled as monistic and immanentist. Whereas the description "monistic," in general, is used to refer to the absence of radical dualisms, including the dualism between mind and matter, the

---

[12] In what has become the philosophical duo's most well-known piece, "1730: Becoming Intense, Becoming Animal, Becoming Imperceptible," Deleuze and Guattari aim to shift the emphasis away from taxonomic categories to movements between symbioses, assemblages, and alliances (i.e., processes of "becomings"). See Gilles Deleuze and Felix Guattari, *A Thousand Plateaus: Capitalism and Schizophrenia*, trans. Brian Massumi (Minneapolis: University of Minnesota Press, 1987), 232–309. This gesture has roots in an oft-cited proposition from Spinoza's *Ethics*, which states that "if a number of individuals so concur in one action that together they are all cause of one effect, I consider them all, to that extent, as one singular thing" (EIIdef7). One might argue that Spinoza's allowing of assemblages of individuals to count as one singular entity, insofar as together they generate certain effects, is perhaps less motivated by a determination to undermine traditional notions of individuality than by a desire to prepare the metaphysical underlay for his political theory that participates in the tradition of the "body politic" (where the entirety of the state is described as one super-individual). This point is further developed in chapter 7, section 7.2.

[13] As explained in chapter 6, section 6.2, Spinoza thinks of empowering affects in terms of changes in the degree of adequate knowledge one has. Spinoza's embracing of the affective side of the thinking mind has not escaped the attention of contemporary scholars such as Armstrong, who points out that the Western intellectual tradition has privileged reason over affect, while simultaneously associating humans, and male humans in particular, with reason. See Aurelia Armstrong, "Autonomy and the Relational Individual: Spinoza and Feminism," in *Feminist Interpretations of Benedict Spinoza*, ed. Moira Gatens (University Park: Pennsylvania University Press, 2009), 43–64. Although Spinoza does undermine the reason-affect dichotomy, as chapter 10, section 10.2 demonstrates, he still associates women in particular with certain sad passions.

[14] For examples of influential works that use Asian intellectual traditions as conceptual resources for environmental philosophy, see J. Baird Callicott and Roger T. Ames, eds., *Nature in Asian Traditions of Thought: Essays in Environmental Philosophy* (Albany: State University of New York Press, 1989); Po-Keung Ip, "Taoism and the Foundations of Environmental Ethics," *Environmental Ethics* 5, no. 4 (January 1983): 335–343; Bill Devall and George Sessions, *Deep Ecology: Living as if Nature Mattered* (Salt Lake City: Peregrine Smith Books, 1985). A more recent work by Tucker and Grim admits in a footnote that East Asian traditions of thought, like all ideologies, "have at times been used for purposes of political power and social control" and that "they have not been able to prevent certain kinds of environmental destruction, such as deforestation"; but the work still announces Confucianism and Daoism to be the most life-affirming of all intellectual traditions due to their allegedly monistic and immanentist outlook. See John Grim and Mary Evelyn Tucker, *Ecology and Religion* (Washington, DC: Island Press, 2014), 23n35.

label "immanentist" is generally employed to refer to the absence of an external cause of the world (such as the Abrahamic God, who also exists in a dualistic relationship with the world He created). The argument goes, since "monistic" and "immanentist" philosophical systems do not posit a transcendent principle or a guarantor of difference (such as a God who creates man in His image and then empowers him to name and rule the world), such systems are expected to challenge the human-animal binary (which also has implications for other interlocked binaries, such as male and female).[15] The argument goes that when heterogeneity and differentiation are viewed to unfold on a continuous trajectory (without explicitly articulated and finalizing boundaries), this is bound to undermine certain oppressive practices supported by dualistic and transcendentist philosophical paradigms.

Assuming for a moment that we are justified in expecting Spinoza and all of Asian "wisdom literatures" to be promoting liberating practices for the non-human world due to some broader ontological features that are attributed to them (namely, being monistic and immanentist), then one inevitably wonders how we could explain the strikingly obvious discrepancy between the expectations we have of such philosophical traditions and what they have actually delivered over the course of their histories. Oppressive species, race, and gender relations still prevail in the societies where many of these traditions and texts have been revered. Furthermore, prescriptions for oppressive dynamics are sometimes articulated within the texts themselves.

That the practice of looking to the "East" or to the heterodox offspring of European philosophy for insight and wisdom has persisted for decades invites us to critically confront the historicity of our own modes of inquiry when we do history of philosophy. Perhaps the very habit of construing the so-called monistic and immanentist texts as greener pastures in the field of world philosophies demonstrates the strong hold that dualistic patterns still have on us, because we somehow feel compelled to construe monism and immanence (however defined) as the polar opposite of anything that dualism and transcendentism stand for—even when the evidence tells us otherwise.[16]

---

[15] This interpretive gesture is employed by Jonathan Israel who claims that "only monist systems could supply the criteria capable of consistently underpinning a comprehensive doctrine of female equality." Jonathan I. Israel, *Enlightenment Contested: Philosophy, Modernity, and the Emancipation of Man 1670–1752* (Oxford: Oxford University Press, 2006), 576.

[16] A similar point is made by Ziporyn who notes that rejecting the possibility that Chinese thinkers had any notion of what we would loosely call transcendence "is itself premised on a transcendent exception" in that "it assumes an absolute separability between transcendence . . . and interdependence." See Brook Ziporyn, *Ironies of Oneness and Difference: Coherence in Early Chinese Thought: Prolegomena to the Study of Li* (Albany: State University of New York Press, 2012), 60. In

Likewise, viewing the alleged absence of an ontological dualism as the collapse of the entire system onto one side of a dualism ("it is all about relationality, not individuality," "it is all about affect, not reason," "it is all about continuity with nature, not anthropocentrism")[17] simultaneously betrays the strength of the dogma that if something makes no difference at the level of absolute concepts, then it makes no difference whatsoever. Thus, even when the presence of certain anthropocentric or misogynist remarks within these appropriated and idealized texts themselves are acknowledged, it is not uncommon to consider such remarks as lodged somewhere in the margins of the work at hand, leaving untainted the general metaphysical picture that has been painted.[18]

Idealized interpretations of non-Western and heterodox intellectual traditions have not gone unchallenged. Spinoza's anthropocentrism and misogyny have already been brought to our attention by Lloyd, Melamed, and Sharp, among others.[19] Furthermore, a scathing criticism of the habit of seeking inspiration in Asian philosophical texts has been offered by Russell

---

a more recent study, Brown and McLeod problematize approaching early Chinese thought with a disjunctive framework in mind (which they describe in terms of an "immanence/nature" versus "transcendence" divide). See Joshua R. Brown and Alexus McLeod, *Transcendence and Non-Naturalism in Early Chinese Thought* (London: Bloomsbury, 2021). For an overview of the history behind disregarding expressions of transcendence in interpretations of early Chinese texts—a topic closely connected with the constrictive and disjunctive applications of the labels "religion" versus "philosophy" to characterize early Chinese traditions—see Filippo Marsili, *Heaven is Empty: A Cross-Cultural Approach to "Religion" and Empire in Ancient China* (Albany: State University of New York Press, 2018): 23–58.

[17] Certainly, the inclination to read Chinese philosophical traditions as valuing the undervalued side of the so-called Western dualisms is not confined to the English-speaking academy. For a well-known example of this reading paradigm defended by Fang Dongmei 方東美, see his *Zhongguo ren sheng zhe xue* 中國人生哲學 [*The Chinese Philosophy of Life*] (Taipei 台北市: Li Ming Cultural Enterprise 黎明文化事業股份有限公司, 1980), 69.

[18] As Gatens points out along with Le Dœuff, this certainly is part of a more deeply entrenched habit of overlooking the troubling remarks of the "great philosophers" as merely anecdotal, which maintains the perennial status of their philosophies while ignoring the unconscious dimension of our cultural heritage altogether. See Moira Gatens, *Imaginary Bodies: Ethics, Power and Corporeality* (London: Routledge, 1996), xi–xii.

[19] Spinoza's anthropocentric remarks have been discussed in Genevieve Lloyd, "Spinoza's Environmental Ethics," *Inquiry* 23, no. 3 (1980): 301, and in Margaret D. Wilson, "For They Do Not Agree in Nature with Us: Spinoza on the Lower Animals," in *New Essays on the Rationalists*, ed. Rocco J. Gennaro and Charles Huenemann (New York: Oxford University Press, year), 336–352. Sharp discusses Spinoza's conflicting remarks on sexual equality in Hasana Sharp, "Eve's Perfection: Spinoza on Sexual (In)Equality," *Journal of the History of Philosophy* 50, no. 4 (2012): 559–580. Gullan-Whur also addresses Spinoza's hostile remarks toward women in Margaret Gullan-Whur, "Spinoza and the Equality of Women," *Theoria* 68 (2008): 91–111. Finally, Melamed cites various unsavory passages from Spinoza's corpus along with a broader discussion of the ubiquitous attempts to "domesticate" Spinoza to make his philosophy more palatable for contemporary sensibilities; see Yitzhak Y. Melamed, "Charitable Interpretations and the Political Domestication of Spinoza."

Kirkland, who argues that this common interpretive pattern can be explained by colonialist impulses that view the thinkers of other ages and cultures as existing to serve our needs.[20] To these criticisms one could add the fact that the habit of locating the main features of Spinoza's works or Asian textual traditions solely in terms of their departures from Western orthodoxy has brought with it a high degree of the amalgamation of these texts, so that although we no longer speak of "Oriental philosophy," we still hear of "Daoist or Confucian" wisdom—which assumes that the two are so similar that one might as well refer to them interchangeably.[21]

Aside from the problem of the erasure of differences between distinct philosophical traditions that are all labeled "monistic" or "immanentist," one also wonders how hermeneutically useful it is to employ such labels for Chinese figures when we lump all of classical Chinese philosophical traditions into that same category[22]—which makes it a non-category that tells us little about how the *Mengzi* differs from the *Laozi*.[23] To make matters worse, the applicability of the labels of immanentism and monism to Spinoza's system has also been challenged,[24] which makes one wonder (1) what these labels even do for us when they clearly conceal more about the specific texts and traditions in

---

[20] Russell Kirkland, "'Responsible Non-Action' in a Natural World: Perspectives from the *Neiye*, *Zhuangzi*, and *Daodejing*," in *Daoism and Ecology: Ways within a Cosmic Landscape*, ed. N. J. Girardot, James Miller, and Liu Xiaogan (Cambridge, MA: Harvard University Press, 2001), 302.

[21] See Grim and Tucker, *Ecology and Religion*, 23n35.

[22] It goes without saying that the label "dualism" itself is already defined in a very specific and Christo-European context to refer to a system where the difference between two entities is so radical that explaining how they even interact becomes a problem and often requires the introduction of a third element to the system (such as Christian theology's employment of the trope of Jesus Christ to bridge the gap between God and his creations). This helps explain the urge to label all early Chinese texts as "non-dualistic," despite the fact that early Chinese texts are not without expressions of tensions between humans and the broader cosmos or between different aspects of one's person. Hall tries to address these tensions by speaking of "polarisms" instead of dualisms. See David L. Hall, *Eros and Irony: A Prelude to Philosophical Anarchism* (Albany: State University of New York Press, 1982), 118–119.

[23] Perkins makes a similar point in the context of the assumed continuity between humans and divine forces in Chinese thought, which misleadingly renders the problem of evil (understood simply as bad things happening to good people) irrelevant in the Chinese context and overlooks the complexity of Chinese philosophy itself. Franklin Perkins, *Heaven and Earth Are Not Humane: The Problem of Evil in Classical Chinese Philosophy* (Bloomington: Indiana University Press, 2014), 13–15.

[24] Melamed points out that although Spinoza is not a mind-body dualist, he is still a dualist of Thought and Being (the two attributes of God to which we have access, as will be discussed in chapter 3, section 3.1). See Yitzhak Y. Melamed, "Spinoza's Metaphysics of Thought: Parallelisms and the Multifaceted Structure of Ideas," *Philosophy and Phenomenological Research* 86, no. 3 (May 2013): 636–683. In another article Melamed argues that Spinoza's definition of God has "significant transcendent features" considering that, as will be discussed in chapter 3, section 3.1, we have causal and epistemic access to only two of God's attributes, when we are told that he actually has infinitely many. See Melamed, "Spinoza's 'Atheism.'" Finally, it should be noted that Spinoza himself uses the description "immanence" only once in the context of causation (EIp18).

question than they reveal, and (2) what we actually gain from giving a conceptual makeover to these "alternative" texts and traditions that ultimately are not free from anthropocentric biases.

Instead of being discouraged by these caveats and criticisms, one could still insist that we keep searching through history to unearth an immaculate philosophy that will help us reorient our thoughts and practices.[25] Perhaps one day we will indeed find what we are looking for in the depths of history. However, engaging in a search for the perfect philosophical tradition that does not harbor troubling biases about human and nonhuman groups prevents reflection upon the myriad reasons that have given rise to such biases in the first place. Stated somewhat more bluntly, dreaming of a flawless philosophical panacea for our anthropocentric ills may distract us from thinking through works that are as complicated, and often as disappointing, as ourselves.

What fuels this book's exploration of questions of humanity and animality in its comparanda—that is, Spinoza's oeuvre and the *Zhuangzi*—is the conviction that the truly transformative potential of studying non-canonical texts lies not in their allegedly harmonious view of the world but in the variety of ways they exhibit human uniqueness, foolishness, or superiority. This, in turn, can help us further understand and transform our own biases, contradictions, investments, and priorities about the human-animal binary.

C. Why Compare? Critical Mimesis and New Areas of Inquiry

In turning its attention to Spinoza and the *Zhuangzi*, this project utilizes these works to examine different constructions of the human-animal binary. Juxtaposing Spinoza's oeuvre and the *Zhuangzi* is not an accident. There is a long history of reading Spinoza together with Asian philosophical texts and especially with canonical Chinese texts. This practice actually has its roots

---

[25] This is a possibility that Calarco entertains when he notes: "There is no shortage of extant examples of alternative modes of human-animal relations, especially if we are willing to think beyond the limits of traditional ways of distinguishing human beings and animals. We can find such examples in a wide variety of indigenous and nondominant cultures, both past and present, across the globe." Matthew Calarco, *Thinking through Animals: Identity, Difference, Indistinction* (Stanford, CA: Stanford University Press, 2015), 67–68. For a work that challenges hopeful views of indigenous cultures' treatment of nonhuman animals, see Barbara Noske, "Speciesism, Anthropocentrism, and Non-Western Cultures," *Anthrozoös* 10, no. 4 (1997): 183–190.

in early modern Christian missionary expansion in China, which brought with itself controversies about the extent to which the Chinese should be charged with atheism.[26] Due to the difficulties that came with cross-cultural transmission of ideas and concerns, it was not uncommon to construe the Chinese in the image of a figure who was more familiar to European intellectuals: Spinoza. One of Spinoza's own contemporaries, Pierre Bayle, considered Spinozism as "none other than a particular way of interpreting a doctrine widely diffused in the Indies"; Bayle then followed this with another comparison between Spinoza's philosophy and Chinese Buddhism.[27] Similarly, Nicolas Malebranche, in his *Dialogue between a Christian Philosopher and a Chinese Philosopher on the Existence and Nature of God*, construed Neo-Confucianism in the image of Spinoza on the grounds that they both exhibited similar kinds of "impieties," that is, atheism.[28]

Centuries later, Spinoza is still readily juxtaposed with Chinese philosophical traditions, but this time not because of their perceived shared heresies but because of their perceived shared wisdom that is hoped will provide a much-needed panacea for various urgent problems of the present.[29] According to this iteration of drawing parallels between Spinoza and Chinese philosophical traditions, the similarities between the two boil down to (1) their alleged dismantling of human arrogance (because, after all, they did not think that humans are created in the image of an Abrahamic God); (2) their so-called monism (which allegedly eradicates the perceived discontinuity between the human and nonhuman world); and (3) their alleged emphasis on harmony with nature (because, the argument goes, if humans are not God-like, then

---

[26] For more on this, see Thijs Weststeijn, "Spinoza sinicus: An Asian Paragraph in the History of the Radical Enlightenment," *Journal of the History of Ideas* 68, no. 4 (2007): 537–561.

[27] For more information, see Bayle's Spinoza entry in his *Dictionnaire Critique et Historique*, followed by *remarque* B, where he examines Chinese "Foe Kiao" (*Fojiao* 佛教). See Pierre Bayle, *Dictionnaire Critique et Historique* (Amsterdam: Par la Compagnie des Libraries, 1734).

[28] Nicolas Malebranche, *Dialogue between a Christian Philosopher and a Chinese Philosopher on the Existence and Nature of God*, trans. Dominick A. Iorio (Lanham, MD: University Press of America, 1980), 98.

[29] The most well-known examples of both drawing parallels between Spinoza and Chinese schools of thought and presenting them as better alternatives to "Western" thinking habits are Arne Naess's and George Sessions's works. See Arne Naess, "The Shallow and the Deep, Long-Range Ecology Movements: A Summary," in *Deep Ecology for the Twenty-First Century: Readings on the Philosophy and Practice of the New Environmentalism*, ed. George Sessions (Boston: Shambhala, 1995), 151–155. Also see George Sessions, "Ecocentrism and the Anthropocentric Detour," in Sessions, *Deep Ecology for the Twenty-First Century*, 156–184. Although they aim to celebrate the "others" of philosophy for their wisdom, instead of condemning them for their heresy, such interpretive parallels still blur the distinctions between underrepresented philosophical figures and texts.

there cannot be much of a difference between humans and all the rest they have managed to dominate).

These broad-stroke observations inevitably rely on interpretive smoothing of thorny subjects, such as the so-called ancient Chinese attitude toward harmony with nature (which was an aspirational norm rather than an assumption about the world they lived in, and it did not always erase notions of human superiority) or Spinoza's presumed atheism (which flattens his ample discussions of God into a ruse to gain a hearing for his philosophy).

In juxtaposing Spinoza's oeuvre and a classical Chinese work, the *Zhuangzi*, *Different Beasts* engages mimetically with a common interpretive paradigm in order to affect multiple shifts in dominant comparative methodologies.[30] The first shift concerns my driving goal for this study. When it comes to the range of theses that are typically explored in relation to conceptualizations of human-animal relations, I am less interested in proving the untenability of a human-animal binary than exploring the complex machinery behind ambivalent attitudes toward it.

What seems to characterize the human-nonhuman animal relationship today is ambivalence with regard to how similar the two groups are—instead of a complete denial of similarities between humans and nonhuman animals.[31] If we are doing history of philosophy not only to understand the attitudes of people there and then but also to reflect on our conceptual baggage here and now, then I believe it makes it all the more crucial for us to examine the way similar ambivalences and contradictions appear in works belonging to our collective past. This very interest informed my decision to focus on works that constantly vacillate between decentering and recentering the human, which I believe is what Spinoza and the *Zhuangzi* actually do.

---

[30] My strategy here echoes Irigaray's mimetic engagement with the history of philosophy. Irigaray's essay "This Sex Which Is Not One," published in her collection of essays of the same name, offers an example of such mimetic engagement, in which Irigaray demonstrates the limitations of certain gendered categories by purposefully assuming them. See Luce Irigaray, *This Sex Which Is Not One*, trans. Catherine Porter and Carolyn Burke (Ithaca, NY: Cornell University Press, 1985), 23–33. This study also performs a mimetic analysis, as I follow a certain familiar interpretive paradigm by reading Spinoza together with a Chinese text while purposefully allowing them to pull against each other instead of re-entrenching their alleged similarities. This approach, I believe, also enriches our understanding of each comparandum in its full integrity and of the topic at hand.

[31] I owe this insight to Sharp. Hasana Sharp, "Animal Affects: Spinoza and the Frontiers of the Human," *Journal for Critical Animal Studies* 9, no. 1/2 (2011): 50–51. It could be argued that today this ambivalence partly stems from our desire to support evolution-based scientific thinking without changing our comfortable lifestyles (enabled by anthropocentric resourcism) at the same time.

Despite their ample moments of ambiguity, if not contradiction, in regard to the human-animal binary, scholars of both comparanda have focused on the decentering aspects of these works much more than their moments of recentering humans and have read them to be consistently adopting a particular ontological attitude where differences are formulated on a smooth and continuous trajectory, without discontinuities or leaps.[32] While I do not deny that for the most part the human-animal binary appears to be porous in each comparandum, it should also be noted that porosity of a boundary is not the same as its absence[33] and moments of *qualitative* difference and discontinuity between humans and animals do appear in both comparanda.[34] At the same time, while both Spinoza and the *Zhuangzi* attempt to deflate the human ego (and hence decenter human perspectives), they both also continue to grant a unique status to humans (openly or tacitly). This, I believe, makes them uniquely revealing texts to study for critical animal studies.

Second, by focusing its attention on two specific sets of texts in a contextually conditioned way and setting up the analysis around a topic that is expansive enough to allow for a comparison to begin with, while also being textured enough to prompt different and distinct formulations of it, this study performs what Stalnaker terms a "fine-grained comparison."[35] Doing so, I believe, allows one to move the very axis of a discussion away from broad and smooth observations about traditions and metaphysical outlooks to the microcurrents running through different textual networks.

---

[32] For two recent examples, see Moa De Lucia Dahlbeck, *Spinoza, Ecology and International Law: Radical Naturalism in the Face of the Anthropocene* (London: Routledge, 2019); Graham Parkes, "Zhuangzi and Nietzsche on the Human and Nature," Special Issue: East Asian and Comparative Approaches to the Environment, *Environmental Philosophy* 10, no. 1 (Spring 2013): 1–24. Paul D'Ambrosio explores the limits of the *Zhuangzi*'s anti-anthropocentric dimension but also argues that the animal characters in the text are mainly allegorical or metaphorical. See Paul D'Ambrosio, "Non-humans in the *Zhuangzi*: Animalism and Anti-anthropocentrism," *Asian Philosophy* 32, no. 1 (2022): 1–18, DOI: 10.1080/09552367.2021.1934218. This particular issue—that many animal anecdotes in the *Zhuangzi* might be taken as a rhetorical gesture that uses animals as metaphorical doppelgängers of humans—is addressed in chapter 1, section 1.2.

[33] Equating the two would be an articulation of the same dogmatic attitude mentioned earlier, which asserts that if something makes no difference at the level of absolute concepts, then it makes no difference whatsoever.

[34] This issue is taken up in detail in chapter 1, section 1.1.

[35] See Aaron Stalnaker, *Overcoming Our Evil: Human Nature and Spiritual Exercises in Xunzi and Augustine* (Washington, DC: Georgetown University Press, 2006), 14–21. Lincoln terms a similar methodology a "weak comparison," which denotes "inquiries that are modest in scope, but intensive in scrutiny." Bruce Lincoln, *Apples and Oranges: Explorations In, On, and With Comparison* (Chicago: University of Chicago Press, 2018), 11. I am indebted to Michael Nylan for this reference.

By focusing its attention on specific texts instead of traditions and deep structures, my goal is to avoid perpetuating the amalgamation of different philosophies and to remain within the internal logic of each comparandum to the best of our hermeneutic capacities.[36] A fine-grained and historically grounded comparative analysis also makes it possible to probe into, instead of erase, the divergences between different intellectual contexts. This approach allows us to rethink and rework our concepts and questions by giving them new associations and overtones.[37] Under such comparative scrutiny, our conceptualizations of the human-animal binary multiply, so do our very definitions of "human," "good life," and "order."

Indeed, as will be shown, aside from simply belonging to different intellectual milieus, which inevitably shapes the ways the human-animal binary is posed and undermined in either comparandum, what makes the two—Spinoza's oeuvre and the *Zhuangzi*—particularly convenient examples for a project like this are the dramatically different conclusions that they reach when it comes to issues of personal and group identity, hierarchical modeling of different life forms, human togetherness, and institutional politics. These differences prove to be crucial in laying bare the sheer diversity of the issues and concerns that end up inflecting the question of the human-animal divide.

In the end, what comes to the fore in this comparative study are the distinct, and at times unpredictable, gestures for undermining and re-erecting boundaries between different life forms, as well as the different levels of investment in human togetherness and unity that are imagined in relation to tropes of animality. Of course, the variations of the machinery behind the human-animal binary exceed these two instances of it, but it is precisely this understanding of its multiformity that together they help deliver.

---

[36] This methodology has been carried out by Lee H. Yearley's *Mencius and Aquinas: Theories of Virtue and Conceptions of Courage* (Albany: State University of New York Press, 1990) and has also been skillfully executed by Stalnaker's *Overcoming Our Evil*. As Stalnaker points out, while with such fine-grained comparisons one cannot make inspired claims about some perennial structures in human thinking or the fundamental attitudes of a civilization, one *can* do justice to the theoretical positions and terminologies of the chosen corpora. Stalnaker, *Overcoming Our Evil*, 16–21.

[37] As noted by Detienne: "There is no experimental comparativism that does not force us to think in new ways about what seems spontaneously to belong to the realm of common sense and familiar categories." See Marcel Detienne, "Back to the Village: A Tropism of Hellenists?," *History of Religions* 43, no. 2 (2001): 99–113 (cited in Michael Nylan, "Talk about 'Barbarians' in Antiquity," *Philosophy East and West* 62, no. 4 (October 2012): 580–601).

D. Roadmap

The benefits of a comparative approach to a philosophical debate are obvious, but so are its pitfalls. Over the last decades, comparative approaches to philosophical and/or religious works have drawn well-justified criticism. The primary concern lies in the way they tend to lift the texts they are comparing out of their interface with the world and carry out their analysis with what is admittedly an ahistorical approach. This attitude is sometimes explicitly defended because, the argument goes, only "a level of abstraction that is high enough" will "allow ideas to be compared at all"—which transforms an ahistorical attitude toward world philosophies into a decidedly anti-historical one.[38] Despite the enduring critiques of Cartesian dualisms, disentangling ideas from their contextual underpinnings in our examinations of philosophers and their works is still acceptable, if not expected. As Lincoln complains, such "comparative reprocessing makes different fruits look and taste alike" due to being "distanced from the soil in which they grew, deprived of the specifics that gave them flavor."[39]

In addition to the inseparability of ideas and the circumstances that birthed them, diligent contextualization becomes especially important in the case of the *Zhuangzi* and Spinoza's oeuvre. This is because the two bodies of works have always been perceived to be unusual, if not radical, compared to what else has come down to us from their own milieus. Hence, Part I of the study is dedicated to offering a contextualizing discussion of the two comparanda with an eye toward contemporaneous discourses of humanity and animality. By examining some of the prominent views and arguments specific to their milieus, as well as points of continuity and discontinuity between these texts and their intellectual contexts, we can better appreciate the distinctiveness of the fruits that the soils of early China and early modern Europe have produced while also being able to pinpoint the hermeneutic implications of such a comparison.

---

[38] The quote belongs Scharfstein, cited in Wiebke Denecke, *The Dynamics of Masters Literature: Early Chinese Thought from Confucius to Han Feizi* (Cambridge, MA: Harvard University Asia Center, 2011), 20. Scharfstein's anti-historical approach could be contrasted with Goldin's balanced approach: "A modern reader of classical Chinese texts must strike a fundamental balance: paying due attention to the historical circumstances of each text's transmission without losing sight of its animating ideas—for the ideas are the reason why the texts were transmitted in the first place. It is all too easy for academic interpreters to veer too far in either direction." Paul Goldin, *The Art of Chinese Philosophy: Eight Classical Texts and How to Read Them* (Princeton, NJ: Princeton University Press, 2020), 3.

[39] Bruce Lincoln, *Apples and Oranges: Explorations In, On, and With Comparison*, 9.

As anyone who has taught the two texts to a novice audience can attest, when one places Spinoza's *Ethics*, his most well-known work, next to the *Zhuangzi*, the first thing one notices is not any facts about their metaphysical outlooks but the simple reality that the two texts read very differently as texts. Hence, Part I also pursues this insight and gives attention to literary and textual issues. In doing so, it simultaneously invites readers to reflect on what it means to think through the human condition and its relation to an imagined animal existence through storytelling (the *Zhuangzi*) versus a systematic edifice (Spinoza's corpus). What kinds of "facts" can one present through these different ways of philosophizing? Can animal "fables" tell us anything about animals? Can mathematical modeling of the world tell us anything about the human condition?

Undoubtedly, when they are juxtaposed to each other, the ontological and epistemological features of Spinoza's oeuvre and the *Zhuangzi* also come to the fore in a starker manner. Part II pursues this contrast in its analysis of the kinds of theories of knowledge, action and agency that are expressed and implied in these two sets of texts. In doing so, it also addresses the dominant interpretive paradigms that see Spinoza's *Ethics* and the *Zhuangzi* as undermining human beings' distinct status in the world.[40] Although both indeed take aim at particular visions of human supremacy that were articulated in their respective milieus, to expect a work that undermines one form of human exceptionalism to also resist all forms of it is to step too far.

Part II demonstrates that what emerges in these works is not different erasures of the human-animal split but two different models of human distinctiveness—one that scales different minds and bodies in a way that privileges human beings over less "complex" beings and the other that presents that distinctiveness as a double-edged sword forged by people's propensity for making distinctions. The contrast is not without critical ramifications; it presents a unique opportunity to reflect on the entanglement between ranking some forms of living as indubitably better than others on the one hand and articulating clear standards for progress on the other.

Having examined the ontological and epistemic dimensions of the question of the human animal divide, Part III moves on to examine passages in Spinoza and the *Zhuangzi* that hint at differences between humans and

---

[40] The issues of translation in regard to the crucial notion "human" are addressed in section 1.1 of chapter 1 and section 2.1 of chapter 2. For the present context, within the introduction, I shall employ the generic terms "human" or "human beings" interchangeably when discussing both Spinoza and the *Zhuangzi*.

animals in regard to their tastes, likes, and dislikes. This is accompanied by an examination of the presence and absence of certain anxieties formed around the issue of the communication of affects between humans and animals. Examining the affective and hedonic dimensions of the human-animal binary unveils complexities that challenge the inclination to trace the seeds of the binary to various metaphysical and epistemological questions alone (such as the extensively studied mind-body dualism). This exploration also further reveals the rhetorical aspects inherent in the two contrasting attitudes toward potential overlaps between human and animal affects.

The examination of some of the key passages on human and animal affects in Spinoza's thought and the *Zhuangzi* brings to the fore several other related issues. One such issue concerns the notion of human solidarity (as an assumption and as an ideal), which easily inflects one's approach toward animal affects—namely, whether one regards them with guileless curiosity or disassociates them from human concern altogether in the name of not wasting emotional resources on those less relevant for human well-being.

Often treated in terms of various differences in constitutions, capacities, and proclivities, the question of the human-animal divide is rarely without political considerations and consequences. Hence, Part IV steers the analysis in the direction of political theory, while also exploring the political dimensions and implications of ontological considerations. Particular attention is paid to different constructions of group and individual identities as well as body politic metaphors, which conceive the political "body" as analogous to the human body, intertwining the person and the group. With an eye toward examining different narratives of origin and construction of the political body, Part IV also examines an understudied but arguably critical aspect of its target texts: Spinoza's and the *Zhuangzi*'s imaginations of the nature of unarranged worlds, namely, "the state of nature" and "distant antiquity," which reveal gloomy versus sunny imageries of animality, as well as humanity.

While part of the contrast stems from opposite attitudes toward institutional governmentality and what orderliness represents, Part IV demonstrates that the presence or absence of an "us versus them" binary also shapes the ways political pasts and presents are imagined. Also significant is the presence or absence of a "logic of scarcity" (of resources, power, wealth), which in Spinoza's case often pits people against each other, sometimes even more than it pits them against the animal kingdom.

18 INTRODUCTION

The final part of the study—that is, Part V—tracks a commonly treaded path in critical animality studies and traces the interconnections between exclusionary or (subversively) inclusionary articulations of human perfection, on the one hand, and different usages of animal imageries, on the other. It does so by looking into Spinoza's and the *Zhuangzi*'s descriptions of foreign, gendered, classed, and disabled others. As is well known, despite first gaining traction decades ago, critical animality studies managed to maintain its momentum because of the way conceptions of animality easily open onto questions of gender, race, disability, and so on, in many intellectual traditions. While it is undeniable that reinforcement or undermining of these categories have a way of spilling into each other, Part V argues that the precise reach of the human-animal binary is not so straightforward.

Part V demonstrates that liberatory or oppressive representations of different undervalued groups can sometimes play out in relatively isolated conceptual bubbles, without directly inflecting each other—whether the actual struggles of these groups are interlinked or not. While this serves as a caveat against ready-made conclusions regarding the rhetorical work that animal imageries perform, it also urges vigilant attention to interconnections between tropes, associations, and narratives surrounding questions of difference.

PART I
READING SPINOZA WITH THE ZHUANGZI

Conversations and Toolkits

Suppose you and I get into a debate. If you beat me instead of me beating you, then are you really right and am I really wrong? If I beat you instead of you beating me, then am I really right and are you really wrong?

Zhuangzi 2:112.

Hence, they maintained it as certain that the judgments of the gods far surpass man's grasp. This alone, of course, would have caused the truth to be hidden from the human race to eternity, if mathematics, which is concerned not with ends, but only with the essences and properties of figures, had not shown men another standard of truth.

EIapp.

1
Contexts and Means for Interpreting the *Zhuangzi*

The *Zhuangzi*, in the chapter titled "The Great Source as Teacher" (Da zong shi 大宗師), depicts an exchange between Kongzi 孔子 (Master Kong, or Confucius)[1] and his disciple Yan Hui. The conversation concerns a man named Mengsun Cai, who does not seem to be shedding any tears and appears to be unperturbed by the death of his mother. This upsets Yan Hui who then asks Kongzi what he thinks about it. Kongzi explains to Yan Hui that

> this clansman Mengsun has gotten to the end of the matter, he has advanced beyond knowledge. . . . Mengsun didn't know why he lived and didn't know why he would die. He didn't know which came first [life or death] and which came last. . . . Moreover, people go around telling each other, "I do this," "I do that"—but how do we know that what we call "I" has any "I" to it? You may dream that you are a bird and soar up into the sky, that you are a fish and dive into the depths. We cannot determine whether we who are speaking now are awake or dreaming."[2]

What is the message of this story, or, above all, is there an obvious message? And, what are we to make of Kongzi's answer and the fact that a man like him, who is known to practice and recommend elaborate forms of mourning, is now portrayed as siding with a man who does not appear to be mourning for his mother at all, all the while questioning whether he is even awake or not, recalling the times he dreamed he was a bird and then a fish? Moreover, why is a text named *Zhuangzi* (莊子 Master Zhuang) telling its readers a story

---

[1] c "Confucius" is a Latinized name, coined by Jesuit missionaries, for the appellation "Kong Fu Zi 孔夫子 (Revered Master Kong)." During this study I will be using Kongzi 孔子 (Master Kong), rather than Confucius.
[2] *Zhuangzi* 6:280.

about Kongzi at all? What kind of a work is this *Zhuangzi* and how are we to even approach episodes like this?

This chapter provides interpretive keys for understanding the *Zhuangzi* by examining the intellectual context in which it was written. More specifically, it studies the connections between the human-animal divide and early Chinese discourses about ordering society, as well as the common rhetorical tools used in such discourses, such as staged conversations, anecdotes, and figurative analogies. The chapter demonstrates that grasping this broader intellectual context that birthed the *Zhuangzi* is critical if we wish to understand the function and significance of its multivocal structure, its engagement in parodic and honorific discursive practices, and its penchant for shifting between different positions. The dating of the texts I use ranges from the "Warring States" era of the late Zhou dynastic period to the Qin and early Han empires (c. 500–100 BCE).[3]

As the chapter demonstrates, much of early Chinese elite thought revolved primarily around speculations about human behavior and what human beings could become (for better or worse). In addition, the aspects of human life that the early masters of philosophy extensively addressed reveal the fundamental intertwinement between early Chinese philosophy, discussions of good governance, and the pursuit of unitary rule. The chapter thus argues that the *Zhuangzi*'s oft-mentioned decentering of the human and its interest in animal perspectives is to be understood in relation to the early Chinese logic of governmentality, which was calibrated not only against the notion of humans as a whole, but also against certain types of human beings, leaving room for the subhumanization and animalization of others.[4]

The chapter also contextualizes the *Zhuangzi*'s well-known literary idiosyncrasies. As often noted, early Chinese masters did not employ deductive argumentation to convey their points, instead deploying a variety of rhetorical tools including staged dialogues, anecdotes (fictional or otherwise), parables, and ample analogies and metaphors. The *Zhuangzi*'s peculiarity as

---

[3] It should also be pointed out that many of the so-called Zhanguo 戰國 (Warring States) Masters texts (including the *Zhuangzi*) were compiled over a long period of time, going beyond the Zhanguo period alone, and were produced from disparate sources, sometimes traceable to as late as the late Western Han. In regard to the *Zhuangzi*, as Klein demonstrates, the definitive editor and commentator of the received text, Guo Xiang 郭象 (d. 312), abridged a larger text of fifty-two *pian* (篇; bound set of bamboo slips, each probably corresponding to a chapter) to its current version of thirty-three *pian*. See Esther Klein, "Were There 'Inner Chapters' in the Warring States? A New Examination of Evidence about the *Zhuangzi*," *T'oung Pao* 96, fasc. 4/5 (2011): 299–369.

[4] I owe this phrasing to Philip Howell, "The Trouble with Liminanimals," *Parallax* 25, no. 4 (2019): 403.

a text lies not in its indulging in storytelling but in the multivocal narrative bends it introduces, which diffuse power away from presumed centers of value: from elites to ordinary people at large, and even to animals and plants. Nor does its oft-mentioned deployment of many metaphors give it its famed extravagant flavor; rather, its unconventional *choice* and *use* of metaphors do. Added to these curious features of the *Zhuangzi* is its meta-textual dimension, which is at times mobilized to denounce any kind of textual authority. While the text's nonchalant attitude toward offering anything close to a conclusive statement presents interpretive challenges, its self-reflective engagement with issues of rhetorical choice and orientation gives its readers some clues about how to approach a work like the *Zhuangzi*.

1.1 Inching Out of Animality: Early Chinese Recipes for Power and Teachings for Humanity

The intellectual foundations of the *Zhuangzi* were laid in what is aptly named the Zhanguo 戰國 (the "Warring States") era of the late Zhou 周 period, which is dated from some point in the fifth century to 221 BCE. The period is commonly characterized by constant military conflict among various regional powers, although it also witnessed unprecedented technological and agricultural advancements (such as advanced metalworking leading to better weaponry and efficient agriculture catering to large armies). Still, that so many of these developments unfolded within the context of incessant battling for territorial dominance inevitably led to the perception of the period as one of violent conflict between shifting centers of power. Moreover, along with ever-changing alliances and interests, combined with new people gaining new influence, came the shuffling of class structures.

It is thanks to this mélange of crises and new opportunities that petty aristocrats (*shi* 士; men of service, well-bred men), who would normally occupy lower-level governmental roles (e.g., scribe, ritual specialist), were enabled to stake claims to more prestigious administrative and advising positions in local and royal courts.[5] With aspirations of rising to positions

---

[5] There is, however, the trickier case of Mohists, who were probably members of lower social strata. However, as Fraser notes along with Graham, "there is no evidence that Mohism represents the ideology of a self-conscious craft or artisan class.... Rather, the Mohists are ambitious, capable commoners for whom the passing of the old feudal system and the development of centralized, meritocratic bureaucracies have made promotion to [*shi*] class a possibility." See "Influence of Social

of advising and service to the court, some of these *shi* developed ambitious theories of leadership and social order, leading to what we today refer to as classical Chinese philosophy. Although not all learned *shi* pundits were able to fulfill their aspirations of political patronage, the proliferation of politico-philosophical thought generated communities of learners and thinkers. It is such communities that developed and preserved compilations of texts that conceived the teachings of a "master (*zi* 子)," which were circulated in manuscript form or used as aides to memory.[6] Not only were the authors and compilers of Masters texts (*zishu* 子書)[7] largely from elite backgrounds, but the *de facto* audience of such teachings was the ruling elite, due to the low level of advanced literacy in the society at large.

Although the textbook account of this era presents this proliferation of new ideas and arguments by numerous learned communities as a silver lining amid the chaos,[8] these learned textual communities hardly perceived themselves (or at least did not depict themselves) as engaging in a delightful blossoming of philosophical thought in harsh soils. On the contrary, they drew a connection between ideological disagreement and political fragmentation, and set a lofty goal of expressing the complete and comprehensive wisdom (*zhou dao* 周道, *bei dao* 備道) that would parallel the unification of "All under Heaven" (*yi tian xia* 一天下), which ideally was to be brought about by a sage-sovereign (*xian sheng zhi jun* 賢聖之君).[9]

Such was the intimate and inseverable connection between political power and philosophy, and regardless of the degree, or even the presence,

---

Origins on Mohist Thought," Stanford Encyclopedia of Philosophy, https://plato.stanford.edu/entries/mohism/social.html (accessed December 28, 2022).

[6] Michael Nylan, "Academic Silos, or 'What I Wish Philosophers Knew About Early History in China,'" in *The Bloomsbury Handbook of Chinese Research Methodologies*, ed. TAN Sor-Hoon (London: Bloomsbury, 2016), 92–97.

[7] "Masters texts (*zishu* 子書; alternative translation: Masters' writings)" refer to compilations that are developed and preserved by textual communities that elaborate on, if not create, the teachings of a "master (*zi* 子)." The texts that are archived in the imperial library under the label of "*zishu* 子書" include the *Analects* or the *Lunyu* 論語, the *Mozi* 墨子, the *Mencius*/*Mengzi* 孟子, the *Laozi* 老子, the *Zhuangzi* 莊子, and the *Xunzi* 荀子 among others. A few masters are thought to have produced at least parts of the canon bearing their name, such as Han Feizi 韓非子.

[8] This sanguine narrative is partly explainable by the lingering influence of Karl Jaspers's celebratory depiction of the "axial age." Jaspers coined this term to refer to the concurrent rise of influential intellectual traditions in China, India, Persia, and the Greco-Roman world between the eighth and third centuries BCE. Jaspers describes this period as "a pause for liberty, a deep breath bringing the most lucid consciousness." Karl Jaspers, *The Origin and Goal of History*, trans. Michael Bullock (New Haven, CT: Yale University Press, 1953), 51.

[9] For a discussion of the parallel between textual and political authority, see Mark Edward Lewis, *Writing and Authority in Early China* (Albany: State University of New York Press, 1999), 287–297. Also see Nylan, "Academic Silos," 103–104.

of involvement in courtly affairs, the early masters of philosophy were never free of the influence of political authority.[10] As different masters professed their own teachings to be comprehensive in some ways, they attacked others for allegedly fixating on one corner (*yi qu* 一曲) of the all-encompassing wisdom. For example, while some were accused of overemphasizing kin relations, others faced scrutiny for overprioritizing utility and frugality, and some others were faulted for heavily relying on rewards and punishments.[11] Even the rare gestures of withdrawal from proactive leadership, such as the ones seen in the *Laozi* 老子, were not entirely free of similar aspirations to express a broad-minded vision. For instance, the advice of non-interference was arguably informed by the view that any agenda would inevitably be partial to some private interests and hence would not be as good as the absence of any particular leadership agenda whatsoever.[12]

Regardless of one's ideological leanings and the "corner" one was allegedly obsessed with, in all such accounts proactive leadership (whether it is presented as a positive or negative) is linked to practices of strategic demarcation—between right and wrong, benefit and harm, elegance and uncouthness, ruler and subject, men and women, and so on—that are to be mobilized to establish order and rule the realm.

In the end, these lofty aspirations of achieving comprehensive rule through various acts of demarcation (of values, roles, duties, peoples) ironically end up leaving out various other aspects of governance due to their tacit exclusionary logic. For example, Pines has shown that even the most comprehensive of all terms, "*tianxia* 天下 (All under Heaven)," designating the lands to be unified and ruled, had an unstable and relatively narrow referent, often leaving out various polities on or beyond the fringes of the Zhou world. Of course, what and who counted as alien lands and peoples was also subject to constant negotiation depending on the ever-shifting interstate relations and interests—which meant that the referent of the notion of All under

---

[10] As Defoort observes, the sheer abundance of staged dialogues between rulers and masters in Masters texts alone attests to fantasies of courtly influence. Defoort adds that "however weak the Zhuangzi authors' political aspirations may have been" they still "share in the fantasy of a king humbly learning from a wise master." See Carine Defoort, "Instruction Dialogues in the *Zhuangzi*: An 'Anthropological' Reading," *Dao* 11 (2012): 463.

[11] For an overview of these debates, see Lewis, "Writing and Authority," 291–296. Also see Mark Edward Lewis, *The Construction of Space in Early China* (Albany: State University of New York Press, 2006), 199–202.

[12] See *Laozi* 7, 57. References to the *Laozi* are by chapter numbers in Liu Xiaogan, *Laozi gujin* 老子古今 (Beijing: Zhongguo Shehui Kexue Chubanshe, 2006).

Heaven was also unstable.[13] In the end, the exclusion of certain territories from the envisioned lands to be unified was not always or necessarily an indication of knowing one's administrative limits or a sign of total indifference toward different lands and peoples. Instead, it was sometimes an extension of viewing frontier regions as "a graded zone of waning degrees of civilization" and hence habitability.[14]

It is often pointed out that in early Chinese texts numerous tropes of animality had a way of overlapping with imageries of alien peoples.[15] However, more than speculating about folks living in frontier regions (about whom we see scattered and inconsistent remarks instead of cohesive and sustained interest), early Chinese masters were primarily invested in offering a vision of orderly and sustainable governance. Hence, much of what animates the human-animal divide as a rhetorical shorthand in the politico-philosophical recipes of the masters is the desire to secure a scheme of distinctions, so as to allot roles and duties, clarify social relations, and distribute resources and organize labor. Tropes of animality were largely evoked to criticize prevailing state of affairs as disordered, or to describe the stakes involved in failing to institute proper governance: the ever-gradual descent of people into an unseemly if not wretched existence.[16]

It is fairly clear that the figurative ladder extending from subhumanity to human perfection in early Chinese elite thought was laden with valuations of sociopolitical significance. While the different markers of human identity and civilization varied, all were intertwined with social cohesion and stratification practices. These include the establishment of division of labor, delineating proper familial relations, as well as the pursuit of ideals centered around building a community that protects the vulnerable.[17] These

---

[13] Pines demonstrates that the borders that separated the central plains from the alien peripheral polities were ever-shifting, so even when *tianxia* (All under Heaven) was used in association with *Zhongguo* (central polities), its referent was not always the same territory and the same group of people. Moreover, especially in what Pines deduces to be earlier layers of ancient Chinese texts (which were composite works that were produced over a span of time), we see a tendency to use *tianxia* to designate a "regime of value" and, more specifically, the values and "public opinion" of aristocrats, which represented a much narrower slice of the populace. Yuri Pines, "Changing Views of 'Tianxia' in Pre-Imperial Discourse," *Oriens Extremus* 43 (2002): 101–116.

[14] Roel Sterckx, *Chinese Thought: From Confucius to Cook Ding* (London: Pelican Books, 2019), 46.

[15] For more on depictions of alien peoples in early Chinese texts, see chapter 9, section 9.1.

[16] The relation between the human-animal division and proper governance is taken up in detail in chapter 8, section 8.3.

[17] To give an example or two for each of these points, see, respectively, *Mengzi* (孟子) 3A4; *Liji* (禮記) 11.25/8–10 ("Jiao Te Sheng 郊特牲") or *Mozi* (墨子) 10/9/15–16; *Xunzi* (荀子) 5.4 or *Mengzi* 3A4; *Lüshi Chunqiu* 呂氏春秋 ("The Annals of Lü Buwei") 20/1.3. Citations to the *Mengzi* are standardly given by the chapter number (1–7), followed by the letter "A" or "B" to designate the "upper" or "lower" part of the chapter and then the section number within that part. References to the *Liji* follow the chapter, section, and line numbers in D. C. Lau and Fanzheng Cheng, eds., *A Concordance to the*

practices were frequently mentioned in narratives about the collective ascent of humanity from an animal-like existence in ancient times.[18] Moreover, in a closely related context, they were also used to describe the conditions that might lead to people's taking on an animal-like existence again should they fail to adhere to the established distinctions and guiding norms for society.

Given the aforementioned observations, the contours of early Chinese notions of personhood and humanhood—*ren* 人 —should be discernible. *Ren* 人 is most appropriately rendered as people/person, placing emphasis on the sociopolitical dimension of the discussions that employed this term; or, on occasion, to avoid semantic awkwardness in English, as human/humans or humanity—but *not* if the latter is taken to refer to a trans-historical biological category.

This interweaving of what we today refer to as the historical and biological dimensions of human existence is a gesture that is both intuitive and intricate at the same time. In the context of early Chinese philosophy, it amounts to an approach that not only recognizes certain affinities and family resemblances in the world but also sometimes attributes inborn tendencies to particular groups of beings. Still, not only did early Chinese thinkers acknowledge that there could be more than one way to structure the world and establish a scheme of distinctions and rankings; as Ziporyn notes, it was also admitted that "by making distinctions about which ways to group things . . . actual changes occur in the real world."[19] This also translates into a view that emphasizes what people *could* evolve or devolve into depending on the kind of ethos promoted in their communities.[20]

Such conceptualizations of *ren* 人 as pliant and ever-evolving are, in the end, what make possible the discourses of role-bounded responsibility, hierarchies, and social relations that make the persons who enact and

---

Liji (Hong Kong: Commercial Press, 1992). Citations to the *Mozi* give page, book, and line numbers in *Mozi Yinde* 墨子引得 [*A Concordance to Mo Tzu*], Harvard-Yenching Institute Sinological Index Series, Supplement no. 21 (Cambridge, MA: Harvard University Press, 1956). Citations to the *Xunzi* follow chapter and section numbers in John Knoblock, trans., *Xunzi: A Translation and Study of the Complete Works*, 3 vols. (Stanford, CA: Stanford University Press, 1988–1994). Citations to the *Lüshi Chunqiu* give book, chapter, and section numbers in John Knoblock and Jeffrey Riegel, trans., *The Annals of Lü Buwei* (Stanford, CA: Stanford University Press, 2000).

[18] This point is discussed in detail in chapter 8, section 8.3.
[19] Ziporyn, *Ironies of Oneness and Difference*, 125.
[20] This particular issue is explored in the exchange between Donald J. Munro and Sonya Özbey. See Donald J. Munro, "When Science Is in Defense of Value-Linked Facts," and Sonya Özbey, "The Plasticity of the Human and Inscribing History within Biology: A Response to Donald J. Munro," *Philosophy East and West* 69, no. 3 (2019): 900–917, 918–926.

perform them. Early Chinese visions of world order (whether as an ideal or an actuality) and people's place in it, then, are not only a matter of disinterested world-description but also of world-making with a conspicuous agenda for configuring and solidifying people's names and titles, roles and functions, commitments and responsibilities.[21]

The self-serving character of such teachings should be obvious given the ways they legitimize social hierarchies and promote behavioral constraints and incentives that primarily serve the interests of the courtly circles and the refined elite. Still, both the social class boundaries operating within humanity and the boundaries separating humanity par excellence from those who are deemed inferior to it were constantly shifting. This was partly due to social mobility, along with occasional shifts in class dynamics, and partly due to the fact that different ideologies gained traction in different and changing power centers. However, a common rhetorical tendency underpinning these shifting discursive grounds is the resort to animality tropes to criticize one's behavior and to describe one's position on the figurative ladder extending from brutish behavior to exemplary conduct.

Although animality clearly implies being less than human in texts that promote social hierarchy, the range of imageries employed parallels the variety of markers of one's humanity and the different ways one could fail to exhibit these markers. To give an example, whereas being like tigers and wolves can convey a sense of greedy or brash conduct, being like docile domestic animals (which is implied in the analogies drawn between the administrative success of the rulers and the herding of animals) implies the masses' inability to be the masters of their own lives.[22] There is also the more general category of *qin shou* 禽獸 (birds and wild animals), which is sometimes invoked figuratively when describing people with behavioral shortcomings or situations resulting from administrative failures. For instance, the *Mozi* compares a society without proper management of its resources to the conditions of birds and wild animals; the *Xunzi* describes the absence of respect in attending

---

[21] That early Chinese attempts at schematizing distinctions and groupings were embedded in structures of governance and accountability is a topic well explored, especially in the context of early Chinese philosophy of names/titles (*ming* 名). The most detailed study of the issue is in John Makeham, *Name and Actuality in Early Chinese Thought* (Albany: State University of New York Press, 1994). This point does not deny that early Chinese masters had a "disinterested" fascination with their surroundings as well, as seen in their observations about routine versus aberrant behaviors of animals, people, and even of stars. On this point, see Michael Nylan, "Humans as Animals and Things in Pre-Buddhist China," *Religions* 10, no. 6 (2019): 360, https://doi.org/10.3390/rel10060360, 2n8.

[22] The use of different animal imageries to describe various groups and their perceived behavioral patterns is discussed in chapter 9, section 9.1.

the burial ceremonies for a deceased parent as being close to the behavior of birds and wild animals; while the *Liji* describes the absence of a distinction between husband and wife as the way of birds and wild animals (*qinshou zhi dao* 禽獸之道).²³

At this juncture, the performative and conventionally constructed dimension of the human-animal divide in early Chinese elite thought should be clear. This, however, does not mean that there was not much weight given to this divide or that it was viewed as something that could be dismantled and rebuilt at whimsy. Neither does the porosity of the human-animal boundary translate into a celebratory attitude toward it.

Three observations must be raised here. First, as mentioned earlier, although many masters of philosophy seem to hold that the distinctions that people employ bring about actual changes in the world, we also see mentions of spontaneous and pre-discursive affinities in the world, which limit and inflect one's constructions. The *Xunzi*, for example, notes, "When a horse neighs, horses respond. When a cow moos, cows respond. This is not because of any wisdom; it is just the way things go."²⁴ Such observations convey the sense that the world is not simply one amorphous mass that one can whimsically carve up into different systems of understanding, as there are spontaneously occurring resemblances and connections in the world.

Second, attempts to police the human-animal binary abound in early Chinese philosophy. This is reflected in the fact that comparisons in which people are said to be similar to or are like birds and wild animals (which is different from being *identical* to birds and wild animals)²⁵ often feature in the context of shaming people into acting smarter, nicer, or more proper. Hence, such comparisons assert, if not fortify, differences between people and animals (as they are imagined), considering that they serve to point out that

---

[23] *Mozi* from 14/11/4 to 15/11/5 and 16/12/3–4. *Xunzi* 19.5a; *Liji* 11.25/10 ("Jiao Te Sheng郊特牲").

[24] *Xunzi* 3.8. For this quote from the *Xunzi*, I largely followed Ziporyn's translation in *Ironies of Oneness and Difference*, 205 (in Chinese the line reads: 故馬鳴而馬應之，牛鳴而牛應之，非知也，其勢然也。). *Lüshi Chunqiu* similarly notes: "Things of one kind inherently call each other up; things of same energy join together; sounds that are comparable resonate with each other" (13/2.1).

[25] Expressions such as *similar* to/being *like* birds and wild animals include *ruo qinshou* 若禽獸, *ruo qinshou ran* 若禽獸然, *ru qinshou* 如禽獸, and *zhi ru qinshou ran* 至如禽獸然. Sometimes we also see comparisons of a specific form of *conduct* to that of birds and wild animals (*qinshou zhi xing* 禽獸之行). In a similar vein, the *Xunzi*, in fact, cautions us against taking human-animal comparisons as assertions of identity when it says: "I wish to classify them [people who engage in brawling] as birds, rodents, or wild animals, but that would not be permissible, because their form is nevertheless human, and their likes and dislikes are largely the same [as those of humans] (我欲屬之鳥鼠禽獸邪？則又不可，其形體又人，而好惡多同。)." *Xunzi* 4.3.

one's conduct falls short of the group expectations so much so that one can be compared to *even* birds and wild animals.

Finally, and of greater significance, the kind of porosity expressed in early Chinese elite attitudes toward the human-animal boundary has its limits and is not to be equated with a full-fledged continuum or spectrum approach. This is particularly true if we define a continuum or spectrum as consisting solely of quantitative differences between people and animals (e.g., people are simply more moral, more perceptive, or more dexterous than animals).[26] The porosity in the human animal boundary certainly does not translate into the possibility of upward mobility for animals. Despite the assumed presence of overlapping commonalities between people and animals,[27] we also see unexplained discontinuities and leaps that set people apart from other earthlings, be it the assumption of a cluster of innate dispositions that people are said to have, or the tension that is assumed to exist between the decrees of Heaven and human affairs (especially when human affairs are not aligned with the workings of Heaven).[28]

There are, of course, cases of liminality[29] and a spectrum existing largely *within* humanity (i.e., some folks are considered to be more fully human

---

[26] This is also known as being different in degree, not in kind. The prevalent description of early Chinese attitudes toward the human-animal binary as an example of a continuum/spectrum approach seems to stem from a concern to differentiate early Chinese approaches from dominant Greco-European attitudes, which is important. For instance, Sterckx, who penned the most comprehensive and deservedly influential work on animality in early China, appears to be using the term "continuum" as a placeholder for a non-essentialist approach (i.e., an approach that does not argue for entirely preestablished differences between animals and humans, potentially unfolding in a "dualistic" universe with different laws and constraints applying to different beings). See, for instance, Roel Sterckx, *The Animal and the Daemon in Early China* (Albany: State University of New York Press, 2002), 240–241. While it is critical (and perhaps overdue) to not allow early Chinese discourses to be swallowed into Greco-European frameworks, perhaps what is particularly intriguing about early Chinese approaches to the human-animal split is the fact that they do not seem to fall on either side of an "either-or" dichotomy, where they either serve as examples of hard-and-fast essentialism or they view all differences to unfold on a smooth, continuous trajectory. The situation is "grittier" than that, perhaps partly because the extant sources we have do not happen to culminate in a unified theory about all living things.

[27] Including, sometimes, a shared basic moral ground, such as care for one's kin. For a discussion of this point, see Sterckx, *The Animal and the Daemon*, 88–91.

[28] A well-known example of an assumption that certain innate dispositions (*xing* 性) separate people from animals is the Mencian claim that people, unlike animals, are endowed with the "sprouts" (*duan* 端; beginnings) of certain virtues. On this see Dan Robins, "The Warring States Concept of *Xing*," *Dao* 10 (2011): 31–51. For a succinct overview of the tension between Heaven and people in early Chinese thought, see A. C. Graham, "Heaven and Man," in *Chuang-Tzu: The Inner Chapters* (Indianapolis, IN: Hackett, 2001), 15–19.

[29] An important case of liminality is Shun 舜, an ancient sage-sovereign who features in narratives of pre-dynastic antiquity (before the civilization-building acts of demarcation between animals and people took place). Shun initially appears to have an affinity with wilderness and animal life but eventually achieves full humanity. His continued exercise of control over the animal world is expressed in narratives about the ministers serving him, who are seemingly human but have animal names (hence

than others, which is the way differential processes of humanization tend to work). Furthermore, there is some degree of mobility in this hierarchical structure, where people can emancipate themselves from less-human or liminal statuses to achieve full humanity. However, perhaps because so much of the focus is on harvesting the rhetorical power of animal imageries to guide human behavior, we do not see speculations on (or an interest in) whether animals can climb up that ladder and acquire personhood (*ren* 人), nor do we see examples of, let us say, a common animal that manages to achieve the status of a sage through hard work and self-cultivation.[30] Hence, at the end of the day, one might, at best, describe early Chinese conceptualizations of the human-animal hierarchy a "continuum with leaps" or an "uneven ladder"—though, either way, it is very obvious who can aspire to reach the top.

Now, given the way animality tropes were employed to rank and judge people's performance of various deeds, which reveals assumptions about animality being "less than," it should not be surprising that a text that undermines a ranked approach to the world also mobilizes animal imagery differently. The *Zhuangzi* is often described in terms of its mischievous jabs at ideologues of the time, who are depicted as having a penchant for imposing norms and hierarchies on others. In the *Zhuangzi*, we indeed see many characters who efficaciously navigate the world by letting go of firm commitments to certain social roles, values, and obligations. Instead of striving to establish themselves in various vocations, callings, and stations in society, such characters excel at pivoting from one value system to another.[31] This approach, which emphasizes the plurality of vantage points, might seem prudent in an era marked by opposition and conflict. However, the *Zhuangzi* often pushes this plurality to its limits and includes the vantage points of people from humble occupations, alien peoples, ex-convicts, and even animals and plants.

---

also occupying positions of liminality themselves). For more, see Mark Edward Lewis, *The Flood Myths of Early China* (Albany: State University of New York Press, 2006), 33–37.

[30] There are, as Sterckx details, more modest examples of animals responding to music (Sterckx, *The Animal and the Daemon*, 129–137), which is crucial as music was believed by some to have a moral impact on its listeners. Of course, one could also argue that the point of these examples is to praise the skill of the music player whose influence reaches *even* to birds and wild animals. However, these examples use imageries of animals, instead of plant life or lakes and rivers, as the audience of the moralizing influence of a music master; this tells us something about a perceived proximity between people and various animals. Finally, there are, for what it is worth, also mentions of fabulous animals, but as Nylan points out, many thinkers in early China doubted their existence, although some thought they were "good to think with" (Nylan, "Humans as Animals and Things," 2n6).

[31] This point is discussed in more detail in chapter 4, section 4.2.

While this gesture bears a subversive aspect, even acts of subversion pay homage to that which they react against, and the *Zhuangzi* is no exception to this. Indeed, the *Zhuangzi*'s gesture of drastically multiplying vantage points on life's core issues could be seen as its own way of performing the aforementioned goal of completeness and comprehensiveness. The only difference is that the text pushes this to an extreme in order to invite the readers to roam outside of the usual confinements of society.

When so much of philosophizing and society-building is tied up with acts of demarcation, what kind of a text can actually roam and make us "roam outside the limits" (*you fang zhi wai* 遊方之外)?[32] This very question is continually visited and explored in the text itself. Certainly, the *Zhuangzi* is not the only early Chinese text with a meta-discursive dimension, nor is it the first one that reflects on its own limits.[33] However, it surely is one of the few extant Masters texts that make a point of letting go of claims to credibility, which perhaps is the shrewdest rhetorical trick in the book, as it enables the text to undermine dominant forms of power without being cornered into a definitive ideological position itself.

The next section explores the toolkits the text employs when moving among positions without being pinned down to one. These include the multiplication of "master" positions, sometimes in a way that also muddies the boundary between parody and homage; the deployment of new metaphors, not in order to convey a new teaching but to carry the reader to a meta-discursive level that exposes underlying assumptions of prevailing teachings; and self-referential gestures that announce the text's letting go of textual and political authority altogether. Moreover, since so much of this study concerns animal anecdotes, the section also probes the limits and possibilities of the animal "fables" featured in the text.

1.2 Loitering Idly with Zhuangzi's Big but "Useless" Words

For a text that touches on so many aspects of life, it is striking how little the *Zhuangzi* says in the way of a normative framework for evaluating things. Instead of instructive answers on the pressing questions of its age, the

---

[32] *Zhuangzi* 6:273.
[33] See *Laozi* 1, 25; or *Xunzi* 21.9.

Zhuangzi often offers a constant reminder—expressed through many stories, "fables," anecdotes, and staged conversations—of the tenuousness of any value position. Some of the episodes present us with fast-paced debates that function in a manner similar to Platonic dialogues, except that the argument is often carried to absurdity to show the limits of one's understanding.

When compared with other Masters texts that were compiled around the same period, what makes the *Zhuangzi* stand out is not the non-deductive character of its discourse, or all the anecdotes and stories it contains. In fact, as Paul R. Goldin points out, early Chinese philosophical reasoning relied mostly on analogies, appeals to examples (including anecdotes), and sometimes also parables and paradoxes, as opposed to deductive argumentative chains.[34] That the text lacks an identifiable author also places it in good company. As noted by Lewis, many early Chinese philosophical texts are penned and preserved by broader textual communities that elaborate, stage, and create "the master" in the act of producing "his" canon.[35] It is due to their composite nature that even the texts that revolve around the persona of a master, such as Kongzi, resist our modern expectations of coherence and closure.[36] Just as with any other early Chinese text that went through a long process of addition, subtraction, and adaptation—which sometimes takes more than a century, if not longer[37]—the *Zhuangzi* too presents us

---

[34] Paul R. Goldin, "Non-Deductive Argumentation in Early Chinese Philosophy," in *Between History and Philosophy: Anecdotes in Early China*, ed. Paul van Els and Sarah A. Queen (Albany: State University of New York Press, 2017), 41–62.

[35] See Mark Edward Lewis, *Writing and Authority*, 54–58. Moreover, as noted by Harbsmeier, there was also a division of labor in ancient China between the scribe, the "originator of the linguistic content of the text" (which comes closest to the person/people serving the authorial function), and the editor/compiler of the text. See Christoph Harbsmeier, "Authorial Presence in Some Pre-Buddhist Chinese Texts," in *De l'un au multiple. Traductions du Chinois vers les langues Europennes*, ed. Viviane Alleton and Michael Lackner (Paris: Fondation Maison des Sciences de l'Homme, 1999), 222.

[36] Contemporary scholars agree that the *Analects* was brought together over the course of more than two centuries and that not only is the work unreliable as a "recording" of Kongzi's own words, but it also presents various stylistic and argumentative inconsistencies. For a sample of controversies, see Weishu tongkao 偽書通考 (Comprehensive Investigation of Forged Writings) comp. Zhang Xincheng 張心澂 (Shanghai: Commercial Press, 1939), 454–459. Hence, Eno observes that the *Analects* should be regarded as a "collection of enduring thematic material, the product of many strata of composition and editing, representing a rough consensus text." See Robert Eno, *The Confucian Creation of Heaven: Philosophy and the Defense of Ritual Mastery* (Albany: State University of New York Press, 1990), 80.

[37] As Boltz explains, when we look at received texts with manuscript counterparts, we notice that the received texts are constructed of individual and movable textual units of about a "paragraph," which then facilitates the process of composition and recomposition of these texts as they are used by teachers, students, and disciples. See William G. Boltz, "The Composite Nature of Early Chinese Texts," in *Text and Ritual in Early China*, ed. Martin Kern (Seattle: University of Washington Press, 2005), 58–61. To describe the material conditions of early Chinese texts, Maeder uses the helpful analogy of "the loose-leaf ring binder into which miscellaneous material, including both class notes by different hands and documentary handouts, can be entered, only later to be rearranged, shortened

with a multivocal structure and a range of different positions on the topics it discusses.

What sets the *Zhuangzi* apart from many other examples of early Chinese Masters texts is its refraining from claims to credibility and its embrace of multivocality as a philosophical position. The text is overabundant with imaginary dialogues that involve characters ranging from a tree or a skull, to the Yellow Emperor or Kongzi. The character of Kongzi, in fact, appears more frequently than the character of Zhuang Zhou (Zhuangzi).[38] Moreover, he is used as a mouthpiece for a wide range of (and sometimes contradictory) positions,[39] which pays homage to and/or satiricizes the practice of quoting an authority figure to lend weight to one's arguments.[40]

Of course, giving voice to a variety of characters ranging from respectable to objectionable is not explainable simply as gestures of either parody or homage and nothing more. Indeed, the same multivocality also forces readers to wander among different vantage points instead of firmly settling on one position—which, very often, is also something that the *Zhuangzi*'s many characters themselves do as they pivot from one position to another according to the demands of the situation, rather than promoting or following a conclusive vision of the ideal life or the ideal society.[41]

---

or expanded as new material is found which is deemed pertinent, and as the compilers' concerns change." Erik W. Maeder, "Some Observations on the Composition of the 'Core Chapters' of the *Mozi*," *Early China* 17 (1992): 27–28.

[38] Moreover, as Lewis also notes, the *Zhuangzi* is "distinctive in the minor role given to its eponymous master," compared to how often Kongzi and his disciples appear as characters in the text. Lewis, *Writing and Authority*, 89. Klein also recently challenged, with success, the view that the "inner chapters" might have come from a single hand, which might be the historical Zhuangzi, by demonstrating that there probably were not "inner chapters" during the Warring States period to begin with. See Klein, "Were There Inner Chapters?" Throughout this book I will avoid making claims about the historical Zhuangzi, about whom we know virtually nothing. In fact, given the way the text mocks and parodies other texts and figures of the period, it is possible that the name of the text is, in fact, a humorous salute to the tradition of naming a collection of writings after a sagacious master whose ideas it is intended to capture.

[39] For a detailed examination of the ways Kongzi is portrayed in the *Zhuangzi*, see Ronnie Littlejohn, "Kongzi in the Zhuangzi," in *Experimental Essays on Zhuangzi*, ed. Victor H. Mair (Dunedin: Three Pines Press, 2010), 177–194.

[40] For some, such as Chong Kim-Chong, the *Zhuangzi* is certainly critiquing Kongzi and his followers, while for others, such as Chen Guying and Wang Bo, the *Zhuangzi* is paying homage to them. See Kim-chong Chong, *Zhuangzi's Critique of the Confucians: Blinded by the Human* (Albany: State University of New York Press, 2016). CHEN Guying 陳鼓應, *Lao-Zhuang Xin Lun* 老莊新論 [New theories on Laozi and Zhuangzi] (Beijing 北京: The Commercial Press 商務印書館, 2008). WANG Bo 王博. *Zhuangzi zhexue* 莊子哲學 [The philosophy of Zhuangzi] (Beijing 北京: Peking University Publishing 北京大學出版, 2004).

[41] This reading, which views multivocality as a philosophical approach and literary strategy, is, in fact, upheld in a chapter titled *Yu Yan* 寓言. The chapter title translates to "Imputed Words," or more literally, "Lodging Place Speech," which involves expressing various viewpoints through the mouths of different figures.

Instead of trying to persuade the reader of a certain didactic vision, the text frequently ponders how various phenomena might seem to different people and even to different creatures. In fact, the very first chapter of the received text opens with the tale of a fish that transforms into a large bird that soars in the sky, only to pause and wonder (from the vantage point of the bird) what the true color of the sky might be. Is it blue or does it only appear that way from a distance? We never get an answer to that question, as the text quickly shifts perspective again and this time joins a little cicada and a turtledove in wondering why the large bird flies so high.[42]

As mentioned earlier, this frequent change of vantage points can be seen as the text's own version of the performance of a comprehensive approach to life that rises above limited and limiting positions. Instead of speculating on the nature of shared dispositions among people or offering codes of behavior that are expected to be effective across different corners of All under Heaven, the *Zhuangzi* multiplies the vantage points from which one can view various phenomena. This includes considering the vantage points of different animals.

At this juncture, the question that demands our attention is this: To what extent can one do justice to the uniqueness of different vantage points, without assimilating them into one's own epistemic and affective horizon? Such concerns become more salient when the gesture of paying heed to others' judgments, needs, and emotions is extended to animals. Furthermore, in the *Zhuangzi*, differences among people are sometimes juxtaposed with those among animals,[43] which might be taken as a rhetorical gesture that uses animals as metaphorical doppelgängers of humans in order to draw attention to different positions within the human community—and nothing more. This begs a related question: Do the animal anecdotes in the *Zhuangzi* tell us anything about the animal experience itself?

This question is a familiar one for scholars of animal fables and is relevant to *Zhuangzi* studies given how often the animal anecdotes in the work are described as animal "fables." Although it is true that some of the animal stories in the text have an allegorical function, given the overwhelming prevalence of imageries used by La Fontaine and Aesop, it should perhaps be clarified from the outset that in the *Zhuangzi* we do not see violin-playing

---

[42] *Zhuangzi* 1:10.
[43] See, for instance, the first chapter of the transmitted text, where the opening episode that juxtaposes different vantage points of various animals is later followed by an episode about regional differences between people of Song 宋 and Yue 越. *Zhuangzi* 1:2–13, 35.

grasshoppers or hares challenging tortoises, and the animal characters in the text are very rarely humanized. They never wear human clothing, they rarely speak, and for the most part we are told of their likes and dislikes based on the requirements of their habitats and their observable behavior (e.g., getting visibly upset, violent, or sick, or fleeing a scene, and so on).[44] In other words, many animal anecdotes take note of the animality of their characters instead of introducing them to the readers as "little men disguised," as Foster puts it.[45]

This approach also relates to the text's deployment of a much greater variety of animal imageries than the typical few that are often used in early Chinese philosophical discourse as shorthand for various human virtues, vices, or privation (e.g., wolves for aggressive folks, or horses for subjects awaiting care and direction).[46] In fact, as Liu Chengji once counted, the Zhuangzi includes references to birds of 22 species, 15 kinds of aquatic life, 32 species of land animals, 18 kinds of insects, 37 kinds of plants, and 34 species of fantastic divine creatures.[47] What primarily motivates this level of interest in many different life forms is not the desire to enliven our poetic imagination à la the Book of Odes (Shi Jing 詩經) but to entertain how life might seem to different beings and to try to view them on their own terms, without moralizing their behavior or ranking them in comparison to human beings.

This still leaves us to address the animal anecdotes in the Zhuangzi that have possible or obvious allegorical layers and to ask whether they merely

---

[44] An explicitly anthropomorphic depiction of an animal takes place in the Wai Wu外物 (External Things) chapter, which features a carp (fu yu 鮒魚) speaking to the character of Zhuangzi after introducing itself as the minister of the Eastern sea waves (donghai zhi bo chen 東海之波臣) (Zhuangzi 26:917). Even in this tale, however, the carp is portrayed as needing water to survive, in the character of a fish. There are a few other examples of animals depicted to be speaking (yue 曰), albeit to each other and while being bounded by their natural habitats and unique characteristics. This includes a cicada and a turtledove who talk about how short a distance they can travel by hopping and flying (1:10); or a frog talking to a turtle about the difficulty of surviving in a broken well (17:597–598). In addition, the distinctiveness of speech (言 yan) as a human-specific activity is also challenged in the text when we are asked whether there is any difference between speech (of humans) and the chirping of fledglings to begin with (2:68). As for the other animal characters whose various judgments and preferences are gathered from their observable behavior or from well-known facts about their habitats, the examples are plenty, but they include monkeys who become upset about their meal portions (2:76); considerations about what loaches, elks, deer, snakes, monkeys, birds, and fish find comfortable, tasty, or pleasing (2:98–99); and observations about the behavior of fish in and out of water (6:247).
[45] Cited in Naama Harel, "Constructing the Nonhuman as Human: Scientific Fallacy, Literary Device," in Restoring the Mystery of the Rainbow: Literature's Refraction of Science, 2 vols., ed. Valeria Tinkler-Villani and C. C. Barefoot (Leiden: Brill, 2011), 906.
[46] Of course, sometimes the Zhuangzi also resorts to imageries of animals that are associated with human characteristics (e.g., tigers and horses, which, respectively, connote ferocious and domesticable behavior).
[47] Liu Chengji, Wuxiang Meixue 物象美學 [The image of aesthetics] (Zhengzhou: Zhengzhou Daxue Chubanshe, 2002), 381.

employ animal imageries as placeholders for different peoples. First, much of the possibly allegorical dimension of animal anecdotes in the *Zhuangzi* stems from the fact that, as mentioned earlier, we see instances of describing alien peoples as animal-like in early Chinese philosophical discourse. Hence, in the context of the *Zhuangzi*, an implied or alleged parallel between an animal suffering at the hands of a human's assimilative impulses (i.e., treating the animal like a human) and a non-Zhou outsider being uncomfortable with the norms of political power centers speaks to, if anything, the interconnections between the domineering practices of folks who impose their norms on others.[48]

Second, as Harel points out, "every analogy necessarily contains both similarity and difference—otherwise the two contents would not be analogical, but identical," adding that ignoring this differential gap and taking the animal experience in a story to be nothing more than a colorful way of speaking about human experience is a bias on the part of the reader[49] (a reader who assumes that animals do not have judgments, perspectives, and preferences of their own).[50] Such a reductionist reading choice becomes even more problematic when we consider that the human-nonhuman distinction features as a major theme of its own in the *Zhuangzi*, suggesting that the animal characters in the text do more than simply serve as sounding boards for human conditions.[51]

Finally, there is the larger question of whether one can *ever* do justice to the vantage point of an animal (or human, for that matter). The *Zhuangzi*, in fact, addresses this specific question in a passage where Zhuangzi, as an embedded character, is seen to be strolling on the Hao bridge, looking over

---

[48] For more, see chapter 5, section 5.1

[49] Naama Harel, "The Animal Voice behind the Fable," *Journal for Critical Animal Studies* 7, no. 2 (2009): 17–19.

[50] Traditional commentaries on the *Zhuangzi* are, in fact, broad-minded at large about how to approach animal anecdotes, as they do not fall on either side of an interpretive divide, that is, viewing animal anecdotes to be primarily allegories about the human condition versus taking them to be genuine reflections on animal life and how it contrasts with that of humans. At times we see commentaries that side with the latter interpretational choice (*Zhuangzi* 17:605–606), at times with the former (*Zhuangzi* 17:598); and at times with both, giving both a literal and an allegorical reading of an animal anecdote (*Zhuangzi* 4:173).

[51] An example of viewing animal "fables" in the *Zhuangzi* as episodes that are "meant to be read analogically as instructions for human thought and behavior" can be seen in Richard John Lynn, "Birds and Beasts in the Zhuangzi, Fables Interpreted by Guo Xiang and Cheng Xuanying," *Religions* 10 (2019): 445, https://doi.org/10.3390/rel10070445. The fact of the matter is that one could also easily argue that some of the examples Lynn gives from Guo Xiang's and Cheng Xuanying's commentaries actually view the animal fables in a non-analogical fashion—that is, as literal reflections on animal life and animal perspectives (see, for instance, the commentary quoted on page 5 of Lynn's piece).

fish swimming in the river. Zhuangzi, the character, says, "The fish come out and swim at ease, this is the joy of fish." When pressed to explain how he knows about the joy of fish, he says, "I know it from above the Hao (*wo zhi zhi hao shang ye* 我知之濠上也)," acknowledging the positionality of his knowledge claims.[52] In other words, his observation is not about understanding how a fish feels as a fish but about how a human would feel as a fish—which acknowledges Zhuangzi's imperfect ability to enter into the inner lives of others.[53]

Zhuangzi's answer also sums up what is at stake when the text—just like the character of Zhuangzi in it—wanders among different positions. It is not an exercise in walking in others' shoes but in seeing others as being the centers of their own worlds. This way, although one may not be able to see *through* the eyes of fish, or quail, or praying mantises, one is still *seeing* animals as producers of perspectives, judgments, and evaluations.[54] Such an attitude expands one's epistemic purview not by transcending one's situatedness but by acknowledging it.

Having noted that the *Zhuangzi* features a wide variety of marginalized groups as central characters of various anecdotes, a few words must be said about *how* they are featured. It is crucial that in the *Zhuangzi* some of these characters also end up teaching a new insight to someone in a position of higher power and authority. Well-known examples include a butcher inspiring a ruler to navigate the demands of life with ease, Kongzi getting lectured by his own disciple, and a skull helping Zhuangzi relax his grip on life.[55] These obvious gestures of role reversal not only take jabs at the perceived pomposity of the elite and the wise, but they also undermine the power of privileged sites of knowledge production by multiplying master positions. What results is a proliferation of opinions and arguments that do not culminate in a finalizing conclusion.

This particular feature of the text is not simply an accidental byproduct of the enterprise of anthology-building, which, one might say, necessarily

---

[52] *Zhuangzi* 17:606. This episode is analyzed in detail in chapter 5, section 5.1.

[53] I owe this insight to ethologist Frans de Waal, who, in response to Thomas Nagel's famous essay "What Is It Like to Be a Bat?" notes that "Nagel did not seek to know how a human would feel as a bat: he wanted to understand how a bat feels like a bat." See Frans de Waal, *Are We Smart Enough to Know How Smart Animals Are?* (New York: W. W. Norton, 2016), 9.

[54] I owe this insight to Harel. Cited in Tua Korhonen, "Anthropomorphism and the Aesopic Animal Fables," in *Animals and Their Relation to Gods, Humans and Things in the Ancient World*, ed. Raija Mattila, Sanae Ito, and Sebastian Fink (New York: Springer, 2019), 222.

[55] *Zhuangzi* 3:123–130, 6:288–290, 18:616–618.

involves bringing together many stories with many characters.[56] Not only the dilution of privileged centers of wisdom is built into the stories themselves, but the *Zhuangzi* also invokes self-referential metaphors of not settling on a viewpoint. One such metaphor is *zhiyan* 卮言, goblet speech, commonly taken to refer to a vessel that tips over when full, pouring out its contents—which, in the context of speech acts seems to refer to being prolific and open-ended.[57] In other words, the same way this vessel never gets completely filled and comes to a halt, one's discourse never reaches a finalizing conclusion.

This deliberate embracing of an ever-mobile and flexible attitude forms an obvious contrast with the prevailing emphasis on distinction clarification and nominal consistency that we see in early Chinese philosophical discourse. This too is not a coincidence. As a number of scholars have shown, so much of what goes by the description "early Chinese theories of language" revolves around establishing how to bind names and titles to situations and deeds in order to ensure social cohesion and political order.[58] This is because in a milieu where political and textual goals are so conjoined, aspirations for clarifying hierarchies, relationships, roles, and jobs also demand clear and "correct" ways of speaking about them.[59] Instead of attempting to sort out

---

[56] For a discussion of the view that describes the *Zhuangzi* as an anthology, see Esther Sunkyung Klein, "Early Chinese Textual Culture and the *Zhuangzi* Anthology: An Alternative Model for Authorship," in *Dao Companion to the Philosophy of the Zhuangzi*, ed. Kim-chong Chong (New York: Springer, 2022), 13–42.

[57] Guo Xiang's commentary suggests that *zhi* 卮 is a type of vessel that tips over when full. See *Zhuangzi* 27:939. For a detailed examination of not only the expression "goblet speech" (卮言) but also the evolution of the metaphor of the goblet across early Chinese texts, see Daniel Fried, "A Never-Stable Word: Zhuangzi's 'Zhiyan' 卮言 and 'Tipping-vessel' Irrigation," *Early China* 31 (2007): 145–170.

[58] This point is central to John Makeham's study, *Name and Actuality in Early Chinese Thought*. Also see Hans-Georg Moeller, "Chinese Language Philosophy and Correlativism," *Bulletin of the Museum of Far Eastern Antiquities* 72 (2000): 91–109; and Jane Geaney, *On the Epistemology of the Senses in Early Chinese Thought* (Honolulu: University of Hawai'i Press, 2002), 121. The two exceptions to the observation about the sociopolitical dimension of early Chinese theories of language are the School of Names (*ming jia* 名家) and the later Mohist canon. In a later work Geaney points out that the School of Names—a group that is credited for initiating a discussion about language solely for its own sake—seems to "mostly refer to figures whose works are unknown, lost, obscure, and/or forged." Jane Geaney, *Language as Bodily Practice in Early China: A Chinese Grammatology* (Albany: State University of New York Press, 2018), xvii–xviii. Finally, about the later Mohist canon, Makeham observes that their "overriding concern was not that a name accurately and faithfully represents some object, but rather that the distinctions invested in that name be maintained." Makeham, *Name and Actuality*, 52.

[59] My emphasis on "speech" and "speaking" about names and titles has to do with the fact that, as Geaney demonstrates, early Chinese theories of language focused on tallying two aspects of reality: aural (that is, one's name, title) and visual (such as one's actions and performance of duties). See Geaney, *Epistemology of the Senses*, 121. It should also be noted that masters' teachings were memorized and recited in early China, which is perhaps why, as Geaney observes, books are said to "speak (*yan* 言)." Jane Geaney, "Grounding "Language" in the Senses: What the Eyes and Ears Reveal about Ming 名 (Names) in Early Chinese Texts," *Philosophy East and West* 60, no. 2 (2010): 252.

distinctions and solidify names and titles, the *Zhuangzi* promises its readers the absence of such stability in the text *and* in the kind of realm imagined in the text.

It is not uncommon (and frankly tempting) to attribute the *Zhuangzi*'s destabilizing and playful style to its frequent use of metaphors. Although it is indeed true that there are quite a number of metaphors used in the text, all the other extant Masters texts make ample use of metaphors as well, and yet none of them reads like the *Zhuangzi*. It is also worth noting that despite the modern tendency to associate figurative speech with creativity, purposeful ambiguity, and imaginative thought, [60] many masters tapped into a common pool of metaphors and analogies (which tells us that the prevailing motive behind their usage might not be literary originality). Moreover, as will be shown, the context in which these metaphors and analogies were often employed does not quite suggest a desire to help readers unshackle themselves from traditionalist thought patterns, either.

When we contextualize the *Zhuangzi*'s use of metaphors with an eye on the text's own intellectual context, what stands out is not that the text uses metaphors but that it so often mobilizes metaphors differently, either to offer an intertextual critique or to carry the readers to a meta-discursive level. While the former nudges them to think about prevailing patterns of thinking, the latter prompts them to reflect on the text's own modalities of thinking.

To flesh out these points about metaphor usage in the *Zhuangzi*, in the final pages of the chapter I will give a brief contrastive analysis of one of the most common types of metaphors in early Chinese Masters texts and Classics, namely, plant metaphors. The reason I focus on plant metaphors is their pervasiveness in relevant early Chinese texts, which makes them convenient cases for an intertextual analysis. Furthermore, in a crucial episode, the *Zhuangzi* also employs such metaphors in a critical way that gives readers clues about how to approach a text like itself.

In much of early Chinese textual culture, metaphors were mobilized to largely discuss fundamental moral-political and administrative issues. Botanical metaphors, in particular, commonly featured in discussions about the arts of governance of people. These discussions covered a wide range of

---

[60] Of course, this common approach that views metaphors as artistic deviations from literal usage, which traces as far back as to Aristotle, has also been challenged by George Lakoff and Mark Johnson. In their seminal study *Metaphors We Live By* (Chicago: University of Chicago Press, 2003), they demonstrate the wide array of ways metaphors permeate human thought beyond mere instances of poetic evocation.

topics, such as long-term moral-psychological practices of guiding people's dispositions in desirable directions, or the practical management of their labor and services. The examples of botanical metaphors vary but include the *Liji*'s description of a gentleman's self-cultivation practices as the chiseling and polishing of bamboos; the *Chunqiu fanlu*'s (春秋繁露) discussion of bringing out the goodness of people by using the imagery of rice plants, which, through patient efforts turn into refined rice; and the *Guanzi*'s (管子) advice to employ people the way one makes use of plants (*caomu* 草木).[61]

Although such botanical metaphors are employed to convey different pedagogical and managerial attitudes—some gentle, some stern—they share the common assumption of the initial likeness and pliancy of the people that are to be cultivated and managed. This optimistic or wishful attitude, which is rarely inflected with the possibility of resistance on the part of the cultivated and managed, is also folded into the authors' choices of specific plant imagery: neat bamboo shoots looking ever-elegant as they are polished; dainty rice plants lending themselves to refinement; and commonplace vegetation that provides food, fuel, and so on.[62]

As is well known, metaphors in general never exist in isolation but emerge from shared codes and structures of meaning, which is also true of the metaphors employed in the *Zhuangzi*. To this point, one might want to add that, when dealing with a text like the *Zhuangzi*, paying attention to the wider textual practices of the time becomes especially crucial, as the text's reactionary streak necessarily renders it parasitic on the texts and traditions it parodies and undermines. Hence, it is not a coincidence that within the intertextual ecosystem of plant metaphors, commonly populated by imageries of cultivable and manageable plants, the *Zhuangzi* picks imageries of anomalous and unruly trees as its alternative metaphors of choice. As will be shown,

---

[61] See *Liji* 43.1/4-5 ("Da Xue 大學"); *Chunqiu fanlu* 36.1; *Guanzi* 2.6:112 ("Qi Fa 七法"). References to the *Chunqiu fanlu* follow the section numbers given in Sarah A. Queen and John S. Major, trans., *Luxuriant Gems of the Spring and Autumn* (New York: Columbia University, 2016). References to the *Guanzi* follow book (*juan* 卷), chapter (*pian* 篇), and page numbers in *Guanzi jiaozhu* 管子校注, Li Xiangfeng 黎翔鳳, ed., Beijing 北京: Zhonghua shuju 中華書局, 2004. For a broader examination of botanical metaphors in early Chinese literature, see Sarah Allan, *The Way of Water and Sprouts of Virtue* (Albany: State University of New York Press, 1997), 10-25, 99-122. Also see Albert Galvany, "Discussing Usefulness: Trees as Metaphor in the *Zhuangzi*," *Monumenta Serica*, 57, no. 1 (2009), 71-97.

[62] An interesting exception to this trend (of choosing metaphors of pliant plants to discuss issues of the cultivation and administration of the people) is *Han Feizi*'s pruning metaphor, used in the context of the need to curb ministerial powers of patronage. Although the analogy does not suggest resistance on the part of the individual, it does suggest that if trees grow too thick and their branches become interlocked (i.e., if officials start building cliques), they can pose a threat to the ruler. The analogy is discussed in Albert Galvany, "Discussing Usefulness," 76-77.

when examined with an eye toward the wider intertextual context, what surfaces is not merely the gesture of stimulating readers' fancy by employing metaphorical language alone but the hijacking of their sociopolitical imagination and textual expectations by employing imageries of atypical trees that resist the logic of governmentality.

One such anomalous and unruly tree imagery appears in the closing episode of the first chapter of the transmitted text. The episode starts with Huizi, Zhuangzi's sparring partner, telling him,

> I have a huge tree of the kind people call ailanthus (*chu* 樗). Its trunk is swollen and gnarled, impossible to align with a plumb line (*shengmo* 繩墨). The branches are twisted and bent, impossible to align to a compass or square (*guiju* 規矩). Even if it were standing right by the road, a carpenter would not give it so much as a second glance. Now your words too are big but useless, which is why people join in spurning them.[63]

As a response, the character of Zhuangzi suggests that instead of worrying about the uselessness of the big tree, Huizi should "plant it in the region of not-even-anything, in the wilderness of vast nowhere. There [you] could loiter idly, doing nothing by its side, or ramble around and fall asleep beneath it."[64] Since both Huizi's accusation and Zhuangzi's response are packed with implicit expectations, disappointments, and renouncements that are also conveyed through discursively loaded imageries, they require an equally layered and contextual analysis.

First, in what ways could Zhuangzi's discourse be "useless"? Given the aforementioned connection between Masters texts and political power, we would expect the uselessness of Zhuangzi's words to have to do with the futility of using them for management and administrative purposes. This reading is supported by Huizi's use of yet another cluster of metaphors—namely, plumb line, compass, and square—which were also widely employed in early Chinese texts when talking about establishing norms and standards that would bring order to people's behavioral patterns and serve as correctives to wrongdoings.[65] Of course, this correctional attitude extends to

---

[63] *Zhuangzi* 1:45.
[64] *Zhuangzi* 1:46.
[65] Lisa Raphals, "Craft Analogies in Chinese and Greek Argumentation," in *Literature, Religion, and East/West Comparison: Essays in Honor of Anthony C. Yu*, ed. Eric Ziolkowski (Newark: University of Delaware Press, 2005), 181–201.

one's speech as well, which, as mentioned earlier, is replaced in the *Zhuangzi* with an approach that emphasizes instability (conveyed with the metaphor of a spillover goblet). Hence, it is not surprising that to attack Zhuangzi's manner of speech, the character of Huizi invokes the image of a gnarly tree that does not align with the corrective tools of moral-political enterprises. Zhuangzi's words are lofty, he admits, but simply too odd and extravagant to align with any message that would be morally and/or politically useful.

It is not uncommon for texts with critical teeth to devour themselves along the way, and the *Zhuangzi* is no exception. The character of Zhuangzi does not try to demonstrate to Huizi that he is, in fact, deserving of recognition as a man of worth. Instead, he simply lets go of discursive and political authority at the same time.[66] Moreover, that Guo Xiang—the definitive editor of the text—chose to close the very first chapter of the *Zhuangzi* with this episode is perhaps not a coincidence; and perhaps the lofty but useless metaphorical tree is not only the character of Zhuangzi in the episode but also the text of the *Zhuangzi*. If so, we the readers are urged to disabuse ourselves from the outset of the usual expectations of use and utility. Moreover, in the episode, Zhuangzi does more than give a shrug to Huizi's accusations; he tells him what to do with the literal and metaphorical tree in question: He is to idly wander in its shade and enjoy its directionless turns and twists.

Now, although Zhuangzi the character and *Zhuangzi* the text let go of claims of discursive and political authority, an invitation to repose and wander is not without textual and political significance. On the contrary, the suspension of the effort to win a place for oneself in circles of power seems to actually clear space for unprofitable truths to reveal themselves.

Recalling that botanical metaphors in early Chinese philosophy relate to ideals for the effective management of the realm and the governance of its people, the imagery of an anomalous tree serves as a reminder of the diversity of the plant *and* the sociopolitical realm at the same time. In other words, the totalizing impulses of self-avowedly comprehensive texts, which aim to bring together a fragmented land through instructive and administrative measures, perhaps conveniently leave out that which resists cultivation and management. If the bamboo stands for the male civic ideal, then the gnarly tree serves as a reminder of all that is marginalized or excluded from

---

[66] A similar parallel is also drawn by Galvany, namely, one between the lofty but "useless" tree and the *Zhuangzi*'s "discursive modality" that departs from "the logic of efficiency, benefits, and utility that permeates the circles of power." Galvany, "Discussing Usefulness," 86.

dominant centers of power: peoples of foreign lands, humble craftsmen, ex-convicts, disfigured folks, mad men, and, of course, all kinds of animals that constitute and sustain the much-cherished boundaries around and within humanity at large.

That the character of Zhuangzi simply embraces the peculiarity of the tree thus serves as a gesture for letting the realm (and its many different and overlooked corners) be instead of advancing exclusionary fantasies of order and cohesion. Zhuangzi too wants to be allowed to be as he is, instead of being forced into some programmatic agenda (resulting in frustration for Huizi when such efforts prove unsuccessful).

It should be noted that this nonchalant attitude toward participation in the moral and political order is, in fact, attested by not only other dialogues of a similar nature but also by many of the literary settings used in the text. As Perkins points out, many of the episodes in the *Zhuangzi* are set in woods or along streams, and the character of Zhuangzi himself is portrayed as lounging under trees or strolling alongside rivers instead of, like Mengzi, spending his time "in courts, or waiting around to get into courts, or talking about whether or not to go to court."[67] Hence, if there is one final orienting insight to be gleaned about the text, it is that in the *Zhuangzi* the primary context for human activity becomes not simply various strata of organized society (e.g., the family, community, the local court, the royal court) but all the nooks and corners of the known world. It is thanks to this broader context that even when one is operating within the confines of stratified and hierarchical polities, one's heart and mind (*xin* 心)[68] can still roam outside of them by not being overly committed to the roles and duties one has been allotted.

Finally, if the concluding episode of the first chapter, featuring a frustrated Huizi and a carefree Zhuangzi, also serves as our reading guide, then this self-avowedly gnarly and unruly text, fit for a gnarly and unruly realm, is also to be enjoyed without trying to pin it down to a final position. We are to resist our totalizing impulses as readers and instead wander through this text without seeking final verdicts on how to manage our and others' lives. Only then can we perhaps allow ourselves to repose and relish in its fanciful

---

[67] Franklin Perkins, "Following Nature with Mengzi or Zhuangzi," *International Philosophical Quarterly* 45, no. 3 issue 179 (2005): 334.

[68] This point is developed in detail in chapter 4, section 4.2, but it should be briefly noted here that although *xin* 心 refers to one's heart, the heart was considered to be the center of one's understanding and cognition in addition to one's affective states. For this reason, many translations render it as "heart-mind."

anecdotes, stories, and aphorisms, and entertain gnarly questions and out-of-the-ordinary viewpoints. These might include the viewpoint of yet another unruly tree that gives a new spin on its own uselessness (!), of another incarnation of Zhuangzi who makes a fool of himself as he is lost in watching a little praying mantis, or of a bird that wonders what the real color of sky is. In the end, instead of giving easy answers about rights and wrongs, we are invited to ponder, together with another *Zhuangzi* character named Wang Ni, whether there is anything that all things can affirm as right—and to not be alarmed if the answer turns out to be "I do not know."

2
Contexts and Means for Interpreting Spinoza

Spinoza in his *Tractatus de Intellectus Emendatione* (*Treatise on the Emendation of the Intellect*; henceforth TIE) shares the following sentiment: "It is part of my happiness to take pains that many others may understand as I understand, so that their intellect and desire agree entirely with my intellect and desire. To do this it is necessary . . . to form a society of the kind that is desirable, so that as many as possible may attain it as easily and surely as possible" (TIE 14). Despite the common perception of Spinoza as a thinker stuck in an epistemic ivory tower contemplating eternal truths and universal laws,[1] it is this ambitious civic-minded goal—that is, making others understand as he understands, so they too can be filled with a refined joy—that fuels much of his multifaceted oeuvre. How did Spinoza go about seeking this lofty goal of achieving collective understanding and alignment with mankind?[2] Furthermore, why did his works ironically provoke so much disagreement and criticism from his contemporaries?

This chapter offers an overview of Spinoza's works in the context of the contemporaneous debates around the proper content and purpose of "natural philosophy" and its relation to "Cartesianism" in the Dutch Republic in the late seventeenth century. Despite being known for its radicality, Spinoza's

---

[1] This reading stems from (mis)interpreting Spinoza's epistemology in terms of completely turning one's attention away from particulars to underlying commonalities and eventually to God—sometimes to the point of adopting God's perspective. A well-known defense of this view is offered by Scruton, who argues that for Spinoza true freedom demands that we rise above the "illusory perspective" of inadequate ideas to "the absolute viewpoint, which is God's." See Roger Scruton, *Spinoza* (Oxford: Oxford University Press, 1986), 73. As Nadler notes as well, however, knowing something adequately or inadequately in Spinoza is rather a matter of considering it in relation to different causal relations. See Steven Nadler, *Spinoza's Ethics: An Introduction* (Cambridge: Cambridge University Press, 2006), 165. Spinoza's epistemological views are discussed in more detail in Part II, chapter 3.

[2] In my treatment of Spinoza's philosophy, I will largely retain his gendered language. Spinoza uses the broader "human" only as a qualifier when talking about, let us say, "human mind" (*mens humana*), "human nature" (*natura humana*), or "human race" (*humanum genus*); but he always uses "men" (*homines*) or "man" (*homo*) when simply referring to the actual group of "humans" as a collective unit. Hence, I too will be following this practice while discussing his works. Spinoza's views on gender are treated in detail in chapter 10, section 10.2.

philosophy certainly also shares many of the characteristics of the natural philosophy of the period, including a profound fear of religious discord and a penchant for inquiring into new methodologies, such as the mathematico-mechanical modeling of nature, that would ideally secure universal access to certain indubitable truths about the world.[3] Of course, redefining mankind's approach to nature also has implications for man's understanding of his very place in the world as well as his relation to God, the creator of said world.[4] In many ways Spinoza largely pursued these implications in his works. However, as will be shown, his pursuit unfolded against the background of a campaign to leave theological matters to theologians alone, which did not help his cause as a natural philosopher. Neither did some of his conclusions, such as his denial of human free will, aid in gaining acceptance for his ideas.

Perhaps due to his awareness of the radicality of some of his conclusions, but also because of the period's investment in "clear and distinct" knowledge and in forms of exposition that would ideally render one's conclusions beyond challenge, Spinoza left behind a remarkably methodical and systematic edifice. Hence, the latter part of the chapter examines issues of methodology and literary format in Spinoza's philosophy while at the same time paying special attention to the pedagogical features of his works. As will be shown, methodological and elocutionary concerns were important for Spinoza particularly because they related to his commitment to uplift mankind by expounding and disseminating truths about their existence in a vast yet intelligible universe. Also crucial for this analysis is Spinoza's approach toward not only systematic forms of exposition but also what he perceived as a less desirable alternative: figurative language. The chapter also pays attention to this understudied subject, which facilitates a deeper exploration of Spinoza's thought beyond the mere identification of his self-coherent arguments and helps reveal inadvertent truths about his philosophy.

---

[3] Wiep Van Bunge, *From Stevin to Spinoza: An Essay on Philosophy in the Seventeenth-Century Dutch Republic* (Leiden: Brill, 2001), 123. Although the chapter will largely focus on Spinoza's immediate historical context, it is worth noting that neither the high regard for mathematics nor a profound fear of religious wars was limited to intellectuals of the Dutch Republic. These elements of natural philosophy were palpable in varying degrees across early modern Europe.

[4] Since for most seventeenth-century writings, the "subject position" was primarily imagined to be male, when discussing Spinoza's intellectual context I too will often refer to "man" and "mankind" instead of using the gender-inclusive "humans" or "humankind." As Shapin notes, "The man of science was... almost always male, and to use anything but this gendered language to designate the pertinent early modern role or roles would be historically jarring. The system of exclusions that kept out the vast numbers of the unlettered also kept out all but a very few women." See Steven Shapin, "The Man of Science," in *The Cambridge History of Science*, vol. 3, *Early Modern Science*, ed. Katharine Park and Lorraine Daston (New York: Cambridge University Press, 2016), 179. Also see footnote 2.

2.1 Lifting Up and Placing Down the Man into the Machine-World: Contested Routes to Knowledge and Salvation

It is tempting to study Spinoza's philosophy, especially his ontology, in the way we commonly take him to approach the natural world: with the disinterested eye of reason. This is partly due to the prevalent tendency to contextualize early modern European philosophers within the history of the "scientific revolution" and its involvement in assumptions and ideals of objectivity.[5] While it is undeniable that early modern natural philosophers in the Dutch Republic and beyond aspired to decipher the Book of Nature in a way that would look the same to whoever was studying it with the "right" method, what intimately inflected, if not inspired, such lofty ideals of universally true knowledge were fantasies of ending all kinds of disagreement once and for all, so as to finally put an end to all wars.

Indeed, much of the natural philosophy of the period unfolded against the background of disruptive religious and political discord, including the devastating Thirty Years War of 1618–1648. The concomitant and resulting ardor for ending all disagreements not only bolstered the continuation of lively scriptural debates and fueled a boom in encyclopedic writing in Europe, but it also supplied the normative foundation for the search for methodologies that would enable mankind to comprehend all the mysteries of God's creations.

The multifaceted scope of God's alleged designs squarely matches the broad and shifting range of inquiries covered by "natural philosophy" (*philosophia naturalis*) in early modern Europe. This encompassed inquiries into celestial objects, elements (especially for alchemical interests), the nature of change and motion, the nature of matter, the nature of space and time, as well as the proper method for obtaining knowledge about the world. What goes by the broad term "natural philosophy" was also carried out by men in a relatively wide variety of social and professional roles, such as clerks, tutors to members of the gentry and aristocracy, secretaries, librarians, highly skilled artisans (e.g., lens grinders like Spinoza), and sometimes

---

[5] There is, of course, the additional interpretive misstep of over-identification on our part with their universalist aspirations, when these European figures clearly had a limited and "provincial" understanding of "universality" that was formulated in culturally specific terms and shaped by their own particular historical realities. For more on this, see Dipesh Chakrabarty's influential work *Provincializing Europe: Postcolonial Thought and Historical Difference* (Princeton, NJ: Princeton University Press, 2007).

professors in universities, where the study of philosophy primarily served "higher" faculties (theology, medicine, and jurisprudence) by providing them frameworks for formulating their findings.[6]

The so-called revolution that natural philosophy went through in the seventeenth century concerns a gradual shift in these learned men's treatments of the more fundamental causal questions that informed all the aforementioned variety of inquiries. More specifically, the period witnessed the slow but eventual replacement of the Scholastic-Aristotelian model, in which things were thought to move toward their intended forms and natural directions (the boy becomes a man, heavy bodies move downward), with a mechanical framework that incorporated both experimentation and mathematization into its workings (which translated into reducing causality to the contact and impact of material bodies in a uniform space).[7] Of course, this change did not happen overnight through revolutionary eruptions of genius. The new mechanical model ultimately succeeded not necessarily because it was indubitably compelling at first glance, but because there were only so many new approaches that the Scholastic-Aristotelian model could accommodate, despite all its flexibility.[8]

In Spinoza's immediate context of the Dutch Republic (or the United Provinces of the Netherlands), the new model was associated with "Cartesian" philosophy—a term that was coined pejoratively by the Cambridge Platonist Henry More.[9] Descartes spent most of his adult life in the Dutch Republic, which, as Blair notes, "harbored some of the earliest university interests in Descartes."[10] As is well known, the Dutch Republic during Spinoza's lifetime had also become a gathering place for major thinkers of the period,[11] due to

---

[6] See Richard Tuck, "The Institutional Setting," in *The Cambridge History of Seventeenth Century Philosophy*, vol. 1, ed. Daniel Garber and Michael Ayers (Cambridge: Cambridge University Press, 2003), 9–32. Also see Shapin, "The Man of Science," 179–191.

[7] Margaret J. Osler, *Reconfiguring the World: Nature, God, and Human Understanding from the Middle Ages to Early Modern Europe* (Baltimore: Johns Hopkins University Press, 2010), 95.

[8] On this point, see Lynn S. Joy, "Scientific Explanation from Formal Causes to Laws of Nature," in Park and Daston, *The Cambridge History of Science*, 70.

[9] Brian Copenhaver, "The Occultist Tradition and Its Critics," in *The Cambridge History of Seventeenth-Century Philosophy*, vol. 1, ed. Daniel Garber and Michael Ayers (Cambridge: Cambridge University Press, 1998), 485.

[10] Ann Blair, "Natural Philosophy," in Park and Daston, *The Cambridge History of Science*, 398.

[11] Aside from René Descartes taking residence in the United Provinces, Bayle too spent twenty-five years there. As Bertrand Russell notes, Hobbes also had his five books printed there while Locke spent the five-year period during which he was exiled from England (1684–1689) in the Dutch Republic. This leads Russell to conclude that "it is impossible to exaggerate the importance of Holland in the 17th century" for history of philosophy. Bertrand Russell, *A History of Western Philosophy* (New York: Simon and Schuster/Touchstone, 1967), 559.

its relatively tolerant atmosphere in an era that was marked by clashes of religious factions. Still, it was not the case that natural philosophers, especially in the universities, enjoyed unlimited freedom of speculation in their search for understanding the workings of nature. In fact, the Dutch Republic at the time was a hot spot of significant and sometimes career-ending discussions surrounding the alleged dangers of the new (Cartesian) philosophy, which then sparked debates about philosophy's proper relation to metaphysics and theology. These debates eventually turned Spinoza and his circle of friends into props used by theologians and defenders of *philosophia recepta* to illustrate the grave dangers of Cartesianism *and* into foils for academic Cartesians who sought to define themselves in opposition to what they were not.

Of course, Descartes actually owed much to the Scholastics in the development of his own philosophy of nature.[12] More crucially, Cartesianism took on a life beyond the ideas of Descartes himself even during his lifetime and hence Cartesians were diverse in the way they imagined "Cartesianism."[13] If we lay out the actual terms of the debate, instead of assuming the presence of self-coherent feuding groups (Scholastics versus Cartesians), we can say that a major concern at stake was the altered meaning of machinery that accompanied the gradual rise of the new mechanical philosophy. Here it should be noted that although "Cartesianism" is often credited (or blamed) for understanding the physical world in mechanical terms, both the ancient and the Scholastic traditions were abundant with analogies between living bodies (and parts of bodies) and all kinds of machines that were perceived to be responsive to and engaged with their surrounding structures (the way bodies are).[14] As Riskin points out, the precise shift that happened in the early seventeenth century rather concerns getting rid of the Aristotelean-Scholastic *spectrum* of soul and matter, according to which plants, animals,

---

[12] Tad. M. Schmaltz, *The Metaphysics of the Material World: Suarez, Descartes, Spinoza* (New York: Oxford University Press, 2020), xv–xvii. As Garber notes as well, the continuity between Descartes's thought and late Scholasticism is not just a matter of terminological overlap but also involves the continuity of ideas, such as the denial of a vacuum and the infinite divisibility of matter. Daniel Garber, "Descartes, the Aristotelians and the Revolution That Did Not Happen in 1637," *The Monist* 71, no. 4 (October 1, 1988): 476.

[13] Tad Schmaltz, *Early Modern Cartesianisms: Dutch and French Constructions* (New York: Oxford University Press, 2017), 5–12.

[14] As Riskin observes, from Aristotle and the Hippocratic Corpus to the writings of Galen and Aquinas, many figures drew parallels between animal physiology and artificial devices, such as bellows, furnaces, irrigation systems, and fountains. Comparisons between an entire physiological system and machine-like devices were also present, such as Aristotle's likening of animals to automatic puppets that transmitted motion. See Jessica Riskin, *The Restless Clock: A History of the Centuries-Long Argument over What Makes Living Things Tick* (Chicago: University of Chicago Press, 2018), 50–53.

and humans shared a vegetative soul that was responsible for life and growth while animals and humans in particular shared a sensitive soul that was responsible for sensation and motion.[15] In lieu of this spectrum approach, what we see in Descartes is the removal of the soul from the machinery of the physical world altogether and the granting of souls to humans alone.

Getting rid of intermediate positions between matter and spirit created an unbridgeable chasm between humans and animals, which actually irked some learned men across Europe at the time, including Descartes's well-known correspondent Arnauld.[16] Of course, the mechanization of animal sensation also took on a life beyond what Descartes might have intended and actually proved pivotal in an era that witnessed the introduction of radical techniques in animal experimentation, including vivisection.[17] However, a bigger problem, in the eyes of its critics, was that Descartes's model also inflated the status of humans to a disproportionate degree, lifting them up to an almost God-like existence. It did not help that Descartes indeed seemed to be giving humans *unlimited* free will, which was viewed as a gesture toward obliterating the difference between God and humans.[18]

Aside from the hubris that such an approach implies, within Descartes's (and also Spinoza's) immediate context, that is, the Calvinist Dutch Republic, not limiting the extent of human free will meant leaving no room for divine grace. Hence underneath all such discussions, a more fundamental criticism also showed its head: Shouldn't such matters be left to theologians alone? For the seventeenth-century Dutch academic philosophers who were enchanted by Descartes's ideas, a way to sidestep such matters of theological significance was to discard the metaphysical dimension of the Frenchman's works (sometimes to his chagrin) and to focus on Cartesian physics (such as the laws of motion)—thus ultimately limiting what philosophers could say about the world and man's place in it.[19]

---

[15] Riskin, *The Restless Clock*, 54.

[16] In the *Fourth Set of Objections* to Descartes's *Meditations*, Arnauld expresses his dissatisfaction with Descartes's claim that animals do not have souls by providing the example of a sheep that sees a wolf and starts fleeing it. Arnauld protests that this cannot simply be explained by various movements in the sheep's optic nerves "reaching the brain" to take flight. See Descartes, *The Philosophical Writings of Descartes*, vol. 2, trans. John Cottingham, Robert Stoothoff, and Dugald Murdoch (Cambridge: Cambridge University Press, 1985), 138–178.

[17] See Anita Guerrini, "The Ethics of Animal Experimentation in Seventeenth-Century England," *Journal of the History of Ideas* 50, no. 3 (1989): 391–407.

[18] This view was attributed to Descartes for good reasons. As Schmaltz points out, Descartes's *Les Passions de l'Âme* do argue that our actions derive from a free will that "renders us in a certain way like God by making us masters of ourselves." Schmaltz, *Early Modern Cartesianisms*, 48.

[19] Alexander X. Douglas, *Spinoza and Dutch Cartesianism: Philosophy and Theology* (Oxford: Oxford University Press, 2015), 1–3. Schmaltz, *Early Modern Cartesianisms*, 39.

While such theoretical battles were fought on the academic front, from non-academic sources came the dissemination of bolder views that threatened to undermine the conciliatory efforts of Cartesians who were trying to secure their future in Dutch universities. Prominent examples of such radical voices included Lodewijk Meijer (also Meyer) (1629–1681), who argued that Cartesianism, the crux of which he located in the inquisition of nature from mathematically deduced principles, should also take over theological discourse and even scriptural interpretation so as to put an end to all religious (and hence also political) disagreements.[20] The same Lodewijk Meijer also edited and wrote the preface to Spinoza's 1663 debut, *Renati Descartes principia philosophiae, more geometrico demonstrata* ("The Principles of René Descartes's Philosophy, demonstrated in geometrical order"; henceforth *Principles*). As Meijer notes in his preface, Spinoza's work does more than simply lay out Descartes's ideas in a way familiar to geometricians ("whereby conclusions are demonstrated from definitions, postulates, and axioms"), but also goes beyond Descartes's own views by rejecting freedom of the will altogether.[21]

With respect to the two different gestures of missing the Calvinist sweet spot of granting humans free will while at the same time limiting its scope, it is not clear which was perceived to be worse: granting humans God-like status by giving them unlimited free will or denying them free will altogether and extending mechanical and mathematical methods of inquiry to include *everything* in the universe, including human actions. What *is* clear is that the work did not bring Spinoza swaths of followers, and additional troubles were to come with the publication of a more controversial work: *Tractatus Theologico-Politicus* ("Theological-Political Treatise"; henceforth TTP).

In the TTP Spinoza offers a critical exegetical analysis of Scripture and argues for the separation of natural philosophy and theology, not because the former does not have anything to say about metaphysical matters but because theology concerns practical matters of pious action alone whereas natural philosophy investigates nature and truth. Moreover, to some, the gist of the book still suggested that perhaps philosophy should be the interpreter of Scripture after all (something Meijer openly defended).[22] The TTP sealed

---

[20] Van Bunge, *From Stevin to Spinoza*, 95–96.
[21] *Principles*, Preface.
[22] This reading is not without textual basis, as in chapter 6 of TTP, which concerns miracles, Spinoza explains miracles by common laws of nature alone (TTP 6.15). Spinoza openly acknowledges this interpretive move in TTP 6.21 noting that because the subject matter is "wholly philosophical," he is justified in reading it with the eye of a natural philosopher instead of taking the Scripture at its word.

Spinoza's reputation as not simply a radical Cartesian but also as a straight-out atheist (which is an accusation he protested),[23] because, in it, he also denied creation *ex nihilo* and the possibility of miracles, and drew attention to the human author of what was supposed to be God's own words.[24] As often noted, TTP was published anonymously, but that did not prevent people from soon learning who the author was. Nor did its eventual ban prevent it from becoming known all over Europe.[25]

The rest of Spinoza's works were not published in his lifetime, which sometimes leads to the mistaken assumption that Spinoza was insignificant as a thinker in the seventeenth-century Dutch Republic, as well as in the larger European context. However, as Richard Tuck points out, Spinoza's milieu emphasized philosophers' participation in the international *respublica litterarum*, and reputations could be made (and sometimes ruined) almost entirely on the basis of manuscripts and letters that were distributed and exchanged across the continent with remarkable speed *and* in a semi-public manner.[26] This was true of Hobbes, Gassendi, and even Descartes.[27] From Spinoza's correspondences, it is clear that, from the very beginning, parts of his major work, *Ethica* (the *Ethics*), were already circulating among fellow learned men,[28] and so were copies of his other works[29] and some of his letters.[30] Moreover, the circulation of the manuscripts was clearly not limited to a small circle of trusted friends, given that a very hostile refutation of the TTP also included references to Spinoza's then unpublished works—which not only reaffirms the non-anonymity of the TTP but also suggests a wider (and uncontrolled) access to copies of Spinoza's other works that were not published at the time.[31]

---

[23] Ep.30. In spite of his contemporaneous critics and much of the contemporary scholarship on Spinoza, I do not take Spinoza's "atheism" to be obvious. As Melamed points out, it is still common to present Spinoza to be reacting against a "Judeo-Christian" God, which not only assumes that early modern Europeans verbally and conceptually hyphenated "Judaism" and "Christianity," but it also erases the entire Kabbalah tradition (which also has a panentheistic streak) from the equation. Melamed, "Spinoza's 'Atheism.'"

[24] To be more specific, Spinoza in the TTP invites the reader to study Moses's imagination to make sense of claims like "God is fire" or "God is jealous" (TTP 7.5).

[25] Van Bunge, *From Stevin to Spinoza*, 114n.87.

[26] Richard Tuck, "The Institutional Setting," 23. There was clearly some etiquette around wide circulation of correspondences though, given that Leibniz was not pleased with the fact that the letter he wrote to Spinoza (Ep.45) was published in *Opera Posthuma*. See Piet Steenbakkers, *Spinoza's Ethica, From Manuscript to Print: Studies on Text, Form and Related Topics* (Assen: Van Gorcum, 1994), 62.

[27] Tuck, "The Institutional Setting," 23–24.

[28] Ep.8, Ep.28, Ep.72.

[29] Ep.70.

[30] Ep.82.

[31] As van Bunge notes, Bredenburg's refutations against Spinoza's TTP included references to *natura naturans* and *naturans naturata*—terms that appear in the KV and the *Ethica*. Van Bunge,

Among Spinoza's works, perhaps the one that proved to be the most provocative is his *Ethics*, which famously equates God with Nature and subjects humans to the same mechanical laws of causation as the rest of the universe (and hence deprives humans of free will). Much of the work's immediate critical reception in the seventeenth century concerns Spinoza's equation of God with Nature[32] and the details of substance metaphysics that Spinoza offers in his treatment of God's nature.[33] In the same work, Spinoza also happens to be granting a mental aspect to everything in the universe, to humans and nonhuman beings.[34] Yet it took a few centuries for Spinoza's "enminding" of the world to gain traction, first in the context of late eighteenth-century idealism—with its endorsement of the "world-soul" of which everything is part[35]—and then again in the contemporary context of critical studies on human-nonhuman relations, which has a tendency to view panpsychism in general, including Spinoza's version of it, as a celebration of nonhuman vitalities.[36]

Despite our wishful thinking about all the epistemic bounties that a panpsychist approach to reality can offer, it befits us to acknowledge that at least Spinoza's own version of it offers underwhelming results. In fact, Spinoza happens to police the human-animal split with an ardor that is not seen

---

From Stevin to Spinoza, 135. Steenbakker's findings on the manuscript circulation of Spinoza's works suggest that it was *Ethica*, not KV, that Bredenburg was referring to. See Steenbakkers, *Spinoza's Ethica*, 125).

[32] As Melamed notes, the Nature with which Spinoza equates God is not the nature that we are familiar with. Spinoza's God/Nature has infinitely many attributes, while we have access to only two of them (namely, Extension and Thought). Melamed, "Spinoza's 'Atheism.'" Spinoza's ontological terminology will be fleshed out in more detail in Part II, chapter 3.

[33] More specifically, in claiming that God is one, but its attributes (i.e., essential facets) are many, Spinoza was accused of actually presenting us with many Gods (Van Bunge, *From Stevin to Spinoza*, 119–120). The accusation relied on a feature of Cartesian metaphysics which asserts that each substance can have only one attribute. Second, in claiming that the things that make up the world are all modes—i.e., modifications—of God, Spinoza was accused of attributing not only extension, but incongruent phenomena to God. As Bayle has famously asked in disbelief: According to Spinoza, when we say "The Germans have killed ten thousand Turks," do we mean that "God modified into Germans has killed God modified into ten thousand Turks?" (Bayle, *Dictionnaire Critique et Historique*, 211).

[34] This is discussed in detail in chapter 3.

[35] For an examination of the history of world-soul (*weltseele*) theories and their association with Spinozism, see Miklós Vassányi, *Anima Mundi: The Rise of the World Soul Theory in Modern German Philosophy* (Dordrecht: Springer, 2011). I owe thanks to the anonymous reviewer for bringing this point to my attention.

[36] For an examination of the deep ecology movement's interest in panpyschism in general and in Spinoza in particular, see Michael Hampe, "Explaining and Describing: Panpsychism and Deep Ecology," in *Contemporary Perspectives on Early Modern Philosophy: Nature and Norms in Thought* (Heidelberg: Springer, 2013), 179–202. A more broad-stroke celebration of panpsychism in general (without narrowing it down to Spinoza) is offered in Steven Shaviro, "Consequences of Panpsychism," in *The Nonhuman Turn*, ed. Richard Grusin (Minneapolis: University of Minnesota Press, 2015), 20.

in oft-criticized Descartes. Take, for instance, this delightful passage from EIVp37s1:

> The law (*lex*) to refrain from slaughtering beasts is founded more on groundless superstition and womanly compassion than on sound reason. The rational principle of seeking our own advantage teaches us the necessity of joining with men, but not with beasts, or with things whose nature is different from human nature.[37] (*translation modified*)

Perhaps the more curious issue, as will be shown, is that Spinoza's ontology, in fact, allows formulations of the human-animal binary on a much more flexible and continuous trajectory. Yet, time and time again, Spinoza cautions against assumptions of shared similarities between mankind and beasts.[38]

The manifold of reasons behind Spinoza's exclusionary attitude toward animals requires a book-length study (such as this one). One of the reasons, I will argue here, is the pedagogical imperative to emphasize human togetherness ("joining with men" as Spinoza tells us in the passage above). At times, this translates into invoking the imagery of mankind's constitutive outside (the beasts) in order to further cement the bonds among all men.

The next section will explore Spinoza's commitment to uplifting mankind as a collective by analyzing the pedagogical tone and literary formats of his works. Examining Spinoza's methodological and elocutionary preferences—which are decidedly deliberate and meditated[39]—also gives us a further glimpse into Spinoza's own answer to the profound fear of discord among mankind that informed much of philosophical discourse as it developed

---

[37] For this passage (and other quotations from EIVp37s1), I largely follow Shirley's translation. In Latin it reads: "Legem illam de non mactandis brutis magis vana superstitione et muliebri misericordia, quam sana ratione fundatam esse. Docet quidem ratio nostrum utile quaerendi necessitudinem cum hominibus iungere; sed non cum brutis aut rebus, quarum natura a natura humana est diversa." I owe thanks to the anonymous reviewer for their helpful suggestion to render "*lex*" as "law."

[38] That Spinoza's ontology allows flexible formulations of differences is discussed in chapter 3, section 3.4, and in concluding remarks to Part II. Spinoza's cautionary remarks regarding associating with beasts is discussed in chapter 6.

[39] As Steenbakkers points out, rhetoric played a dominant role in the education of the period, which is reflected in Spinoza's writings (Steenbakkers, *Spinoza's Ethica*, 176). That Spinoza took a suspicious view of particular rhetorical strategies and appeals such as florid oratory (TTP Preface 9), while praising mathematical formalism as the language of reason, shows due deliberation on his part about which literary formats he should be using in his writings.

from the late sixteenth century onward in the Dutch Republic and Europe at large.

2.2 Seeking True Philosophy, in the Proper Order, with Spinoza

Spinoza declares that the goal of his famous *Ethics* is to disabuse his readers of false assumptions about men's place in nature, because their salvation is only possible through proper knowledge of God, of themselves, and of their place in the world.[40] While the *Ethics* came to be the most well-known work of Spinoza, its main goal—men's salvation—is, in fact, a thread that runs across all of Spinoza's works. In the TTP, Spinoza aims to achieve this goal by providing "a fresh examination of Scripture with a free and unprejudiced mind" (TTP Preface 10) and detailing what he considers to be the freest and most enabling kind of polity for mankind, which would be a democracy (TTP 16). These two means to help men achieve salvation—namely, offering a truthful interpretation of Scripture and being an advocate for the right kind of polity for men's collective empowerment—are also explored, separately, in Spinoza's *Compendium Grammatices Linguae Hebraeae* (often translated simply as "Hebrew Grammar") and in his *Tractatus Politicus* (*Political Treatise*; henceforth TP), in that order. His early work *Korte Verhandeling van God, de Mensch en deszelf's Welstand* (*Short Treatise on God, Man, and His Well-Being*; henceforth KV) is seen as a proto-*Ethics* and rightly so, because despite various terminological differences, it shares with the *Ethics* the same goal and a similar ordering of main themes.[41] His TIE, in which Spinoza lays out his epistemological positions and rules for obtaining true knowledge, also simultaneously serves as a defense of the life of reason—which is the highest good (*summum bonum*) and is something that one should attempt to arrive at "together with other individuals if possible" (TIE 13). Even his debut, which is chiefly an explicatory analysis of Descartes's philosophy, is

---

[40] EIapp. Note that the title of this section, "Seeking True Philosophy, in the Proper Order, with Spinoza," refers to Spinoza's own definition of "true Method" (*vera Methodus*) in TIE 36, which aims to facilitate the attainment of this knowledge.

[41] KV was also originally penned in Latin and then translated into Dutch by a friend of Spinoza. There is no extant copy of the Latin manuscript Spinoza composed, which poses unsolvable interpretive difficulties when it comes to the oft-mentioned terminological differences between the *Ethics* and KV.

interrupted by calls to truly understand the attributes of God so that "we" can get to love Him properly, which is the highest blessedness.[42]

Despite being known for his fondness for the geometric format, Spinoza also experimented with other kinds of literary styles as he pursued his multifaceted project of helping men achieve salvation. In fact, overall, four of his seven works are described as presenting a systematic treatment (*tractatus*; treatise) of a subject, while two are described as being written in a "geometric manner."[43] Spinoza also penned a grammar compendium on Hebrew, which explains the grammatical structure of the target language using Latin as a model.[44] Despite the variation in formats, all of these works present the reader with systematic treatments of various subjects and are intended to improve the readers' understanding of target topics, persuade them of a point of view, and establish authority on certain debates.

---

[42] *Principles*, Part I, Proposition 5, scholium (henceforth *Principles* Ip5s). Here too Spinoza adds that mankind together should strive toward this end.

[43] The opening page of Parts I and II of *Principles* includes the description "demonstrated in the geometric method" (*more geometrico demonstrata*). Similarly, the opening page of the posthumous Latin first edition of his *Ethics* tells the reader that it is "demonstrated in the geometrical order" (*ordine geometrico demonstrata*). Certainly, we do not have conclusive knowledge of how much control Spinoza had on the titles of his works, especially granted that most of them were published after his death and the only surviving manuscripts of Spinoza's writings are a few letters; two copies of the KV (and not the Latin original, but the Dutch translations); and a recently discovered, non-autograph manuscript of the *Ethics*. However, we do know that not only was the publication process carried out by a small circle of friends who were familiar with Spinoza's philosophy and were recipients of the manuscripts he circulated; before he died, Spinoza also left explicit instructions about what was to be done with the manuscripts. He himself had also made preparations for the publication of his *Ethics* and was involved in the production of the fair copy. For more on the editorial processes behind the publication of Spinoza's works, see Steenbakkers, *Spinoza's Ethica*, 7, 27, 50–57. In regard to the titles of his works, it should also be noted that in his letters (Ep.2, Ep.13), if not inside the texts in question (EIIIpref.), Spinoza himself describes the methodology he employed in the *Ethics* and in the *Principles* as "geometric." He also calls his *Theologico-Political Treatise* "my treatise" (Ep.43, Ep.69) and "this treatise" TTP 20.18; and refers to his *Political Treatise* as "this treatise" (Ep.84, TP 2.1) suggesting agreement with the titles of the works. Of course, Spinoza (and/or the editors of his works) was not particularly restrained when it came to using the word "treatise" (*tractatus*). As will be discussed in more detail in the present section, his *Treatise on the Emendation of the Intellect* actually has an autobiographical tone and reads like a philosophical meditation *à la* Descartes, Augustine, and many other medieval precedents. In addition, His KV is written as expository prose but is interrupted by two dialogues and is appended with a piece on God written in the aforementioned "geometric" manner. In a letter addressed to Oldenburg, he refers to *The Principles of René Descartes' Philosophy* (which has the subtitle "demonstrated in geometrical order") as a "treatise" (*tractatus*) as well, suggesting again that a treatise can also accommodate his geometric style. A large portion of TTP actually engages in close exegetical analysis of biblical passages. Finally, he uses the term "treatise" in the title of his TP, which is written in expository prose and evaluates various types of government (monarchy, aristocracy, democracy) according to their suitability for human nature. All of this suggests that by "treatise" (*tractatus*) Spinoza largely understood systematic treatment of a subject.

[44] Spinoza presents a mini-treatment of the Hebrew grammar in the seventh chapter of TTP as well, with the goal of giving a more accurate interpretation of the scripture without relying on clerical authority.

The literary formats that Spinoza employed in his works were employed by many of his contemporaries and predecessors as well; and although the texts read differently from one another, a certain common epistemological comportment undergirds them all. Spinoza's most "personal" work, TIE, which has many seemingly autobiographical details in it, partakes in the long tradition of philosophical meditation, which consists of presenting the reader with what Rorty describes as a "staged reflection" that walks the reader through the author's own intellectual journey in which the author simply stands for Everyman.[45] Any reader who follows through the author's explication of his process of attaining various kinds of knowledge is expected to be experiencing the same epistemic breakthroughs, as the order and objects of thought of those who are committed to the philosophical life are expected to be alike. The assumption regarding the comparative similarity of "our" minds is the reason the voice of the "I" of Everyman quickly gives way to the language of "we." This "we" often designates the learned men who are the target audience and are tasked with teaching and uplifting others. It sometimes also refers to a broader populace, especially when Spinoza is discussing matters of public good, such as the education of children.[46]

Spinoza does not simply teach his readers a set of correct propositions in the TIE but also discusses the modes of understanding that would direct them toward certain and eternal truths (TIE 10, 30). This approach is pursued in his *Ethics* as well, which, Spinoza points out, has the advantage of teaching (*docere*) enabling manners of comportment to deal with the hardships of life that are beyond one's power (e.g., bad fortune, difficult people). The secret, he explains, is understanding all such things as following from God's eternal decree "with the same necessity as from the essence of a triangle it follows that its three angles are equal to two right angles" (EIIp49s). In the end, what Spinoza aims to do is provide his readers the tools to understand and contextualize their own lives in relation to principles of necessity.[47]

---

[45] I owe this insight to De Dijn, who demonstrates that the TIE "should not be taken as strictly biographical" as it "clearly is meant as a paradigm, in which one can in principle recognize oneself." Herman De Dijn, *Spinoza: The Way to Wisdom* (West Lafayette, IN: Purdue University Press, 1996), 11. For "staged reflection" as a rhetorical strategy, see Amelie Oksenberg Rorty, "Experiments in Philosophic Genre: Descartes' 'Meditations.'" *Critical Inquiry* 9, no. 3 (March 1983): 549,

[46] TIE 15. Going back to the point about the similarity of "our" minds, in the same work Spinoza also discusses the nature of the intellect and understanding (among other things, such as thought, mind, imagination) either in an indeterminate (e.g., *intellectus*; "the intellect") or collective way (e.g., *noster intellectus*; "our intellect").

[47] Spinoza himself suggests an analogy with tools when he discusses the method by which one arrives at true knowledge in TIE 30–32.

Although Spinoza positions himself as a teacher who aims to help mankind achieve salvation, he is clear that what makes his overall philosophy reliable and helpful is not his own unique genius. Instead, his philosophy relies on certain modes of orderly thinking, which simply reveal the logic of the world.[48] This combination of humility with regard to his own individual contribution to knowledge production, on the one hand, and over-confidence with regard to the results of his study, on the other, is expressed in a letter addressed to Albert Burgh:

> You ask . . . me, "How I know that my philosophy is the best among all that have ever been taught in the world, or are being taught, or ever will be taught?" a question which I might with much greater right ask you: for I do not presume that I have found the best philosophy. I know that I understand true philosophy. If you ask in what way I know it, I answer: In the same way as you know that the three angles of a triangle are equal to two right angles: that this is sufficient, will be denied by no one whose brain is sound. (Ep. 76)

True philosophy is something that Spinoza understands, not something that he has discovered. This ingenious gesture, which simultaneously indicates epistemic humility and authority, is the reason Spinoza invites those who disagree with him on some matter to simply reflect on it more carefully and "consider properly the chain of [his] demonstrations" (EIp33s2). For Spinoza, truth carries its own weight and his methodology derives its force not from his own unique brilliance but from the lawful order of nature itself through which all things unfold.[49]

---

[48] In fact, in EIIIpref., Spinoza mocks Descartes's treatment of human emotions for showing "nothing else but the brilliance of his own genius" and goes on to announce that he will treat human emotions in the geometric manner as if he were conducting "an investigation into lines, planes, or bodies." His own method is part of a larger approach that aims at the proper ordering and management of our perceptions, so that our minds "will reproduce Nature as closely as possible; for it will possess in the form of thought the essence, order, and unity of Nature." (TIE 99).

[49] Although the importance of methodology for Spinoza's epistemological program is undeniable, the exact relation between the two is still debated. Some describe Spinoza as a metaphysicalist, arguing for the traceability of Spinoza's epistemological views and tools to his formulation of the mind-world relation. Others label Spinoza as an epistemological methodist, arguing that Spinoza makes his metaphysical discoveries through self-evident ideas and logical necessity, from which other true principles follow. A less common position categorizes Spinoza as a particularist who prioritizes what is commonly known over criteria of knowledge. For an examination of all three views and a defense of the latter view, see Daniel Schneider, "Spinoza's Epistemological Methodism," *Journal of the History of Philosophy* 54, no. 4 (October 2016): 573–599.

Spinoza's philosophical program, therefore, involves the distribution of epistemic authority to his readers by laying out a methodology and its applications for understanding God and human life—which is a process that the readers can reproduce themselves. Beyond the element of reproducibility, Spinoza's works also seem to endeavor to attain broader accessibility by adopting a methodology that proceeds from what could (allegedly) be more distinctly known, ultimately arriving at the knowledge of the less known.

To be more specific, the works that are written in the geometric format start with definitions and axioms (as is required by the format); thematically both the KV and the *Ethics* follow the advice of TIE and begin with a discussion about the existence and nature of God, which the readers are allegedly able to grasp clearly and distinctly; and his *Hebrew Grammar* attempts to teach Hebrew as if it were Latin (a language that is more familiar to his target audience).[50] Both TTP and TP open with treatments of several foundational themes (e.g., the notions of prophecy, miracles, and divine law in TTP; concepts of natural right and sovereign power in TP).[51] Likewise, both the TTP and TP are also built on the underlying foundational knowledge of the cognitive-affective makeup of mankind (which Spinoza also examines in detail in the second and third parts of the *Ethics*). Finally, his *Principles of René Descartes' Philosophy* begins with Descartes's own foundational principle, which is the knowledge of oneself as a thinking thing.

Evidently, for Spinoza, this systematic deduction of true philosophy from what is more easily known and certain can accommodate a combination of various literary formats, including a treatise with an introspective dimension (TIE), a treatise written with expository prose (KV, TP, parts of TTP),[52] staged dialogue (parts of KV,[53] parts of TTP that deal with biblical hermeneutics),[54] and Euclidean geometric style (*Ethics, Principles*, and the first appendix to the KV). Spinoza, however, seems to have developed a preference for the geometric format for discussing ontological issues. As described earlier, the geometric format in question amounts to employing the expositional structure

---

[50] This strategy results in a very peculiar but possibly pedagogically useful work that downplays the irregularities of an ancient language for the sake of giving a systematic account of it and making it accessible to a Latin-reading audience.

[51] TTP 5.14 also explicitly speaks of the need to start with "clear intellectual concepts" and "basic ideas" when persuading one's (learned) audience of "something which is not known by itself."

[52] More specifically, the last five chapters of TTP.

[53] The work includes two dialogues that are placed right between chapter 2 and chapter 3. The dialogues serve to thematically bridge the two chapters and further explicate the themes discussed in both chapters.

[54] More specifically, the first fifteen chapters of TTP.

of Euclid's *Elements*, which consists of first laying out definitions, axioms, and postulates, followed by propositions and their demonstrations.[55] Spinoza resorts to this format for ontological subjects because of its perceived ability to lay out a subject matter in a manner that aligns the ordering of Nature with the workings of the higher registers of understanding.[56]

Spinoza also seems to assume a high degree of translatability of various other literary formats into the Euclidian geometric format,[57] which is expected to render the claims of these works even clearer.[58] This assumed translatability of insights from one format to another is due to Spinoza's conviction that words, although potentially misleading,[59] can still be connected

---

[55] As explained by Lodewijk Meijer in his preface to Spinoza's *Principles*, demonstrating a subject matter according to a geometric framework amounts to employing the format of Euclid's *Elements* "wherein Definitions, Postulates, and Axioms are first enunciated, followed by Propositions and their demonstrations." It should be noted here that, as noted by Steenbakkers, what is referred to as the "Euclidean model" is, in fact, "the result of a long historical process of transmission, reception and interpretation," which is to say that "the captions over the principles—'definitions', 'postulates', 'axioms'—are interpolations of a later date." Piet Steenbakkers, *Spinoza's "Ethica,"* 140.

[56] The association Spinoza draws between mathematical thinking and clarity of exposition is the reason he often resorts to mathematical examples to convey certainty on various subjects. As an example of the way in which Spinoza resorts to mathematical examples to explain how adequate thinking—which delivers certitude—works, see TIE 22, in which Spinoza gives the case of knowing that "if two lines are parallel to a third line, they are parallel to one another" as an example of adequately knowing something. It is for this reason that in TIE 79, Spinoza also announces that "if we do possess such knowledge of God as we have of a triangle, all doubt is removed." While the terms "mathematical" and "geometrical" are not interchangeable, Steenbakkers notes that "Euclidean geometry for a long time was the height of exact mathematical reasoning"; thus, in the context of the seventeenth century (and before), the difference between the two tended to be blurred. Steenbakkers, *Spinoza's Ethica*, 148n2 and 173n2. Moreover, Spinoza himself uses the two interchangeably (see, for instance, his usage of the term "*mos mathematicorum*" in his preface to part III of *Principles*).

[57] A clear exception to this is his TTP, approximately 75 percent of which concerns biblical hermeneutics. Aside from the exegetical nature of the work, Spinoza also tells his readers that scripture teaches piety and not philosophy (TTP 15.1) and hence its meaning cannot be derived from the investigation of nature, which admits of mathematical expression. Spinoza adds that the principles underlying theology and scriptural authority cannot be demonstrated with mathematical order and certainty (TTP 15.7).

[58] It is this assumption that informs Spinoza's exegetical work on Cartesian philosophy, which, as Meyer (Spinoza's friend and the author of the preface to the work) puts it, presents the works of Descartes, who "laid the unshakeable foundations of philosophy," in the style used in Euclid's *Elements*. This is expected to rectify the understanding of those who can "only prate and chatter" about Descartes without any proof (*Principles* Part I Preface). Moreover, as Michael L. Morgan also points out in his introduction to Shirley's translation of KV, both the thematic structure and many of the conclusions of Spinoza's *Ethics* were already anticipated in his KV. The *Ethics*, however, not only introduces further nuances in terminology but also revisits many of the themes of the KV, presenting them in a format that was deemed superior. Spinoza, *Complete Works*, trans. Shirley, 31–32.

[59] Spinoza conveys apprehensions about broad generalizations and linguistic signs, which are informed by random experience (*experientia vaga*) that varies from person to person—as in the example of the man who thinks that all sheep have short tails, only to be surprised at the sheep from Morocco, which have long ones (KV Part II, Ch. 3). Aside from variation in words' referents, Spinoza also worries about the possibility of combining words randomly in accordance with various fabricated concepts one might feign, which then can cause great errors (TIE 88). Regarding the arbitrary nature of the signification of words, also see TIE 88–89 and EIIp18s.

in a way that follows the order of the intellect.⁶⁰ Not surprisingly, as someone who believed in the possibility of universal access to truths about the world, Spinoza prioritized what he deemed to be obvious bearers of facts, namely, literal utterances (as opposed to figurative language) that are arranged in a systematic fashion (that is, in a manner that can aid the proper ordering and management of the reader's perceptions so as to align their mind with the order of Nature) (TIE 99, TTP 7.17).⁶¹

The underlying assumption behind the alleged reliability and iterability of the structures of the argumentative and demonstrative processes that Spinoza deploys is the similarity of (hu)man aptitudes.⁶² Time and time again, Spinoza notes that the means by which to attain true knowledge lie in the "entirety of the human race" (*totum humanum genus*) (TTP 3.5, 3.7; TP 7.27). Yet, he is also clear that, in reality, his unambiguous articulations of true ideas are still not fit for everyone. In fact, he notes that when conclusions are "deduced from intellectual axioms alone, that is, solely by the power of the understanding," then one "will be writing only for the learned, that is, he will be intelligible only to what is, in comparison with the rest of the mankind, a very small handful of people" (TTP 5.14). This is because following through "a long chain of linked inferences" requires "supreme mental discipline" that many people do not possess (TTP 5.14).

Spinoza explains the apparent variation observed among men's epistemic and affective powers as the influence of accepted customs (*mores recepta*),

---

⁶⁰ This is exactly the point made in an important passage from Ep. 17, where Spinoza states: "For, as we know from experience, in all things it [imagination] follows the traces of the intellect and concatenates its images and words in a certain order, and interconnects them, just as the intellect does with its demonstrations; so much so that there is almost nothing that we can understand of which the imagination does not form some image from the trace thereof." Here it could be added that "imagination" relates to perceptions of *experientia vaga* (random experience) and although Spinoza views reason as a superior mode of knowledge, as chapter 3 will show, he does not suggest that the operations of imagination shall (or could) be transcended. Imagination can coexist together with higher orders of knowledge, which then enables us to also put language in touch with the order of reason. Here I disagree with Savan's contention that Spinoza considered both language and even mathematics to be "fundamentally inadequate to the formulation or direct expression of philosophical truths" and that his own writings were not even meant to be a literal exposition of his vision. See David Savan, "Spinoza and Language," *Philosophical Review* 67, no. 2 (1958): 212–225.

⁶¹ This is to say that not only literal utterances (as opposed to figurative language) are obvious bearers of facts for Spinoza, but also a specific systematic arrangement of such utterances could further aid the proper ordering and management of "our" perceptions in ways that would align the mind with the order of Nature (TTP 7.17).

⁶² Spinoza's infamous remarks about the necessary servitude of women in the last paragraph of TP are examined in chapter 10, section 10.2. He also has critical views on universals (such as "human") and shared essences, which are discussed in chapter 3.

laws (*leges*), and refinement (*cultus*) (TTP 17.26; TP 7.27),[63] as well as the corrupting sway of clerical power (TTP 7.1). In fact, much of the TTP aims to debunk theologians' self-ascribed sole authority over knowledge of God and the salvation of mankind. This authority, Spinoza argues, relies on a pernicious campaign to mystify religion and Scripture and to turn knowledge of God into "ridiculous mysteries" (TTP Preface 9) that can only be deciphered by a few. This is, however, partly because common people, we are told, do not place value on the natural knowledge that is available to everyone and are instead more drawn to narratives of strange and wondrous events that surpass their judgment (TTP 1.2, 1.26).[64] For Spinoza, this prevalent yet problematic phenomenon seems to be as ancient as the Old Testament itself, which, he notes, is why revelation has come to people in the form of colorful and corporeal metaphors, parables, and allegories (TTP 1.29, 4.10).[65]

While such devices allegedly make certain truths more enticing to an audience of low intellectual caliber (as Spinoza views it), it does not make them clearer. In fact, it is the same figurative and poetic nature of biblical narratives that renders common folks in need of "pastors or church ministers to explain these to them" (TTP 5.18), which then enables the same clergy to exploit people's confusion to intimidate them and at times turn them against their fellow men who are deemed heretics, all in the name of religion (TTP Preface 9, 10). It is because the kind of life fit for mankind is not a life of sanctioned ignorance and discord but a life of understanding and togetherness that Spinoza tasks himself with expounding truths using clearer methodologies.

In the context of Spinoza's biblical exegesis, the discussions that seek clarity end up involving yet another form of translatory effort—this time from figurative speech into literal speech, because poetic narratives speak "in

---

[63] I follow Steinberg's rendering of "mores recepta" as "accepted customs" (instead of Israel and Silverthorne's translation of it as "morality") and of "cultus" as "refinement" (instead of Shirley's translation of it as "culture." See Steinberg, *Spinoza's Political Philosophy*, 35.

[64] Moreover, sometimes, we are told, biblical commentators render clear passages "obscure and impenetrable" because the literal reading might be too bold, if not blasphemous (e.g., the literal reading might suggest that most prophets were ignorant of many things) (TTP 2.13).

[65] This view is visible in the entirety of the TTP, when Spinoza examines the language of the Scripture with the Calvinist accommodationist approach in mind. Spinoza, in fact, also speaks of different layers of accommodation in the process of the formation of the Scripture itself. These involve God accommodating certain truths according to the limited understanding of the prophets (TTP 1.26, 1.27, 2.9, 2.13, 2.14, 2.15, 2.19, 4.9), except for Christ, who, we are told, was able to communicate with God mind to mind (TTP 1.19, TTP 4.10); prophets accommodating what they know to their even more feeble-minded audience, which doubly removes common folks from straightforward truth (unless the prophet is Christ) (TTP 2.15, 3.2); and sometimes God accommodating certain truths with the limited understanding of the common people (not just the prophets) in mind (TTP Preface 10, 1.25, 1.29).

a wholly inexact manner about God and things" as they are not "seeking to sway men's reason but to influence and captivate their fancy and imagination" (TTP 6.15). Spinoza renders in literal terms the meaning of sentences like "God opened the windows of the heavens," concluding that "it just means that a lot of rain fell" (TTP.6.20).

Now, aside from the fact that his rendering of metaphors in literal terms leaves out more than he acknowledges,[66] at times, Spinoza also employs the literary tools he deems inadequate for expressing eternal truths. To illustrate, in the *Ethics* Spinoza frequently breaks the order of deduction by making ample use of *scholia*, adding illustrative and at times graphic notes that would not normally fit in "demonstration proper."[67] In *scholia*, Spinoza comments further on the demonstrated material with examples, anecdotes, and hypothetical scenarios, which enliven the work itself. Moreover, although Spinoza does not appear to see great use in figurative forms of speech, he certainly does not deprive himself of them either. For instance, on multiple occasions, he likens humans' relation to God to "the clay in the hand of the potter," calls the Dutch republic—which, at the time, was a confederation of seven provinces—a headless body with many limbs, and draws parallels between ordinary people's relation to laws and horses' relation to bridles.[68] Spinoza also very frequently speaks of laws of nature, while admitting that the word law (*lex*) can be applied to natural phenomena only metaphorically (TTP 4.2).

That Spinoza shifts between different registers of speech in his works and resorts to figurative speech itself is not necessarily a contradiction on his part. Figurative speech does not by itself pose a threat when it is in collaboration with and kept in check by higher registers of understanding. In fact, for Spinoza, different registers of understanding, and hence apparently

---

[66] Spinoza's rendering "God opened the windows of the heavens" as "a lot of rain fell" in TTP.6.20 obviously downplays the fact that the metaphor of God parting the skies is employed in the Scripture to convey momentous occasions that are marked by abundant blessings and misfortunes that are certainly more out of the ordinary than a heavy rainstorm. For instance, in Genesis 7.11–12 we are told that God opened the windows of Heaven, which initiated the great flood.

[67] I owe this point to Laura Bryne. See "The Geometrical Method in Spinoza's *Ethics*," *Poetics Today* 28, no. 3 (2007): 469n26.

[68] For what might be termed the "divine potter" metaphor, see Ep.75, TP 2.22, and annotation 34 to chapter 16 in the TTP. For Spinoza's body politic metaphor regarding the Dutch Republic, see TP 9.14. For the analogy between subjects and horses, see TTP 4.2. Examples such as these can be multiplied. For instance, the TIE is rich with tool-making metaphors used to describe the epistemic development of the intellect (see, for instance, TEI 31, 32). As another example, in the KV, Spinoza describes reason as a staircase by which one can ascend to supreme happiness in union with God (KV Part II, chapter XXVI).

the speech patterns corresponding to them, can coexist instead of negating one another.[69] Ultimately, what matters is being able to distinguish the perceptions evoked by these "lesser" rhetorical devices from those of true understanding.[70] When Spinoza employs different registers of speech, figurative speech plays a subsidiary and dispensable role to literal utterances that are organized in a systematic fashion and that speak to learned men who have the rare mental discipline to grasp it.

Two observations should be made here. Although Spinoza's stated goal is the collective salvation of mankind, his target audience still remains limited to learned men.[71] At times, there is also an insidious aspect to his speaking to an admittedly narrow audience, which is the lack of reserve afforded by in-group language. This certainly makes it easier for Spinoza to employ zoological tropes to speak of ordinary folks in terms of equine analogies or to describe people of some other cultures as brutish (TTP 5.7) or barbaric (TP 6.4).[72]

Second, despite the fact that Spinoza views figurative speech as an expedient but inadequate tool of world-description rather than a creative tool of world-making,[73] some of the figurative analogies he employs arguably do

[69] Spinoza's views on different registers of understanding are examined in detail in chapter 3, sections 3.3 and 3.4.

[70] TTP 2.1. Also see TTP 1.29–31. As mentioned earlier, Spinoza also at times explicitly points out the metaphorical nature of the expressions he is using. In addition to his use of the word "law" (*lex*) when talking about the eternal order of nature (which he admits in TTP 4.2 to be a metaphorical expression), he also helps himself to the story of Adam—which he declares to be a parable instead of a straightforward narrative—to illustrate some of his points (TTP 4.11).

[71] TTP is explicitly addressed to the "philosophical reader," who is described as being "capable of rational reasoning" and is contrasted with the "common people" who tend to be superstitious and obstinate (TTP Preface 15). Parts of KV and the entirety of the *Ethics* and *Principles* are written in the geometric method that consists of long chains of linked references, which, as noted earlier, are not viewed as accessible to the common people who allegedly do not have the mental discipline for them. Even in the TIE, Spinoza's urging of learned men to speak according to the limited understanding of the multitude is made in the context of avoiding unnecessary conflict and trouble while pursuing a life of knowledge (his urging is followed by the call to "do whatever does not interfere with our attaining our purpose" [TIE 17]).

[72] For more, see chapter 10, section 10.1. The same kind of insider talk affords Spinoza the liberty to talk about women disparagingly as well (see chapter 10, section 10.2). This is obviously not to suggest that the relation between Spinoza's target audience and his disparaging remarks about people outside of that audience is a relation of direct causation, especially given that the *Zhuangzi* does not use animal pejoratives to describe people of humble backgrounds, despite the fact that its audience was elite folks with advanced literacy.

[73] This is also partly because Spinoza confines their source to imagination, referring largely to haphazard experience-based learning and sometimes to confused fantasies (TTP 1.29). This is not trivial given that for Spinoza imagination is not a creative but merely a reproductive aspect of our mental lives. It is for this reason that fictional notions, such as speaking trees, men changing into stones, Gods changing into men and beasts, and corpses that reason, walk, and speak (TIE 57, note x; 58; 68) have nothing new or original about them. What appears to be new, claims Spinoza, is nothing but the remnants of perceptions in the imagination that are recalled to memory and combined together in a confused manner.

more than simply embellish or elucidate speech and, at times, end up revealing perhaps more than he intended. This point merits a brief exploration because it offers a glimpse into the tension-oriented reading that this study will give to Spinoza's works. In the final pages of this chapter, I will examine two figurative analogies that Spinoza employs, which also provide preliminary insights into his views on the fundamental markers of one's humanity and of human perfection.

The first is the aforementioned equine analogy that Spinoza employs to describe ordinary folks' relation to law. Equine (as well as bridling) analogies trace back to the ancient Greeks and are often used in the context of training and taming people who allegedly lack an understanding of what is good for them, which then necessitates various contrivances and disciplinary measures (e.g., laws for people, bridling for horses).[74] The analogy, of course, is not without subsidiary connotations; some of these reinforce existing threads of thought (e.g., the association of absence of understanding with beast-like existence) and some potentially invite fresh associations, depending on how the equine imagery operates in a particular milieu's "experiential gestalt" (Spooks easily? Dangerous when threatened? Primarily a labor resource for an increasingly industrialized society?).[75]

Notably, Spinoza switches from animality tropes to those of automata when speaking of skeptics (*sceptici*), whose minds are so "blinded ... either from birth, or from prejudices" that they refrain from affirming or denying anything and hence should be regarded as mere "automata."[76] Though both

---

[74] For a contextually grounded study of equine analogies in Plato, see Jeremy Bell, "Taming Horses and Desires: Plato's Politics of Care," in *Plato's Animals: Gadflies, Horses, Swans, and Other Philosophical Beasts*, ed. Jeremy Bell and Michael Naas (Bloomington: Indiana University Press, 2015), 115–130.

[75] Johnson uses the term "experiential gestalts" to refer to "structured meaningful wholes within experience" that consist of recurring patterns and sub-patterns of associations that interrelate with each other. Mark Johnson, "Introduction: Metaphor in the Philosophical Tradition," in *Philosophical Perspectives on Metaphor*, ed. Mark Johnson (Minneapolis: University of Minnesota Press, 1981), 30–31. Regarding the possible associations about ordinary people I suggested above (e.g., that they are prone to be stirred up easily, or that their labor supply is a matter of crucial interest), in Spinoza's writings we see remarks about how ordinary people's susceptibility to superstition is intertwined with their living in a state of fear and insecurity (TTP Preface 5). This is combined with the warning that "the mob (*vulgus*) is terrifying, if unafraid" (EIVP54s). As for the comment concerning people possibly being seen as a labor force, one of the main draws of living in an organized polity, for Spinoza, is the division of labor it affords (TTP 5.18–20).

[76] TIE 47–48. Spinoza did not think animals were automata, so this trope does not have obvious associations with zoological tropes in Spinoza's writings. However, in a different context, Spinoza uses the expression "beasts or automata" to describe polities that "control people by fear or subject them to the authority of another" (TTP 20.6). The Latin phrase is "bestias, vel automata" where "vel" connotes disjunction (instead of equivalence, as with "sive"), although it is not *necessarily* an exclusive disjunction either (as with "aut").

figurative analogies, one involving horses and the other involving automata, suggest shortcomings in one's performance of key markers of humanity, namely, understanding and agency (which, as chapter 3 will show, go hand in hand), a horse would still be receptive to training that would sharpen its various capabilities, whereas there is no such hope for the automaton.[77] One implication of this contrast is the view that educational sophistication does not necessarily bring one closer to human perfection.[78] Whether Spinoza intended it or not, looking at the various tropes he employs, together with the set of implications they highlight or generate, gives us additional glimpses into the kernels of what Spinoza thinks make a man a man of understanding and wisdom.

These last points bring us to the final question concerning the kind of reading strategies Spinoza's oeuvre requires in general. First, although some of us may not exactly match the profile of the "learned men" Spinoza had in mind when he was imagining his audience, we are still required to approach his system with the mental discipline he explicitly demands from his readers so that they can follow what are, at times, long chains of linked inferences. Given that Spinoza had a unified understanding of truth and also seems to have imagined his works to be complementing each other,[79] we need to trace the interlinks between Spinoza's ontology, epistemology, affect theory, and political thought. In regard to Spinoza's treatment of the human-animal binary (whether animals are viewed in their own right or as tropes for various epistemic or affective failures), given that Spinoza is a systematic thinker, it behooves us to inquire into the systematic grounds of his treatment of this very binary. Moreover, for the same reason he is a systematic thinker, it

---

[77] This reading is supported by TIE 77, where Spinoza blames sustained doubt on skeptics' unrelenting stubbornness. Here it is also worth reiterating that unlike many other early modern thinkers, Spinoza never says animals are automatons. This also supports the aforementioned interpretation and explains why the two tropes function differently in Spinoza.

[78] When attacking "skeptics," Spinoza clearly has philosophical skepticism in mind and his targets are learned men who might oppose his demonstrations due to a deeply entrenched epistemological stance (TIE 47–48). That being learned, for Spinoza, is not a sufficient condition for openness of the mind is also clear from his wish for his writings to be ignored by theologians, who, he notes, do nothing but bring harm to those who do not subordinate reason to theology (TTP Preface 15).

[79] For a discussion of the relation between TIE and *Ethics*, see De Dijn, *Spinoza*, 9–14, 195. For a discussion of the relation between TP, TTP, and *Ethics*, see Justin Steinberg, *Spinoza's Political Psychology: The Taming of Fortune and Fear* (Cambridge: Cambridge University Press, 2018), 9–11. Moreover, both his *Hebrew Grammar* and his TTP overlap in their examination of the Hebrew language, with the former delving more substantially into this analysis. The relationship between *Principles* and his other works is more difficult to establish, due to the fact that separating the "Cartesian proper" aspects of Spinoza's reconstruction of Descartes's philosophy from Spinozist interpolations already requires one to refer to Spinoza's other works (which is a gesture that is premised on the assumption of continuity among his works, creating a circle in reasoning).

equally befits us to address the areas where he falls short of his own goal of consistency.

This much-needed attention to tensions in Spinoza's writings is not simply due to a philosopher's appetite for catching a systematic thinker's moments of weakness. On the contrary, it is an act of taking seriously Spinoza's own invitation to carefully study the operations of different registers of understanding. As mentioned earlier, for Spinoza, different perceptual abilities and mental constructs can coexist; and he himself also employs different registers of speech, targeting his learned readers' different epistemic powers. This multifaceted approach to one's powers of understanding shall be extended to him as well, especially when his oeuvre is replete with statements betraying his own biases, investments, and anxieties as a thinker.

A very remarkable feature of Spinoza's systematic edifice is the fact that in it Spinoza gives his readers ample tools to study not only human capabilities but also human flaws and oversights, which are to be mobilized together to understand the human mind in its entirety. Hence, perhaps what makes Spinoza's edifice so captivating is not its ability to lead its readers to new heights of philosophical consistency, but the fact that—in yet another brilliant gesture of combining epistemic humility and confidence—Spinoza offers us the very tools to critique his own thought and urges us to use them. Spinoza's comprehensive scrutiny of man's nature, with all its potential for achieving great wisdom or wallowing in pathos, is central to the pursuit of collective salvation. However, this pursuit also contributes to his dismissiveness, if not antagonism, toward what he deems as lying outside the boundaries of mankind. Although we may not agree entirely with Spinoza's vision of collective salvation or the constituents of the particular "collective" that he had in mind, holding him to his own critical standards and giving his philosophy in-depth scrutiny does, in the end, enrich our understanding of the many possible and remarkably intricate machineries behind the human-animal split.

Conclusion

Strange Companions—Thinking about Animals with Spinoza and the *Zhuangzi*

It is a truism that philosophical works are informed by the intellectual and sociocultural contexts within which they are born. However, as also evinced by our comparative analysis, like many works, both the *Zhuangzi* and Spinoza's oeuvre are shaped in the space between external constraints and individual choice. Indeed, both sets of writings emerged out of conflict-ridden sociopolitical settings, yet the ways in which these works responded to their environments could not be more different. These differences, as will be shown, speak to each comparandum's particular sensibilities about what holds value and what is worth pursuing in life. Also evident is the authors' and compilers' choice to perform through, but sometimes also against, the culturally legitimate literary conventions of their time, which conveys indispensable clues about their own epistemic and affective comportments and investments.

In a study such as this one, which compares two collections of writings around the issue of the human-animal split, it also befits us to entertain the possibility that the ways in which this issue is treated within Spinoza's corpus and the *Zhuangzi* are also, to some extent, folded into the way these texts operate as texts. Inevitably, the two demand different types of hermeneutical vigilance from their readers and impose different standards of analysis, which will have a bearing on the way we approach and analyze their "content." At the same time, the sheer historical distance between us and the *Zhuangzi* versus Spinoza invites different modes of contextualization, which can be utilized to reveal fresh lines of interpretive framing.

A. Form, Context, and Function

The *Zhuangzi* emerged from an intellectual tradition that both presumed and aimed for a vision of cohesion and agreement, aligned with a political agenda focused on asserting sovereignty and consolidating territories. Within this context, the human-beast divide afforded critical rhetorical force to philosophical justifications for promoting an extensive array of hierarchical social arrangements, which were credited for humans' emancipation from an animal-like existence. When considered against this background, it is significant that the *Zhuangzi* refrains from offering a unified and ostensibly unifying ideology, drawing attention instead to a multiplicity of viewpoints. At the same time, as Graziani notes, the text often attempts to "imagine relationships between humans and animals from the standpoint of animals" while rejecting a "socio-centric vision of the world."[1] With its many stories told from the vantage points of different characters, all of whom are acting in a complex and unpredictable world, the *Zhuangzi* also offers ample opportunities for readers to reconsider what they once thought as dear, important, or noble. Storytelling, when used to relate to and move among positions and situations different from one's own, can thus also expand the epistemic and affective purview of the audience and compel them to rethink long-held habits of the mind and its evaluative hierarchies, rankings, and orders.[2]

Emphasizing the plurality of vantage points in a diverse and fragmented world can also deepen the reader's appreciation of how divisions, differences, and ranks are mediated through one's own explanatory interests, biases, and habits. It is not necessarily the case that there are no pre-discursive similarities and differences among various beings, but as one of the many incarnations of the figure of Kongzi in the *Zhuangzi* tells us:

---

[1] Romain Graziani, *Fiction and Philosophy in the Zhuangzi: An Introduction to Early Chinese Taoist Thought* (London: Bloomsbury, 2020).

[2] Several moral philosophers have already noted the unique use of storytelling in inviting readers to participate in different scenarios that display the difficulty of making a judgment or making a choice. See Martha C. Nussbaum, *Love's Knowledge: Essays on Philosophy and Literature* (New York: Oxford University Press, 1992), 3–53. Also see Chris J. Cuomo and Lori Gruen, "On Puppies and Pussies: Animals, Intimacy, and Moral Distance," in *Daring to Be Good: Essays in Feminist Ethico-Politics*, ed. Bat-Ami Bar On and Ann Ferguson (New York: Routledge, 1998), 133–134. Although a moral dimension is largely absent in the *Zhuangzi*, its preoccupation with distinction-making is obvious.

Looked at from the point of view of their differences, even your own liver and gallbladder are as distant as Chu in the south and Yue in the north. But looked at from the point of view of their sameness, all things are one.[3]

In a world marked by unpredictability and conflict, being mindful of the framing through which one perceives and engages with their surroundings can surely be helpful for navigating through challenging circumstances. This approach also allows one to better relate to different vantage points, which then expands the sheer repertoire of reactions available to one.[4] The effect of this expansion is not a quietist attitude toward what can be said about the world, but endlessly multiplying voices and opinions about all that is unfolding in the world, without elevating any particular voice to the status of authority.[5]

That the *Zhuangzi* not only thinks along with animals but also views them as being on par with human vantage points instantly shifts the conversation away from rituals, values, and distinctions between refinement and vulgarity—and all the other contrivances that are recruited to establish social order—and toward the vast diversity of existence and the tenuousness of all such distinctions. This, of course, renders the text useless for purposes of improving the world according to a certain vision of good governance, which is acknowledged in the text itself. In the end, this same "uselessness" of the text is what clears space for overlooked corners of the world to reveal themselves, as was demonstrated earlier through an analysis of the imagery of an anomalous and gnarly tree.

---

[3] *Zhuangzi* 5:196.
[4] For more on this point, see Lee H. Yearley, "Daoist Presentation and Persuasion: Wandering among Zhuangzi's Kinds of Language," *Journal of Religious Ethics* 33, no. 3 (September 2005): 511, 519.
[5] Two passages in the *Zhuangzi* (namely, *Zhuangzi* 22:746–747 and *Zhuangzi* 25:916–917) have led some interpreters to believe that the text must have a quietist streak. See, for instance, Youru WANG, *Linguistic Strategies in Daoist Zhuangzi and Chan Buddhism: The Other Way of Speaking* (New York: Routledge, 2014), 102. However, what is being conveyed is the view that words are not apt tools for speculating about the primordial sources and processes underneath the formation of things and events. Not only can we still talk about things and events (*wu* 物), and, more broadly, whatever has substantiality (*shi* 實, lit: that which has come to fruition), but other passages also suggest that we can extend the reach of words by engaging in more efficacious forms of speech (e.g., "goblet speech," which is discussed in chapter 1, section 1.2). Also see descriptions of Zhuangzi's speech in the chapter titled "All under Heaven" (Tianxia 天下). The all-or-nothing approaches to the *Zhuangzi*'s treatment of language seem to either stem from employing the Greco-European "language versus reality" dichotomy when examining early Chinese texts (as in the case of WANG's treatment of the *Zhuangzi*) or Buddhist notions of emptiness and ineffability (which risks anachronism). See chapter 4, section 4.3 for a critique of associations of notions of emptiness with the *Zhuangzi*'s treatment of the heart (*xin* 心).

With that imagery of the unruly gnarly tree, the *Zhuangzi* subverts norm-imposing craft and plant metaphors, thereby undermining aspirations of regularity and consistency. That the work was produced in an era that witnessed great political instability does not prompt its authors and compilers to seek agreement among different groups and peoples. Instead, the work goes in the opposite direction of explicitly embracing the multiplicity of worldviews. At the same time, the text unsettles an established social dynamic that is ingrained in the fabric of the elite society of its time, namely, the master-disciple relationships that are sometimes sustained over a lifetime. It does so by parodying the very idea of authority (including textual authority) and locating sites of insight in random encounters with unlikely masters (in other words, embracing chance and accidentality).[6]

The authors and compilers of the *Zhuangzi* are not system-builders, in the way that Spinoza is, because they did not view the world as having an intelligible order, the patterns of which are accessible through privileged entry points. What is emphasized instead are the surprises that life offers. As the *Zhuangzi* repeatedly emphasizes the overwhelming complexities of life, it, on the whole, offers only snapshots of life instead of cohesive and integrated treatments of ritual and human behavior, or binding codes of conduct and standards. Because the work suggests that enabling interactions can occur with all kinds of actors and locates sites of thriving in many different settings and habitats, it leaves no privileged sites of knowledge unscathed. The authors and compilers admit this has implications for the *Zhuangzi* as a text and they disabuse their readers of any hope of extracting conventional forms of utility from it.

If the *Zhuangzi* envisioned (at least some) people as gnarly trees that prosper according to their own logic, without easily aligning with tools of measurement and calibration, Spinoza studied people's actions and emotions "just as if it were a question of lines, planes and bodies" (EIIIpref.) and sought to understand their place in the machine-world. It is tempting to interpret this difference in terms of organic versus mathematico-mechanistic conceptions of people, groups, and the conditions surrounding them. The fact of the matter is the *Zhuangzi* also occasionally resorts to mechanical metaphors,[7] just like Spinoza helps himself to organic (and even botanical)

---

[6] The fleeting and fickle nature of human encounters and teaching relations in the *Zhuangzi* are explored in detail in chapter 5, section 5.2.

[7] The metaphor of the wheel is well known and well studied and it is also briefly examined in chapter 4, section 4.2. For a study of mechanical metaphors in early Chinese texts, see Boqun Zhou, "Mechanical Metaphors in Early Chinese Thought" (PhD diss., University of Chicago, 2019).

ones.⁸ Hence, the difference between the two attitudes is much finer than generalized assumptions about organic versus mechanistic ways of envisioning the world and its denizens.

When we look at the two comparanda's portrayals of human beings and human behavior in context and consider what work these depictions do for the texts in question, what stands out as the origin of contrast is something much simpler: the presence or absence of strong assumptions of similarity among people. The *Zhuangzi* uses botanical metaphors in subversive ways to counteract the prevalent rhetorical tendency of employing such metaphors to show similarities among people. Spinoza, on the other hand, gives a mathematico-mechanistic explanation of everything in the universe, including human actions, rendering mankind without free will. While that undermines a long-established wall between men and beasts, Spinoza still holds onto epistemic and affective differences between the two *and* similarities among each as he prioritizes human salvation above all else.⁹ That goes hand in hand with his promotion of a clear understanding of man's place in the world, which he hoped would ultimately bring an end to conflict and discord.

Certainly, for Spinoza, different groups of people came with different capacities of understanding. His preoccupation with the epistemic limits of different audiences lays bare the shifting borders around the community Spinoza identified with, and the borders around "us" as he imagined them. Regardless of how broadly or narrowly Spinoza imagines his fellow men at different moments in his writing, their salvation and their togetherness are what fuel his thinking. Hence, perhaps it should not be surprising that in this decidedly human-centered philosophy, we do not see sustained engagement with animal vantage points in the manner of the *Zhuangzi*.¹⁰

Spinoza developed this penchant for human togetherness in war-torn early modern Europe, which, in his case, brought with it a concern for dissolving disagreements through the pursuit of true knowledge. Spinoza's interest in expressing the world in a way that "we" all can ideally agree on (as opposed

---

⁸ For instance, Spinoza is fond of the imagery of fruition, as can be seen in phrases such as "fruit of the understanding (*fructus intellectus*)" (TTP 4.12) or "fruits of liberty" (*libertatis fructus*) (TTP 20.15).

⁹ Spinoza opens the second book of his *Ethics* by declaring that although infinitely many things follow from God, he will only study that which can lead us to "the knowledge of the human mind and its highest blessedness" (EIIpref.).

¹⁰ There are, however, sporadic mentions of non-human perspectives. An example including the vantage point of a worm is discussed in chapter 3, section 3.4; and of a stone is discussed chapter 3, section 3.2.

to endlessly multiplying meaning structures and interpretations of the world we share) is also intertwined with his view of figurative language as an entertaining deviance from literal usage that can be brought "back on track" with translatory efforts. Of course, according to Spinoza, figurative language can help convey certain truths to the feeble-minded in concrete and vivid ways, but it can also yield disagreement about the meaning of the truths it is supposed to convey—a scenario that is sure to threaten the collective salvation of men, which is premised on uniting around accurate knowledge of their place in the world.

That literal statements are seen to be more obvious bearers of truth speaks to Spinoza's ontological and epistemological assumptions regarding the possibility and desirability of uniform access to reality—had we just managed to align our thinking with the preestablished order of nature. Accordingly, what might similarly be described as a vision of "expansion" is affected by Spinoza's works too, but of course, in a way that corresponds to fundamental aspects of life as he viewed it. For Spinoza, expanding one's epistemic purview is a matter of the mind reproducing "Nature as closely as possible" and discerning uniform and omnipresent patterns of reality through the proper ordering and management of ideas (TIE 99).

This mimicry of Nature's logic, though within reach and sight, still rarely happens by chance,[11] which adds a final explanatory layer to Spinoza's didactic, if not disciplinary, tone as a writer. Spinoza's tone is informed by a concern to actively guide the mind in the direction of acquiring ideas in the proper order (*debitus ordo*),[12] without leaving this to chance. Hence, Spinoza calls for *restraining* (*cohibere*) the mind from those perceptions that do not provide true ideas, such as perceptions of random experience (*experientia vaga*) that come to us by mere chance;[13] or *directing* (*dirigere*) the mind according to the standard of a given true idea,[14] such as the idea of God.[15]

---

[11] TIE 44. Spinoza adds that he has "been forced to lay things down" in the "proper order (*debitus ordo*)" so that "what we cannot acquire by fate, we may still acquire by a deliberate plan (*quod non possumus fato, praemeditato tamen consilio acquiramus*)."

[12] TIE 44.

[13] TIE 19, 49; TTP 2.1

[14] TEI 43: "A good Method is one which shows how the mind is to be directed according to the standard of a given true idea (*bonam Methodum eam esse, quae ostentit, quomodo mens sit dirigenda ad datae verae ideae normam*)."

[15] This is why Spinoza finds great relief in the geometrical method, which illustrates what orderly thinking looks like. However, in the end, no method can immediately trigger people to put aside old habits and jump over epistemic hurdles of prejudice, credulity, and superstition. Their surrounding conditions also need to be conducive to developing their understanding. Hence, as will be discussed in detail in chapter 10, in his political thought, Spinoza promotes elaborate organization of human societies in ways that foster togetherness, so that men can enhance each other's intellectual and

CONCLUSION 75

In the end, there is no obvious choice to be made between Spinoza's machine-like systematicity and the *Zhuangzi*'s topsy-turvy trove of stories and musings as the more apt way of discussing the human condition and its relation to animality. However, they do inevitably translate into different attitudes toward the world and the myriad beings in it. Spinoza tells a community of learned men about the regularities one can observe in the world and the lawful characteristics of nature, craving their agreement (TIE 14). As will be shown, however, Spinoza's investment in building intellectual camaraderie with his fellow mankind also inflects his dismissive, if not hostile, remarks against what he deems to be outside of, if not insidious threats to, human fraternity.

If the *Zhuangzi* appears to be more pluralistic, this is as much because it is not fueled by aspirations to uplift a community, if not mankind *en masse*, as it is because the *Zhuangzi* emphasizes the enriching and even empowering aspects of the ability to think along with others, including animal others. These two different attempts at reorienting thought—one aiming to align it with the order of Nature, the other unmooring it from familiar perceptions of reality—demand different kinds of engagement from their readers. Moreover, reading them together calls for great hermeneutical vigilance, while also opening up fresh lines of interpretive approach.

B. Hermeneutical Challenges and Opportunities

The way any text situates itself against different "horizons of expectation"[16] is linked to different views on how to communicate what one thinks is worth knowing about the world.[17] The dissimilar ways that Spinoza's corpus, on one hand, and the *Zhuangzi*, on the other, operate as texts also force us to bring different standards to bear on evaluating their conclusions. To put it simply, whereas Spinoza's corpus allows the reader to search for coherence and closure (and to be intrigued by moments of tension), the *Zhuangzi* offers a

---

affective powers (TP 5.2, 5.5) as well as their material stability. This stability is to be sustained with civil laws (TTP 16.5, TP 1.3) so that people will not feel at the mercy of forces of fortune (which could breed credulity and superstition [TTP Preface 1–5]).

[16] I borrow the phrasing from Todorov's oft-cited 1974 article on literary genres. See Tzvetan Todorov, "Literary Genres," in *Current Trends in Linguistics*, vol. 12, *Linguistics and Adjacent Arts and Sciences, Part 3*, ed. T. A. Sebeok (The Hague: Mouton, 1974), 958.

[17] I owe this insight to Nussbaum. See Nussbaum, *Love's Knowledge*, 7.

disjointed and incongruous discourse, which matches its vision of the world as heterogenous, fragmented, and unpredictable. Another obvious difference in the hermeneutical methodologies that the two sets of writings demand has to do with the presence or absence of an investment to laying claim to knowledge and authority. For a philosophical monograph that critically assesses the assets and liabilities of various positions, it is the not-knowing and, more significantly, the not-even-caring that proves to be especially challenging.

The obvious "weakness" of the *Zhuangzi*—that it lacks common types of use one would expect from a Masters text—is, in the end, already addressed and acknowledged within the text itself. Of course, this acknowledgment may not be enough to satisfy a reader who, after reading stories of and about many characters expressing their divergent understandings of the world, might still ask: Where do we go from here? Moreover, this question itself presumes the presence of a "we," which, as will be shown, is also undermined.[18] Certainly, notions of companionship are not absent in the text, but the same cannot be said about notions of community. In that vein, it is not an exaggeration to say that a community-oriented "we" is lost in the *Zhuangzi*—or perhaps it was not really there but was rather enforced by unificationist discourses serving fantasies of all-encompassing sovereignty, and the text is merely exposing that. As for the obvious follow-up question: "Then where do I go from here?," the answer, for better or worse, seems to be: Wherever you want.

On the other hand, taking a definite position on any issue invites dissatisfaction, if not disagreement, regardless of one's powers of persuasion. Even with the greatest system-builders in the history of philosophy, there are moments of tension, if not contradiction, even within the same work, which merit attention. Moreover, one's articulation of a position can also evolve over time or become inflected by the nature of the discussion at hand, which requires an interpreter to attune her assessment of a proposition accordingly. In regard to Spinoza's edifice, I am more of a lumper than a splitter, as Steinberg puts it, in the sense that I do take Spinoza's political, theological, ontological, and epistemological views as largely aligning with each other (as Spinoza seems to have intended and to a great degree succeeded in doing).[19] However, despite the fact that Spinoza developed his fairly large oeuvre in a relatively short span of time (about fifteen years), there are, at

---

[18] See chapter 5, section 5.2. Also see concluding notes to Part III.
[19] Not only are Spinoza's unitary impulses in his search for truth obvious, but he also explicitly notes the complementary nature of his works. See Steinberg, *Spinoza's Political Psychology*, 10n39. Also see chapter 2, footnote 79.

times, differences in tone.[20] When relevant, such tonal differences will be highlighted for the ways they potentially reveal facts about the author's aims and sensibilities within that specific textual context.

That philosophers are people with their own biases, investments, and inconsistencies should not be controversial. Neither is the fact that philosophers' ideas are fashioned in relation to their own historical and intellectual circumstances, as well as interactions with prevailing circles of power. However, a further challenge for a study like this is that we have access to different breadths and depths of detail for Spinoza's works and for the *Zhuangzi*.

As the previous chapter has shown, it is relatively easy to contextualize a seventeenth-century figure like Spinoza, sometimes at the level of specific dates, people, and places. With ancient works like the *Zhuangzi*, all we can say by way of contextualization will be zoomed out, since what we know about early China and its elite intellectual culture is very much fragmented. Hence, in the absence of conclusive information regarding issues of dating and exact philosophical targets (especially considering that the extant Masters texts themselves were largely compiled over long periods of time by broader textual communities), one can, at best, broadly surmise the intellectual and political sensibilities that were symptomatic of the time.

Although the disadvantages of the absence of precise contextual information are obvious, it can be argued that in the absence of an identifiable author behind the philosophical texts of early China, one is also emboldened to further question unitary understandings of such texts. Even with a single, identifiable author behind a set of writings (such as Spinoza), one encounters moments of incongruity within a corpus, because individuals, just like their works, are complicated, changing, and not always self-coherent. When a work is produced by a larger and anonymous authorial group, expectations of unitary meaning fail more easily, even when the work in question revolves around the persona of one master. With a text like the *Zhuangzi*, possibly named after a fictitious master in a double gesture of mimicry and satire, one has no choice but to leave aside consolidatory interpretations. However, this allows the reader to read the text fragmentarily, which is fitting for a text that is also polyvocal and is known to frequently shift perspectives.

For a comparative project like this one, fragmentariness also allows one to strategically bring out the features of the comparison one wants to emphasize.

---

[20] See chapter 10, section 10.1 for an overview of the argument that TTP employs a harsher tone against common folks than TP.

As discussed in the introduction, given that so many comparative approaches to Spinoza (including ones carried out by his own contemporaries) "orientalize" him and liken his philosophy to texts and traditions of Asia, the luxury of reading the *Zhuangzi* fragmentarily serves as a corrective measure against such prevalent reading habits by bringing into focus layers of the *Zhuangzi* that serve as obvious contrasts to aspects of Spinoza's philosophy.

Of course, this is not to suggest that continuous threads of thought in the *Zhuangzi* should be or could be overlooked. Neither are we prevented from studying moments of similarity between the comparanda. As mentioned in the introduction, one reason to study Spinoza's corpus and the *Zhuangzi* within the context of critical human-animal studies is that both, I believe, "vacillate between decentering and recentering the human"—which runs counter to the still-prevalent interpretive angle that focuses on moments of decentering the human in Spinoza's corpus and the *Zhuangzi*.

Part of the overemphasis, if not exclusive emphasis, on antianthropocentric dimensions of Spinoza's corpus (especially the *Ethics*) and the *Zhuangzi* stems from their fame as non-conformist works of philosophy. As the previous two chapters have shown, the two sets of writings indeed have a way of standing out when set against the background of the philosophical fabric of their own time. However, as we have also shown, this does not warrant reading them as "going against the grain" in their treatments of everything.

The next two chapters—chapters 3 and 4—pursue this insight further by delving into Spinoza's *Ethics* and the *Zhuangzi* with an eye toward their ontological assumptions as well as their theories of action and agency. As will be shown, what emerges out of this examination are not different erasures of the human-animal split, but two different models of human distinctiveness—one that ranks different minds and bodies in a way that privileges humans over less "complex" beings, and the other that presents human distinctiveness as a double-edged sword forged by humans themselves owing to their propensity for making distinctions.

PART II
PORTRAYALS OF HUMAN DISTINCTIVENESS

Thus, salvation (*salus*) is good for men, but neither good nor bad for animals or plants, for which it has no relevance.

Principles[1]

Is human life always and everywhere such a daze? Or could it be only me who is dazed, while there are also others who are undazed? Of humans is there anything or anyone undazed?

Zhuangzi 2:61[2]

---

[1] *Principles*, Appendix Containing Metaphysical Thoughts, Part 1, chapter 6.
[2] For this line, I follow Ziporyn's translation. Ziporyn, *Zhuangzi: The Complete Writings*, 13. In Chinese, the line reads: 人之生也，固若是芒乎！其我獨芒，而人亦有不芒者乎！

3
Rich in Complexity
Human Distinctiveness in Spinoza

What shall we make of declarations of human exceptionality, if not superiority, in texts that are celebrated for the way they take aim at their contemporaries' views of human supremacy? Or perhaps a more pertinent question here concerns whether it is warranted to expect a work that undermines one form of human exceptionalism to also oppose all forms of it. Spinoza has long been celebrated for striking a blow against human hubris, when he, in fact, largely reacted against specific biblical claims of human superiority. Admittedly, the *Zhuangzi* strikes a more unsparing blow against human pomposity by persistently undermining people's presumed role as the valued center of life. Yet, it still does concede the exceptional status of the human condition, which, nonetheless, often translates into being worse off than other beings in crucial ways.

The preceding two chapters have already examined some of the onto-epistemological assumptions of Spinoza's corpus and the *Zhuangzi* while deliberating on the kind of reading attitudes the two sets of writings demand. Part II delves further into the ontological and epistemological layers of Spinoza's corpus with a focus on his *Ethics* (which most conspicuously reveals the interlinkages between the two dimensions of his thought) and the *Zhuangzi*. A key aim of this examination is to highlight their vacillation between deflation and reflation of human significance, if not human achievement. In this vein, a large portion of Part II is devoted to examining two different theories of action and agency, which, as will be shown, both yield sentiments of human distinctiveness in their own ways.

The current chapter examines some of the fundamental assumptions employed by Spinoza about the world and mankind's place in it as knowing and acting subjects. It shows the ways in which Spinoza steps away from a common variety of biblical conceptions of God and free will by formulating human agency around understanding one's conditions (instead of the ability to act without the constraints of necessity), while also divorcing man's epistemic and agential powers from God's grace. Also significant is his panpsychic view of the world, which distributes mental powers to everything in the world. Yet, as will be shown, neither of these features of Spinoza's thought translates into an effort to undermine man's (mental and/or bodily) superiority over beasts. Spinoza's views on the human-animal distinction are still very understudied, perhaps due to the fact that his views on animals had less of a historical impact than the Cartesian beast-machine theory. However, they certainly merit careful attention because of their uniqueness in demonstrating how one could extend the powers of the mind to everything while also exalting man's epistemic and corporeal capabilities.

3.1 "That Eternal and Infinite Being We Call God, or Nature"

Spinoza is best known for his *Ethics*, in which he attempts to provide a coherent and true account of man's place in the world, which is necessary to attain true happiness.[1] Since an ambitious project like this necessitates an account of the fundamentals of reality in its ontological and phenomenological characteristics, Spinoza opens the *Ethics* by laying out his definition of God and what it entails. God, as Spinoza defines it, is an infinite being with infinite attributes, which means he is all that exists and there is nothing outside of him. Since God is all there is, and he cannot be finite (which presupposes being limited by something else), Spinoza concludes, God must have all the possible attributes, including extension (EIp15). Spinoza later also equates God with Nature, which is followed by the qualification that God is the dynamic aspect of Nature[2]—all of which further cements Spinoza's status as a heretic for his contemporaries and as the champion of immanentism for scholars of later centuries.

Spinoza's equation of God with Nature might strike one as an "immanentist" gesture, indicating that God exists within the world he generated

---

[1] The section title is quoted from EIVpref.
[2] Spinoza often uses the phrase "God or Nature," where the word that is translated as "or" is *sive*, which connotes equivalence, not disjunction. Spinoza further qualifies his identification of God with Nature when he notes that God is rather the generative and active aspect of Nature (EIp29s). Through his characterization of the creator God versus God's productions as two aspects of Nature (considered in its active versus passive aspects), Spinoza eliminates any kind of temporal gap between cause and effect, giving a radical twist to the issue of God's causation: God is the cause of all things in the same sense that he is the cause of himself.

instead of being beyond and outside of it. However, it is worth noting that aside from the fact that Spinoza refers to God's immanence only once and in the more specific context of causation,[3] the "Nature" with which Spinoza equates God is not the nature given in human experience (i.e., the realm of bodies and minds).[4] God (or Nature) in Spinozist ontology has infinitely many attributes (EId6) while the denizens of the world have access to only two of these attributes, namely, the attributes of Thought and Extension (EIIax5).[5] This, by itself, introduces a significant epistemic and experiential gap between God and his creations, which is akin to a "transcendent" conception of God—not in the sense that God is beyond the material world, but in the sense that he lies beyond ordinary human experience.[6]

What does it mean to perceive Nature either in terms of Extension or Thought? In a nutshell, according to this view, given a particular phenomenon, one can explain its history and interactions as either unfolding out of mental processes (i.e., in terms of ideas relating to each other) or out of material processes (i.e., in terms of extended bodies relating to each other). To describe this from a different angle while elaborating further on Spinozist terminology, let us take a person. Being an individuated phenomenon, Spinoza calls this person a "mode." This "mode" is one of many particular "modifications" of God and is, as far as we can tell, a thinking and extended being. Taken as a body, this person expresses Extension; taken as a mind, he expresses Thought. We can also think of the smaller constituents of his body or mind as modes of God that express God's attribute of Extension or Thought.

---

[3] Spinoza notes that God is the immanent, not transitive, cause of things (EIp18) in the sense that he is an "indwelling cause" and hence is inseparable from its effects. To be more specific, Spinoza likens this to the way in which the nature of a triangle gives rise to its own essential properties: "From God's supreme power, or infinite nature, infinitely many things in infinitely many modes, that is, all things, have necessarily flowed, or always follow, by the same necessity and in the same way as from the nature of a triangle it follows, from eternity and to eternity, that its three angles are equal to two right angles" (EIp17s1).

[4] I owe this point to Melamed. See Melamed, "Spinoza's 'Atheism.'" Henceforth I shall capitalize "Nature" especially when it is crucial to differentiate it from the nature that we experience (the realm of bodies and minds).

[5] Of course, that Nature/God has infinitely many attributes poses an interpretational difficulty regarding the relation between Thought and all the other attributes (e.g., is there also an attribute of Thought corresponding to each of the other unknown attributes?). In order to resolve this interpretational tangle, Melamed argues that "modes of thought, unlike modes of any other attributes, are multifaceted" in the sense that "each idea has infinitely many aspects (or facets), so that each aspect of the idea represents a parallel mode under another attribute." See Yitzhak Y. Melamed, *Spinoza's Metaphysics: Substance and Thought* (Oxford: Oxford University Press, 2013), 155.

[6] I owe this insight regarding the two senses of the notion "transcendence" to Mark Csikszentmihalyi, *Material Virtue: Ethics and the Body in Early China* (Leiden: Brill 2004), 161. For a description of Spinoza's philosophy as transcendent, see Melamed, "Spinoza's 'Atheism.'"

A crucial aspect of this ontological picture is that these two ways of understanding the world, Thought and Extension, are both legitimate in their own right and there is no causal interaction between the two. To every idea, that is, to every mental state, corresponds a physical state, and vice versa.[7] However, an idea, by virtue of being an idea, cannot cause a change in the material dimension, as it can only interact with other ideas (EIIp7s).

That Thought and Extension are causally closed to each other has the crucial implication that, for Spinoza, there is no such thing as free will (where the mind is seen to be capable of ordering the body into various states and positions). That every physical state has a corresponding mental state (and vice versa) has another significant implication as well: According to Spinoza, a stone could also be said to have a mental life. The ways these controversial views inform his conceptualization of mankind are manifold and they require a two-sided analysis of Spinoza's concurrent undermining of envisioning God and mankind in each other's image.

3.2 Eliminating the Anthropomorphic God and the Theomorphic Man

Spinoza's introduction of the critical phrase "God or Nature" (*Deus sive Natura*) is part of a broader attempt to equate God's providence with the laws of Nature. This has the direct consequence of eliminating teleological conceptions of God's actions, according to which all things happen for a deliberate reason (EIapp, TTP 6.1). Spinoza's undermining of teleological views of the world can largely be traced to the development of a new conception of a mechanical universe. This new notion allowed the application of mathematics to physical phenomena while spurring the retirement of teleological and theological explanations for the properties and movements of natural objects.[8] However, what is crucial in Spinoza's case is not simply his

---

[7] Although many commentators have used the term "parallelism" to describe the relation between minds and bodies, as Hasana Sharp notes, along with Macherey, the imagery of parallelism could be interpreted to imply that ideas are "representations" of extended modes. However, this depiction does not accurately reflect Spinoza's vision as it implies that "ideas exist in order to represent bodies and are valid insofar as they do so accurately." See Hasana Sharp, *Spinoza and the Politics of Renaturalization* (Chicago: University of Chicago Press, 2011), 28; Pierre Macherey, *Introduction à l'éthique de Spinoza. La Seconde partie: la réalité mentale* (Paris: Presses Universitaires de France, 1997), 72. It is not that one order of relations represents the other order but that there is only one causal order that is expressed both by bodies and by thoughts (which also explains their symmetry).

[8] The fundamental developments concerning the rise of the new mechanical philosophy in seventeenth-century Europe is explained in chapter 2, section 2.1.

rendering of God's will as irrelevant for explanatory purposes (which could also be achieved by strategically separating theology from natural philosophy, limiting what the latter can say about God),[9] but also his discarding of the difference between God's will and intellect (EIp17s)—in other words, eliminating God's free will, along with human free will.

As examined in chapter 2, amid the deconstructions and reformulations of what it means to be a man, a question that became a major subject of philosophical discussion in early modern Europe concerned the presence or absence of the animal soul. The dominant views largely fell into two groups. One was the view of the Schools, referring to late Aristotelian-Scholastic philosophers, who granted animals sensible but not rational souls (where only the latter is considered to be immaterial); and the other was the Cartesian beast-machine approach, which infamously held that animals are similar to machines and are governed by the laws of matter alone.[10] According to both views, however, free will and the rational powers of the mind imply each other, which means that only mankind can be said to have free will.[11] In other words, although the new mechanical philosophy struck a blow to Scholastic formulations of man's dominion over creation, it did not fully challenge notions of man's superiority over animals and anthropocentric resourcism; instead it led to justifications of these notions in new and non-religious terms.

Spinoza's approach differs from both the Scholastic and Cartesian paradigms in that he grants a mental dimension to all the phenomena in the world, while also subjecting everything (including mankind) to a deterministic order. It is for this reason that Spinoza famously warns against conceiving of man in nature as a "dominion within a dominion" (*imperium in imperio*)— a view according to which men can act independently of the natural order rather than following it like everything else does (EIIIpref). Moreover, unlike Descartes, who envisioned mankind as consisting of distinct, yet coexisting

---

[9] As mentioned in chapter 2, section 2.1, this was the route taken by many Dutch Cartesians working in universities in order to secure institutional space for Cartesian philosophy.

[10] Scholars disagree on whether (or to what extent) Descartes himself viewed animals as mere automata. Some argue that it was, in fact, Nicholas Malebranche who adopted a more radical interpretation of Cartesian philosophy to explain away the suffering of animals, popularizing what came to be known as the "Cartesian beast-machine" approach. For more on this debate, see Nathaniel Wolloch, "Christiaan Huygens's Attitude toward Animals," *Journal of the History of Ideas* 61, no. 3 (July 2000): 417–418.

[11] For a detailed examination of the history of debates concerning the presence and absence of different types of souls in different beings and the extent to which various living beings can be understood as machine-like, see Jessica Riskin, *The Restless Clock: A History of the Centuries-Long Argument over What Makes Living Things Tick* (Chicago: University of Chicago Press, 2018).

and causally interacting, mental and physical substances—namely, the mind and the body (where the former was seen to be controlling the human body without being bounded by physical laws)[12]—Spinoza declared that human thoughts, emotions, and conduct follow the same common laws of Nature as does everything else (EIIIpref.). In other words, as Della Rocca puts it, the kind of metaphysical system Spinoza proposed is one in which everything "plays by the same rules."[13]

As explained earlier, having a mind is not a distinctively human quality in Spinoza's system particularly because of the view that Thought and Extension are representations of one and the same causal order. This view entails two crucial implications. First, owing to its granting of a mental dimension to everything in the world, it presents a serious challenge to the early modern humanist goal of relocating the dignity of mankind from its closeness to God to its exclusive possession of mental capacities. Second, if there is one causal network (expressed either in mental or physical terms) and everything is an inseverable part of it, then this has the direct consequence of stripping mankind of its privilege to act independently of natural determinations.[14] This latter implication brings forward two fundamental features of human existence: dependence and interconnectedness.

Spinoza observes that despite being part of an inescapable chain of causation, many people still imagine themselves to be the free and sole causes of their own actions simply because they are only conscious of their volitions, but not the myriad causes behind those volitions (EIapp, EIIp35s). In fact, in one of his oft-cited letters, Spinoza draws a humbling comparison between the situation of mankind and that of a stone flying while thinking that it is the sole cause of its own motion:

> Furthermore, conceive if you please, that while continuing in motion the stone thinks, and knows that it is endeavoring, as far as in it lies, to continue its motion. Now this stone, since it is conscious only of its endeavor (*conatus*) and is not at all indifferent, will surely think that it is completely free, and that it continues in motion for no other reason than it so wishes. This, then, is that human freedom which all men boast possessing, and

---

[12] See René Descartes's "Fourth Meditation: Truth and Falsity," in Descartes, *The Philosophical Writings of Descartes*, vol. 2, 37–43.
[13] Michael Della Rocca, *Spinoza* (New York: Routledge, 2008), 5.
[14] For examples of Spinoza's necessitarianism, see EIp29, EIp33, and EIIp48.

which consists solely in this, that men are conscious of their desire and unaware of the causes by which they are determined. (Ep.58)

The stone and mankind are embedded in the same chain of causation. Neither of them can stand above and outside of the infinite chain of causation of which they are part, and neither can control their own destiny independently of the world around them. In wryly suggesting that not only are men foolish in imagining themselves to be free, but that the degree of their delusion and arrogance is on par with that of the hypothetical stone, Spinoza takes audacious aim at deflating human hubris and putting mankind where it belongs: in the natural world.

Spinoza's insistence that men are subject to the same necessities that govern the rest of nature, combined with his elimination of the gulf that had divided reasoning mankind from the irrational nonhuman world, are the main reasons his philosophy has experienced a recent posthumous rebirth and has been appropriated by various philosophical programs aiming to undermine anthropocentric thinking. Perhaps the most well-known attempt to utilize Spinoza's philosophy to undercut "human-centered thinking" has been made by the deep ecology movement, whose chief goal is to formulate a notion of an "ecological self" that identifies not only with other humans but also with other beings (a doctrine known as "wide-identification").[15]

Spinoza's view that men are part of an interconnected causal chain along with other beings (who also have mental dimensions of their own) indeed makes his philosophy seem directly relevant for discussions regarding how to build an egalitarian relationship with the rest of nature. However, as the next section shows, for Spinoza, mental experiences still unfold on a hierarchical scale, where men are said to have more complex minds than others, which makes it easier for them to attain true understanding and "freedom." As chapter 6 further demonstrates, this has direct implications for the kind of identification that men can and should cultivate for other beings, according to Spinoza. For now, however, let us first look into another passage from the *Ethics* on the absence of free will, which will provide a glimpse into Spinoza's own particular vision of the "free" man—which is, in fact, still formulated

---

[15] See Arne Næss, "Identification as a Source of Deep Ecological Attitudes," in *Deep Ecology*, ed. M. Tobias (San Diego: Avant Books, 1985), 363. Also well known is Althusser's Marxist "anti-humanism" and its indebtedness to Spinoza. For an analysis of Althusser's interpretation of Spinoza, his antihumanist reading of Marx, as well as their connections and limitations, see Yitzhak Y. Melamed, "Spinoza, Althusser, and the Question of Humanism," *Crisis and Critique* 8, no. 1 (2021): 170–177.

around familiar tropes of mental ability and strength. This will be followed by a brief account of Spinoza's theory of knowledge, which will demonstrate the ways in which Spinoza is still able to preserve the superiority of mankind over other beings, without implying that man is separate from nature.

3.3 What Distinguishes a Man from an Ass

Since Spinoza denies any interaction between the mind and the body, it is clear that the mind cannot propel the body to act in certain ways. Notably, Spinoza not only nullifies the mind's grip over the body, but also rejects the view that there are different faculties within the mind, namely, the will and the intellect (where the former faculty freely makes judgments concerning the data provided by the latter). Spinoza insists that there are no such things as faculties of intellect and will, but only particular *acts* of the mind (EIIp48s), which are all located within the same chain of causation.[16]

Spinoza illustrates his own view—that "will and intellect are one and the same thing" (EIIp49c)—by presenting his reply to a version of the paradox of Buridan's ass. The scenario involves a donkey that is equally hungry and thirsty, placed midway between a stack of hay and some water.[17] Spinoza writes that

> it can be objected that if man does not act from freedom of the will, what will happen if he is in a state of equilibrium, like Buridan's ass? . . . [In reply] I grant entirely that a man placed in such an equilibrium (viz. who perceives nothing but thirst and hunger, and such food and drink as are equally distant from him) will perish of hunger and thirst. If they ask me whether such a man should not be thought an ass, rather than a man, I say that I do not know—just as I also do not know how highly we should esteem one who hangs himself, or children, fools (*stulti*), and madmen (*vesani*), and so on. (EIIp49s)

---

[16] This is generally interpreted as a criticism directed against Descartes, who argued that the human mind had two separate domains consisting of the intellect (the operations of which result in ideas) and the will (which gives rise to volitions). See Descartes's Fourth Meditation in *Meditations on First Philosophy*.

[17] For a history and different variations of the paradox, see Justin Clemens, "Spinoza's Ass," in *Spinoza Now*, ed. Dimitris Vardoulakis (Minneapolis: University of Minnesota Press, 2011), 67–71.

Aside from assuming the possibility of a perfect equilibrium where the incentives to action are completely equal, the scenario, for Spinoza, is founded on a false separation between will and intellect. The two are inseparable, which is to say that a man's difference from a donkey does not lie in such an erroneous division. If not having freedom of the will—that is, not having an excess of the mind giving rise to volitions—makes a man not different from a donkey, then perhaps the two are not different after all.

The fact that Spinoza imagines his opponents to be asking whether such a man really deserves to be called a man or an ass shows how closely tied "freedom of the will" and one's "humanity" are for some of Spinoza's contemporaries. The fact that Spinoza says he does not know the answer, adding that he also does not know whether someone who hangs himself—or fools, madmen, and children as well—deserves to be called a man, shows who else Spinoza thinks might be considered closer to an ass than a man. Although this extended list of dupes is informed by associative inclinations that were symptomatic of the time,[18] Spinoza is not one to challenge such associations. The examples that Spinoza throws into the mix—children, suicidal people, and those who are deemed mad or foolish—offer suggestive hints into his vision of mankind's "freedom." Although it does not involve a separation between will and intellect, it is still closely related to being able to conduct a certain type of reasoning (hence his use of examples connoting intellectual disability and debility).

Given the kind of intellectual labor Spinoza asks of his narrowly conceived audience,[19] who are set on a path to grasp the Book of Nature written according to mathematical constraints, his casual distancing of "madmen," "fools," and "children" from the category of "men" perhaps should not be that surprising. Although Spinoza's example of the man who hangs himself is laden with underlying assumptions that merit a closer look,[20] the exclusionary logic of his theory of freedom, particularly as it relates to his conceptualization of intellectual ability and growth, is apparent. As will be discussed, Spinoza reformulates freedom in terms of the mind's adequate

---

[18] Three of these examples—fools (*stulti*), children, and madmen (*vesani*)—are also used by Hobbes in chapter XXVI of his *Leviathan*, in the context of a discussion about people who are not different from brute beasts in that they, too, are incapable of making a covenant to obey laws. Cited in Clemens, "Spinoza's Ass," 79.

[19] Spinoza time and time again admits that his works' intended audience is learned men and not common people. For more, see chapter 2, section 2.2.

[20] More specifically, the example relates to his theory of "sad passions," which is examined in chapter 6, section 6.2.

understanding of things, which is also intertwined with his scaling of different minds and bodies in a way that privileges men with (conventionally) strong intellectual skills.

Going back to the way Spinoza shifts the focus of the discussion away from the distinction between a donkey and a man who cannot choose between two options, toward the equally blurry (for him) distinction between a donkey and madmen or fools, this gesture is not coincidental, given the long history behind associations drawn between mental atypicality and subhuman status.[21] Such associations inform Spinoza and his interlocutors alike.[22] In the end, the distinction between mankind and other beings remains intact for Spinoza, with the crux of the differentiation lying not in the concept of "freedom of the will," but rather in the notion of freedom understood in different terms.

Spinoza's alternative notion of freedom is defined not in relation to the separation between will and intellect, nor in terms of the mind ordering the body into acting in this or that way. Rather, it is defined in terms of the degree of activity (or power) of the mind *and* the body, which Spinoza relates to having an "adequate" understanding of one's situation achieved by grasping the necessary laws of Nature. The more one "adequately" understands things, the more active one's mind (and hence also one's body) becomes. To understand what Spinoza means by one's understanding being adequate or inadequate, it is imperative to take a brief look at his theory of knowledge. This will also lay bare the correlation Spinoza draws between the complexity of one's body and the degree of the adequacy of one's understanding, which then factors into man's relative superiority over other beings.

Since, according to Spinoza, the mind and the body are simply two different ways of expressing one and the same causal order, it should already be clear that different kinds of knowledge for Spinoza are not the products of the mind relating to the physical world in different ways, but the body relating

---

[21] A well-known study of the association between intellectual disability and animality has been offered by Foucault, who observes that "madness took its face from the mask of the beast." See Michel Foucault, *History of Madness*, ed. Jean Khalfa (New York: Routledge, 2006), 147.

[22] In a series of letters exchanged with Blyenbergh, Spinoza addresses the accusation that by merely arguing for the absence of a separation between will and intellect, he might be reducing mankind to the level of plants and stones. See Ep.20–21. Moreover, in his recapitulation of Descartes's *a posteriori* proof of God, Spinoza draws parallels between intellectual defects, visual disability, and beastliness: "There are some who deny that they have any idea of God, and yet, as they declare, they worship and love him. And though you were to set before them the definition of God and the attributes of God, you will meet with no more success than if you were to labor to teach a man blind from birth the differences of colors as we see them. However, except to consider them as a strange type of creature halfway between man and beast, we should pay small heed to their words" (*Principles* Ip6s).

to other bodies and ideas relating to other ideas in different ways. The lowest kind of understanding, namely, imagination, refers to the confused awareness of one's own body *as* it is affected by external bodies. It should be noted here that imagination, as used in Spinoza's *Ethics*, does not refer to an illusory state that contrasts with concrete reality. When speaking of imagination, Spinoza often uses the noun *imago*, which conveys the idea of images.[23] Formulated in ocular-centric terms, imagination primarily refers to a kind of knowledge that solely relies on haphazard experiential learning from which, depending on one's causal history, one could draw wildly different associations among different things. One could think of the process as one of being bombarded with random images that give rise to different arbitrary connections in the mind. Spinoza provides a well-known example in which the sight of horse traces on sand evokes thoughts of war in a soldier and thoughts of fields in a farmer (EIIp18s).

Since, for Spinoza, the knowledge of an effect requires the knowledge of its cause (EIax4), it is impossible for anyone to have complete knowledge of events that are perceived via imagination alone (as it would require one to trace the complete causal history of events by following endless "images" of singularities). All one has in this state is "conclusions without premises" (EIIp28d) and the mind is passive in the sense that it does not have an adequate understanding of its own experiences (EIIId2).

For Spinoza, one could still form ideas of abstract notions by drawing generalizations based on the ideas of these experiences. However, abstract ideas that are solely formed via imagination will reflect its random character, and thus different people will form different conceptions of the same thing (one of Spinoza's commonly cited examples is the different conceptions of mankind as laughing animals, featherless bipeds, or rational animals [EIIp40s1]). Such generalizations, which are generally referred to as "bad" universals, owe their origin to one's failure to hold all the instances of a being in the mind, which then makes one start to conveniently erase the differences among them (EIIp40s1).

Fortunately, aside from bad universals that are based on the confused and mixed awareness of various phenomena, one can also grasp what those experiences have in common with others—in other words, one can form "common notions." Common notions are defined as notions that are "common to all things" and exist "equally in part as in the whole" (EIIp38);

---

[23] Spinoza's treatment of imagination in EIIp17s also explicitly reveals its connection to images.

the obvious examples are motion and rest, from which one can also derive the general laws of nature (EIp22). Common notions and general laws of Nature are things that one can understand adequately, as they are omnipresent features of the world.

Although it is not uncommon for scholars to view Spinoza's process of attaining higher forms of knowledge as a case of turning one's attention away from finite particularities to common notions themselves (and eventually to God or Nature),[24] Spinoza himself holds that one can also develop an adequate understanding of finite, local phenomena by situating them in relation to common notions and the laws of the nature.[25] One can also break down a complex "imaginary" perception into aspects shared by other bodies and see it as an expression of the common laws of Nature[26] (which is bound to transform one's experience of reasoning itself as well, by diversifying the ways certain commonalities and laws of nature manifest themselves).[27] Given that understanding all the diverse manifestations of the commonalities and laws of nature is what Spinoza means by having a more "active" mind, having a more complex mind and body (consisting of more diverse configurations of components) is bound to have some significance for his epistemological system.

Regarding the complexity of minds and bodies, it should be noted that, for Spinoza, bodies are not differentiated from each other because they are made of different "stuff," but because they are constituted through different configurations and degrees of motion (EIIp13L1)—which is also a direct consequence of his substance monism.[28] Motion, as a necessary

---

[24] Scruton, *Spinoza*, 73.

[25] Spinoza, in the *Ethics*, as well as in TIE and KV, gives the example of solving a mathematical problem that consists of finding the fourth proportional to a series of three numbers. Spinoza argues that one could solve the problem by mechanically applying a rule that one has memorized in school (which would be a case of haphazard learning that relies on the operations of the imagination alone), or one could infer the solution by applying one's knowledge of the common property of the proportional (EIIp40Sc2, TEI 23; KV Part 2, chapter 4).

[26] Spinoza occasionally resorts to more mundane examples as well, such as the process of making butter out of milk, which one can understand as a local expression of the common laws of motion, where stirring the milk causes it to acquire "a new motion to which all the parts composing the milk cannot accommodate themselves," which results in the differentiation of "heavier" [i.e., butter] and "lighter" [i.e., buttermilk] parts (Ep.6).

[27] This point is often overlooked and, as Yovel notes, gaining adequate ideas in Spinoza is often viewed as a matter of "acquiring a piece of fixed property" when there is in fact a constant effort, an ever-active *conatus intelligendi* that recreates those ideas again and again in new and different situations. Yirmiyahu Yovel, "Incomplete Rationality in Spinoza's *Ethics*: Three Basic Forms," in *Ethica IV: Spinoza on Reason and the "Free Man,"* ed. Yirmiyahu Yovel and Gideon Segal (New York: Little Room Press, 2004), 17.

[28] Spinoza's substance monism and his formulation of everything as "modes" of God or Nature implies that things that are perceived as independent bodies are in fact simply different modifications of the same substance, which is one and indivisible (EIp15s). One of the clearest explanations of

and omnipresent feature of the extended world, is at the origin of different modifications of Extension. Spinoza argues that what ultimately modifies extension are motion and rest, and that the other qualities that we perceive are *all* reducible to them. Other sensible qualities of matter, such as hardness, coldness, or weight, all feature as secondary qualities, which means that they are also explainable through relations of motion and rest (EIIp13ax3; Ep.6).[29]

Thus, when Spinoza refers to certain bodies (in fact, only human bodies) as examples of highly complex bodies (EIIp13post1) and points to the presence of a wide variety of hard, soft, and liquid parts within them (EIIp13post2), he is talking about the greater range and variety of configurations of motion and rest that these complex bodies can accommodate (which Spinoza also explicitly points out in EIIp13L3ax3). It is this very terminology of complexity that Spinoza mobilizes to formulate man's superiority over animals, without resorting to biblical arguments for man's exclusive possession of the soul or to a Cartesian separation of the thinking man from the mindless universe. However, although one can easily argue that some minds/bodies are more complex than others, it requires a much bigger argumentative leap to claim that human minds/bodies are more complex than others. Yet, as the next section explores, Spinoza takes this very leap, despite the numerous interpretive difficulties it single-handedly introduces.

---

modal distinction appears in EIp15s, where Spinoza states that "matter is everywhere the same, and that parts are distinguished in it only insofar as we conceive matter to be affected in different ways, so that its parts are distinguished only modally, but not really." A direct outcome of this notion of modal distinction is Spinoza's denial of the idea of a vacuum in space, which also implies that annihilation of one body (that is, one mode of extension) requires the whole extension to vanish with it (Ep.4). It should be clarified that modes still have singularity (in that they are not reducible to each other). An example Spinoza gives in EIIp8s is helpful in illustrating this point. The example involves a circle (representing the substance) with two intersecting chords, D and E, drawn within it (representing the modes). The chords, Spinoza says, owe their existence to the existence of the circle. Moreover, the chords' existence implies all the other intersecting chords and shapes that could be drawn within the circle (which extends to infinity). Every mode is implicated in the existence of every other mode, which still does not make them reducible to each other. Chord D is different from chord E, or any other mode that exists in the circle, and if there were any other mode that existed at the exact spot where D was, then it would simply be identical to chord D (like some of his contemporaries, Spinoza adhered to the principle of the identity of indiscernibles).

[29] As Lecrivain notes, Spinoza here is clearly following the Cartesian "primary versus secondary qualities" distinction. His account of the individuation of bodies echoes Descartes, who proposed that a body is defined by "the different parts that are transported together." André Lécrivain, "Spinoza and Cartesian Mechanics," in *Spinoza and the Sciences*, ed. Marjorie Grene and Debra Nails (Dordrecht: D. Reidel, 1986), 39.

3.4 A Ladder of Complexity: From Worm to Man

Due to Spinoza's envisioning of the mind and the body as two sides of the same coin, having a complex body directly translates into a more complex mind. For most people, this complexity is articulated only at the level of a complex imagination[30] (which means that they are affected by a wide variety of mixed affections [*affectiones*] of the body).[31] However, since "there is no affection of the body of which we cannot form a clear and distinct concept" (EVp4), having a complex variety of affections also makes possible the formation of a greater variety of adequate ideas (even when those affections are initially confused).[32] As one forms adequate ideas of a greater variety of phenomena, one's understanding of the common principles of nature becomes enriched and diversified.

Certainly, the minds of less complex bodies, in principle, could develop ideas of common notions too, given that common notions are described as being equally present everywhere. This point does not escape Spinoza's attention. In fact, in an exchange with Henry Oldenburg, where he describes how we often take the bodies surrounding us as independent wholes and forget that they are determined by the greater whole of which they are part, he draws another humbling comparison between man's situation and that of a tiny worm living in the blood, stating that

> [the worm is] capable of distinguishing by sight the particles of the blood-lymph, etc. and of intelligently observing how each particle, on colliding with another, either rebounds or communicates some degree of its motion, and so forth. (Ep.32)

---

[30] Spinoza's view that most people simply live according to the guidance of their imagination, and his derogatory remarks concerning the "multitude" (*vulgus*) are discussed and criticized by Smith and Wetlesen. See Steven B. Smith, *Spinoza, Liberalism, and the Question of Jewish Identity* (New Haven, CT: Yale University Press, 1997) and Jon Wetlesen, *The Sage and the Way: Spinoza's Ethics of Freedom* (Assen: Van Gorcum, 1979). For a response to the charges of "elitism" brought against Spinoza, see Hasana Sharp, "'Nemo non videt': Intuitive Knowledge and the Question of Spinoza's Elitism," in *The Rationalists: Between Tradition and Innovation*, ed. Carlos Fraenkel, Dario Perinetti, and Justin E. H. Smith (New York: Springer, 2011).

[31] As Curley notes, Spinoza follows Descartes in using *affectio* (*affectiones* when plural) as a synonym for quality or mode. *Affectus* (translated as either affect or emotion) is usually used for a specific kind of *affectio*. Spinoza, *Collected Works*, trans. Curley, 625.

[32] On this point, also see EIIp13s, where, after discussing the complexity of the human body, Spinoza states that "in proportion as a body is more capable than others of doing many things at once, or being acted on in many ways at once, so its mind is more capable than others of perceiving many things at once. And in proportion as the actions of a body depend more on itself alone ... so its mind is more capable of understanding distinctly."

Here the remark on the worm's intelligently observing how cells communicate different motions to each other does not seem accidental, because, in principle, the worm *can* indeed have an adequate understanding of those minute particles *if*, let us say, it manages to view them as aspects of motion in general (which, again, is an omnipresent feature of nature for Spinoza).[33] However, even then, the scope of this worm's adequate understanding will be very limited, assuming that, having a simpler body, it will, in general, have a limited variety of the affections of the body, which translates into a limited variety of adequate and/or inadequate ideas.[34] This forms a contrast with how a human knower interacts with the world, given Spinoza's statement that human bodies excel over all others in their complexity (EIIp13s).

Assuming that a human body accommodates a greater range of configurations of motion and rest than a worm living in the bloodstream is perhaps not as controversial as placing humans at the top of a general ladder of complexity. To be more specific, Spinoza correlates the superiority of a mind with the body's capacity "to act or be acted upon simultaneously in many ways" (EIIp13s).[35] As Wilson notes, from this understanding of the superiority of a body (and its mind) alone, it is not clear how "even a brilliant human mind, let alone an average one, is 'superior' to the minds of all beasts." In particular, Wilson entertains the example of a theoretical physicist with physical impairments[36] and points out that it is not unambiguously clear that that person's body would be superior (by Spinoza's own formulation) to the body of an eagle, wolf, or whale—unless, by "more capable bodies" we merely understand "the physical substratum of theoretical understanding."[37]

---

[33] In EIIp38, Spinoza states that what is common to all can only be adequately conceived. Here I disagree with Lloyd's suggestion that the mind's capacity to form common notions requires it to be the mind of a body that has a "sufficiently complex structure." (*Part of Nature*, 159). For a detailed critique of Lloyd's reading, see Margaret D. Wilson, "'For They Do Not Agree in Nature with Us,'" 340–343.

[34] Moreover, Grey argues that, according to Spinoza, nonhuman beings can form adequate ideas but that "such understanding and reason would be alien to our own." John Grey, "'Use Them at Our Pleasure': Spinoza on Animal Ethics," *History of Philosophy Quarterly* 30, no. 4 (October 2013): 373.

[35] I follow Shirley's translation of EIIp13s in this passage.

[36] Wilson here only mirrors Spinoza's own ableism as Spinoza himself associates physical debilities with a weak mind when he says in EVp39s: "He who, like an infant or child, has a body that is capable of very few things, and very heavily dependent on external causes, has a mind which, considered solely in itself, is conscious of almost nothing of itself, of God, or of things."

[37] Wilson, "'For They Do Not Agree in Nature with Us,'" 350, 351n28. Wilson also notes that if we take Spinoza to only be talking about "the physical substratum of theoretical understanding" then that makes his phrasing about complex bodies (that they have the capacity to affect and be affected by many things) very peculiar.

Another peculiarity in regard to Spinoza's placing of human minds/bodies at the top of a ladder of complexity and superiority is that such a claim is simply not demonstrable through the geometric method.[38] In fact, the only way one can reach such a conclusion is through observing (via imagination) that men (a "bad universal") tend to exhibit higher registers of understanding and activity than other beings (however one defines the word "higher" here), followed by reasoning backward and reaching a conclusion about the complexity of their minds and bodies.[39]

Spinoza's reliance on bad universals, which are the direct products of imagination, is not, on its own, problematic. In fact, imagination, for Spinoza, is not something that is left behind once one forms an adequate understanding of a situation. Rather, different registers of understanding coexist and complement each other.[40] Moreover, one could always rework various abstractions of the imagination and fill in the content of these generalizations differently as one goes through different experiences (the way one might choose to move away from the definition of mankind as "bipedal animals" after seeing other primates that can also stand upright on their hind legs).[41]

That Spinoza chose to speak of men in general as the most complex of creatures is simply reflective of the operations of his imagination—that is, it is a result of the impressions he has accumulated through his own experiences. Since inadequate ideas "follow with the same necessity" (EIIp36) as adequate ideas (i.e., ultimately there is only one causal story to be told, which could simply be expressed in different ways), there are reasons why one's imagination operates in certain ways (which do not finalize but explain its

---

[38] Wilson's aforementioned criticism of Spinoza (that it is not obvious how a human mind is superior to the minds of all animals) relies on a similar diagnosis. See Wilson, "For They Do Not Agree in Nature with Us."

[39] Bennett makes a similar point in regard to Spinoza's claims about humans' alleged likeness and the collaborative morality that Spinoza draws from it. Bennett notes that such statements "must depend on contingent facts about human nature and perhaps human societies; it cannot be derived in a few short steps from basic, abstract metaphysics." Jonathan Bennett, *A Study of Spinoza's Ethics* (Indianapolis, IN: Hackett, 1984), 306.

[40] I owe this point to Lloyd, who notes that "the goal is not to transcend and spurn the imagination but to complement it and collaborate with it." Genevieve Lloyd, *Routledge Philosophy Guidebook to Spinoza and the Ethics* (London: Routledge,1996), 62. In an oft-cited example, Spinoza mentions experiencing the sun as 200 feet away due to our ignorance of the causes behind this perception. This experience can be supplemented with the knowledge of the sun's true distance, but that still would not make the eye see it as farther than 200 feet away (EIIp35s).

[41] Some scholars have moved into the more speculative direction of not only de-emphasizing Spinoza's own comments regarding mankind as a group but also attempting to give an altogether post-humanist interpretation of the *Ethics*. An obvious example of this is the late works of Deleuze and Guattari, in which the category of the human and other species-specific categories are disrupted altogether in favor of an immanentist cartography of power and affects. For further reading, see Deleuze and Guattari, *A Thousand Plateaus*, 232–309.

operations). By understanding those reasons, one develops an adequate understanding of a situation (and becomes more "active"). However, in this particular case, when speaking of human minds and bodies surpassing all others in complexity, Spinoza seems to be allowing inadequate ideas of the imagination to carry the whole weight of the argument without that being accompanied by an understanding of why they appear that way.

Certainly, having the body and mind of a man does not guarantee acquiring high levels of understanding and activity—as evidenced by Spinoza's placing of a fictional donkey in the same mix as "fools" and "madmen." In fact, recalling that imagination registers all the diverse changes taking place in one's body caused by the impingement of other bodies,[42] the extreme variety of things in the human body also makes possible the greater confusions of the imagination (unless one is able to connect its perceptions to the common laws of nature). Having a complex mind and body can translate into favorable or unfavorable outcomes, and, as Sharp correctly points out, strictly speaking, nothing prevents some animals from exhibiting greater capabilities than a man in Spinozistic ontology.[43] That makes Spinoza's unequivocal exaltation of mankind a relatively more curious case than that of many other philosophers, because the initial premises of Spinoza's ontology *do* allow him to formulate differences in more radical terms, but that is simply not the direction that he chooses.

The discrepancy between what Spinoza could have said and what he ended up saying could easily be attributed to various extra-doctrinal factors (personal biases, explanatory interests, pedagogical goals, and so on). What is important is that Spinoza's unwarranted declaration of man's higher levels of mental and material complexity is not an isolated or accidental remark. While Part III will explore its connections to Spinoza's emphasis on human solidarity, the rest of Part II will turn its attention to a less hierarchical (if not non-hierarchical) view of reality that still manages to introduce a distinction between people and other denizens of the world.

The next chapter opens with an examination of some of the fundamental ontological assumptions of the *Zhuangzi*, which will be followed by

---

[42] As EIIp16c2 explains, imagination tells us about the condition of our own bodies more than the nature of an external body. It is for this reason, Spinoza notes, that we imagine God to have human emotions or imagine trees to speak like humans when we perceive them through our imagination.

[43] Sharp, *Spinoza and the Politics of Renaturalization*, 27. After all, for Spinoza, one's capabilities are never fixed and they develop as the body and the mind become more powerful and more active (EIIp13–14), which is also captured in the famous phrase we "do not know what a body can do" (EIIIp2s).

a discussion of the debilitating and enabling models of knowledge and action that are laid out in the text. As will be demonstrated, for the *Zhuangzi*, what could be described as self-empowerment corresponds to cultivating the ability to do many things at high levels of competence *and* with enjoyment and ease. This necessitates increased attentiveness to the sheer variety of ways to view and live in the world (instead of seeking what we can know about the world with certainty). This particular feature of the text translates into a different model of human flourishing and, as a result, a different articulation of human exceptionality that maintains people's seemingly distinct status in the world without introducing an obvious hierarchy between people and other beings.

4
Pinnacles of Versatility
Human Distinctiveness in the *Zhuangzi*

One of the obvious effects of the *Zhuangzi*'s multiplication of vantage points from which to view the world is that it strips human perspectives of their unquestioned weight. That is partly why numerous contemporary attempts have been launched to repurpose the *Zhuangzi* for "green politics," interpreting its polyvocal feature as a call to focus on the value of the broader "nature," of which humans are also a part.[1] Although the anti-anthropocentric streak of the text is undeniable, as several sinologists have been quick to point out, the specific question of whether humans are part of or apart from "nature" does not arise—that is, not in those terms—in early Chinese philosophical discourse.[2] Sometimes this has also been interpreted as evidence that the ancient Chinese wisely took for granted human beings' continuity and harmony with nature instead of as a glaring indication that the question itself is simply formulated in European terms.[3] Aside from overlooking the fact that "an absence of a theory

---

[1] See, for instance, J. Baird Callicott, *Earth's Insights: A Multicultural Survey*, 72, 78. Another reason the *Zhuangzi* was deemed relevant for environmental philosophy is a perceived contrast between human interventionism and "following nature," where "nature" is taken to stand for *Tian* 天 (sky, Heaven), *dao* 道 (way, ways), or even *ziran* 自然 (self-so) (or all three, taking them to be interchangeable). Clarification on key terminology is offered in Section 4.1; also see footnote 2. Finally, it should be mentioned that very often the *Zhuangzi* is appropriated by eco-philosophers not in isolation but together with the *Laozi* and the *Liezi*, as part of a framing decision that focuses on "Daoist" insights for environmentalism. Despite the presence of some overlapping philosophical positions, none of these three texts exhibit a sense of belonging to a unified school of thought called Daoism, let alone mention a *Daojia* 道家 (school of the *Dao*) and *Daojiao* 道教 (teachings of the *Dao*).

[2] More specifically, scholars have noted the absence of a notion that squarely corresponds to "nature" in classical Chinese philosophy. See Perkins, "Following Nature with Mengzi or Zhuangzi," 328–331; Paul D'Ambrosio, "Rethinking Environmental Issues in Daoist Context: Why Daoism Is and Is Not Environmentalism," *Environmental Ethics* 35, no. 4 (2013): 408–411.

[3] It goes without saying that looking for the absence of certain Greco-European views and notions in Chinese texts keeps our interpretational paradigms anchored within Greco-European parameters, even when the purpose is to celebrate the "Chinese wisdom" for the alleged absence of specific dichotomies. For a fresh attempt at reversing this interpretational gesture by seeking the presence of ancient Chinese notions within ancient Greek philosophy, see Eric L. Hutton, "柏拉图论'仁'" [On Confucian "benevolence" in the philosophy of Plato], trans. 刘旻娇 Liu Minjiao, in 伦理学术 *Academia Ethica* 4, ed. 邓安庆 Deng Anqing (June 2018): 29–45.

is not a theory of absence," as Williams aptly puts,[4] it is also not very difficult to imagine articulations of similar tensions in different terms.

In regard to notions of human exceptionality, especially within the early Chinese texts that were later canonized as "Confucian" classics, we see unambiguous statements declaring that people are "the heart of heaven and earth," or that they are the most valuable among all the creatures of heaven and earth.[5] These statements of people's status as the cherished center of the cosmos are joined with calls to form a unity with Heaven and Earth—which is posited as a goal instead of an assumption, suggesting that the current, if not the default, state of human existence was seen to be marked by discontinuity, rather than continuity, with the rest of the cosmos.[6]

It is against such statements about people's central status in the cosmos, which clearly bear marks of human pomposity, that the *Zhuangzi* throws into question prevalent values and rankings in general. This then yields the inevitable result of undermining people's status as the valued center of life and the moral conscience of the cosmos. If there is no indisputable criterion that would justify the superiority of one thing over another, then notions of human supremacy as well (regardless of whether that superiority is viewed to be preestablished or acquired) come into question.

Undermining the centrality of human values and concerns does not render untenable any bias toward people's distinct status in the world. In fact, several stories in the *Zhuangzi* formulate people's exceptional status around their ability to see their own positionality. This very ability is rooted in weakening the hold that established views and values have over one's heart-mind (*xin* 心), which also paves the way for new ideas, skills, and possibilities. As this chapter demonstrates, the *Zhuangzi* serves as a unique example of how a work with such a strong skeptical streak can still formulate—albeit in

---

[4] Bernard Williams, *Shame and Necessity* (Berkeley: University of California Press, 1993), 27. Cited in Edward Slingerland, *Effortless Action: Wu-Wei as Conceptual Metaphor and Spiritual Ideal in Early China* (New York: Oxford University Press, 2003), 307n5.

[5] The Chinese for the first example reads: 故人者，天地之心也 (*Liji* 9.26/22; "Li Yun 禮運"). The second example is a rendition of the line "天地之性，人為貴," which is from the "Sagely Governance" (*Shengzhi* 聖治) section of the *Xiaojing* 孝經 (*The Classic of Filial Piety*), reprinted in Donald Sturgeon, Chinese Text Project (2011), https://ctext.org/xiao-jing/government-of-the-sages. For a detailed examination of portrayals of human exceptionality within the classical Ru discourse, see Qianfan Zhang, "The Idea of Human Dignity in Classical Chinese Philosophy: A Reconstruction of Confucianism," *Journal of Chinese Philosophy* 27, no. 3 (2000): 299–330.

[6] Hence, we see statements calling for the gentleman (*junzi* 君子) or the sage (*shengren* 聖人) to join with Heaven and Earth (*can yu tiandi* 參於天地) in the *Liji* (9.18/15 "Li Yun 禮運" and 30.4/22 "Kongzi Xian Ju 孔子閒居") and in the *Xunzi* (3.5, 8.11, 23.5a). For a study that challenges the still ubiquitous assumption that the early Chinese worldview was devoid of tensions and discontinuities between different aspects of the cosmos, see Michael J. Puett, *To Become a God, Cosmology, Sacrifice, and Self-Divinization in Early China* (Cambridge, MA: Harvard University Press, 2004).

paradoxical ways—people's unusual place in the world. Identifying the text's peculiar formulations of human uniqueness, however, first requires a look into the definitional framework through which the authors and compilers viewed the world and people's place in it as knowing and acting subjects. The next section overviews the relevant ontological assumptions implied in the *Zhuangzi*, followed by a discussion of the debilitating and enabling models of knowledge and action laid out in the text. The chapter concludes with an analysis of formulations of human uniqueness in the *Zhuangzi*.

4.1 The Ten Thousand Things under Heaven

When examining any early Chinese Masters text in comparison to works of an early modern European figure, it is requisite to first note that many of the ontological disputes that occupy Spinoza's writings are either absent or appear in significantly different terms in classical Chinese philosophical discourse. For instance, a tension that often features across all Masters texts concerns Heaven's (天 *tian*; sky) relation to other dimensions of the cosmos and to the actions of people. Heaven, as a term, can simply refer to the sky, but sometimes it also appears as a supreme force with specific moral preferences, while at other times it connotes what is simply given and cannot be changed.[7]

In the *Zhuangzi*, the term Heaven is mainly used in three interrelated contexts: when literally referring to the sky; when referring to Heaven and Earth together to talk about the cosmos as a whole; and when referring to the broader patterns and forces of the world, which unfold of their own accord and without any regard for human values. The notion of Heaven's indifference to human concerns and values is pronounced in relation to another very crucial view: that people are ultimately things among the myriad things (*wanwu* 萬物; ten thousand things) in the world.[8]

The *Zhuangzi* emphasizes the "thingness" of people to draw out several humbling implications. One is the simple fact that things are many and, in comparison to all the things in the world, people are few. It is for this reason that we are told, "in comparison with the ten thousand things, [people] are not even like the tip of a hair to the body of a horse."[9] Moreover, as Perkins notes,

---

[7] For a study of the motif of *tian* in early Ru literature and beyond, see Eno, *The Confucian Creation of Heaven*.

[8] The "Autumn Waters" (Qiu shui 秋水) chapter of the *Zhuangzi* states: "In counting the number of things we say 'ten thousand.' Human beings are just one of them" (號物之數謂之萬，人處一焉) (*Zhuangzi* 17:563).

[9] 此其比萬物也，不似豪末之在於馬體乎。(*Zhuangzi* 17:563).

in addition to the multiplicity of things, the authors draw on the equality of things, which is articulated in the straightforward explanation given for what it means to be a "thing": "what has appearance, image, sound and color."[10] This phenomenological description is perhaps purposefully simple so as to pose the rhetorical question in the end: "Between things, how could there be much distance?"[11] In being a thing that has appearance, color, and so on, all things are equal and there is no reason to rank them among each other.

This view that places people on par with all other things is expressed in many humbling stories in the text, where human perspectives are placed on equal footing with those of animals and even plants. An example of the latter features in the "In the Human World" (*Renjian shi* 人間世) chapter, in a story about a carpenter and a giant tree. The story opens with a scene in which a carpenter and his apprentice run into a giant old tree when they are traveling in the state of Qi. While the apprentice admires the sheer size and ancientness of the tree, the carpenter is unimpressed with what the tree could offer if used as material for carpentry. Using emphatic language, the carpenter says: "This is cast-off lumber. As a boat, it would sink; as a coffin, it would soon rot; as a tool, it would soon break; as a door, it would leak sap; as a pillar, it would bring infestation. This is a worthless tree."[12] The tree later appears to the carpenter in a dream, offended and defiant. It says to the carpenter: "You and I are each a thing, how can things rank each other? How could a worthless man with one foot in the grave know what is or isn't a worthless tree?"[13]

The tree's words serve as reminders of the carpenter's status as simply a thing among things, which is then mobilized to undercut the weight of his value judgments (and his implicit anthropocentric resourcism) and to use the carpenter's standards of evaluation against himself. There is more to that tree than being raw material for a ship or a door and, by the carpenter's own conventional standards of worth and worthlessness, there is perhaps not that much worth to a man who is himself very old. If the tree's words are mean-spirited, so were the carpenter's; and neither party—neither the tree

---

[10] Franklin Perkins, "What Is a Thing (*wu* 物)? The Problem of Individuation in Early Chinese Metaphysics," in *Chinese Metaphysics and Its Problems*, ed. Chenyang Li and Franklin Perkins (Cambridge: Cambridge University Press, 2018), 65. In Chinese, the aforementioned line reads: 凡有貌象聲色者，皆物也。(*Zhuangzi* 19:632).
[11] 物與物何以相遠? (*Zhuangzi* 19:632).
[12] *Zhuangzi* 4:176.
[13] In Chinese, the tree's response reads: 若與予也皆物也，奈何哉其相物也？而幾死之散人，又惡知散木！(*Zhuangzi* 4:178). This episode forms a contrast with the other mention of a useless tree that was discussed in chapter 1, section 1.2. Here, the useless tree comments on its own alleged uselessness.

nor the carpenter—possesses a privileged position as the ultimate producer of values.

With such gestures of making a human-nonhuman comparison from the vantage point of the latter, the *Zhuangzi* decenters the human not by degrading human actors to a status that is ostensibly lesser than that of animals but by shifting the very angle from which one makes such comparisons. However, although it is true that the *Zhuangzi* makes it difficult to draw a clear hierarchy among different beings by shaking up the discursive ground on which such comparisons usually pivot, the text is not entirely devoid of notions of people's uniqueness.[14] As will be shown, people stand out not only negatively through the way they dare to unduly arrogate themselves to a higher status than other things but also in the way they are able to efficaciously blend in with others to the extent that their seamless continuity with their surroundings becomes a source of awe in itself.

This is a peculiar and paradoxical formulation of people's uncanny status in the world, which rests on two key notions that are invariably invoked in early Chinese discussions on human understanding and agency. The next section gives a brief intertextual analysis of the notion of *xin* 心 (heart, heart-mind), which is at the center of the *Zhuangzi*'s discussions of people's radical continuity versus discontinuity with their surroundings. Section 4.3 takes a look at another key notion, namely, *dao* 道 (way, ways, teachings), in relation to the *Zhuangzi*'s take on enabling forms of knowledge and action. Section 4.4 further delves into the text's depictions of human exceptionality, while adding another layer of complexity to the discussion by exploring the way the text both posits and problematizes at the same time the very category of the human.

4.2 Dethroning the Heart

Although we are told that, in being a thing, all things under Heaven are equal, the *Zhuangzi* still bears witness to a perceived sense of discontinuity between people and their surroundings, in the sense that people seem to be caught up in hierarchies and established conventions that bring them frustration and

---

[14] As argued in chapter 5, I take the *Zhuangzi* to be employing provisional definitions to refer to various groups of beings in the world instead of offering stable and normative definitions of them. See chapter 5, section 5.1.

cause them to struggle with their surrounding conditions. This self-inflicted discontinuity with one's surroundings is expressed in the *Zhuangzi* in terms of a human-Heaven(ly) binary, in which the former is associated with striving to manage and exert control on one's situation, whereas the latter is associated with letting things take their own course.[15] Before delving into the mechanism behind this dynamic, it is imperative to review a notion that takes center stage in classical Chinese theories of knowledge and action: the heart (*xin* 心; mind, heart-mind).

The term *xin* 心, which is often translated into English as "heart," "heart-mind," or "mind," is central to some of the dominant discussions of Warring States thought, owing to its association with mental functions. The heart's unique status in the body is emphasized especially in early Ru[16] texts such as the *Wuxing* 五行 (Five Forms of Conduct), the *Mengzi*, and the *Xunzi*.[17] The distinctive status of the heart is explicitly formulated in the *Mengzi* along the lines of its moral and reflective capacities, which constitute the more "valuable" (*gui* 貴) and "greater" (*da* 大) part of the person (6A:14–15). The heart is viewed as occupying a privileged status among all the organs due to its perceived ability to reflect (*si* 思; to think, to attend) on things and ideally develop a stable commitment to specific choices without being easily moved by external stimuli, which can be achieved through a process of cultivation.[18]

Within the early Ru literature, a large part of the heart's commitments has to do with morally significant values, although whether these values have roots in the heart itself (in the form of certain innate, moral predispositions)

---

[15] As Guo Xiang suggests: "What is so of itself is called what is so of Heaven. The Heaven-so is what is not purposefully done. Hence, we use 'Heaven' to talk about it. (自己而然，則謂之天然。天然耳，非為也，故以天言之。)" (2:55–56). On the human-Heaven(ly) binary in the *Zhuangzi*, also see Franklin Perkins, "The *Zhuangzi* and the Division Between Heaven and Human," in *Dao Companion to the Philosophy of the Zhuangzi*, ed. Kim-chong Chong (New York: Springer, 2022), 119–134.

[16] Throughout this study, I follow the common practice of using the term Ru 儒, rather than "Confucianism," to designate the group of scholars and intellectuals who had expertise in traditional texts and ceremonial practices—and who may or may not directly label themselves as followers of Confucius.

[17] In looking at these texts, I am not making any chronological assumptions about which one of these texts (and how much of each) was known to the authors and compilers of the *Zhuangzi*. My goal is rather to give a general idea about certain sensibilities that were symptomatic of the time, in order to lay the ground for discussions regarding the *Zhuangzi*'s epistemological outlook.

[18] For a detailed analysis of the distinctive status of the heart, in comparison to other organs of the body (and sometimes the entire body), see Edward Slingerland, *Mind and Body in Early China: Beyond Orientalism and the Myth of Holism* (New York: Oxford University Press, 2019), 100–142. Although I am not arguing in this section that the heart's status is somewhat "super-material," as Slingerland phrases it on page 103 of his study, I do agree with his observation that the fact that *xin* 心 primarily refers to an organ in the body does not obliterate its special status in early Chinese discussions of agency, motivation, and moral responsibility.

or are learned is open to debate. Also critical is the heart's perceived ability to command other parts of the person and their associated functions. As will be discussed shortly, this ability is not given or guaranteed, but it is still emphasized as a crucial function in many early Chinese texts.[19] Well-known examples include the *Wuxing*, which expresses the heart's authority in terms of how it can command other organs with such power that when it makes a judgment, none "dares" to oppose it,[20] as well as the *Xunzi*, which emphasizes the heart's self-reliance along with its impressive resoluteness in regard to its own choices, as seen in the following passage:

> The heart is the ruler of the body, and owner of intelligence. It issues a command, but does not receive commands. On its own it forbids, enables, grabs, receives, initiates, and stops. Thus the mouth can be coerced and made to be silent or speak, the body can be coerced and made to be bent or extended, but the heart cannot be coerced and made to change its thoughts. If it affirms something, it accepts it. If it rejects something, it dismisses it. (21.6a)

Although the heart can still take input from the world, the *Xunzi* makes it clear that it is capable of distinguishing, affirming, and ordering things instead of being merely dragged around along with the other organs. Given such capabilities' relevance for moral-political agendas to cultivate people into moral subjects, it is no surprise that discussions around the heart became so crucial in an era that is marked by contending viewpoints about upright conduct.[21]

---

[19] See Lisa Raphals, "Skilled Feelings in Chinese and Greek Heart-Mind-Body Metaphors," *Dao* 20 (2021): 69–91, for an examination of various accounts of the heart as a ruling authority in the *Mengzi*, the *Xunzi*, the *Xing Zi Ming Chu* 性自命出 (Inborn Inclinations Derive from [Heavenly] Decree]), the *Guanzi*, the *Zhuangzi*, the *Sunzi Bingfa* 孫子兵法, and the *Huangdi Neijing* 黃帝內經 (Yellow Emperor's Classic of Internal Medicine). The last text, which is an early medical text, presents a particularly complex account of the heart, viewing it within a network of visceral systems, consisting of both organs and "channels" (*jingluo* 經絡) running throughout the body. Although *Huangdi Neijing* also refers to the heart's ruling authority, it evenly distributes various effects to different systems within the body, making the mechanics behind the heart's alleged ability to rule other parts of the body more difficult to decipher.

[20] In more detail, it says: "Ears, eyes, nose, mouth, hands, feet—the six are (all) servants of the heart. When the heart says 'yes', none dare to say 'no.' When the heart says 'approve', none dare to not approve. When it says 'advance', none dare to not advance (耳目鼻口手足六者，心之役也。心曰唯，莫敢不唯；〔心曰〕諾，莫敢不諾；〔心曰〕進，莫敢不進)." See PANG Pu 庞朴, *Zhu Bo "Wu Xing" Pian Jiao Zhu Ji Yan Jiu* 竹帛五行篇校注研究 (Taibei 臺北: Wanjuan Lou 萬卷樓, 2000), 经 22.

[21] Here one could add that, similar to how the formulation of mind-body dualism in Europe was intertwined with certain moralizing agendas, such as the Christian view of eternal punishment premised on the notion of free will, the formulation of the heart as a distinguishing, determining, and

The *Zhuangzi* remarks on different values and functions of different body parts as well, which gains a pointed significance when evaluated against this backdrop. In opposition to giving the heart sovereignty over other organs, the *Zhuangzi* asks:

> One hundred bones, nine orifices, six storehouses, they are together and exist here [in my body]. Which one do I take to be closest to me? Are you pleased with them all or is there one to which you are partial? Like this, do you take them all as servants and concubines? Are these servants and concubines insufficient to govern each other? Or do they take turns serving as the ruler and servants? If there is a genuine ruler existing among them, then, looking for and obtaining facts about it or not, would not add to or decrease its genuineness. (*Zhuangzi* 2: 61)

The passage takes a pointed jab at the discursive practice of elevating an organ to the status of the ruler of others, which is part of the text's broader attack on hierarchy-building in general. While the implications of this passage for the body politic and monarchical sovereignty will be discussed in Part IV,[22] its undermining of the capacities associated with the heart should be unpacked here.

First and foremost, in regard to the ruler status of the heart, it is certainly not the case that Ru thinkers ignored the view that the heart does not always seem to act as the ruler of other parts of one's person[23]; in the same way they clearly did not ignore that people do not always act as the moral center of the universe. An obvious example of acknowledging the heart's occasional failure to manage other organs with its reflective and supervisory prowess can be seen in a story told in the *Xunzi*, in which a man named Ji decides to live in a cave just so that his thinking will not be distracted by the hankerings of the eyes and the ears.[24] In fact, it could be easily argued that it is precisely because the heart is not always the ruler that there was a perceived need to

---

determined organ is ultimately informed by a desire to safeguard and bolster ideals of civic and moral agency in a period perceived to be rife with sociopolitical and moral challenges.

[22] See chapter 8, section 8.1.

[23] The fact that the heart's commitments and ruling capacities were not taken for granted also ties into considerations about moral integrity and its limitations in difficult circumstances. For a study that argues against the tendency to read early Ru texts as offering an idealistic account of moral agency that is "invulnerable" to tragic circumstances, see Michael D. K. Ing, *The Invulnerability of Integrity in Early Confucian Thought* (Oxford: Oxford University Press, 2017).

[24] *Xunzi* 21.11.

convince people of its supreme capacities to rule and encourage them to engage in cultivation practices, ensuring that it was indeed ruling the rest of the body. This is, in fact, what the last part of the *Zhuangzi* passage seems to be trading on when we are told that if there were a genuine ruler among those organs, then the endeavors to either strengthen or rob it of its authority would be ineffective.

As observed earlier, the heart's special status in the eyes of some early Chinese thinkers lies in its reflective and supervisory capacities. Of course, this also relates to the aforementioned description of people as the heart of Heaven and Earth. To be clear, there is no indication that animals were thought to be devoid of hearts. In fact, there is some textual evidence suggesting that they do have hearts.[25] However, while birds and wild animals (*qin shou* 禽獸) are sometimes said to make various distinctions and have awareness (*zhi* 知), they are still viewed as lacking higher sensibilities, such as a sense of right and dutiful conduct (*yi* 義) or hierarchized relations.[26] In undermining the heart's ruler status, the *Zhuangzi* targets its commonly praised ability to settle on value-laden distinctions—and, at times, goes as far as criticizing committing to any set of distinctions in general.

Indeed, the text often discusses the limits of debating (*bian* 辯) and discoursing (*lun* 論), both of which include a sense of making distinctions and settling on one side. *Bian* 辯 in particular has the sense of disputation over two opposite claims, where one party tries to persuade another about the correctness of certain differentiations and identifications.[27] The *Zhuangzi*

---

[25] For instance, in a passage on "applying the heart in an undivided manner" (*yong xin yi ye* 用心一也) when pursuing an endeavor, the *Xunzi* gives the example of an earthworm that uses its determination to survive (*Xunzi* 1.6). This is not an isolated case; in numerous early Chinese texts, including *Xunzi*, *Liji*, *Huainanzi* 淮南子, and *Liezi* 列子, creatures of "blood and qi (*xueqi* 血氣)," which include animals and human beings, are said to be endowed with cognitive and affective functions that are associated with the heart (*xin* 心), such as awareness (*zhi* 知). For an examination of the association between having blood and qi on the one hand and having various cognitive and affective functions on the other in the aforementioned texts (and beyond), see Sterckx, *The Animal and the Daemon*, 73–76. The description of animals and human beings having "blood and qi" is revisited in chapter 5, section 5.2.

[26] For a few examples, see *Xunzi* 5.4 and 9.16a; *Liji* 1.6/18–20 ("Qu Li Shang 曲禮上") and 39.2/11–14 ("San Nian Wen 三年問"); *Lüshi Chunqiu* 16/1.4 and 20/1.1.

[27] It should be noted here that the graph 辯 (debating) is used interchangeably with 辨 (distinction-making) in early Chinese texts. As Fraser points out, a likely explanation for this is that "the two graphs were conceptually so deeply intertwined that they were considered alternate ways of writing a single word that referred both to drawing distinctions and to the process of discussing or debating how to draw distinctions." See Chris Fraser, "Distinctions, Judgment, and Reasoning in Classical Chinese Thought," *History and Philosophy of Logic* 34, no. 1 (2013): 8. It is hard to overlook the contrast that disputation (*bian* 辯) forms with the motif of goblet speech (discussed in chapter 1, section 1.2). Whereas disputation (*bian* 辯) aims to firmly settle on one view, on one side of an opposition, goblet speech resists being pinned down to a fixed position, as it always offers the possibility of further contestation rather than a culmination (and, for this reason, generates endless conversation).

presents us with numerous passages in which the context-dependent nature of discriminative judgments is betrayed and we are explicitly told that "a thing is so by calling it. How is it so? In so-ing it, it is so. How is it not so? In not-soing it, it is not so."[28] It is not that one cannot pass judgments on any situation, but there is always an alternative way of seeing a situation, which is evidenced by the presence of debates about it. It is due to this view that the audience is told: "If so were really so, then so's difference from not-so would not be debated."[29] In other words, the existence of a debate on any issue undermines the obviousness of the plausibility of one's position.

The text's resignation to disagreement among people is developed alongside the view that every judgment is shaped by a previously absorbed judgment. It is for this reason that in a passage proposing the hypothetical scenario of two people arguing, the narrator asks:

> Whom should we have to straighten out the matter? Someone who agrees with you? But since he already agrees with you, how can he straighten it out? Someone who agrees with me? But since she already agrees with me, how can she straighten it out? Someone who disagrees with both of us? But if he already disagrees with both of us, how can he straighten it out? Someone who agrees with both of us? But since she already agrees with both of us, how can she straighten it out? (*Zhuangzi* 2:113)

One can simply answer, "Just bring in a non-partisan person"; but does such a person exist? Another line suggests that assuming one is able to pass a judgment without having a position first is as absurd as "saying you left for Yue today and arrived there yesterday."[30]

When one's heart is molded in specific ways, that can certainly create limitations. However, the counterargument would be that the heart, in the end, is simply absorbing the most proper, commonsensical, and/or socially beneficial set of judgments. Still, the fact that there is no agreement as to which set of judgments is the one that fulfills such criteria undercuts the weight of the counterargument. The *Zhuangzi* does not give a consistent explanation for the presence of disagreement among people. Sometimes it is mentioned as a spontaneously occurring phenomenon[31] and sometimes as a product of

---

[28] 物謂之而然。惡乎然？然於然。惡乎不然？不然於不然。*Zhuangzi* 2:75.
[29] 然若果然也，則然之異乎不然也亦無辯。*Zhuangzi* 2:114.
[30] *Zhuangzi* 2:61.
[31] See, for instance, the final chapter of the received *Zhuangzi*, which presents a story of decline from ancient times when the understandings of the people were complete (*bei* 備). However, some

disorder brought about by pedants who have arrogated to themselves the position of knowledge producers.³² However, either way, there is no privileged and pure domain from which one can proclaim knowledge.³³ What is the alternative then? The next section briefly explores the notion of having a tenuous heart in the *Zhuangzi* while also clarifying the text's treatment of another key term, namely, *dao*.

4.3 Finding the Pivot of all *Daos*

Regardless of the origins of disagreement, by not assuming or actively seeking agreement among people, the *Zhuangzi* seems to embrace what someone like Mozi considers to be a nightmare: "If there is one person, then there is one rightness (*yi* 義), ten people then ten rightnesses, a hundred people then a hundred rightnesses."³⁴ To complicate matters further, not only do people disagree on things at any given moment, but we are also sometimes told that different situations simply call for different approaches to things. If one instead insists on the cross-situational efficacy of certain divisions, then that necessarily conceals other ways of seeing a situation. Such a firm commitment to various distinctions and evaluative judgments potentially generates friction between people and their environment due to the simple fact that things and situations change.³⁵

If we have nothing but many distinctions and judgments in an ever-changing world, the best one can do is to occupy different positions within various discourses and go along with different views and values without

---

people begin to develop their own ideologies, which are merely partial understandings of "the way." There is no causal explanation given for such a development, and it is presented as a phenomenon that simply happened to have unfolded.

³² See, for instance, the *Mati* 馬蹄 [Horse Hooves] chapter, which accuses Ru folks of making people doubt themselves by introducing normative values into a community that was living happily before their arrival. The episode is discussed in detail in chapter 3, section 3.5.

³³ The positionality of knowledge claims is explicitly acknowledged at the very end of the "Autumn Waters" (Qiu shui 秋水) chapter in a dialogue between the characters of Zhuangzi and Huizi about the joy of fish. The dialogue is briefly discussed in chapter 2, section 2.1 and then in greater detail in chapter 5, section 5.1.

³⁴ *Mozi* 15/12/2. This line appears in the context of Mozi's depiction of ancient times before there was a ruler. It forms a sharp contrast with the *Zhuangzi*'s portrayals of ancient times, which are discussed in chapter 8, section 8.3.

³⁵ A well-known example is offered in the opening chapter of the received *Zhuangzi*, which tells the story of a man from Song who goes to sell ceremonial caps to a community that is culturally different from his and has no use for such things. See *Zhuangzi* 1:35. This passage is discussed in greater detail in chapter 9, section 9.1.

letting any of them take hold in one's heart. Some of the characters in the *Zhuangzi* manage to do just that by exploiting the pliability of the heart and adjusting their distinctions and labels to different situations in a way that enables them to multiply the variety of ways they can view a given situation and lead their lives.[36] The high levels of flexibility regarding the variety of approaches one is able to adopt are sometimes described in terms of making the heart tenuous (*xu* 虛)[37] or recalibrating the heart (*xin zhai* 心齋; fasting of the heart).[38] Both expressions connote a sense of not over-committing to certain values, which enables one to adapt to different situations with ease. The text sometimes also employs metaphors of turning or pivoting, as seen in the expression "[finding] the pivot of ways" (*dao shu* 道樞).[39]

The term that is translated as "ways" (or sometimes "the way") is *dao* 道, which primarily refers to a teaching or a guiding discourse (as in, for

---

[36] In an under-studied episode, we are told about the story of Lady Li who was kidnapped by a nobleman. Although initially she cries until her clothes are soaked with her own tears, she later manages to deal with her own subjugation by reconsidering her judgment of the situation after she fills her stomach with meat dishes and experiences the comfort of her new bed (*Zhuangzi* 2:109). Lady Li's reconsideration of her situation is presented in a longer series of arguments about how we can give a positive twist to even the most horrible-looking situations, including one's own death. This episode is revisited in chapter 9, section 9.2.

[37] Here I agree with Fraser's decision to translate *xu* 虛 as "tenuous" or "tenuousness" instead of "empty" or "emptiness." With regard to the state of *xu* 虛, Fraser insightfully points out that it is "less likely to connote emptiness in the sense of a void as much as insubstantiality, indeterminacy, and receptiveness." Chris Fraser, "Psychological Emptiness in the *Zhuangzi*," *Asian Philosophy* 18, no. 2 (2008): 125. An analogy Ziporyn uses to describe the kind of flexibility that the tenuousness of the heart entails is that of having a "wild card" in a poker game. See Brook Ziporyn, *Ironies of Oneness and Difference*, 179–192.

[38] In regard to my translation of *xin zhai* 心齋 as "recalibrating the heart," instead of adopting the common translation of it as "fasting of the heart," a couple points must be explained. First, as Nylan notes along with Trenton Wilson, the characters *zhai* 齋 and *qi* 齊 were conflated in pre-Han and Han texts, which is to say that the phrase in question might also be *qi xin* 齊心 (balancing the heart). See Michael Nylan, *The Chinese Pleasure Book* (New York: Zone Books, 2018), 217. However, since in the "In the Human World" (*Renjian shi* 人間世) chapter of the *Zhuangzi* the phrase is discussed in relation to dietary purification, I do take the text to be talking about *xin zhai* 心齋 there. Even so, I still choose to avoid translating it as "fasting of the heart" or even as "cleaning out the heart" due to such notions' associations with spiritual regimes of strict austerity (Nylan also makes this point in *The Chinese Pleasure Book*, 217.). Moreover, especially in the chapters organized into the Inner Chapters (including the same "In the Human World" chapter) in the received *Zhuangzi*, the text consistently points in the direction of increasing our sensitivity and receptivity to a multiplicity of distinctions, values, and judgments instead of telling us to purge our heart of them. In rendering of the phrase as "recalibrating the heart," I aim to acknowledge that the focus is on loosening the grip of the heart's fixations and allowing different distinctions and judgments to be tentatively adopted by the heart without taking hold in it—and one could argue that this is also what fasting does: it recalibrates one's approach to various desires, pleasures, and emotions, loosening the grip they have on one's person. For more discussion on the phrase, see chapter 5, section 5.3. I owe special thanks to Erica Fox Brindley who suggested "recalibrating the heart" as an alternative English rendering of the Chinese phrase.

[39] *Zhuangzi* 2:71. Grammatically, *dao shu* 道樞 could also be translated as the "pivot of the Way." However, I take the text to be utilizing the pivot metaphor to give the sense of moving from one position to another, which is why I rendered *dao* 道 in the plural.

instance, "Kongzi's way" or "Mozi's way") or, relatedly, to a way of going about things (as in, for instance, "the way of a hegemon [*ba dao* 霸道]"). As Hansen notes, when used in this sense of teaching, *dao*s are about teaching people to lead their lives in a certain way by shaping their tastes, preferences, and overall discriminative attitudes.[40] These meanings of *dao* are preserved in the *Zhuangzi* as well, where it often refers to a way of doing things, a way of valuing things, or sets of values themselves.[41] Finding the "pivot of ways" thus refers to a situation where one does not settle on a particular set of values and discriminative attitudes, and instead shifts between different positions, which makes one "respond [to things] endlessly" (*ying wu qiong* 應無窮).[42]

The term *dao* is sometimes also used to refer to the primordial and dynamic aspect of the cosmos, as seen in a line in the "The Great Source as Teacher" (Da zong shi 大宗師) chapter, where we are told that *dao* "produces Heaven, produces Earth (*sheng tian sheng di* 生天生地)."[43] The relation between the usages of *dao*—generative activity by which things arise and a way of doing things—may not be straightforward. In a later chapter of the received text we are told that the *dao* that generates things (literally "that which things things") is not a "thing,"[44] which suggests that it is an activity, a dynamic process that is not easily identifiable.[45] If we also take pivoting

---

[40] Chad Hansen, *A Daoist Theory of Chinese Thought: A Philosophical Interpretation* (Oxford: Oxford University Press, 2000), 213.

[41] Examples include a dialogue between Kongzi and a swimmer (which is discussed in the next section) that has the former asking about the *dao* for treading the water as a means to inquire whether there is a method to his swimming (*Zhuangzi* 19:655); an episode in the "Being There and Giving Room" (Zai you 在宥) chapter that describes the way(s) of people (*ren dao* 人道) as being about taking forced action (based on a chosen set of values) (*Zhuangzi* 11:408); and a discussion of Hui Shi's *dao* in the "All under Heaven" (Tianxia 天下) chapter, which is portrayed as being about wordplay and sophistry (*Zhuangzi* 33:1095).

[42] *Zhuangzi* 2:71. Another metaphor of turning, namely, "resting on the potter's wheel of Heaven" (*xiu hu tian jun* 休乎天鈞), refers to employing discriminative judgments in a flexible and harmonizing manner (*Zhuangzi* 2:76). As Robins points out, the metaphor echoes an image found in the *Mozi* and the *Guanzi* of a spinning potter's wheel used to determine the directions of sunrise and sunset. While both texts use this analogy to criticize not acting according to fixed standards, the *Zhuangzi* uses the same analogy to praise not committing to a specific set of norms. See Dan Robins, "It Goes Beyond Skill," in *Ethics in Early China: An Anthology*, ed. Chris Fraser, Dan Robins, and Timothy O'Leary (Hong Kong: Hong Kong University Press, 2011), 114. Finally, the emphasis on flexibility here, as opposed to providing standards, forms a sharp contrast with the square and compass metaphors (discussed in chapter 1, section 1.2), which are prevalent in early Chinese Masters texts.

[43] *Zhuangzi* 6:252.

[44] The full line reads: "But if there were something before Heaven and Earth, could it be a 'thing'? What things things is not a thing (有先天地生者物邪？物物者非物)" (*Zhuangzi* 22:759).

[45] This also relates to another tension, often expressed in the text, which concerns the difference between determinate and identifiable phenomena, on the one hand (things [*wu* 物], forms [*xing* 形], names [*ming* 名], affairs [*shi* 事], anything that has come to fruition [*shi* 實]), and the indeterminate, undifferentiated forces and sources underneath them, on the other (e.g. *dao* 道, or tenuousness [*xu* 虛]). See, for instance, *Zhuangzi* 2:61; 25:909; and 22:742.

from one *dao* into another as an anti-reification gesture, where one does not settle on a fixed set of norms, then residing at the pivot of *dao*s could be taken as a meta-*dao* where one taps into how way-making itself works and recognizes all the different paths one could take in a given situation.[46] In that sense, finding the pivot of *dao*s is being equidistant to all the distinctions that generate things[47] without limiting oneself to one truth regime[48] and its prevailing norms of conduct. The next and final section examines the flexibility entailed in pivoting from one *dao* to another, and how this informs the human-Heaven and human-animal binaries that are both expressed and challenged in the text.

4.4 What Distinguishes People from Turtles and Fish

As observed in section 4.2, the *Zhuangzi*'s dethroning of the heart is an anti-hierarchy gesture, which also implies dethroning people as the heart of Heaven and Earth. However, as Perkins observes, the *Zhuangzi*, in a way, still makes the heart central to its own discourse, in the sense that it emphasizes the need to render its distinctions and judgments tenuous.[49] What is the implication of this paradoxical centrality for the presumed heart of Heaven and Earth? Just like the *Zhuangzi* emphasizes the need to loosen the heart's grip on other organs, so that many different drives can surface without being controlled and guided by the heart (in other words, take turns being the servant versus ruler), it also presents us with many examples of people who

---

[46] I owe this point to Fraser, who makes a convincing case for taking "meta-*dao*" as one of the meanings of *dao* in the Zhuangzi. See Chris Fraser, "Wandering the Way: A Eudaimonistic Approach to the *Zhuāngzǐ*," *Dao* 13, no. 4 (2014): 541–565.

[47] As Perkins demonstrates in his article on the discourse of individuation, structured around the term *wu* 物 (things), many passages in the Zhuangzi—and in other texts, such as in the *Xing Zi Ming Chu*—point toward the simultaneity of our activities of distinction drawing, on the one hand, and the appearance of formed, distinguished things, on the other. The term *wu* 物 (things), does not fall on either side of the "objective data" versus "subjective construct" distinction, either, as can be seen in the line from the *Xing Zi Ming Chu* that says: "Whatever appears/seen (*jian/xian* 見) is called a thing" (*jian/xian* 見 could mean both "to see" and "to appear"). *Wu* 物 thus names a way of appearing/seeing things as individuated. See Franklin Perkins, "What is a thing (*wu* 物)?," 62. The *Xing Zi Ming Chu* line is from LIU Zhao 劉釗, *Guodian Chujian Jiaoshi* 郭店楚簡校釋 (An interpretation with corrections on the Guodian Chu Slips) (Fuzhou 福州: Fujian Renmin Chubanshe 福建人民出版社, 2003), strip 12.

[48] I use the term "truth regime" in the Foucauldian sense to draw attention to the fact-value entanglement (which is very much present in early Chinese philosophical discourse as well) and to the view that the authorized speakers of truths may also coincide with power-holders. Michel Foucault, "Truth and Power," in *Power*, ed. J. B. Faubion, vol. 3 of *Essential Works of Foucault 1954–1984*, ed. Paul Rabinow (New York: New Press, 2000), 111–133.

[49] Perkins, *Heaven and Earth Are Not Humane*, 169.

have a knack for blending in (instead of trying to impose mastery on a situation so as to control it) and do such a good job of adapting to any given context that they actually stand out.[50]

While only human characters are portrayed as being able to adapt to a wide range of situations in a way that defies expectations (which translates into an alternative gesture for highlighting human uniqueness), when these people's hearts lose their resolute character, their humanity becomes suspect in the eyes of others. What we are left with is a distorted notion of the heart, which excels at not committing to its distinctions, and a distorted notion of the "human," marked by their ability to let go of their humanity.[51]

One of the clearest articulations of these lines of thought appears in a story in the "Grasping Vitality" (Da sheng 達生) chapter. The story features the character of Kongzi who is sightseeing at the Lüliang waterfall. He sees a man diving into the water from a place that is impossible to navigate, even for fish and other aquatic creatures. Taking the swimmer for a suicidal man, Kongzi orders his disciples to save him. However, before they can try to pull him out, he gracefully emerges from water with "his hair streaming down, singing a song." Kongzi runs after him and tells him that he thought the man was a ghost (gui 鬼) instead of a man, and asks if he has a *dao* for treading the water like that. The swimmer answers:

> No, I have no *dao*. . . . I go in along with the swirls and come out as a companion to the eddies. I follow along with the *dao* of the water and make no private one of my own. This is how I do my treading.[52]

---

[50] Valmisa's analysis of "adapting" in early Chinese discourse differentiates this notion from replicating "the natural spontaneity of the non-human world." Valmisa takes adapting—which she uses in a precise sense, corresponding to the term *yin* 因 when conceptualized—to involve not simply flexibility and blending in, but also being innovative about the way one makes use of available resources, engaging in purposive action while abandoning fixed patterns of thinking, and turning obstacles into conditions of possibility. Mercedes Valmisa, *Adapting: A Chinese Philosophy of Action* (New York: Oxford University Press, 2021), 35, 53–60. As I will argue in the following pages, even what one might consider to be simpler acts of blending in and/or going along with things appear to require a particular form of engagement with distinction making and *dao*-following. This could help explain why the text uses only human characters in the episodes analyzed below, despite its abundant engagement with animal characters otherwise.

[51] This issue is revisited at the concluding segment of Part III, in the context of a passage on a "person without affects (人而無情 *ren er wuqing*)."

[52] In Chinese, the line reads: 「亡，吾無道。(...) 與齊俱入，與汩偕出，從水之道而不為私焉。此吾所以蹈之也。」 *Zhuangzi* 19:655.

The humorous and satirical aspect of this story has been noted before.[53] It is surely amusing to imagine Kongzi presuming that a swimmer needs his assistance only to be proven wrong *and* getting lectured by the swimmer— one that also happens to wear his hair loose (*pi fa* 被髮), which suggests his cultural otherness.[54] As with many of the humorous stories in the *Zhuangzi*, this one harbors a sober insight hidden in the answer of a humble nobody who proves to be wiser than famous masters strutting around with their disciples.[55] The swimmer's answer is a clear commentary on not imposing onto actual situations a pre-set way of doing and thinking about things—which is exactly what the character of Kongzi had done earlier. The swimmer does not have a *dao* in the sense that he does not have a predetermined *dao*[56] and, furthermore, in being so adaptable to different *dao*s, he also appears to Kongzi as something different than a man. This very reaction of Kongzi's to the man invites a loaded question: What makes a man a man?

The swimmer's answer—that he does not have a *dao*—already gives us a glimpse into conventional markers of one's humanity. They concern having various discriminative attitudes and set ways of leading one's life, which translate into deliberate methods and planning tools. The swimmer, however, does not rely on that type of a *dao* and instead goes along with different ways of navigating the world that are built into myriad situations. This ability to to adapt to a wide variety of circumstances and make one's abode anywhere[57] parallels the affirmative gesture of accepting whatever life brings, as seen in stories of characters who calmly accept losing a body part, or even losing their own life.[58] Whether such people should be called humans, or

---

[53] A very similar story appears in the *Liezi* and is analyzed in Shirley Chan, "Identifying Daoist Humor: Reading the *Liezi*," in *Humour in Chinese Life and Letters: Classical and Traditional Approaches* (Hong Kong: Hong Kong University Press, 2011), 85.

[54] For more on the association between unbound hair and cultural otherness, see Erica Fox Brindley, *Ancient China and the Yue: Perceptions and Identities on the Southern Frontier, c. 400 BCE–50 CE* (Cambridge: Cambridge University Press, 2015), 143–148. Sterckx also notes that it was often southern "barbarians" who were employed as swimmers. Sterckx, *The Animal and the Daemon*, 189.

[55] As Defoort notes, the *Zhuangzi* often presents us with "objectionable masters," such as people from humble professions, ex-convicts, young disciples of Kongzi, and so on. See Defoort, "Instruction Dialogues in the *Zhuangzi*," 466–467. This gesture clearly serves the function of challenging the entanglement of authority and power.

[56] I owe this interpretation of the swimmer's answer to Dan Robins, who notes that the swimmer's not having a *dao* should be understood in terms of his not relying on a fixed *dao* and his adjusting to the particularities of water that he may not have anticipated in his training. Robins, "It Goes Beyond Skill," 108–109.

[57] Also see *Zhuangzi* 2:102 for an example about making a dwelling in the skies.

[58] The examples about losing a body part and losing one's life appear, in order, in *Zhuangzi* 5:196 and 6:267.

ghosts, or something else surely depends on the definition of such categories, since one could also suggest that being so flexible *is* part of being human. The *Zhuangzi*, as is often the case, does not offer us a final answer on the issue, but instead unsettles the very categories upon which such a discussion operates.

As discussed earlier, a consistent thread running through the *Zhuangzi* concerns employing a flexible attitude, so that one "constantly goes by the self-so (*ziran* 自然) and does not add anything to life."[59] By contrasting Heavenly versus human ways of acting, the *Zhuangzi* also expresses the difference between going with what unfolds on its own accord versus taking labored and contrived action. The *Zhuangzi* later ambiguates the Heavenly-human distinction as well, remaining faithful to its own critique of settling on final distinctions. The text asks: "How do I know that what I call Heavenly is not human and that what I call human is not Heavenly?"[60] Perhaps this ambivalent attitude toward the Heaven-human distinction itself is the strongest argument against the stability of a human identity.

In fact, it could be said that the work both posits and problematizes the category of the human on two levels. The first level concerns the text's treatment of ordinary people who are locked into various perspectives, cultural codes, and social roles. What unites them is their commitment to a particular way of life; however, due to the presence of different norms and codes in the world, there is still a great variety and a great deal of disagreement among them.[61] Here it is safe to assert, in general, that any enhanced emphasis on disagreement within a group is bound to blur the imagined boundaries surrounding the group. After all, if there is indeed so much diversity among people, then to what extent can we talk about them as a group? In fact, as chapter 5 further explores, the *Zhuangzi*'s comparison of different viewpoints takes a curious turn when the difference between a person and a fish is considered to be on par with the difference between two people—suggesting, perhaps, that we are simply all others to one another.

Aside from folks who set their hearts on specific norms, cultural codes, and social roles, the work also presents us with people who are awe-inspiring in their ability to go along with and adapt to a wide variety of circumstances.

---

[59] 常因自然而不益生也。(*Zhuangzi* 5:227).
[60] In Chinese the line is 庸詎知吾所謂天之非人乎？所謂人之非天乎？(*Zhuangzi* 6:231)
[61] In fact, the work sometimes juxtaposes disagreements among people with those among animals from different habitats, which accentuates the sheer epistemic and value plurality within human communities. An example of that gesture can be seen in the opening chapter of the transmitted text, which juxtaposes different vantage points of different animals with the different cultural codes of the Song and Yue territories (*Zhuangzi* 1:35).

One might be inclined to simply describe such folks as aligning with the Heaven side of the Heaven-human binary,[62] except to be reminded of the fact that the *Zhuangzi* also asks: Who is really to say what is Heavenly and what is human? Moreover, the adaptability of people like the swimmer suggests an even greater amount of diversity among people, to the extent that this diversity throws into question what such groupings even entail.

Regardless of how one views the Heaven(ly)-human tension, the human condition seems to be marked by its relation to *dao*-following.[63] Many people limit themselves to the specific *dao*(s) they adhere to, whereas some manage to pivot from one *dao* to another, multiplying the circumstances in which they can flourish. That it is the latter group of people who inspire awe in others is partly a mockery of more conventional role models who try to elevate humanity to greater heights by promoting a specific set of lofty norms and values. However, there is also a positive dimension to such stories of flexibility that goes beyond mere satire of rival intellectual trends.

As noted in chapter 1, when the *Zhuangzi* offers many stories of different characters acting in an unpredictable world, it also inevitably expresses its own sense of what aspects of the world merit being talked and written about.[64] Given the *Zhuangzi*'s emphasis on the complexity of the world that eludes one's grasp, it is only to be expected that the enabling modes of knowledge and action in the *Zhuangzi* are formulated around resistance to epistemic closures and that people's exceptionality lies in their ability to go along with what they are given. However, perhaps a more curious aspect of such formulations is the fact that such people's ability to blend in with their surroundings is so great that the radicality of their adaptability makes them stand out.

Earlier it was observed that the *Zhuangzi* decenters the heart only to recenter it in a different way. At the same time, the text undermines people's uniqueness by reminding the readers that they are, after all, part of the ten thousand things populating the world, but only to reinstate their unique status formulated around their ability to successfully blend in with those ten

---

[62] This gesture can be observed in the "Heavenly Way" (Tiandao 天道) chapter and "The Turning of the Heavens (Tianyun 天運) chapter in the text.

[63] This is also explicitly suggested in the "The Great Source as Teacher" (Da zong shi 大宗師) chapter with the line "fish come together in water, people come together in the *dao*." (魚相造乎水，人相造乎道。) (6:277). I follow Ziporyn's 2009 translation of "相造" as coming together. See Brook Ziporyn, trans., *Zhuangzi: The Essential Writings with Selections from Traditional Commentaries* (Indianapolis, IN: Hackett, 2009), 47.

[64] I owe this observation about storytelling to Martha Nussbaum. See Nussbaum, *Love's Knowledge*, 3–4.

4. HUMAN DISTINCTIVENESS IN THE ZHUANGZI   117

thousand things and with their environment. In other words, the *Zhuangzi* undermines and then reestablishes as the center of focus the unique status of the heart and of people, but in distorted forms.

The same is true for the Heaven(ly)-human binary. As the *Zhuangzi* posits, nullifies, and announces the insolvability of this binary, one thing remains certain: The text cannot stop hovering around this very tension. Whether there is indeed a discontinuity between people and what is deemed Heavenly, that the issue proves so enticing to the authors and compilers of the text still evinces people's (preestablished or acquired) unusual standing in the world for the *Zhuangzi*.

Conclusion
Admiring and Humbling Humanity

One of the most noticeable things chapters 3 and 4 demonstrated is that the two formulations of human exceptionality unfold in evidently different terminologies, in line with the different ontological categorizations that are peculiar to their corresponding milieu. Hence, in this final portion of Part II, instead of diving directly into a theoretical comparison, which risks overburdening the analysis with conceptual observations and beclouding what is at stake, I will initiate the comparison between Spinoza and the *Zhuangzi* with the illustrations examined in chapters 3 and 4. To this end, the next section revisits the aforementioned illustrations and examines what the seemingly humbling human-nonhuman comparisons precisely do for Spinoza and the *Zhuangzi*. The relation between our findings and the broader threads of thought within each comparandum is explored in section B. The final section carries the discussion into the domain of critical human-animal studies and explores the stakes implied in Spinoza's and the *Zhuangzi*'s different epistemic positions regarding what human actors can know about the world. Additionally, it explores the different sensibilities around human uniqueness, if not human superiority, expressed in Spinoza and the *Zhuangzi*.

A. Like a Worm, Like a Tree

What better way to deflate the human ego than to draw comparisons between humans, on the one hand, and donkeys, stones, worms, or trees, on the other? The juxtaposition of a person and a seemingly unimportant being is a powerful and well-known rhetorical gesture employed both by Spinoza and by the authors and compilers of the *Zhuangzi*. All these aforementioned comparisons have been examined in secondary scholarship on Spinoza and the *Zhuangzi* using a similar angle—that they take jabs at the human ego.[1] Although it is undeniable that all such comparisons do harbor an obvious element of ridicule directed against human actors, it should not be overlooked that human-nonhuman comparisons—including those that seemingly equalize humans and nonhumans—could be, and indeed were in the case of Spinoza and the *Zhuangzi*, mobilized to different ends.

As discussed in chapter 3, Spinoza presents us with comparisons of mankind to a stone, a tiny worm, and a fictional donkey. The initial context of the latter comparison, that is, the mechanics of action in a deterministic cosmos, argues for the fundamental equality between all things in the world. Mankind is not different from an ass, in the sense that both are embedded in a vast chain of causation which they cannot "will" their way out of. Spinoza's treatment of the paradox of Buridan's ass comes across as hasty and dismissive, perhaps because it is an unlikely scenario, verging on sophistry. Is it possible for a donkey, let alone a man, to be placed between two perfectly equal choices? If a man, who is also expected to have a more complex set of drives due to having a more complex mind/body than other things, finds himself stumped by such a simplistic scenario of causal bifurcation, then can he be called a man? "I do not know," Spinoza says. Nonetheless, the paradox itself was initially concocted to prove that there is an excess of free will over understanding in men, but then Spinoza himself does not locate man's difference from animals in the presence or absence of free will anyway. However, Spinoza then digresses into offering other close candidates to a donkey, all of whom have various intellectual disabilities and debilities. This foreshadows the fact that the animal-human comparisons in Spinoza are less of a humbling gesture against humanity *en masse* and more of a discriminative move that targets specific groups of people.

Whereas Spinoza's example about the flying stone pokes fun at men who are boasting about having free will (and who are as delusional as the flying

---

[1] For a thorough examination of Spinoza's undermining of human hubris, see Yitzhak Y. Melamed, "Spinoza's Anti-Humanism: An Outline," in Fraenkel, Perinetti, and Smith, *The Rationalists: Between Tradition and Innovation*, 147–166. For an examination of the history of "anti-humanistic" interpretations of the *Zhuangzi* (and a rebuttal of this reading paradigm), see Eric S. Nelson, "The Human and the Inhuman: Ethics and Religion in the *Zhuangzi*," *Journal of Chinese Philosophy* 41, no. 5 (2014): 723–739.

stone that takes credit for the movements it is going through), his example about the worm serves as a rhetorical tool to criticize those who share the ignorance of the worm that takes the blood in which it lives for the entirety of the world. Both these examples target various epistemic failings in mankind that can be remedied instead of arguing that, on a fundamental level, all these beings are on the same tier. For Spinoza, there is, in the end, a way out of being like a foolish stone or a narrow-minded little worm, which is grasping the laws of causation that are all embedded in a world wider than our immediate surroundings.

There is a similarity between what we see in Spinoza's comparison of various people to a stone or a worm and the episode in the *Zhuangzi* that juxtaposes a carpenter and a tree. The carpenter too suffers from an epistemic failure: He judges the tree according to human-centric paradigms of value. However, in the end, not only does the carpenter realize that he is ultimately not that different from a tree by virtue of each being a "thing" among myriad things (*wanwu* 萬物), his humbling discovery is made possible by imagining how the human-tree comparison would look from the perspective of the tree.[2] Moreover, their ultimate parity is not a position to which the carpenter *descends* due to his intellectual inadequacies. It is a given, which he initially did not realize because he was hung up on a dogma that ranks things among each other.

This very contrast between the two ways in which a juxtaposition between humans and nonhumans unfolds is certainly not coincidental. Neither could it be explained away by appealing to possible differences in the literary habits of different milieus.[3] The difference has to do with the internal logic of each set of writings and the ways in which the human situation is codified within each. The next section fleshes out the contrasts between the two approaches to epistemic and agential empowerment, which ultimately also feeds into different formulations of human exceptionality.

---

[2] Whether it could really be said that the tree itself brought awareness to the carpenter is ambiguous, given that it appears in a dream. On the one hand, the *Zhuangzi* also undermines the difference between dreaming and being awake in the "The Discourse that Levels Things" (Qi wu lun 齊物論) chapter (*Zhuangzi* 2:20–21, 28). On the other hand, the text also displays sensitivity to what does not "speak" by virtue of their own particular endowments. Hence, the tree speaking in a dream could be a case of the authors taking note of the treeness of the tree. Similarly, when a skull is portrayed to be speaking directly to the character of Zhuangzi, that conversation also takes place in a dream (*Zhuangzi* 18:616–618).

[3] In fact, one could argue that there are many parallels between Spinoza and some early Ru thinkers in the ways they employ animal pejoratives to criticize human shortcomings.

B. Finding Empowerment in a Univocal versus Polyvocal World

If one were to seek parallels between the two paradigms of knowledge and action, one would find plenty of easy points of comparison. One point concerns the shared aversion toward broad generalizations, which we observe in both the *Ethics* and the *Zhuangzi*. Spinoza criticizes "bad" universals for reflecting the random character of the imagination, whereas the *Zhuangzi* warns against applying certain distinctions and values in a pan-contextual way and forgetting that different circumstances call for different distinctions, evaluations, and actions.

This parallel breaks down when one recalls that the *Zhuangzi*'s aversion toward generalizations is tied up with themes of the fickleness of life and the incommensurability of different worldviews. Such themes are rather muted in Spinoza, who instead emphasizes the lawfulness and orderliness of nature, as well as agreement among the people who have an adequate understanding of the world. Given his emphasis on the regularities of nature, Spinoza's model of empowerment very much relies on understanding the lawful dimensions of nature. Not surprisingly, when it comes to empowering forms of thinking and acting in the *Zhuangzi*, a dominant theme is cultivating the ability to roll with the punches, so to speak, without becoming overly attached to specific values and distinctions.

Another obvious parallel concerns Spinoza's notion of adequate understanding and the *Zhuangzi*'s emphasis on adaptive responsiveness. In both accounts we see an emphasis on the commonalities that underlie particular phenomena and the co-presence of different levels of understanding. As explained earlier, according to Spinoza, imagination and adequate understanding coexist and one can perceive a phenomenon to be unfolding out of the common laws of nature while still continuing to draw random associations between various phenomena, depending on one's personal history. This might be seen as analogous to the kind of double-perspective exhibited by various characters in the *Zhuangzi*, which involves attending to the uniqueness of each thing while also being aware of the "thingness" of all things, which places them on par with each other. The two—acknowledging the uniqueness of each thing and placing them on par with each other—are not contradictory. To be a thing is also to have a vantage point on life and there is no obvious way to rank different vantage points among each other. To complicate matters further, one's judgments and values are also subject to change over time, simply because people change and so do their surroundings.

Ultimately, unlike Spinoza, the *Zhuangzi*'s world is one that is always already mediated through one's interests, values, purposes, and so on. As such, it is oversaturated with different ways of viewing it, which are all legitimate in their own right. Empowerment comes with not having access to favored entry points but with multiplying one's "ins."[4] This also relates to an earlier point made about finding "the pivot of all *daos*." One can tentatively rely on a *dao* (a way of doing things and evaluating things) while also being aware that in simply being a *dao*, no *dao* is indubitably better or worse than another— the same way that in being a thing, no thing is indisputably better or worse than another thing.

The fact of the matter is, in the *Zhuangzi* only human actors are portrayed as being capable of such flexibility. Although, as mentioned earlier, "an absence of a theory is not a theory of absence," that we do not see animal actors exhibiting high degrees of adaptability to different circumstances, at minimum, shows a lack of interest in the subject matter (which is surprising given the authors' and compilers' interest in animal lives).

It is also plausible that a particular feature of humanity functions as both a debilitating and empowering factor, depending on how one makes use of it. Namely, the different ways people make use of labels and evaluations inform whether they are limiting themselves to one way of life (one *dao*) or thriving in many contexts and environments. The difference maps on to the contrast between having a very resolute or well-formed (*cheng* 成) heart versus a tenuous heart, and the two extremes might also relate to the human condition. After all, the text does exhibit a sensibility that views people as peculiar in the way they manage to create so much struggle for themselves, which forms the basis of the pesky Heaven-human binary. It is not too surprising then that human beings occupy the center stage in episodes about carrying out a 180-degree reversal on trying to manage one's surroundings and, instead, being at ease everywhere.

Finally, a feature of mankind that acts as a double-edged sword is explicitly articulated in Spinoza, in the context of the complexity of the human body, which makes possible both the greater confusions of the imagination and the

---

[4] I owe the description of multiplication of one's entry points as having more "ins" to Cuomo and Gruen, "On Puppies and Pussies," 133–34.

higher forms of knowledge.⁵ Spinoza's model exhibits a clear fascination with the complexity of human minds and bodies, which can lead mankind both to great confusions and to great insights. Likewise, the *Zhuangzi*'s model shows a preoccupation with the capacities and shortcomings of the heart, which, certainly in people's case, causes both great rigidity and great flexibility. It is easy to be biased toward the latter, especially from a critical animal studies perspective, because even when the *Zhuangzi* admits people's peculiarity in the world or invites us to marvel at various awe-inspiring human actors, it still avoids presenting us with obvious rankings of people, animals, or plants (especially given that one's increased adaptability relies on letting go of these rankings). However, as the next and final section explores, the absence of such rankings come with a price, just as the presence of them does.

C. Certainty with a Bias, Humility without an Agenda

At the heart of the *Zhuangzi*'s undermining of a clear hierarchy among different denizens of the world is its rendering of all distinctions and rankings in general as tenuous, thereby also conveying the limitations of one's certainty about the world. It is tempting to draw a moralizing message from such themes of epistemic humility, as well as from the text's other persistent preoccupation with the singularity and alterity of different situations and beings. Indeed, gestures of epistemic humility are commonly celebrated by critical animal theorists, such as Behnke, who hails "not-knowing" as key to having a more "responsive comportment that allows differences to emerge."⁶ Such a sentiment does, in fact, apply to the *Zhuangzi*, which is why attempts to utilize the *Zhuangzi* to develop a philosophical basis for non-reductive and ecocritical ethics have also been made.⁷

---

⁵ Genevieve Lloyd makes a similar point in her *Routledge Guidebook to Spinoza and the* Ethics, 55.

⁶ Elizabeth A. Behnke, "From Merleau-Ponty's Concept of Nature to an Interspecies Practice of Peace," in *Animal Others: On Ethics, Ontology, and Animal Life*, ed. H. Peter Steeves (Albany: State University of New York Press, 1999), 107. Also see Aragorn Eloff, "Do Anarchists Dream of Emancipated Sheep? Contemporary Anarchism, Animal Liberation and the Implications of New Philosophy," in *Anarchism and Animal Liberation: Essays on Complementary Elements of Total Liberation*, ed. Anthony J. Nocella II, Richard J. White, and Erika Cudworth (Jefferson, NC: McFarland, 2015), 208.

⁷ For a nuanced and self-conscious attempt, see Eric Sean Nelson, "Responding with *Dao*: Early Daoist Ethics and the Environment," *Philosophy East and West* 59, no. 3 (July 2009): 294–316.

An obvious problem with repurposing the *Zhuangzi*'s content for such a platform is that the text's emphasis on allowing alterity and difference to emerge hardly translates into agenda-laden plans and practices. Instead, it seems to help one cultivate uncertainty about the world and appreciation of the manifold and unrankable differences between things and situations. The absence of an explicit, normative message is built into the text's skeptical attitude toward finalizing knowledge claims, which means it is difficult to isolate and celebrate themes of radical epistemic humility without acknowledging the morally apathetic conclusions that come with them.

In the end, what the *Zhuangzi* offers is an unmistakable highlighting of this very entanglement instead of an ecocritical and post-humanist manifesto. In fact, as a text that is better at multiplying our questions than presenting answers to our various problems, the *Zhuangzi* proves to be an excellent resource for reflecting on the price that such gestures of radical epistemic humility exact from us: They open up capacious space for inquiry without providing any clear standard for how to measure progress.[8]

Spinoza's corpus does not frustrate its audience in the same way—that is, by deliberately resisting our desire for clarity and closure. The frustration with Spinoza lies in the discrepancy observed between all the radical conclusions he could have arrived at and his actual conclusions. Although his assertion that human minds and bodies excel above all others presents interpretational difficulties, the very presence of a ladder of complexity does not. Such proto-Darwinian constructions of heterogeneity and difference that unfold on a hierarchical axis have attracted both praise and criticism within critical human-animal studies.

The praise concerns such constructions' ability to articulate the apparent overlapping similarities found among human and nonhuman animals, albeit on a hierarchical continuum where some beings are claimed to possess more complex configurations of similar components (e.g., an adult human brain is more complex than that of an ape). The criticism concerns the linear way these hierarchical continuums are often imagined, which, simply and too conveniently, depicts nonhuman animals as lesser versions of humans.[9] We see an early modern articulation of this familiar phenomenon in Spinoza,

---

[8] The wording is borrowed from Weil, *Thinking Animals*, 24.
[9] Cary Wolfe raises this criticism against the "Great Ape Project," which measures the cognitive and linguistic skills of the great apes according to their closeness to humans, without seeing much value in their difference and uniqueness. See Wolfe, *Animal Rites*, 192.

who seems to be biased toward a certain kind of intelligence, which he associates with adult men without the type of neurodivergencies that might earn them the title of "madmen" or "fools."

One can here reiterate that for Spinoza, not only can abstract categories that rely on generalizations of one's imagination be reworked, but (relatedly) the complexity of the affections of the body is subject to change. In fact, Spinoza explicitly notes that our capabilities are never fixed and they develop as the body and the mind become more powerful and active (EIIp13–14), which is captured in the famous phrase that we "do not know what a body can do" (EIIIp2s). However, it must also be noted here that, at least initially, the diversity of the ways one can use one's body and mind is a matter of a certain inborn power (*vis nativa*).[10] This power can be improved upon, as Spinoza describes through an analogy with tool-making.

Spinoza asserts that from certain basic tools we are born with, we can make more and more complicated and advanced tools. Similarly, by working on certain inborn intellectual powers, we can produce intellectual tools that can help us acquire the capacity to generate more intellectual works. This, in turn, enables us to create further tools and continue the process until we reach the "summit of wisdom" (*sapientiae culmen*) (TIE 31). Hence, strictly speaking, the ladder of complexity that Spinoza offers should not necessarily run unidirectionally from human to animal, although possession of certain inborn powers does seem to give one a leg up.

Aside from certain biases that are the products of Spinoza's imagination, one also wonders whether there is a rhetorical element to his speciesist language. In EIIIp12s, Spinoza states that the mind endeavors to think of things that increase its power. Moreover, in the preface to Book IV of the *Ethics*, he states that although setting an exemplary model of human nature (*naturae humanae exemplar*) before ourselves is problematic, we inevitably do it anyway. It thus merits consideration whether Spinoza's discussions around a specific group of bodies (namely, human bodies) as the most complex might have such a rhetorical dimension.

The possibility that there might be a rhetorical element to Spinoza's remarks about human exceptionality gains further weight when one considers Spinoza's investment in human unity and togetherness. In Spinoza's philosophy, understanding one's conditions in life as unfolding out of eternal laws of nature is, by itself, expected to have a unifying function among men

---

[10] TIE 31.

who follow reason, given that "we" are not expected to have disagreements over laws that are omnipresent. However, as chapter 6 demonstrates, Spinoza also attempts to seal off the porous borders separating mankind from beasts due to an anxiety regarding what "leakage" between different life forms could develop into: the possibility that one might actually prefer the company of beasts over that of mankind and begin restraining "our" power because of considerations of sympathy. This betrays an unambiguous investment in human solidarity, which Spinoza fears could be threatened if men start feeling too close to beasts.

This emphasis on agreement—as an assumption and as an ideal—is absent in the *Zhuangzi* due to three interlocking features of the text: multivocality, not laying claim to knowledge, and not ranking some values as indubitably better than others. Although, as chapter 5 discusses, the *Zhuangzi* does not exhibit anxiety regarding human-animal companionship and does not argue for the intrinsic value of human solidarity. The text clearly acknowledges the implications of its emphasis on diversity and pluralism. A line from the "The Great Source as Teacher" (Dao zong shi 大宗師) reads: "Fish forget one another in the rivers and lakes, and people forget one another in the arts of *daos*."[11] Given that people can come together through many ways of valuing and doing things, the *Zhuangzi* is hinting at the inevitable result of the culmination of people's versatility and ability to thrive in many different conditions and environments: the loosening of all commitments to unify and cement human society more closely together.

Part III explores issues of human bonding and solidarity, together with the affective dimension of neutral and negative depictions of animality in Spinoza and the *Zhuangzi*. In doing so, the next two chapters—chapters 5 and 6—also address different philosophical treatments of the communication of affects between different beings. This topic is still relatively under-studied in a field that largely focuses on tracing the seeds of the human-animal binary to assumptions about humans' rational capacities. As Part III examines key passages in both sets of writings in which the tastes, lusts, and joys of different beings are compared, it also explores another related and equally under-studied topic, namely, the role humor and laughter play in one's affective empowerment and in bonding different life communities together. While exploration of the topic of humor is indispensable for any study that

---

[11] In Chinese the line reads 魚相忘乎江湖，人相忘乎道術 (*Zhuangzi* 6:277).

deals with a text like the *Zhuangzi*, which is known for its playful dimension, paying focused attention to this topic in a comparative context also reveals the rhetorical dimensions and affective investments (or lack thereof) of Spinoza and the *Zhuangzi*, as they are cementing or undermining human bonding.

PART III
ANIMAL AFFECTS
Curiosity Versus Threat

The Invocator for the Ancestors, dressed in his solemn black robe, approached the pigpen and addressed the pigs saying: "Why should you object to dying? I'll feed you for three months, I'll practice austerities for ten days, fast for three days, then put down the mats of white reeds and lay your shoulders and rumps on the carved stand. Surely, you'd be willing to go along with it?" But someone who was planning things from the point of view of the pigs would say, "It would be better to eat bran and chaff, and be left right there in the pen." Planning things from his own point of view, he is willing to go along with having the honors of cap and carriage while still alive and a fine hearse to carry him to his stately funeral when he dies. Planning things from the point of the pigs, he rejects these things. Planning from his own point of view, he chooses them. Why does he think he's so different from the pigs?

Zhuangzi 19: 646[1]

The law to refrain from slaughtering beasts is founded on groundless superstition and womanish compassion rather than on sound reason. . . . I do not deny that beasts feel; I am denying that they are on that account debarred from paying heed to our own advantages and from making use of them as we please and dealing with them as best suits us, seeing that they do not agree with us in nature and these emotions are different in nature from human emotions.

EIVp37s1

---

[1] For this passage, I followed Ziporyn's translation. See Ziporyn, *Zhuangzi: The Complete Writings*, 152.

5
Zhuangzi and the Happy Fish
Animal Affects in the *Zhuangzi*

What role do affects play in bonding human communities together and imagining alternative life-enriching futures? And, as we imagine more inclusive life communities, what are the limits and price of the enthusiasm for unsettling the boundaries between "us" and "them"? Part III examines the human-animal binary in Spinoza and the *Zhuangzi* in the context of their affective similarities and differences. Of particular focus is the presence or absence of anxiety around communication of affects between different beings in the two comparanda and the connection that such anxiety has to different views on human solidarity as an ideal.

As will be shown in the next two chapters, neither Spinoza's investment in human bonding nor the *Zhuangzi*'s disinterest in bringing people together as a sociopolitical community is trivial, as the former's investment sometimes enables him to police species-borders, while the latter carries its dismantling of all group borders to uncomfortable extremes, including divestment from human welfare as a collective goal altogether.

The first section of the present chapter offers an analysis of key episodes in the *Zhuangzi*, where the likes and dislikes of different beings are compared. The section examines the ways in which the text mobilizes curiosity about different beings' tastes and preferences to both blur and affirm a human-animal binary, which perhaps destabilizes one's distinctions and groupings even more than a consistent denial of the binary. In the end, what unites these episodes in the *Zhuangzi* is a concern for developing sensitivity to the multiplicity of different needs and preferences, which results in a greater degree of efficacious action.

Section 5.2 moves on to examining the conditions leading to heightened awareness of others' likes and dislikes. These involve letting go of the desire to gain mastery of a given situation and continually recalibrating the heart (*xin zhai* 心齋) to hear others' likes and dislikes without them being overwritten with one's established affective dispositions. A less studied but crucial feature of the text's description of the cultivation of such skills is that the process does not depend on reliance on a master's sustained tutelage or the sages' legacy. This very feature sets the *Zhuangzi* apart from many other early Chinese Masters texts.

The final section takes up this observation to explore the obvious question: What happens to human bonding amid this heightened awareness of each other's differences, which at times translates into a radical view that puts differences among people on par with the difference between a man and a fish? The section demonstrates that although the *Zhuangzi* does not explicitly promote a master-disciple dynamic, and at times also emphasizes the radically diverse nature of human beings, it does not lack an appreciation for human companionship. Fleeting in nature, human bonds in the *Zhuangzi* tend to rely on a shared sense of humor that trades on incongruity. However, I argue that, ultimately, the types of human friendships articulated in the *Zhuangzi* and the enthusiastic engagement with the perspectives of myriad animals both unfold out of the same openness to the unfamiliar and the same playfulness that undermines established hierarchies.

5.1 Wandering with the Fish, Zhuangzi, and Huizi

Chapter 4 discussed the *Zhuangzi*'s portrayal of the double-edged nature of humanity, which relates to the way people navigate different *dao*s in different manners. Some become engrossed in a single *dao* whereas others remain noncommittal and pivot from one *dao* to another and flourish in many ways of living—*if*, of course, they can render their heart and its distinctions and judgments tenuous (*xu* 虛). Several passages from the *Zhuangzi* also compare the tastes and preferences of humans and various animals, which suggests that it is not only people's hearts (or their ability to render the heart noncommittal) but also their mouths, ears, and eyes that make them different from other earthlings.

One of these comparisons appears in the context of a conversation between Nie Que and Wang Ni, in which the latter is asked whether there is anything that all things affirm as right. Wang Ni responds:

> When people sleep in a damp place, their waists get sick and twisted to death, but is this so of loaches? If people live in trees, they tremble with

worry and fear, but is this so of monkeys? Of these three, which one knows the right place to live? People eat the flesh of their livestock, elks and deer eat grass, snakes relish centipedes, owls and crows crave mice. Of these four, which one knows the right thing to eat? Monkeys take their females for mates, elks and deer pair up, loaches play with fish. Now, Mao Qiang and Lady Li are taken to be beautiful by humans, but when fish see them they dive deep, when birds see them they soar into the skies, when elks and deer see them they run away. Which of these four knows what is rightly alluring in the world?[1]

The theme of the diversity of experiences and vantage points is a recurring one in the text and was discussed in the previous chapter. Wang Ni's response clearly aims to demonstrate the silliness of taking one's own judgments as standard, due to the obvious disagreements one would find among different creatures over the proper criteria for comfort, gastronomical pleasures, and beauty. While challenging the centrality of the human perspective, Wang Ni's response still seems to presuppose the existence of specific differences among different groups of beings. In fact, similar affirmations of such differences make appearances in other chapters of the text;[2] however, because such comparisons are sometimes presented along with differences between two people, it is difficult to offer any general and conclusive statement about group-specific differences in the *Zhuangzi*.

One of the instances in which borders between different groupings are both endorsed and unsettled appears in the "Utmost Joy" (Zhi le 至樂) chapter, which offers a story featuring Kongzi. Kongzi is worried about what the future holds for Yan Yuan (Yan Hui) who goes to the state of Qi to talk with a nobleman about the ways of ancient sages. More specifically, he fears that the nobleman might not be able to gracefully receive the Yan Yuan's well-intentioned efforts and might even put the man to death. He elaborates on the kind of miscommunication that he thinks could transpire between the

---

[1] *Zhuangzi* 2:98. After pointing to the existence of such different perspectives for even the most basic concepts, Wang Ni and Nie Que conclude that given such divergent views, one can neither be sure what virtues such as "humanity" or "dutifulness" (*ren yi* 仁義) refer to, nor can one distinguish benefit (*li* 利) from harm (*hai* 害). Humanity and dutifulness, and benefit and harm, are conceptual pairs that make frequent appearances in Ru texts such as the *Mengzi* and the *Xunzi*, as well as in the *Mozi*.

[2] Such as the story of a bird who dies as a result of a nobleman's efforts to be a good host by feeding it human food and entertaining it with human music (*Zhuangzi* 18:620). The example is revisited below.

two people by giving an example about the absurdity of expecting animals to respond to human music in the way that humans do. The passage reads:

> When the Xian Chi (咸池) or Jiu Shao (九韶) music is displayed in the wilds of Dongting (洞庭), birds fly away upon hearing it, beasts run away, and fish dive deep. When human masses hear it, they gather and come back to see it. When fish are in water, they live. When humans are in water, they die. Therefore they are most certainly (*bi* 必) different from each other and their likes and dislikes are different. Hence the former sages did not consider their abilities as one and did not consider their affairs alike. (*Zhuangzi* 18:620–621)

Putting different auditory preferences on par with different survival needs is a bold gesture, since it suggests that assuming that other animals would enjoy human music and would share human likes and dislikes is as absurd as expecting people to breathe under water. At the same time, Kongzi's observation about people's inability to do certain things (like breathe underwater) is undermined by other passages in the *Zhuangzi* suggesting that some people can adapt to alien habitats and life styles—such as feeding on just wind and dew,[3] riding on air,[4] or feeling at home in water.[5] In the passage above, however, Kongzi points to the differences between people and various animals in order to elaborate on a possible difference between two men. Although this very analogy is mobilized to ultimately make a point about the limits of the nobleman's openness to the advice he is about to be given—and analogies, in general, always have their limits—literal comparisons between inter- and intra-group differences are offered elsewhere in the text as well.

A well-known instance of an argumentative gesture that puts the difference between two people on par with the difference between a human and an animal appears in what is often referred to as the "happy fish" passage. The passage features a dialogue between the character of Zhuangzi and his friend Huizi, which unfolds as follows:

---

[3] *Zhuangzi* 1:31. The description of the dietary regimen is significant because it includes obvious allusions to practices of longevity. An explicit formulation of the specific practice of replacing grains with subtler matter appears in the *Mawangdui* medical texts, particularly in a text named *Que Gu Shi Qi* 卻穀食氣, which are thought to have been buried around 200 BCE (and we could perhaps, along with Harper, speculate that earlier manuscripts might have been circulating even before that date). See Donald Harper, trans., *Early Chinese Medical Literature: The Mawangdui Medical Manuscripts* (London: Kegan Paul International, 1998), 4, 305–309.

[4] *Zhuangzi* 1:31. The passage includes details about the same man living on a mountain and riding the clouds, which is a clear reference to the motif of *xian* 仙- beings who were believed to reside on the mountains and live for hundreds of years.

[5] *Zhuangzi* 19:654–655.

Zhuangzi and Huizi were wandering (*you* 遊) on the Hao bridge. Zhuangzi says: "The fish come out and swim at ease (*you* 遊), this is the joy of fish." Huizi says: "You are not a fish, whence do you know about the joy of fish?" Zhuangzi answers: "You are not me, how do you know that I do not know about the joy of fish?" Huizi says: "I am not you, surely I do not know you; you surely are not a fish, so you do not know the joy of fish, that is the whole point." Zhuangzi says: "Let's go back to your original point. You said 'whence do you know about the joy of fish?'—that presupposes you know that I know it [the joy of fish] and asked me [about it]. I know it from above the Hao River." (17:605–606)

Zhuangzi utilizes Huizi's mode of argumentation against him to point out that his initial question relied on the assumption that he was able to know what Zhuangzi was thinking.[6] Although the entire dialogue here is carried out in a humorous and playful way, we can see an ongoing concern in the text about what one can and cannot know about the world (which includes other beings' dispositions, experiences, and vantage points).

Though it is not obvious in the aforementioned passage how much each knows about the fish and about each other, it is clear that everyone involved in the story is engaging in a similar activity. This is perhaps especially true considering that the two words *you* 遊 (to wander, to roam) and *you* 游 (to swim) were also often used interchangeably in early Chinese texts and are etymologically connected with each other.[7] This lingual and notional affinity underscores the similarity between what Zhuangzi, Huizi, and the fish are all doing: wandering, be it in the water or on the Hao bridge.[8] However, the fact that the character of Zhuangzi later qualifies his claim that the fish seem joyful, by adding that they seem so only from where he is standing, suggests an acknowledgment that the fish might be both like *and* unlike him—but we could perhaps say the same for

---

[6] In addition, Zhuangzi's final reply ("I know it from Hao River") is also a wordplay on *an* 安 (whence).

[7] The *you* 斿 in both *you* 遊 and *you* 游 refers to "pendants of a banner" and connotes a sense of flowing or float. See William H. Baxter and Laurent Sagart, *Old Chinese: A New Reconstruction* (Oxford: Oxford University Press, 2014), 122, 372. As Goldin notes, a common misconception in Chinese studies is to resort to speculations about "the graphic components used to represent the word in the writing system" instead of paying attention to the history of the word. Goldin, *The Art of Chinese Philosophy*, 286n2. Hence, when making etymological notes, I will largely be building on the system of Old Chinese reconstruction developed by Baxter and Sagart.

[8] It should be noted that "*you* 遊" is a recurring term in the *Zhuangzi* (in fact, it appears in the title of the opening chapter of the transmitted text) and seems to have an affinity with two other recurring motifs in the text: *wuwei* 無為 (non-contending action) and *ziran* 自然 (so of its own). I render *wuwei* 無為 as "non-contending action" to highlight the fact that what is being denied is not any and

Huizi. Thus, the passage can be taken to affirm both the idea that we are all similar *and* the idea that we are all "others" to one another.

The two threads that run through the text, one pointing in the direction of a human-animal difference (as seen in Wang Ni's comparison of humans' and fishes' criteria for beauty) and the other telling us that we are all simply others to one another can be explained in several ways. The relatively easy explanation would be to simply point out that the *Zhuangzi* was written over a period of time by multiple authors who may not have been as like-minded as we might want to assume. One could also attempt to reconcile the two views into a larger, overarching view by suggesting that these comparisons between humans and animals as groups *and* the gesture of putting the differences between two humans on par with the difference between a human and a fish unfold out of the same simple aim to induce epistemic humility in general. After all, it is through cultivating an awareness of the limits of our knowledge that we can acknowledge we perhaps do not know much about others' affective states—whether the other is a human or an animal. Moreover, sometimes referring to humans as a group and at other times emphasizing the diversity among humans are not necessarily contradictory gestures, since one could argue that humans as a group simply enjoy more diversity than fish do—which is a direction that was explored in chapter 4.[9] One could even push the emphasis on intra-human diversity in the direction of arguing that humans' differences from each other *are* what make them human.

Another possible interpretive route is to embrace the tension between the two views (one view endorses and one view disturbs the human-animal binary *and* human identity), and to interpret this tension as a possible attempt to hijack the desire to give a coherent and finalizing reading of these distinctions and groupings (because, after all, what is more unsettling than sometimes affirming and sometimes negating a distinction?).[10] As noted in chapter 4, this purposeful ambivalence is, in fact, employed for the Heaven(ly)-human distinction, which the text then muddies by asking whether we could know what is from Heaven and what is from human.[11] Such gestures serve to

---

all action, but striving (for a particular outcome, in a fixed mindset) in opposition to broader factors and forces. Other translations include non-interfering action, non-coercive action, non-striving. "Non-contending action" has been suggested in Ziporyn's glossary entry for *wuwei*. See Ziporyn, *Zhuangzi: The Complete Writings*, 287.

[9] See section 4.4 of chapter 4.

[10] Ziporyn makes a similar point when he states that the *Zhuangzi* avoids the problem of "instantiation by negation" by dwelling in doubt (*Ironies of Oneness and Difference*, 169).

[11] See section 4.4 of chapter 4.

destabilize "human" identity altogether, when both the ordinary earthliness of humans and their seeming oddity when compared to other earthlings are incorporated. Regardless of the interpretational framework one follows, the comparisons that the text makes between the preferences and pleasures of humans and various animals serve a clear function, namely, providing a critique of imposing one's own set of standards onto others.

Keeping in mind the sentiment conveyed by Wang Ni, the attempt to employ certain distinctions (whether these are distinctions between right and wrong, or beautiful and ugly) in a pan-contextual way is often criticized in the text. Given that different beings have different preferences, one can easily see how generalizing one's own likes and dislikes to others could breed communication failures. The text is notably rich with bleak stories in which displays of even the most well-intentioned, sympathetic acts of care end up harming others. Examples include the story of Hundun, a creature with no eyes, ears, nose, or mouth, who dies after its friends open seven holes in its head as a favor, thinking this is something Hundun would want;[12] or the story of the bird who dies as a result of a nobleman's efforts to make it happy by feeding it human food and entertaining it with human music.[13] At the root of both Hundun's and the bird's unfortunate deaths lies people's presumption that their own preferences and tastes are universal and thus must be shared by everyone.

It is no coincidence that these stories of failed communication often appear in the context of extending one's standards of appropriateness to other parties with a kind of confidence that is sometimes physically aggressive. The story of Hundun could easily be read alongside other stories of physical mutilation, where people's noses or feet are cut off, or their faces are tattooed, because they do not live up to certain expectations that society places on them.[14] As for the bird, though it is easier to see how inappropriate nourishment could kill a bird, it might not be immediately obvious that exposing a bird to human music could harm it. Concerning early Chinese views of human music and its possible impact on other beings, Roel Sterckx points out that music was thought by some to have a moral force,[15] and he observes that "domestication of the animal world and the triumph of human governance over the natural world at large were presented as a process of moral

[12] Zhuangzi 7:315.
[13] Zhuangzi 18:620.
[14] Zhuangzi 5:207–208. Also see Zhuangzi 6:284 for a critical reference to practices of physical mutilation that associates them with standards of humaneness and dutifulness (ren yi 仁義) and notions of right and wrong (shi fei 是非).
[15] Sterckx, The Animal and the Daemon, 124.

transformation rather than an act of physical conquest."[16] Given that aesthetics and morality were often intertwined, especially in early Ru discourse, it is not surprising that the authors' wariness of the imposition of certain aesthetic standards parallels their critique of the norm-imposing character of moral discourses. Of course, one might ask here, what makes the character of Zhuangzi, who judges the fish to be joyful, different from a nobleman playing human music to make a bird happy? Perhaps the difference lies in the fact that the former does not assume that because something is enjoyable for him, it should be enjoyable for the fish as well, and hence he does not try to force the fish to take a stroll on the Hao bridge. This certainly presupposes a difference between the character of Zhuangzi and the fish: Although they are all *you*'ing (遊; to wander), they *you* in different circumstances.

This last reading still leaves open the possibility that humans might share more similarities with each other than they do with fish; but given the general criticism of assimilative assumptions of similarity between one and the other (as we see in the story of Hundun), it seems that a line remains between giving provisional definitions of various groupings and giving stable and normative definitions of them. It should also be added here that passages hinting at diversity among humans include stories about awe-inspiring people who manifest excellent adaptability to different circumstances, including situations that require the mimicry of nonhuman beings. Examples include a cicada catcher who cultivates the ability to stand like a tree in the forest and a swimmer who leads an aquatic lifestyle that is suitable for turtles and fish.[17] Although it is tempting to interpret these stories as instances of letting go of one's humanity, one could also argue that such flexibility is part of being human,[18] which is to suggest that the cicada catcher's using his body like a tree, or the swimmer's ability to swim like fish and turtles, is, in fact, part of the human experience.[19]

Regardless of what one makes of group similarities and distinctions in the *Zhuangzi*, there seems to be an agreement that we should not be too sure about

---

[16] Sterckx, *The Animal and the Daemon*, 123.

[17] *Zhuangzi* 19:637–638, *Zhuangzi* 19:654–655. The latter episode is discussed in more detail in chapter 4, section 4.4.

[18] This point was also made in chapter 4, section 4.4, as part of the analysis of the story in which Kongzi takes a swimmer to be a ghost.

[19] This point goes against Eno's suggestion that the cicada catcher's "body replicates an object of nature apart from humanity" and "conduit[s] away from the human perspective into a holistic engagement with nature." See Robert Eno, "Cook Ding's Dao and the Limits of Philosophy," in *Essays on Skepticism, Relativism and Ethics in the Zhuangzi*, ed. Paul Kjellberg and Philip J. Ivanhoe (Albany: State University of New York Press, 1996), 141–42. One can also argue that what makes us human is our ability to be not like a human. For an example of this argument, see Franklin Perkins,

the rightness of our own likes and dislikes, unless we want to make fools of ourselves or end up harming others in our attempts to please them. Different affective states, however, are not without shared commonalities and, in the end, what facilitates successful affective engagement with others is attentiveness to underlying similarities combined with loosening the hold that one's own likes and dislikes might have on one's heart. The next section examines several episodes in which attending to others' affective states does not result in harm to either party. Additionally, it probes into the factors that facilitate successful communication of affects.

5.2 Effective and Affective Communication in the *Zhuangzi*

As explored in section 5.1, many stories in the *Zhuangzi* point to a deep concern about being presumptuous about what one can and cannot know about others' likes and dislikes. This worry about affective differences among different beings, however, does not necessarily lead to a communication deadlock. A well-known example of hearing others' likes and dislikes in their own terms is an episode that features a monkey trainer who manages to successfully navigate the frustrations of his captive monkeys. The episode goes like this:

> A monkey trainer was distributing chestnuts. He said, "I'll give you three in the morning and four in the evening." The monkeys were angry. "Well then," he said, "I'll give you four in the morning and three in the evening." The monkeys were pleased. Name (*ming* 名) and actuality (*shi* 實)[20] were not lost, but pleasures and angers were used. He just went along with *this* (*yin shi* 因是). Therefore, sagely people harmonize them using so and

"Of Fish and Men: Species Difference and the Strangeness of Being Human in the Zhuangzi," in *Zhuangzi and the Happy Fish*, ed. Roger T. Ames and Takahiro Nakajima (Honolulu: University of Hawai'i Press, 2017), 182–205. Perkins's article offers a discussion of how humans' exceptional status in the *Zhuangzi* might be located in their freedom from being human.

[20] The *ming* 名/*shi* 實 pairing in early Chinese texts is a much-debated issue. Against the tendency to interpret this pair in terms of a language versus reality distinction, Geaney demonstrates that although the character *shi* 實 does sometimes connote a sense of honesty and authenticity (which connotes "reality"), when paired with *ming* 名, it often has a sense of the fulfillment of a name (for instance, one's actions matching one's title). As such, the two actually map onto two aspects of reality: the aural (that is, one's name, title) and the visual (such as one's actions and performance of duties). See Geaney, *Epistemology of the Senses*, 121. Makeham similarly puts the 名 *ming*/實 *shi* pair

not-so (*shi fei* 是非), yet rest on heaven's wheel.²¹ This is called walking both (ways). (*Zhuangzi* 2:76)²²

The monkey trainer harmonizes his vantage point with that of the monkeys (without losing his own) by simply acknowledging that his is one among many.²³ Although to him it does not make a difference whether a bigger meal is consumed in the morning or in the evening, it does to the monkeys, and he understands why they are angry about the initial arrangement. One might still want to argue that perhaps the monkey trainer's successful negotiation of the situation was the result of mere luck instead of his ability to harmonize with the monkeys' vantage points. However, as will be shown, in several other stories the stakes are much higher than angering a few captive monkeys, which makes it unlikely that chance factors alone could plausibly account for successful communication with beings whose preferences and proclivities are different from one's own.

In the "In the Human World" (Ren jian shi 人間世) chapter, right before the story of a horse trainer who fails to understand the likes and dislikes of his own horses,²⁴ we are told a brief story about a successful tiger trainer:

> He [the tiger trainer] does not dare to use live animals to feed it [the tiger], for its killing of them would provoke its fury; [he] does not dare to use the

---

at the center stage of his survey of the history of the ancient Chinese philosophy of names, where the two often map onto a title/performance dynamic. This is central to one of Makeham's main argument that the linguistic domain in early China was closely intertwined with the creation and maintenance of the sociopolitical, moral, and cosmic order. See Makeham, *Name and Actuality in Early Chinese Thought*.

²¹ As Yearley notes, the image of the wheel resonates with expressions such as the pivot or axis of *daos* (道樞 *dao shu*), which was discussed in chapter 1, section 1.5, in relation to themes of flexibility and adapting to different situations. Lee H. Yearley, "Zhuangzi's Understanding of Skillfulness and the Ultimate Spiritual State," in *Essays on Skepticism, Relativism, and Ethics in the Zhuangzi*, ed. Paul Kjellberg and Philip J. Ivanhoe (Albany: State University of New York Press, 1996), 161. The imagery of the wheel in the story is explicitly tied to harmonizing different affects by making use of *shi/fei* judgments in affective ways (which confirms Yearley's reading); this is then described as walking both [ways] (*liang xing* 兩行).

²² The last three lines in Chinese read: 名實未虧，而喜怒為用，亦因是也。是以聖人和之以是非，而休乎天鈞，是之謂兩行。

²³ I owe this point to Ziporyn who notes that "merely staying fully within any single perspective actually brings with it the power to open outward into interaction with other perspectives, and to accommodate other viewpoints and other types of 'rights' and 'wrongs.'" Brook Ziporyn, "Zhuangzi as a Philosopher," hackettpublishing.com, https://hackettpublishing.com/zhuangziphil (accessed July 27, 2022).

²⁴ The horse trainer expresses his care for horses by collecting their excrement in a basket, only to be later kicked by them for swatting away a gadfly at the wrong time.

entirety of animals to feed it, for its rending of them would provoke its fury; [he] times out when to satisfy its hunger and comprehends its ferocious heart. Tigers and humans are of different types, but they fawn on and obey those who raise them. Thus, those who are killed are the ones who cross them. (4:172–173)

Considering the tiger's fatal temperament when aroused, it is safe to assume that the tiger trainer did not develop his technique on a trial-and-error basis. Moreover, his arrangements are as precise as determining the conditions of the food that is fed to the tiger so as not to provoke it to harm him, which requires a fitting sense of its affective dispositions. The tiger story appears as part of a larger story, which is placed among two other similar stories, all of which are about how to effectively serve a tyrannical person in a position of power.[25] All such stories are framed alongside the familiar theme of making the heart tenuous, which is credited with enabling one to achieve higher levels of sensitivity toward one's surroundings, leading to an ability to better hear others' affects as well. The chapter also gifts us with a convenient metaphor for such receptivity: recalibrating the heart (xin zhai 心齋).[26]

The metaphor appears in the context of a story about Yan Hui going to Kongzi to discuss his desire to travel to the state of Wei to reform a tyrant. After Yan Hui shares two different strategies that he has in mind, both of which involve forcefully interfering with the activities of the tyrant, he is

---

[25] The imagery of the tiger is generally used in early Chinese texts to refer to behavior that is violent and anti-social and is sometimes used to describe disagreeable people as well. For instance, Dadai Liji 大戴禮記 (Records of Rites compiled by Elder Dai) tells us that tigers and wolves, by birth, have covetous and violent hearts (Dadai Liji, 3.1/22/17–19 ["Bao Fu" 保傅]); the Liji draws a parallel between living among tigers and living under an oppressive government (Liji 4.56/15–18 ["Tan Gong Xia 檀弓下"]); the Xunzi describes a petty person as having the heart of wolves and tigers in addition to being chaotic and disagreeable (Xunzi 2.1); and Lunheng 論衡 (Discursive Weighing) offers an account of a meeting with Wei Liaozi (who is credited with having written a book on the methods war) and Qin Shi Huang (the first emperor) in which Wei Liaozi wisely gathers from the tiger-like appearance of the king that he has a bad character (Lunheng 121 ["Gu Xiang骨相"]). The story in the Zhuangzi is no exception, given that the story of the tiger-trainer appears alongside stories of dangerous people in positions of power. As explained in chapter 1, section 1.1, when interpreting the Zhuangzi, I avoid taking the "allegorical" and "literal" dimensions of the text to be mutually exclusive and instead take them as coexisting aspects that occur in many of the stories in the Zhuangzi, including the story of the tiger-trainer. References to the Dadai Liji give section, page, and line numbers in D. C. Lau, ed. A Concordance to the Dadai Liji (Hong Kong: Commercial Press, 1992). Citations to the Lunheng give page numbers to Huang Hui 黃暉. Lunheng jiaoshi 論衡校釋 (The explanations and annotations of the Discursive Weighing), (Beijing北京: Zhonghua Shuju 中華書局, 2011).

[26] For a discussion of different translations of xin zhai 心齋along with an explanation of my decision to render it as "recalibrating the heart," see Chapter 4, footnote 38.

advised to stop taking his heart as the master (*shi xin* 師心) and allow his heart to be recalibrated (*xin zhai* 心齋). When he asks what is meant by this phrase, Kongzi continues:

> Unify your resolve (*zhi* 志), do not listen with your ears, but listen with your heart; do not listen with your heart, but listen with your vital energy (*qi* 氣). Hearing stops at the ears, the heart stops at symbols (符 *fu*). As for vital energy, it is tenuous (*xu* 虛) and thus awaits (*dai* 待) things. Only the way (*dao* 道) gathers tenuousness. Tenuousness is what the recalibration of the heart is. (4:152)

Kongzi's answer here involves three interrelated pieces of advice, namely, not taking the heart as the master, listening with *qi*, and awaiting things. While these suggestions are meant to guide one's interaction with other beings, they also explain how affects travel between different subjects and beings.

Qi 氣 is an essential notion within Chinese cosmology, although much of how we assume it is used in ancient texts relies on reconstructions of its origins from later usages. Common translations of the term include "breath" but also "vital energy" or simply "stuff" "out of which all things condense and into which they dissolve."[27] Although it is not clear whether the *Zhuangzi* submits to a full-fledged *qi*-based cosmology, there are glimpses in it of the worldview that recognizes *qi* as breath (or what one might call "pneuma") while simultaneously taking different phenomena to be also unfolding out of different configurations of *qi*.[28] The word "phenomena" here is used in its widest semantic scope to include affects as well, which is why *qi* also plays

---

[27] A. C. Graham, *Disputers of the Tao: Philosophical Argument in Ancient China* (Chicago: Open Court, 1989), 101. The exact nature of the relationship between the two senses of *qi* 氣, that is "breath" and "stuff," in early Chinese texts remains ambiguous. As Csikszentmihalyi notes, recent work on oracle bones suggests that "the original use of the term was to describe external influence allied with early concepts of wind (*feng* 風) and that its projection into the body was probably a secondary meaning." Csikszentmihalyi, *Material Virtue*, 144. However, Baxter and Sagart's Old Chinese reconstruction suggests a connection between *qi* 气/氣 and *xi* 吸 (to breathe), which potentially reverses the narrative about which sense came before the other. Baxter and Sagart, *Old Chinese*, 170. At any rate, as Csikszentmihalyi adds, in Warring States and early imperial periods, both senses of the term were used in relation to the body and its proper functioning (Csikszentmihalyi, *Material Virtue*, 144). As I argue in the next sentence, at least some portions of the *Zhuangzi* suggest awareness of a model in which the two senses are connected.

[28] In the chapter titled "Knowing that Wanders in the North" (Zhi bei you 知北游), we are told that "the human life is about accumulation of *qi* 氣. [*Qi* 氣] accumulates and there is life; disperses and there is death" (*Zhuangzi* 22:730). We are also told, "The myriad things are all one.... Thus it is said, 'Throughout all the world is *qi* 氣 and that is all'" (*Zhuangzi* 22:730).

an integral role in early Chinese theories of self-cultivation.[29] In fact, it is not uncommon for early Chinese texts to speak of six cosmic *qi* (originating from a more primordial *qi*) that form the basis of the fundamental affective tendencies: likes, dislikes, pleasure, anger, sorrow, and joy (*haowu xinu aile* 好惡喜怒哀樂). This would explain why Kongzi in the aforementioned dialogue speaks of the cultivation of affective attunement in terms of listening with *qi*.[30]

The heart (*xin* 心), just like the rest of the body, has constitutive roots in and is energized by *qi*. When interacting with things in the world, reactions

---

[29] The fact that *qi* was conceptualized as a force that is operating on multiple and intercrossing levels—where it not only causes construction and destruction of life forms but also enables the material and mental transformations that a particular life form goes through—certainly made it inevitable that it would play a significant role in both medical and moral discourses. The excavated Warring States text *Xing Zi Ming Chu* serves as a good example of the latter context of use, where *qi* is seen to play a key role in the way characteristic tendencies (*xing* 性) give rise to certain affects and judgments. *Xing Zi Ming Chu* also suggests that *qi* could be rearranged and redirected in various directions, which is the reason it also plays an integral role in early Ru moral discourses. On this point, see Franklin Perkins, "Motivation and the Heart in the *Xing Zi Ming Chu*," *Dao* 8 (2009):117–131. Also see Csikszentmihalyi, *Material Virtue*, 5–14.

[30] The relation between *qi*, heart, and affects is mentioned in *Mengzi* 2A2 as well, except that the *Mengzi* gives a central role to the heart and articulates a theory of self-cultivation that is based on regulating the movements of *qi* and one's affective responses. For an in-depth examination of the relation between *qi*, heart, and affects in the *Mengzi*, see Alan Kam-Leung Chan, "A Matter of Taste: Qi (Vital Energy) and the Tending of the Heart (*Xin*) in Mencius 2A2," in *Mencius: Contexts and Interpretations*, ed. Alan Kam-Leung Chan (Honolulu: University of Hawai'i Press, 2002), 42–71. Aside from *Xing Zi Ming Chu* (which is mentioned in footnote 29) and the *Mengzi*, the relation between *qi* and affects is also discussed in the *Chunqiu Zuozhuan* 春秋左傳 (*Zuo's Commentary on Spring and Autumn Annals*; henceforth *Zuozhuan*), which speaks of the six main affects being born out of six *qi* (and in the same work the six kinds of *qi* are also identified as *yin*, *yang*, wind, rain, darkness, and light). See *Zuozhuan*, Zhao 25. 3: 1636–1639 and *Zuozhuan*, Zhao 1.12, 3: 1330–1331. References to the *Zuozhuan* give section, volume, and page numbers in Stephen W. Durrant, Wai-yee Li, and David Schaberg, trans., *Zuo Tradition/Zuozhuan* 左傳: *Commentary on the "Spring and Autumn Annals"* (Seattle: Washington University Press, 2016). When it comes to the *Zhuangzi*, the text refers to "one *qi*" in 6:273 and 22:730 and "six *qi*" in 1:19 and 11:395. There is also a mention of "receiving *qi* from *yin* and *yang* (*shou qi yu yin yang* 受氣於陰陽)" in 17:563 and the statement that "*yin* and *yang* are *qi* that is large" (*yin yang zhe, qi zhi da zhe ye* 陰陽者，氣之大者也) in 25:905. Hence, it seems, at least for some authors and compilers of the *Zhuangzi*, one primordial *qi* comes to be differentiated into *yin* and *yang*, which then eventually differentiate into six kinds of *qi*. It should be noted that the exact enumeration of the basic affects changes in the *Zhuangzi*. In 23:804, for instance, we see *yu* 欲 (to desire) instead of *hao* 好 (to like or be fond of) being listed next to the other five affects. The *Zhuangzi* sometimes also simply refers to "likes and dislikes" (*hao wu* 好惡), "sorrow and joy" (*ai le* 哀樂), and "pleasure and sorrow" (*xi nü* 喜怒) as a shorthand for basic affects in general (see *Zhuangzi* 5:227, 18:620, 11:375, 3:134, 4:161, 6:265, 22: 761). Hence although, as seen earlier in *Xing Zi Ming Chu* and *Zuo Zhuan*, "likes and dislikes" (*hao wu* 好惡) serve as the most basic of the six affects and establish the foundation for the other four affects, the *Zhuangzi* does not take a definitive position on which affects are more primordial than others. Finally, the connection between affects and *qi* is taken for granted not only in the aforementioned dialogue between Yan Hui and Kongzi, but it is also hinted at in the "The Discourse that Levels Things" (Qi wu lun 齊物論) chapter in the context of the parallel drawn between the wind (which Graham takes to be referring to *qi* in general) and the free-flowing movement of various affects. See A. C. Graham, trans., *Chuang Tzu: The Inner Chapters* (London: George Allen and Unwin, 1981), 52.

to likes and dislikes, pleasure and anger, sorrow and joy are animated by *qi* and arise from the heart. None of the affective reactions are necessarily bad.[31] However, when such affects settle deep inside the heart instead of freely moving in and out of it, then our capacity to be in tune with the affective aspects of our surroundings becomes limited. The heart seems to play some role in the mobility of affects by absorbing certain sets of judgments, which are then intertwined with what we become disposed to like and dislike, and so on.[32]

Kongzi tells Yan Hui to recalibrate his heart, render it tenuous, and let *qi* take over, because *qi*, we are told, simply "awaits things." The character that is generally translated as "await" (*dai* 待) conveys a sense of attending to something or depending on other things, which here is used together with (the tenuous) *qi* and the tenuous heart (which is not in the position of the master anymore), further strengthening the meaning of "await" as receptivity to things. Finally, as Fraser notes, these "things" (*wu* 物) that *qi* is awaiting are not limited to physical objects, but include events and states of affairs[33] (and, in fact, anything that is observable and appears as individuated).[34] Hence, human (and nonhuman) beings and their lives are part of "things" (*wu* 物), which means that others' interests, values, and needs will be among the things one "hears" when one "listens with the *qi*."[35] In a nutshell, when one makes the heart tenuous and listens to the world with *qi*, then one can hear the affects of others without them being overwritten with one's established affective dispositions.

---

[31] A possible exception to this observation is a passage in the "The Graven Intentions" (Keyi 刻意) chapter, which reads: "Thus it is said that sorrow and happiness are deviations of potency, that joy and anger are oversteppings of the Way, that liking and disliking are misplacements of potency. It is when the heart is without sorrow or happiness that the potency is ultimate (故曰：悲樂者，德之邪；喜怒者，道之過；好惡者，德之失。故心不憂樂，德之至也). *Zhuangzi* 15:543.

[32] This intertwinement is obvious in the dialogue between Huizi and Zhuangzi that concludes chapter 5 of the received *Zhuangzi*. The dialogue is discussed in section 2.6. Moreover, according to *Mengzi*, the heart's resolution directs the movements of *qi*. *Mengzi* in 2A2 speaks of the way one's resoluteness (*zhi* 志) guides the activity of *qi*: "Your resolution is the master of *qi* . . . when your resolution is settled somewhere, the *qi* also settles there" (夫志，氣之帥也,,,夫志至焉，氣次焉). The dialogue between Yan Hui and Kongzi is often interpreted as a response to *Mengzi* 2A2, in which case Kongzi's advice could be taken to be about not controlling the movements of *qi*.

[33] Fraser, "Psychological Emptiness," 140.

[34] As discussed in chapter 1, *wu* 物 denotes any observable phenomena, anything that has appearance, image, sound, color, and so on. This description could be interpreted to mean that *wu* 物 refers to anything that appears as individuated and distinct. This is, of course, not to suggest that there are preestablished phenomena that are individuated and distinct independently of human observers. Indeed, as Perkins demonstrates, the discourse of individuation, structured around the term *wu* 物 (things), does not fall on either side of the "objective data" versus "subjective construct" distinction (Perkins, "What Is a Thing [*wu* 物]?," 62). See also Chapter 4, footnote 47 on this point.

[35] Fraser, "Psychological Emptiness," 140.

This line of reasoning, which suggests one could cultivate a heightened attunement to the affects of others, begs two questions. First, when a human "hears" the joy of fish or the anger of a tiger, are they similar to the joys and angers of humans? To clarify the question with an example, we do know that different circumstances give rise to the joy of fish versus of Zhuangzi (the former has joy when it wanders in rivers whereas the latter has joy when wandering on Hao bridge together with his sparring pal), but when the affect of joy has been roused, is it a similar kind joy? Second, who can perform this form of heightened listening discussed in the text (i.e., listening with *qi*) and what are the conditions for cultivating it?

The answers to both questions rely on admittedly fragmentary textual evidence that might yet still shed some light on relevant matters. For the first question, across early Chinese texts we see numerous suggestions of affects being tied to, if not being made up of, different configurations of *qi*, which is to say that there are commonalities underlying different affects. In fact, as Csikszentmihalyi observes, this is what enables "weighing" (*quan* 權) of different affective states in quandary situations, where, let us say, one has to weigh the feeling of propriety against the feeling of compassion.[36] As Csikszentmihalyi further notes, this is not to suggest that all affective states are "apples," but that "both apples and oranges may be weighed on the same scale."[37] In other words, affects are both similar and different in the sense that they are different configurations of a shared underlying mechanism. Traces of this line of reasoning can be found in the *Zhuangzi* as well, as one passage draws an analogy between different affects emerging out of the heart and music flowing out of hollows, suggesting that different affects are similar to different tunes or sounds.[38]

What does this imply about the affects of different creatures? Many contemporaneous texts suggest a continuity between affective states of humans and animals so much so that the latter even exhibit affects with moral implications (such as caring for one's kin or mourning after the loss of one's kin).[39] Although this might strike one as a case of anthropomorphizing animal reactions, as Schäfer, Siebert, and Sterckx note, these observed affective similarities between humans and animals were not formulated by using humans as a yardstick but by emphasizing certain features of the cosmos that

---

[36] Csikszentmihalyi, *Material Virtue*, 160.
[37] Csikszentmihalyi, *Material Virtue*, 126.
[38] *Zhuangzi* 2:57.
[39] Michael Nylan, "Humans as Animals and Things," 3–4, 6–7.

underlie everything.⁴⁰ When it comes to humans and animals, for instance, we are often told that both groups are creatures of "blood and *qi*," which is a feature that is also associated with having a heart and hence also various cognitive and affective states.⁴¹ Some sources, however, note that animals have "coarse" (*cu* 粗) or "unregulated" (*luan* 亂) *qi*, which is then contrasted with the ostensibly "fine" (*jing* 精) *qi* of human beings.⁴² Although being endowed with "fine" *qi* is a state to be cultivated, that still does not change the gradation implied in the evaluation of affects, according to which animal affects appear to be not as developed, let alone institutionalized, as those of humans.

In the *Zhuangzi*, we do not see suggestions of animal affects being coarser or less "regulated" than those of humans, while we do see indirect intimations of the absence of such a hierarchy.⁴³ Nonetheless, awareness of a possible difference is still present in the text, as can be seen in Huizi's reaction to Zhuangzi's observation about the joy of fish in the aforementioned episode. Zhuangzi does not counter Huizi's skepticism with a self-assured discourse about the nature of affects but with a playful answer that negotiates the possible similarity and difference between his joy and the joy of fish, which parallels the similarities and differences that might also exist between Zhuangzi and Huizi.

Whereas Zhuangzi's belief that he can tell that the fish is joyful implies assumptions of an underlying commonality between him and the fish (which makes possible the very communication of affects), his qualification of that claim by drawing attention to his own situatedness points to unassimilable differences between him and the fish—which, nonetheless, do not unfold on a hierarchical scale developed around group-specific variances. A similar negotiation between assumptions of likeness and vigilance about differences between one and the other seems to be at work in descriptions of

---

⁴⁰ Dagmar Schäfer, Martina Siebert, and Roel Sterckx, "Knowing Animals in China's History: An Introduction," in *Animals through Chinese History: Earliest Times to 1911*, ed. Roel Sterckx, Martina Siebert, and Dagmar Schäfer (Cambridge: Cambridge University Press, 2019), 6.

⁴¹ See Sterckx, *The Animal and the Daemon*, 73–76.

⁴² See Sterckx, *The Animal and the Daemon*, 74. As Sterckx adds, there is an intersectional dimension to such gestures of hierarchizing affective and cognitive states of different beings as well, given that unregulated *qi* is also associated with alien peoples, such as Rong and Di (Sterckx, *The Animal and the Daemon*, 74).

⁴³ So Jeong PARK observes that *Zhuangzi*'s philosophy of music undermines the conventional hierarchy between sound (*sheng* 聲) and note or tone (*yin* 音), which maps onto the distinction between animals and human beings (in the sense that animals ostensibly only know sounds, but not tones, which then separates them from human beings). This is significant considering that in classical Ru discourse with musical refinement comes affective refinement. For further reading, see So Jeong PARK, "On Sound: Reconstructing a Zhuangzian Perspective of Music," *Humanities* 5 (2016): 3, DOI: 10.3390/h5010003.

recalibrating the heart as well, which enables one to hear the affects of others without one's own deeply entrenched affective states overriding those affects.

This brings us to the other question regarding who can perform this form of heightened listening and the conditions to cultivate it. When we, again, look at contemporaneous texts, we see a pattern of associating perceptual acuity with sagacious people (*shengren* 聖人) who have a heightened ability to perceive *qing* 情—a term that can refer to either circumstances or affective states, depending on the context.[44] Sometimes even prophetic abilities are attributed to such people, which, as Csikszentmihalyi observes, could actually be tied to their heightened ability to take in affects and even subtler affective dispositions, which, after all, could be seen as "incipient manifestations that carry within them a sign of the potential for future events."[45]

As for attaining such sagacious abilities, it requires an expansion of one's horizon, which could be facilitated by familiarity with the legacies of past sages, if not contact with living sages. In texts associated with the Ru, this also implies participation in traditional rites and rituals, with the understanding they were established through a penetrating discernment of the patterns of the world, especially relational patterns that knit together and structure human society. Acculturating oneself in the ways of tradition builders can thus help one understand the very reasoning behind the rituals (the main one being elucidation of human relations) and develop similar insights into the subtle workings of the world, especially of human society.[46]

Markers of sagacity sometimes also include instructing others.[47] This is perhaps also why depictions of close and long-standing relationships

---

[44] This perceptual acuity of sagacious people is often described in terms of their aural abilities. As Ning Chen observes, the word *sheng*聖 (sagacious, sage) itself was used in Shang oracle descriptions to convey the meaning "to hear" and by extension "to listen to the state of affairs." Ning Chen, "The Etymology of *Sheng* (Sage) and Its Confucian Conception in Early China," *Journal of Chinese Philosophy* 27, no. 4 (December 2000): 420. As Brown and Bergeton demonstrate, visual abilities too were sometimes mentioned in relation to sagacity. This agrees with Geaney's broader observation that early Chinese epistemology of the senses emphasized tallying the input of ears with that of eyes. See Miranda Brown and Uffe Bergeton, "'Seeing' Like a Sage: Three Takes on Identity and Perception in Early China," *Journal of Chinese Philosophy* 35, no. 4 (2008): 641–662. Also see Geaney, *On the Epistemology of the Senses*.

[45] Csikszentmihalyi, *Material Virtue*, 170.

[46] This is also why, as Angle points out, paying attention to rituals, along with the roles and duties they imply, inherently helps one attend to the needs and desires of those around us. See Stephen C. Angle, *Growing Moral: A Confucian Guide to Life* (Oxford: Oxford University Press, 2022), 95.

[47] For this reason, we see inquiries, if not assumptions, about the master's sagely status from their own disciples (although the virtue of modesty can require one to deny one's own sageliness, which then serves as yet another marker of one's said sageliness). See, for instance, *Mozi* 87/48/77 and *Mengzi* 2A2 (which include a discussion of the possible sagely status of both Kongzi and Mengzi). It should also be noted that the *Mengzi* sets the standard for the instructive reach of a sage quite high when he notes that "a sage is a teacher of a hundred generations" (聖人，百世之師也). *Mengzi* 7B15.

between masters and their students are abundant in early Chinese texts. The textual communities surrounding a living master or the legacy of a master then take on a self-justifying dimension, which grants further validation to a life of tutelage and further authority to the master helping one converse with the workings of the world. Now, although the *Zhuangzi* has a complicated relationship with the very title of *shengren*, given that it sometimes openly criticizes sages for their pedantry and sometimes offers what seem like satirical alternatives to sages—such as *zhenren* 真人 (genuine people) or *zhiren* 至人 (utmost people)—it does have room for the cultivation of perspicacity.[48] However, the text unfetters the cultivation of perceptual acuity from the bonds of tutelage, which, at the same time (and perhaps for the same reason) democratizes the acquisition of heightened perceptiveness.

Certainly, a large number of stories in the *Zhuangzi* still include what could be seen as "teaching scenes," which is expected given that, as Stalnaker points out, "relations of master to student are simply presumed as the social matrix in which much of life happens in the *Zhuangzi*."[49] However, within these scenes, who and what counts as a teacher is persistently being questioned and reversed, as can be seen in one depiction of Kongzi who asks to be taught by his own student Yan Hui.[50] We also see tentative and objectionable (if not deliberately ridiculous)[51] masters triggering a fleeting teaching moment, which is decidedly different from seeking to become established in the role of a master.[52]

---

[48] For a detailed defense of the argument that what are often taken to be exemplars of authenticity, such as *zhenren* and *zhiren*, are actually satirical alternatives to *shengren* 聖人 (sagely person) and ideals of sageliness, see Hans-Georg Moeller and Paul J. D'Ambrosio, *Genuine Pretending: On the Philosophy of the* Zhuangzi (New York: Columbia University Press, 2017), 112, 135–136, 155–156.

[49] Aaron Stalnaker, "Mastery, Authority, and Hierarchy in the 'Inner Chapters' of the *Zhuāngzǐ*," *Soundings: An Interdisciplinary Journal* 95, no. 3 (2012): 264.

[50] *Zhuangzi* 6:288–290. An even more well-known episode features a butcher who shares his wisdom about how to be a good butcher with a ruler, who then deduces lessons about how to nourish life (*yang sheng* 養生) in general. See *Zhuangzi* 3:123–130

[51] See the episode that features a certain sage named Lady Ju who traces her intellectual lineage to a series of ridiculous-sounding sources, such as "Repeated-Recitation's Grandson" and "Dubious Beginning" (*Zhuangzi* 6:257–261). Another example is Robber Zhi, who in the twenty-ninth chapter of the received text (which is named after him), lectures Kongzi about the entanglement between morality and power. See *Zhuangzi* 29:983–997.

[52] In fact, when we examine the formal traits of the teaching scenes in the *Zhuangzi*, we see that they are set up to upend familiar models of master-disciple dynamics. As Defoort notes, among these traits are depictions of role-reversals; portrayals of objectionable masters (mutilated ex-convicts, women, craftsmen, and so on); and descriptions of these objectionable masters actively engaged in activities other than teaching (fishing, slaughtering oxen, catching cicadas, and so on), which emphasizes the lack of investment in the activity of teaching itself. See Carine Defoort, "Instruction Dialogues." In relation to the lack of investment mentioned by Defoort, a related feature of the alternative-teaching scenes in the *Zhuangzi* is what Levinovitz describes as the "reluctant teacher set-up," in which people find themselves in the position of delivering an awe-inspiring speech even

Given that so much of the discourse on communication of affects in the *Zhuangzi* revolves around a criticism of the pretense to know what is best for others, it is not surprising that the ability to hear others' tastes, preferences, and emotional states in their own terms blooms outside of the power dynamic of a master and a disciple. Here, one cannot help but wonder: What about the companionship of equals? Does it aid one's cultivation of perspicacity? More crucially, with all the seeming tenuousness of human groupings, which makes it difficult to assess the extent of their similarity or difference from each other, how much a shared affective foundation is there for the flourishing of human companionship? It is left unresolved in the text whether Zhuangzi can really relate to the joy of fish or not, but what about his rapport with Huizi? Is there something unique about their liaison or is that also not that different from Zhuangzi chancing upon fish or a praying mantis? The next section explores the status of human companionship in the *Zhuangzi* with a focus on the affect of joy grounded in a shared sense of humor that trades on incongruity. As will be shown, however, the bonds of non-hierarchical human friendship portrayed in the text are often non-committal in nature, and what grounds these transient bonds is also what opens up one's affective purview to nonhuman others.

5.3 Bonding through Banter and Laughter

It could be argued that the very abundance of dialogues that culminate in someone gaining an insight[53] suggests that at least some members of the textual community that produced the *Zhuangzi* thought that people are able to improve each other's various skills. A well-known example of the portrayal of human companionship is the recurrent rapport between Zhuangzi and

---

though they have not sought and sometimes even resent being put in that position. Levinovitz adds that "the reluctant teacher setup can be understood as a metaphor for the structure of the *Zhuangzi*." See Alan Levinovitz, "The *Zhuangzi* and *You* (遊): Defining An Ideal without Contradiction," *Dao* 11, no. 4 (2012): 489.

[53] At the end of such dialogues, the listener often announces that he has gained a valuable insight. Reporting the audience's reaction, which often involves praising the speaker's words, is another literary gesture that the text commonly employs and is possibly used to give weight to the words of an otherwise objectionable teacher who ultimately inspires insight into someone important. As noted in chapter 4, section 4.4, in the context of the story of the swimmer who ends up delivering a mini-lecture to Kongzi, there is also often a humorous and political dimension to such dialogues in the sense that we get to imagine a scene in which someone with a lowly social status lectures a man holding a position of power.

Huizi, who are seen bantering back and forth on a wide array of topics. In fact, as Denecke notes, the *Zhuangzi* is peculiar among received Masters texts for giving to its eponymous master figure a companion "who is certainly often pushed around as a mindless sophist, but who is also truly appreciated as a helping hand for Zhuangzi's own intellectual enterprise."[54]

Aside from the presence of several playful dialogues between the two characters, in which it is not always clear whether Huizi annoys or amuses Zhuangzi (maybe both?), an explicit commentary on their friendship is also presented in a chapter titled "Ghostless Xu" (Xu wugui 徐無鬼), by the character of Zhuangzi himself. The scene opens with Zhuangzi passing the grave of Huizi. Zhuangzi tells the story of an artisan who once managed to remove with his axe a piece of plaster that was stuck on someone's nose. When asked to do it again later, the artisan refused, noting that the owner of that nose was now dead. Zhuangzi then says, "Since the master [Huizi] died, I [too] do not have material to work with, I do not have anyone to talk to."[55]

The analogy Zhuangzi offers to describe his relationship with Huizi is a rich and evocative one. Guo Xiang's commentary interprets the story as conveying the experience of bereavement for a mate or counterpart (*sang'ou* 喪偶),[56] leaving no doubt about Zhuangzi's heartfelt fondness for his sparring partner. Galvany also rightly points out that the simile Zhuangzi uses suggests a high degree of trust on the part of Huizi.[57] However, a more cynical interpretation would point out that the analogy still does not suggest a relationship of two equals, given that it places Huizi in the position of a sidekick.[58] However, even without assuming that Zhuangzi was mourning

---

[54] Wiebke Denecke, *The Dynamics of Masters Literature: Early Chinese Thought from Confucius to Han Feizi* (Cambridge, MA: Harvard University Asia Center, 2011), 267. Another exception Denecke does not count is the sustained exchange between Gaozi and Mengzi in Book VI of *Mengzi*. I owe this observation to Jeremy Huang.

[55] 自夫子之死也，吾無以為質矣，吾無與言之矣。(*Zhuangzi* 24:836). I am indebted to Franklin Perkins for bringing this particular passage to my attention.

[56] *Zhuangzi* 24:837. *Sang'ou* 喪偶 is generally used in the context of being bereaved of one's spouse.

[57] Albert Galvany, "Distorting the Rule of Seriousness: Laughter, Death, and Friendship in the *Zhuangzi*," *Dao* 8, no. 1 (2009), 54n5

[58] The complicated relationship between the two characters is suggested in the opening chapter of the text, which begins with a story about a vast fish transforming into a vast bird. The large bird then gets laughed at by small birds who fail to understand why the large bird flies so high. The chapter ends with Huizi ridiculing Zhuangzi for the vastness (and yet uselessness) of his words, only to be reciprocally mocked by Zhuangzi for the smallness of his understanding. The parallel between the small bird and Huizi, on one hand, and the large bird and Zhuangzi, on the other, is made explicit in the 秋水 [Autumn floods] chapter in which Huizi (who in the story occupies a minor official position and is afraid Zhuangzi might want to steal his job) is likened to an owl that once caught a rat and is now screeching at a phoenix flying past over his head. Of course, the hierarchy between the small bird/small understanding and the large bird/vast understanding could also be challenged, considering that, as Nylan notes, the large bird "despite its extraordinary size and strength, despite its godlike

Huizi's death the way one would mourn the loss of an intellectual companion of equal status, his remark nonetheless highlights the irreplaceable value of his relationship with Huizi.

Aside from the duo of Zhuangzi and Huizi, the text offers other examples of human camaraderie, which are all pointedly fleeting in nature. An example of such a dynamic is offered in a chapter titled "The Great Source as Teacher" (Da zong shi 大宗師):

> Zisanghu, Mengzifan, and Ziqinzhang came together in friendship, saying, "Who can be together in their not being together, do things for one another by not doing things for one another? Who can climb up upon the Heavens, roaming on the mists, twisting and turning round and round without limit, living their lives in mutual forgetfulness, never coming to an end?" The three of them looked at one another and burst out laughing, feeling complete concord, and thus did they become friends. After a short silence, without warning, Zisanghu fell down dead. Before his burial, Kongzi got the news and sent Zigong to pay his respects. There he found them, one of them composing music, the other plucking the zither, and finally both of them singing together in harmony: . . . "You've returned to what we are really, while we're still humans—wow, yippee!"[59]

Many features of the episode align with concurrent motifs in the text. Despite the portrayal of the character of Zhuangzi as mourning for Huizi, the *Zhuangzi*, in fact, is better known for undermining traditional mourning practices,[60] as the two friends in the story do.[61] The characters' calm attitude toward death itself resonates with the way the text throws into question the intrinsic value of many things, which in this story includes the value

---

ability and the superior vantage point from which it surveys all phenomena" "can see no more and no less than the mere mortals below." See Michael Nylan, *The Chinese Pleasure Book*, 232.

[59] *Zhuangzi* 6:269–271. For this passage, I largely followed Ziporyn's translation. See Ziporyn, *Zhuangzi: The Complete Writings*, 59.

[60] As further explored in chapter 8, section 8.2, this is not simply an anti-establishment gesture but is also a critique of clinging onto certain roles (of father, husband, disciple, and/or friend) and relational behavior patterns.

[61] The outrageous nature of what the remaining two friends were doing at the funeral of Zisanghu is acknowledged and highlighted in the story through Zigong's reaction. As Galvany notes, the *Liji* is also rich with passages that do not approve of playing instruments while mourning, including a passage that shows Kongzi praising a man named Meng Xianzi 孟獻子 for refusing to play his instruments even after the end of the three-year mourning period. Galvany, "Distorting the Rule of Seriousness," 56–57.

of human life. It is perhaps also not surprising that the condition for their friendship is that they can be together in not being together (*neng xiang yu yu wuxiang yu* 能相與於無相與) and can live their lives in mutual forgetfulness (*xiang wang yi sheng* 相忘以生). Such a friendship is certainly paradoxical in nature in that these three men "bond" with each other through their ability to not be over-attached to things and people.

Perhaps what stands out as most striking in this episode is the laughter that seals the friendship of the three characters, which is then followed by the surprisingly sudden death of Zisanghu. Later in the episode, the remaining two characters laugh again when Zigong protests that they are not mourning the death of their friend properly. Although much has been said about satire and mockery in the *Zhuangzi*, relatively less attention has been given to the depictions of guileless laughter in the text.[62] The laughter that seizes the three (and then the two) friends right before and after the death of one of them not only highlights the outrageous and the absurd elements of the story, but it also conveys the like-mindedness of men who spontaneously bond with one another.[63] Although the story concerns people who paradoxically bond over their mutual forgetfulness (which perhaps is what they are initially laughing at),[64] they acknowledge each other and their shared sense of absurdity before they laugh (we are told that they look at each other before laughing [*xiang shi er xiao* 相視而笑]).[65]

---

[62] It should be noted that because the semantic range of "*xiao* 笑" includes both "to smile" and "to laugh," the exact number of instances in which characters in the *Zhuangzi* are "laughing" is ultimately open to interpretation. Following Galvany's analysis, I take *xiao* 笑 to be referring to laughter when the characters seem to be placed on stage "to shock and to subvert" or when the story has heavily pronounced elements of incongruity and excess. See Galvany, "Distorting the Rule of Seriousness," 53–54. This applies to passages that deal with the issue of death in ways that defy conventional mourning protocols, not only due to characters' calm attitudes in the face of death but also due to depictions of unabashed singing and music playing at funerals.

[63] In the story right before this we are offered another similar episode: "Zisi, Ziyu, Zili and Zilai, these four men were talking to each other when one of them said: 'Who can take nothingness as the head, life as the spine, and death as the rump? Who knows that life and death, surviving and being lost, are all one body? He shall be my friend.' Then, the four men looked at each other and laughed. None was unwilling in his heart (*mo ni yu xin* 莫逆於心), and so they all became friends." (*Zhuangzi* 6:263).

[64] The affinity between laughter and instances of incongruity has been most famously noted by Schopenhauer. See Arthur Schopenhauer, *The World as Will and Idea: 3 Volumes in 1*, trans. R. B. Haldane and J. Kemp (Scotts Valley: CreateSpace Independent Publishing Platform, 2016), 39. The affinity between incongruity, on the one hand, and humor in general, on the other, in the context of the *Zhuangzi* is studied in detail in Moeller and D'Ambrosio, *Genuine Pretending: On the Philosophy of the* Zhuangzi.

[65] This phrase is repeated twice in the aforementioned story and also in two other analogous tales (that concern norm-defying people bonding with each other) featured in the "Yielding Sovereignty" (Rang wang 讓王) and "The Great Source as Teacher" (Da zong shi 大宗師) chapters. See *Zhuangzi* 28:980 and 6:263.

If one wants to find clear instances of joyful human sociality in the *Zhuangzi*, then stories of odd folks who delight in each other's company and laugh together without committing to lifelong relationship bonds come closest. The transient nature of these odd friendships is not coincidental, given that part of what bonds such people to each other is their shared acceptance of all the changes that life offers.[66] The laughter that erupts spontaneously between them is a testimony to their emotionally unentangled perspective on life, which they preserve in the aftermath of the sudden and fittingly ludicrous death of Zisanghu. As anyone who reads this story in a group setting (such as in a classroom) can testify, the story always induces surprise and laughter in the audience while simultaneously insulating them (just like the friends in the story) from feelings of pity for the character who suddenly dies. This odd bond forged by laughter emotionally distances the laughers (which include both the characters and the audience of the work) from an otherwise troubling situation while also spontaneously and temporarily bringing them closer to one another through the complicity they share in taking something like death so lightly.

This particular type of amusement might be viewed as a typically human-specific phenomenon (both in general and in the context of the *Zhuangzi*). In the *Zhuangzi*, we witness animal lust, joy, anger, frustration, and playfulness, but only once do we see animals laugh. Even then, the animals in question (a cicada and a dove) seem to exhibit sardonic laughter (instead of laughter stemming from delight in the absurdity of a situation)[67] and the whole episode appears to be an allegory about misjudgment of a situation due to one's own narrow-mindedness.[68] Given that it is people who are associated with forming conceptual patterns and expectations about the world, it is perhaps not surprising that both the perception of absurdity (which relies on something going against certain expectations) and the

---

[66] Galvany also points out a possible association of the acceptance of life and death and with the emergence of a friendship, drawing a parallel between the non-hierarchical aspect of a friendship and death as the ultimate equalizer that does not differentiate between social status or rank. Galvany, "Distorting the Rule of Seriousness," 53–55.

[67] These two types of laughter map onto the superiority and incongruity theories of laughter—the former being associated with haughtiness and the latter with wit and the ability to enjoy some violation of our cognitive and affective patterns and expectations. For a brief overview of different theories of humor, see Hans-Georg Moeller, "Humor and Its Philosophical Significance in the *Zhuangzi*," in *Dao Companion to the Philosophy of the* Zhuangzi, ed. Kim-chong Chong (New York: Springer, 2022), 294. Moeller's piece focuses on instances of incongruous humor in the *Zhuangzi*.

[68] To be more specific, the episode concerns small animals not being able to understand the needs and wants of a much larger animal.

accompanying laughter appear to be a typically human phenomenon. Moreover, joining in friendship appears to take place only among human characters.[69]

Certainly, this might be a coincidence or an editing choice on the part of Guo Xiang, but even when one adopts the strong reading and assumes that both delighting in incongruity and the bond that is formed through such shared delight are indeed human-specific phenomena in the *Zhuangzi*, neither of these components of human existence are ever employed as tools to seal the borders separating people from animals. Then again, this latter aspect of the text might also be a mere coincidence. However, considering the conditions that give rise to the kind of laughter we see among the friends portrayed in the *Zhuangzi*, the text's philosophy of humor, so to speak, and its philosophy of intersubjective relations share the same underlying attitude: active affirmation of the unfamiliar and the bizarre. Humor, in the *Zhuangzi*, figures as a tool to gracefully submit to what one cannot understand or control. Moreover, parallel to the way the text turns the stratified structures of the teacher-master relationship upside down by offering us objectionable and ridiculous masters, it mobilizes humor to level hierarchies.[70]

This chapter opened with a story about different creatures having different values and preferences. In its very first pages, the received *Zhuangzi* itself features a similar story about myriad creatures having different vantage points, and also includes a curious reference to an allegedly classic text named the *Equalizing Joke* (*Qi Xie* 齊諧).[71] This is often taken to be a joke in itself (as there is no such known classic), but it could also be a self-reference (to the *Zhuangzi* as the book of jokes that equalizes things). In the *Zhuangzi*, things are not "equal" in the sense that they are the "same" but rather in the

---

[69] At least, there is no mention of animals joining in friendship (*xiang yu you* 相與友) or becoming friends (*wei you* 為友).

[70] As discussed in chapter 4, section 4.1, leveling hierarchies, not only in the sociopolitical sense but in a general sense, appear as a recurring theme in the text. It is no coincidence that a text that gives voice to marginalized vantage points weaponizes humor to dismantle well-established structures of power. As Cynthia Willett notes, subaltern studies also has "established that ridicule and other forms of humor serve not only as accessories of cruelty and props of power but also provide discourses and technologies of reversals." See Cynthia Willett, *Interspecies Ethics* (New York: Columbia University Press, 2014), 30.

[71] Here I am following Ziporyn's translation of *Qi Xie* 齊諧 as "Equalizing Jokebook," which is more in the spirit of the text and its opening chapter (which is where it appears). Ziporyn, *Zhuangzi: The Complete Writings*, 3.

sense that they are difficult to rank.⁷² This applies to their affects as well. Despite their shared commonalities, they also enjoy particularity without gradation. In fact, the only obvious case that admits some semblance of gradation concerns the difference between letting affects seep deep into one's heart (just as the judgments accompanying them do) versus successfully recalibrating the heart (and rendering it tenuous), both of which, at least in the extant text, are used in relation to people.⁷³

In the final analysis, a key consideration for this study revolves around how the discourse around the affects of different beings is actually mobilized in the text. In the *Zhuangzi*, regardless of whether human and animal affective experiences are similar or not, the focus remains on the detrimental consequences of assuming one knows what is best for others. Certainly, attuned sensitivity to the preferences of other beings (for the sake of the efficacy of one's actions, if nothing else) is not the only direction one could take after acknowledging affective variance among different beings. One could also read differences along the lines of an "us versus them"—if not "I versus other"—split and exploit the situation to alienate the affects of others.

This latter line of thought is at times employed by Spinoza, who, instead of being concerned about bringing inadvertent harm to other beings, fears that men might harm themselves by worrying too much about "those" he deems to be different from "men." Chapter 6 examines two difficult passages where this sentiment is explicitly expressed. This analysis is then followed by a discussion of some of the assumptions and possible motivations behind the aforementioned argumentative move.

---

⁷² Chapter 1, section 1.4, discussed in detail the equalizing function of being a "thing" (*wu* 物) among ten thousand things.

⁷³ That both the frustrations and tenuousness of the heart are discussed in relation to people is perhaps not surprising given the recurring Heaven(ly)-human tension in the text. For more on this tension, see chapter 4, section 4.4. About the *Zhuangzi*'s account of human affects, it should be mentioned that along with misleading translations of 心齋 as "heart-fasting" and *xu* 虛 as "emptiness," it is common to portray the *Zhuangzi* as suggesting that we should eliminate all affects. However, instead of purging the heart of its affects, the text often points toward allowing affects to simply come and go. A passage in the *Zhuangzi* reads: "Happiness and anger, sorrow and joy, plans and regrets, change and fixity, pleasant idleness and initiating a position—[they are like] music coming out of hollows, mushrooms formed from mere steams. Day and night they alternate before us, but no one knows from where they sprout" (*Zhuangzi* 2:57). The passage, which is also dramatically agnostic about the origin of affects, suggests that moods and thoughts simply sprout forth without warning (the way mushrooms shoot out of the earth overnight) and, if we let them, they also simply cease without taking hold. Similar lines in the *Zhuangzi* include descriptions of letting one's joy and anger intermingle with the four seasons (see, for instance, *Zhuangzi* 6:235).

6

Spinoza's Serpentine Worries

Animal Affects in Spinoza

Chapter 3 has shown that although Spinoza undermines prevailing biblical assertions of human superiority over the rest of creation by attributing mental powers to everything in the world, he still grants mankind higher epistemic powers due to their more complex minds/bodies. Although this very approach poses some interpretational difficulties (such as the difficulty of demonstrating mankind's overall position at the top of a ladder of complexity using the geometric method), one can still argue that Spinoza, at least, does not explicitly seal the borders separating mankind from beasts. However, Spinoza's attitude toward human-animal relations takes on an alarmist tone when he discusses the affective states of men and beasts. As will be shown, in several key moments Spinoza alienates the affects of beasts from those of men, which, I argue, is not accidental and relates to Spinoza's theory of affects and his commitment to human solidarity.

The next section opens with a brief examination of a passage in which Spinoza argues for anthropocentric resourcism through a deliberate alienation of the affective states of beasts from that of mankind. As section 6.2 demonstrates, Spinoza's main concern appears to be overidentifying with the beasts and wasting "our" affective resources on "them," when the primary goal should be uniting with fellow men. Certainly, this specific concern about identifying with the "wrong" type of being is intertwined with Spinoza's clear association of beasts with passions, which are the affective dimension of inadequate understanding.

As section 6.3 shows, one would still expect Spinoza to allow for enabling interactions between human beings and (passion-driven) animals, given his assertion that passions *can* aid the improvement of one's epistemic powers. However, Spinoza still exhorts mankind to distance themselves from the affects of beasts due to an "us versus them" distinction that inflects his arguments. The same "us versus them" binary also shapes much of his portrayal of animal sympathizers, who he thinks are motivated by misanthropy. In the end, the choice, for Spinoza, is not simply between choosing the company of mankind versus animals but also between self-hatred and melancholy versus the cheerfulness and blessedness that can only be cultivated with and among fellow men.

6.1 Making Use of Beasts as We Please

Chapter 5 analyzed passages from the *Zhuangzi* that emphasize the situatedness of one's likes and dislikes, regardless of whether they are of animal or human origin. That our vantage points in general could be so intimately bound by the material aspect of our lives is acknowledged by Spinoza as well, as seen in the example of the worm, which was discussed in chapter 3.[1] However, the awareness of the perspectival variance between different beings sometimes gives way to putting a deliberate distance between "men" and "beasts," especially when it comes to ostensible differences between their affects. A clear example of this approach was mentioned in chapter 2,[2] which is worth revisiting here. In EIVp37s1, Spinoza notes:

> The law to refrain from slaughtering beasts is founded on groundless superstition and womanly compassion. . . . They [the beasts] do not agree with us in nature, and their emotions are different in nature from human emotions.[3]

The passage poses an interpretational difficulty largely because Spinoza's ontology allows him to lay out the difference between men and animals in terms of degrees, not kinds, and this passage does not quite serve as an example of the former kind of differentiation.

Now, in the passage, where with the same gesture he distances the (hu)man from both women and animals, Spinoza seems to be posing the existence of

---

[1] The example involves a worm that takes the blood it lives in as the entire world. Spinoza uses the example as part of a discussion about how human beings often take the bodies surrounding them as independent wholes. See chapter 1, section 1.3 for more detail.
[2] See section 2.1.
[3] The Latin version of the afore-cited passage reads, "Legem illam de non mactandis brutis, magis vana superstitione, & muliebri misericordia. . . . [N]obiscum natura non conveniunt, & eorum affectus ab affectibus humanis sunt natura diversi."

a fundamental difference between the affects of the former group and the latter, and to be using this to support his point that mankind may treat animals as they wish. The same passage continues:

> We have the same right over them [beasts] as they do over us. Indeed, since every individual's right is defined by its virtue or power, man's right over beasts is far greater than their rights over man. I do not deny that beasts feel (*sentire*); I am denying that we are on that account debarred from paying heed to our own advantage and from making use of them as we please and dealing with them as best suits us, seeing that they do not agree with us in nature and their emotions are different in nature from human emotions. (EIVp37s1)

The motivation behind the assertion that men should not curtail their actions to protect beasts is not surprising given the overall amoral tone of the text. Indeed, when Spinoza asserts that "we have the same right over them as they do over us," he is simply rejecting the Christian stewardship model that suggests that mankind has a responsibility to take care of other beings. This model is inherently rooted in assumptions about man as created in the image of God. When Spinoza continues by stating that "since every individual's right is defined by his virtue or power, man's right over beasts is far greater than their rights over man," he is again keeping with the overall spirit of the text.[4] His explanation that "I do not deny that beasts feel; I am denying that we are on that account debarred from paying heed to our own advantage and from making use of them as we please" also sits well with the rest of the text, where pity is defined as a species of sadness (EIIIp22s) and is said to decrease one's power.[5] Whether Spinoza also needed to add the phrase "they do not agree with us in nature and their emotions are different in nature from human emotions" to support his point, and whether one could even give a substantial account of this discrepancy in a way that would align it with the rest of the text—*that* is the question that merits our attention.

At this juncture it should be mentioned that Spinoza, in fact, sometimes goes in the direction of formulating the affects of men and beasts along a continuous trajectory, thereby rendering comparisons of different groups

---

[4] Spinoza equates right with power, which enables him to say that "man's right over beasts is far greater than their rights over man" (EIVp37s1).

[5] This is why Spinoza later writes that "a man who lives according to the dictates of reason, strives, as far as he can, not to be touched by pity" (EIVp50c).

irrelevant. An example of this line of thought appears in the scholium of EIIIp57, which reads as follows:

> The affects of the animals which are called irrational [*affectus animalium, quae irrationalia dicuntur*] (for after we know the origin of the mind, we cannot in any way doubt that brutes feel things) differ from men's affects as much as [*quantum*; as far as] their nature differs from human nature. Both the horse and the man are driven by a lust to procreate; but the one is driven by an equine lust, the other by a human lust. So also the lusts and appetites of insects, fish, and birds must vary. Therefore, though each individual lives content with his own nature, by which he is constituted, and is glad of it, nevertheless that life with which each one is content, and that gladness, are nothing but the idea, *or* soul, of the individual. And so the gladness [*gaudium*] of the one differs in nature from the gladness of the other as much as the essence of the one differs from the essence of the other. Finally, from P57 it follows that there is no small difference between the gladness by which a drunk is led and the gladness a philosopher possesses.

In the very first sentence, where Spinoza speaks of the irrational affects of animals, which differ from human affects as much as their nature differs from human nature, he reiterates that animals are sentient beings.[6] This forms a contrast with the Cartesian "beast-machine" approach, where all animal agitation was seen as mere mechanical response to stimuli.[7] Unlike the thinkers who viewed animals as senseless automata, Spinoza asserts that "brutes" surely are sentient, which is in line with his view that all beings are, albeit to different degrees, animate (EIIp13s).[8] However, considering his views on slaughtering animals, one could argue that another form of "dissociative

---

[6] The relative pronoun that is translated as "which" (quæ) could be either feminine or neuter, whereas *affectus* is masculine; hence it is the animals that are called "irrational" here, rather than their affects. I owe thanks to Richard A. Lee Jr. for bringing this point to my attention.

[7] Of course, this view did not develop in a vacuum. In fact, it has proved to be especially pivotal in an era that was marked by a boom in animal experimentation and witnessed the introduction of vivisection in experimental work. This, in turn, made the trivialization of animal affects a necessary component of the process. Some of these experiments involved measuring medicine dosages and pain thresholds, which necessitated recording and tabulating indications of (sometimes extreme) agitation. Surely, interpreting animals' affects in a mechanized way made such a process easier on the conscience. For ethical debates on animal experimentation in the seventeenth century, see Guerrini, "The Ethics of Animal Experimentation," 391–407.

[8] As discussed in chapter 3, sections 3.1 and 3.2, instead of an "all or nothing" approach, where one either has a mind or not, Spinoza thinks every physical phenomenon has a mental correlate.

repression" is sometimes at work in Spinoza's philosophy, where animal affects are not denied *à la* the beast-machine approach but are nonetheless distanced by pointing out that they are different enough from "our" affects that we need not worry about them.

Returning to the same passage, the second part of the first sentence—which remarks that the affects of animals differ from those of men "as much as" their nature differs from human nature—is crucial because it seems to point out that differences between men and animals come in degrees. Not only this, Spinoza later moves from the lusts and appetites of different animals to the lusts and appetites of different men and then compares the affects of two men (a "drunkard" and a "philosopher"—on the assumption that the two are mutually exclusive categories) to suggest that the difference between the two could be remarkably large, depending on how much they exercise their power of understanding. In fact, the remark that "the gladness of the one differs in nature from the gladness of the other as much as the essence of the one differs from the essence of the other" goes in the direction of suggesting that the joys of each of us are different simply because we are all different from one another.

Finally, as will also be discussed in chapter 7, strictly speaking, by the "essence" of different individuals Spinoza means the ratio of motion and rest that is specific to each individual.[9] That is to say, because we each have different essences, one person's gladness is different from another person's gladness. Surely, as Wilson notes, we might expect the essences of two humans to be more alike than the essence of any human and the essence of any horse;[10] however, this still potentially gives us a formulation for heterogeneity and difference without finalizing closures (where things are different from each other not in "kind" but in "degree").

Having examined the passage regarding animal slaughter and the passage that compares the lusts, appetites, and gladness of different beings, the crucial question at this juncture is this: According to Spinoza's thought, *can* a man agree with an animal more than he does with another man? This question has two different answers: If we follow the initial premises of Spinoza's ontology to their radical conclusions, then the answer is an unequivocal "yes." Especially given Spinoza's stance against "bad" universals,[11]

---

[9] See chapter 7, section 7.1.

[10] See Margaret D. Wilson, "'For They Do Not Agree in Nature with Us,'" 345.

[11] "Bad" universals are discussed in chapter 3, section 3.3. Briefly, they refer to generalizations that one forms based on haphazard contact with things.

one could easily carry the implications of Spinoza's ontology in the direction of posthumanism, where the very category of man, as well as other group-specific categories, is disrupted altogether in favor of a cartography of power and affects (instead of a taxonomy of species).[12] The second answer to the aforementioned question comes from Spinoza himself: "Apart from men we know no singular thing in nature whose Mind we can enjoy, and which we can join to ourselves in friendship, or some sort of association" (EIVapp26).

Clearly, the open-ended trajectory of similarity that is implicated in Spinoza's comparison of the various affects of different beings does not stop him from making finalizing statements about the difference between man and animals. Spinoza's ambivalent—if not self-contradictory—stance on this difference is particularly curious, given his well-earned fame as a system-builder. The next section explores this tension around human-animal relations further by tackling a difficult passage from the *Ethics* that concerns a peculiar interpretation of the story of the Fall, which offers new insights into Spinoza's theory of affects and his investment in human togetherness.

6.2 Choosing Eve over the Serpent

In a passage on human freedom, Spinoza presents his version of the story of the Fall, in which he again points to a discrepancy between human and animal affects—though, fortunately, this time he does not do so by distancing men from overly compassionate women; perhaps because in the story, which is still told from the man's perspective, there are only two human beings. At any rate, the passage reads as follows:

> The story goes that when man had found woman, who agrees entirely with his own nature, he realized that there could be nothing in nature more to his advantage than woman. But when he came to believe that the beasts

---

[12] Within this Deleuzo-Spinozistic cartography of affects and power, what matters is what a body *does* in relation to others instead of what "horseness" or "humanness" *is*. To illustrate this point, Deleuze gives the famous example that the "draft horse" has more in common with an ox than it has with the "racehorse." Gilles Deleuze, *Spinoza: Practical Philosophy*, trans. Robert Hurley (San Francisco: City Lights, 1988), 124.

[*bruta*] were like himself, he straightaway began to imitate their emotions and to lose his freedom. (EIVp68s)[13]

Adam "finds," "discovers," or "comes upon" (*invenire*) a woman (instead of the woman being handed to him after being created out of his rib)[14] and knows that no one else's companionship can be more advantageous to him. Yet, he believes (*credere*) that he is similar to the beast, and imitates it, which causes him to lose his freedom. Among the peculiar aspects of this passage is the remark that it is Adam's *believing* that he is similar to beasts (not the *fact* of his similarity to beasts) that leads him to imitate beastly emotions.

This peculiar logic of the circulation of emotions is expressed throughout the *Ethics*, especially in the third book, where we are told that imagining something to be similar to us causes us to be affected by similar affects (EIIIp27). Spinoza further explains how the similarity between interacting bodies facilitates the communication of affects between them:

> If therefore the nature of the external body is similar to the nature of our own body, then the idea of the external body in our thinking will involve an affection of our own body similar to the affection of the external body. Consequently, if we imagine something like ourselves to have been affected by some affect, the imagination would express an affection of our body similar to that affect. (EIIIp27d; translation modified)

In this passage, the similarity between the two bodies is taken to be preestablished, and we are told that when we perceive a similar body affected by a certain emotion, our perception of this (the other body's being affected by X or Y) brings out a similar affect in our own body. In an earlier proposition, Spinoza also states that

> it should be noted that we do not pity only a thing we have loved . . . , but also one toward which we have previously had no affect, provided that we *judge* [or "decide" (*iudicare*)] it to be like us. (EIIIp22s; my emphasis)

---

[13] For the translation of EIVp68s, I follow Shirley's translation with minor modifications.
[14] Sharp argues that "it is not unusual to interpret this part of Genesis to imply equality between woman and man" and uses the example of Maimonides, who gives an Aristophanic account of the creation of Adam and Eve. See Hasana Sharp, "Eve's Perfection," 572.

Here one might wonder if there is any significant difference between a "real" similarity and "judging" (or believing; Spinoza's word in EIVP68s) that something is similar to oneself. However, the very way that Spinoza sets up the mechanism behind the operations of the imagination defies any sharp distinction between "objective similarity" and "assumed similarity" (*insofar as* we relate to the other body through the imagination).

As explained in chapter 3, Spinoza primarily uses the term "imagination" to refer to memory and sense perception instead of fictional mental constructs (although they too could be involved).[15] Imagination is a form of awareness of the affections of our body *as* it is affected by other bodies (EIIp17s). Thus, when affects are communicated through this kind of analogizing apprehension,[16] it is neither an act of appropriation where the other being and its emotions are completely assimilated into one's own horizon nor an act of yielding to "factual evidence" that imposes itself so that one cannot help but identify with the other being.

As we are told in Spinoza's version of the Fall, the identification process is not guaranteed by having relatively similar anatomies, since Adam happens to feel closer to a beast than to his human companion. The question thus remains: What initially made Adam identify with the beast, rather than with Eve? To answer this question, along with the question of why this causes Adam to lose his freedom, it is imperative to look at how ideas interact with and support each other in Spinozistic epistemology, as well as the affective side of our thought processes.

Imagination, for Spinoza, is never the work of isolated minds freely forming their private mental pictures of the universe. Ideas (taken, in the Spinozistic sense, as the mental correlates of physical events) are always already in relation with and moved by other ideas. The way in which ideas are interrelated with one another also explains why certain ideas have more force than others; some ideas gain more power by simply combining with other ideas and the combination then becomes harder to remove.[17] Now, given that the ideas of the imagination are formed via the accumulation of certain experiences and are fostered or weakened by surrounding ideas, it is difficult to disagree with Sharp's observation that Spinoza would hardly be surprised

---

[15] For more, see chapter 3, section 3.3.

[16] This term is borrowed from Husserl. See Edmund Husserl, *Cartesian Meditations: An Introduction to Phenomenology*, trans. Dorion Cairns (Leiden: Martinus Nijhoff, 1977), 111–112.

[17] Spinoza discusses the mutually reinforcing nature of ideas in Part II of the *Ethics*, particularly in the scholium to proposition 49.

by the "wolf-child" phenomenon, because repeated contact with something could bring out the result of strongly identifying with that being.[18]

Returning to Adam's preference for the beast over Eve, this too could be the result of a wide variety of factors, ranging from the amount of contact he had with the beast to other experiences that gave rise to particular patterns of association.[19] However, what perhaps makes Adam's identification with the beast more peculiar is the fact that Adam also knows that Eve is more similar to him. Thus, even when we know an idea to be true, certain ideas, and the affects that they give rise to, may give us stronger gratification (EIVp7s) or might be supported by other preconceptions more strongly than true ideas are.[20] One final question still remains to be answered: What makes the nature of the beast's affects so different from the nature of Adam's?

Spinoza's treatment of affects is intimately tied to his theory of knowledge in which the mind's inadequate understanding of the causes of its bodily states becomes the cause of its passive affects (i.e., passions).[21] For Spinoza, the more adequately we understand something, the freer, more active, and more empowered we become. This transition from inadequate to adequate understanding is facilitated by seeing underlying commonalities among various phenomena, including the lawful features of nature that underlie everything. This progression toward greater states of understanding and empowerment does not bring with it an elimination of affects but rather the

---

[18] Hasana Sharp, "The Force of Ideas in Spinoza," *Political Theory* 35, no. 6 (2007): 754n34.

[19] It must be reiterated here that the kind of information provided by the imagination can be highly confused, especially when it belongs to a very complex body such as a human body that shares a great many things with other bodies. Moreover, since ideas are simply the mental counterparts of physical events, just as we do not feel every single movement of the cells in our bodies, we do not have complete knowledge of the history behind any particular opinion (and, as we have seen, this ignorance is the reason many people believe that they have free will or interpret certain events as miracles caused by God). Hence, it is not surprising that we lack the complete causal history of this particular instance of Adam's identification with a particular beast.

[20] As Sharp points out, this self-destructive aspect of Adam's identification with the beast arises in other contexts as well. On several occasions, Spinoza paraphrases Ovid's verse that "I see the better course and approve it, but I pursue the worse course" (EIIIp2s, EIVpref, EIVp17s; Spinoza explicitly cites Ovid only in EIVp17s) and laments the fact that the truth of an idea does not prevent it from being assailed by uncritical beliefs (*opiniones*) (EIVp15–P17sc). Sharp, "Eve's Perfection," 579.

[21] Failing to understand the psychological mechanism behind one's attraction to another person, which could breed infatuation and obsessive love, is one obvious example of how an inadequate understanding of a situation breeds passions. Although an attraction that is not fully understood might still have various enabling and joyful effects, for Spinoza it would still prohibit one from thinking and doing a wider variety of things, because of its fixation on a specific external source (EIVp43s and EIVp44s). Moreover, having one's happiness depend on another's affection always carries the risk of having that joy quickly turn into a sad passion. In fact, Spinoza states that "all love, which has a cause other than freedom of mind, easily passes into hate unless (and this is worse) it is a species of madness" (EIVApp.19).

replacement of passive affects (joyful or sad passions) with the active affect of joy.²²

With respect to how exactly this transition from inadequate to adequate understanding happens, although we know that imagination *aids* reason in getting there, the transition, as Deleuze aptly puts it, still requires a "genuine leap."²³ Deleuze explains why he (in my opinion, accurately) describes it as a leap by pointing out the fact that although certain epistemological and affective circumstances that arise from the operations of the imagination might be advantageous for developing the ideas of the common notions (which are adequate ideas),²⁴ it is not the case that these ideas of the common notions emerge from the accumulation of a threshold amount of inadequate ideas of the imagination.²⁵ Indeed, breaking free from the concatenation of inadequate ideas and forming ideas that are common to all bodies cannot be achieved by the mere accumulation of an even greater number of inadequate ideas.

This suggests that there is something *qualitatively* different about understanding a phenomenon adequately versus inadequately, which is to say that "adequate" and "inadequate" understanding actually name different "kinds" of knowing a thing, not simply different "degrees" of knowing a thing (which is why these forms of knowing can coexist, since one is not simply

---

²² Whereas we can talk about active or passive joys, depending on how much understanding accompanies the idea of the body's activity, there is no such thing as "active sadness" for Spinoza, as transitions to adequate knowledge and activity always result in joy (thus, the phrase "reality hurts" would not make sense for him, because reality does not hurt when one truly understands it; this involves considering it in wider contexts and understanding the necessities that govern these contexts). For an excellent discussion of the process of one's transition from passive joys and pains to active joys of reason, see Amélie Rorty, "Spinoza on the Pathos of Idolatrous Love and the Hilarity of True Love," in Gatens, *Feminist Interpretations of Benedict Spinoza*, 65–86.

²³ Gilles Deleuze, *Expressionism in Philosophy: Spinoza*, trans. Martin Joughin (New York: Zone Books, 1990), 283. The "leap" problem is also raised in De Dijn, Spinoza, 88, 134. The "leap" problem is also raised by De Dijn. De Dijn, *Spinoza: The Way to Wisdom*, 88, 134.

²⁴ As will also be discussed later, in EIVp45c2s, Spinoza presents the joys of pleasant food and drink, scents, decorations, music, sports, and the theater as helping one to participate in the "divine nature." Human companionship matters to a great extent for Spinoza as well, due to the way humans can stimulate each other's minds/bodies in a great variety of ways. For an in-depth discussion of the role that passive, yet joyful, affects play in strengthening the reason, see Syliane Malinowski-Charles, *Affects et Conscience chez Spinoza: L'automatisme dans le progrès éthique* (Hildesheim: Georg Olms Verlag, 2004).

²⁵ Here it is important to recall that our first adequate ideas are common notions, which are already omnipresent features of the world. For more, see Deleuze, *Expressionism in Philosophy*, 281–283. A similar point is made by Yovel, who argues that although initially "reason must be prompted and awakened by other causes than itself... these causes do not actually create reason, they only entice it to come into operation" (Yovel, "Incomplete Rationality," 19).

an advanced version of the other).[26] Given that the process also has an affective aspect, combined with the fact that Spinoza differentiates active joys from passive joys, where the former does not even have an opposite (an active sadness), a similar qualitative difference could be said to exist for these two kinds of joy as well.

It is difficult to conclusively tell whether this qualitative difference between passive and active affects parallels the seeming discontinuity between (hu)man and beasts that is sometimes observed in Spinoza's thought. However, it is clear that not only do certain propositions in EIV (especially p35-37) suggest an association between reason and human nature,[27] but also when we look at the favorable circumstances that can give rise to the joyful condition of being more active and more powerful (which, again, is tied to having an adequate understanding), we see that Spinoza consistently advises coming together with other fellow men. Men are able to affect and be affected by each other in a wide variety of ways; this is what it means to be more active, more powerful, and so on (EIVp18s, EIVp35c1&s, EIVp37s1). Considering this advice together with the fact that Adam's bonding with the beast is seen as the cause of the loss of his freedom, it is clear that mankind is more closely associated with adequate understanding (and hence also with active and empowering joy) for Spinoza.[28] However, Spinoza's warning against associating too closely with beasts is not simply reducible to his bias toward the intellectual powers of (hu)mankind. As the next and final section shows, Spinoza's caution against bonding with animals relies on certain tendencies

---

[26] This point is discussed in detail in chapter 3, section 3.4. To revisit an example mentioned there, Spinoza himself talks of experiencing the sun to be 200 feet away due to ignorance of the causes behind that experience. This ignorance could be supplemented with the knowledge of the sun's true distance but that would still not make the eye see it as farther than 200 feet away (EIIp35s).

[27] I owe this observation to Wilson. See Wilson, "'For They Do Not Agree in Nature with Us,'" 342.

[28] Although strictly speaking, other beings should be able to develop adequate understanding as well. Since the adequate understanding of a phenomenon has to do with seeing that particular mode in relation to common notions, and given that common notions are omnipresent features of the world, nonhuman beings should be able to form adequate ideas as well. Hence, as discussed in chapter 3, section 3.4, even a worm can form adequate ideas. However, having a simpler body, the worm is expected to have a limited variety of affections of the body, which then translate into a limited variety of adequate and/or inadequate ideas. On multiple occasions, however, Spinoza presents having "reason" (*ratio*) or possessing "natural light" (*lumen naturale*) as the distinguishing marker of humanity that separates humans from beasts (see, for instance, TP 5.5 and TTP 5.16). Given that Spinoza denies the presence of faculties such as intellect or will, and that strictly speaking there is nothing but a continuous ladder of complexity, Spinoza's remarks regarding reason as a human-specific phenomenon suggest either the presence of an unsolved tension in his system or the assumption of a "threshold" for powers of the mind. In addition, as explored further in chapter 3, section 3.6, "beasts" sometimes appear as tropes for what is violent and uncivilized (instead of referring to animals in their own right). This observation sets some of Spinoza's exclusionary remarks about beasts in a softer light.

he had observed among what one might call animal sympathizers, namely, sad passions rooted in misanthropy.

6.3 On Misanthropic Melancholy and Fraternal Cheer

Despite what the anachronistic label "rationalist," which is often used to describe him, might connote, Spinoza clearly is not dismissive toward the affective aspect of one's existence. Quite the contrary, reason, for him, already has an affective aspect simply because the act of adequately understanding anything brings one joy. This kind of joy, which accompanies the increase in one's power and activity, is aptly named an "active" joy, distinguishing it from the "passive" affects that are not fully understood because they stem from an individual external stimulus (such as an object of love) instead of being perceived in relation to God (EIVp43s, EIVp44s). For Spinoza, passive affects (i.e., passions) are not eliminated by adequate ideas but by the active affect of joy that accompanies those adequate ideas, which means that the goal of adequate understanding is not to eliminate one's passions but to transform them.

In addition to the possibility of transforming passions, some passions can also aid the life of the reason, whether they are brought under its scrutiny or not. In EIVp45c2s, Spinoza presents the joys of pleasant food and drink, scents, "the beauty of green plants," decorations, music, sports, and the theater as helping one to "refresh and restore himself" and enhance the powers of the human body/mind—which, after all, requires "varied nourishment" due to its complex makeup. In fact, anything that induces the affective state of cheerfulness (*hilaritas*) is good for Spinoza as cheerfulness uplifts the entirety of the body/mind (EIVp42d) and hence agrees with reason.[29] In addition, one could also understand the mechanism behind the cheerfulness that one is feeling and conceive it in relation to God, in which case the affective state of cheerfulness becomes an active affect, that is blessedness.[30] Here one wonders, Why can't animals induce a cheerful state in one? Can't they also

---

[29] This is to say, it is different from "localized" pleasures, such as titillation (*titillatio*), which "consists in one or more body's parts being affected more than the rest" which can hinder the other activities of the body and hence its "ability to be affected in numerous other ways" (EIVp43d). As discussed in chapter 3, section 3.4, the advantage of having a more complex mind/body is being able to affect and be affected in a greater variety of ways, which then aids reason.

[30] Laurent Bove makes a similar point in "Hilaritas and Acquiescentia in se ipso," in *Ethica IV: Spinoza on Reason and the "Free Man,"* ed. Yirmiyahu Yovel and Gideon Segal (New York: Little Room Press, 2004), 218.

bring cheer with, let us say, their beautiful form (just like green plants do) or with the comfort or energy they might provide (just like music or sports)?

There seem to be two concerns, for Spinoza, to consider here. One is that men tend to *identify* with beasts in ways they do not seem to do with plants. This identification poses a problem when one prefers their company over that of human companions. If we go back to what we, for the sake of brevity, might call the "animal slaughter passage," the scholium in which Spinoza condemns as "womanish" people who feel compassion for other animals continues with his warning that the fact that beasts feel pain should not make us curtail our own actions (EIVp37s1). Spinoza clearly sees the issue in terms of an "us versus them" distinction, where showing compassion for beasts somehow results in limiting "our" own actions. A similar approach is at work in Spinoza's version of the Fall, where Adam's imitation of animal affects is portrayed in terms of a choice between Eve and the beast, as if he cannot enjoy the company of both. There too Spinoza's main concern is fostering human solidarity, which he thinks could be disrupted when humans feel strong connections with nonhuman animals and begin arguing on their behalf.[31]

The second concern relates to an empirical observation on Spinoza's part, namely, that human-animal intimacy tends to revolve around feelings of pity for the animal (despite the fact that, as he admits, they are capable of joyful passions, such as lust or gladness) and of self-hatred for oneself for being (hu) man. These concerns make explicit appearance in passages where Spinoza speaks of "satirists" deriding "the doings of mankind" and "melancholics" "disdaining men and admiring beasts" (EIVp35s).[32] Spinoza's association of melancholy (*melancholia*) and preferring the company of beasts might sound odd to a modern reader. However, it is an association that is commonly found in Spinoza's intellectual milieu.

As Gowland notes, there was a "heightened early modern consciousness of the incidence of melancholy," which coincides with the perceived spiritual and political malaise inflicting Europe, but also with the increase of philosophical interest in the passions of the soul (which explains the intellectual preoccupation with the assumed frequency of melancholy).[33] The range of

---

[31] On this point, see Sharp, "Animal Affects," 55, 65.
[32] This point is also discussed in Sharp, "Animal Affects," 55.
[33] Angus Gowland. "The Problem of Early Modern Melancholy," *Past & Present*, no. 191 (May 2006): 83, 100, 117.

characteristics commonly attributed to melancholy includes excessive fear and sadness, delusions, solitariness, denunciation of the world, and misanthropy.[34] At times, these attributes are combined to depict more specific and colorful scenarios. For example, the characteristics of withdrawal from society, misanthropy, and delusions are used together to paint a picture of melancholic individuals who experience delusions of turning into an actual animal.[35]

Spinoza's description of melancholics as people who "admire beasts" and "despise men" echoes some of these associations, while also allowing him to connect the condition of melancholy to his own theory of affects. Since their love of beasts goes hand in hand with their misanthropy, melancholic folks could be said to be under the influence of self-hatred and extreme humility, which are species of sad passions (EIVp54s).[36] That Spinoza juxtaposes melancholics with satirists also sits well with the aforementioned cluster of associations, given that satire, he states, feeds on the belittlement of men.[37] Finally, Spinoza's description of beast-sympathizers as satirists and melancholics also suggests a sharp contrast with the circumstances that aid reason.

Specifically, both melancholy and satire are opposed to cheerfulness, albeit in different respects. Cheerfulness, we are told, clears away melancholy and as such it is the negation of it (EIIIp11s, EIVp42 and d). As for satire, we are told that cheerfulness is incommensurably different from the state induced by satire, even when said satire prompts laughter. It is because satire relies on deriding human affairs instead of understanding them (TP 1.1), and

---

[34] Gowland, "The Problem of Early Modern Melancholy," 88, 90, 94, 97–98, 115.

[35] In *The Anatomy of Melancholy* (1621), Robert Burton notes that the melancholic "howls like a wolf" and "barks like a dog." Cited in Diego Rossello, "Hobbes and the Wolf-Man: Melancholy and Animality in Modern Sovereignty," *New Literary History* 43, no. 2 (Spring 2012): 256. This peculiar characteristic of melancholy possibly stems from the influence of Galenic symptomology on early modern medicine, which links melancholy to the excess of black bile—a characteristic shared with the rabid dog. Also relevant is the lingering influence of demonology and the need to offer an explanation for anecdotes of lycanthropy. See Rossello, "Hobbes and the Wolf-Man," 255–257; Gowland, "The Problem of Early Modern Melancholy," 86–92.

[36] Sharp adds that misanthropic statements also rely on a tendency to oppose humans to nature, or the rest of creation (as if they are even separable), and to favor the latter (nature) over the former (human beings). Regardless of whether Spinoza was indeed also motivated by such a concern, it seems that alienating animal affects by explicitly arguing that they are different in nature from human affects would not alleviate the situation, as that is simply another gesture to separate humans from the rest of nature (which does not resolve their initial separation, but merely changes the nature of that separation). See Sharp, *Spinoza and the Politics of Renaturalization*, 189. I owe this insight to a conversation with Richard A. Lee Jr.

[37] TP 1.1. Moreover, in TTP 1.22, Spinoza attributes a toxic attitude of mind to melancholy as well when he explains that *melancholia* maps onto what in common parlance is called an "evil spirit" (*spiritus malus*), referring to a harmful disposition or attitude of mind. This point is repeated in TTP 1.25.

as such it is not that different from lamenting human shortcomings, which are also informed by dislike for at least a certain aspect of humanity (Ep.30). Although Spinoza also at times adapts a scornful language toward human follies[38] (i.e., not following his own advice), it is clear that he (1) contrasts cheerfulness with melancholy and satire at the same time, and (2) associates sympathizing with beasts with the latter pair.

When freed from sad passions, such as scorn for human affairs and pity for beasts, and when ungrounded identifications with beasts are kept in check, then companionship of beasts should not pose a problem. Still Spinoza's protectiveness of human bonds evinces a special status granted to human companionship in the development of one's epistemic and affective powers. This should not be surprising. Spinoza's penchant for human solidarity was earlier explained in section 6.2 when discussing his other assumption that men can stimulate each other in a wider variety of ways and hence can be advantageous to each other's mental and physical development. While the complexity of their minds/bodies allows for greater reciprocal stimulation, the more men uplift each other in following reason, the more they agree with each other (given that adequate understanding is a matter of tapping onto the eternal and lawful features of Nature that underlie everything). It is, in fact, for this reason that Spinoza sometimes points in the direction of the golden rule and states that men who follow reason "agree in nature" and "seek nothing for themselves that they would not desire for the rest of mankind" (EIVp18s).[39]

Ultimately, although things and circumstances that incite joyful passions *can* aid the life of the mind/body, "nothing is more useful (*utile*) to man than man" as Spinoza puts it (EIVp18s). Spinoza does not stop at emphasizing men's use for each other, which could be taken to refer to their ability to aid each other's material survival only, but also announces that "man is a God to man" (*homo homini Deus est*) (EIVp35s).[40] This impassioned statement

---

[38] In EIIIp39s Spinoza writes: "Experience teaches all too plainly that men have nothing less in their power than their tongue, and can do nothing less than moderate their appetites."

[39] It could also be added here that since people's agreement or disagreement in nature is a matter of the extent to which they follow reason, when Spinoza states in EIVp68s that "man had found woman, who agrees entirely with his own nature," he must mean that both Adam and Eve were following reason and were not governed by passions (which rely on operations of the imagination and the random associations one draws between various haphazard experiences).

[40] Spinoza's assertion counteracts Hobbes's portrayal of humans as lupine creatures, as Hobbes famously asserts that "man is a wolf to man." See Thomas Hobbes, *On the Citizen*, ed. and trans. Richard Tuck and Michael Silverthorne (Cambridge: Cambridge University Press, 1998 [1642]), epistle dedicatory. The phrase, of course, originally appears in Plautus's well-known play *Asinaria* in its Latin version as "Homo homini lupus est."

is sometimes interpreted with the particular Spinozist definition of God in mind and hence as referring to acting from "adequate ideas and rational desires" and in doing so expressing "God's activity."[41] However, the statement does not simply refer to a man's activity as a solipsistic phenomenon, but a man fulfilling the role of God to another man. Hence, it is more likely that this is a figurative statement that employs the conventional definition of God, in which case Spinoza is referring to men aiding each other's salvation, that is, achieving the life of reason.[42] That is also to say, although Spinoza's system is without a caring God, it is not without redemptive hope.

As discussed in chapter 2, the ultimate end of Spinoza's philosophy is not simply giving a disinterested description of the world but understanding the world and man's place in it in order to aid his salvation.[43] Such an outcome will not be brought about by the grace of a personified God but rather by men acting as each other's saviors. Men can induce in each other not only joyful or sad passions but also the understanding of such passions, which is blessedness. A rational man strives to aid others in their salvation, not out of selfless goodwill but because it is in his best interest for others to join him in this endeavor (TIE 14). Furthermore, since such a man will have a better understanding of human actions, he "hates no one, is angry with no one, envies no one, is indignant with no one, despises no one, and is not prone to pride" (EIVp73s). As such, Spinoza declares that his "doctrine contributes to social life insofar as it teaches . . . [that each person] should be helpful to his neighbor, not from unmanly compassion, partiality, or superstition, but from the guidance of reason, as the time and occasion demand" (EIIp39s).

Such statements serve as testimony to the fact that although Spinoza steps outside of the tradition by not formulating human specificity in terms of their God-given moral capacities, the significance of the (hu)man world does not disappear together with the significance of conventional (hu)man values in Spinoza. Neither does his paying attention to the affective aspect of reason eliminate his unease toward certain passions or prevent him from guarding the boundaries between the mankind and those who are associated with the said passions. That Spinoza still exhorts mankind to distance itself from the

---

[41] This is the reading Eugene Marshall gives in "Man Is a God to Man: How Human Beings Can Be Adequate Causes," in *Essays on Spinoza's Ethical Theory*, ed. Matthew J. Kisner and Andrew Youpa (Oxford: Oxford University Press, 2014), 177.

[42] Nadler gives a similar reading when he notes that Spinoza's emphasis in the statement "man is a God to man" is on men helping each other reach rational perfection. Steven Nadler, "The Lives of Others: Spinoza on Benevolence as a Rational Virtue," in *Essays on Spinoza's Ethical Theory*, 54.

[43] See section 2.2 of chapter 2.

affects of beasts perhaps evinces the unique position of beasts in that they are, in fact, similar enough to mankind for strong identifications with them to occur. At the same time, Spinoza's ardor for protecting and fostering (hu)man bonds conveys their importance. However, what is also conveyed in Spinoza's persistent rhetorical policing of the boundaries separating beasts from mankind is the fragility of (hu)man bonds, which are to be protected from the threat of bonding with lesser beings.

Conclusion
Affects, Solidarity, and Power

Our examination of some of the key passages on human and animal affects in Spinoza's thought and the *Zhuangzi* brings to the fore several related issues of relevance. One important concern relates to the concept of human solidarity, both as an assumption and as an ideal. This notion certainly inflects one's perception of animal affects, particularly in terms of whether we approach them with guileless curiosity or regard them as inferior versions of human affects. The latter view also easily leads to disassociating animal affects from human concern altogether in the name of not wasting "our" emotional resources on others who are deemed less relevant for human salvation and self-empowerment.

Second, neither approach is without an open or implicit awareness of the power dynamic between human beings and animal others. Moreover, both approaches actually exhibit a concern around the erasure of the particularity of animal affects. However, whereas Spinoza urges caution against over-identifying with animal others, in the *Zhuangzi* the emphasis is on increasing one's ability to become better attuned to others' affects (not for their own sake alone but to increase one's own efficacy in the world). The mechanisms underlying these findings are intricate but significant for our interpretation of the texts in question *and* for identifying some of the thorny questions still facing critical human-animal studies.

A. The Cementing and Loosening of Human Bonds

Compared to the way Spinoza sets up a distinction between (hu)mankind and animals in terms of their affects, accompanied by a stern warning about the consequences of forgetting this distinction, the *Zhuangzi*'s treatment of the affective dimension of human-animal interactions is bound to strike one as much more carefree. As discussed in sections 5.1 and 5.2, at no point does the *Zhuangzi* alienate the joys and pains of nonhuman animals more than it alienates the affects of humans, and it never suggests that mingling with fish or tigers takes away from one's cognitive and affective empowerment. In fact, much of the discussion about recognizing the uniqueness of the pains and joys of others is intricately linked to the *Zhuangzi*'s resistance to presumptions of similarity among human beings and its critique of the goals of unifying moral-political norms. Instead, we see a thickening of the manifold of differences that exist between and among human beings and animals, as well as an abandonment of ranking beings in terms of their cognitive and affective aptitudes.

It is difficult to rank the joys of different beings in the *Zhuangzi* when they are all simply doing what they are good at—be it wandering on a bridge or swimming in the river. In fact, in the very same passage in which the question is raised of how much a man can know about the joy of fish, the limits of what this man can know about a fish is compared to what another man can know about this man, particularly because the question is *not* about various creatures being at different stages of cognitive-affective refinement. In the end, the character of Zhuangzi thinks he can tell that the fish are joyful as they wander and swim in the water, because he is himself feeling a similar kind of joy as he is wandering on the Hao bridge. In a way, both are performing a carefree and purposeless action and they both seem to share the joy of unimpeded wandering, albeit in different habitats.

Although at a given moment the joy of fish might not be that different than the joy of a man, differences on a diachronic level are suggested in the larger body of the text. More specifically, there is a contrast drawn between the fixity versus the mobility of affects, which maps onto one's rigidity versus flexibility with the distinctions and judgments one employs.[1] The latter determines the extent to which one can be attuned to the affective states of others (be it a tyrant or a monkey) and (at least within the transmitted text) is performed by various human characters. Yet it is this same ability to continually recalibrate the heart—allowing the affects come and go and enabling the reception of others' joys and pains without being overridden by one's own—that makes one's humanity suspect.

---

[1] Here it should be recalled that both flexibility with one's judgments (which feed into one's behavioral patterns) and the mobility of affects are tied up with operations of the heart. I am indebted to Virág for the framing of enabling and debilitating affects in the *Zhuangzi* in terms of the extent to which they enjoy mobility. Curie Virág, *The Emotions in Early Chinese Philosophy* (New York: Oxford University Press, 2017), 135, 154.

Chapter 4 examined a passage in which the humanity of someone who excels in being flexible is questioned.² A similar line of reasoning applies to people without tenacious affects as well. A dialogue between Huizi and Zhuangzi lays bare the implications of letting go of affective resoluteness for one's humanity. The dialogue has Huizi asking:

— A person without affects (*qing* 情)—how can you call that a human being?
— The *dao* gives him appearance, Heaven gives him shape, so why shouldn't he be called a human being?
— But if you've already called him a human being, how can he be without affects?
— Approving and disapproving things (*shi fei* 是非) is what I call "affects" (*qing* 情). When I talk about not having affects, I mean that a person does not allow likes and dislikes to damage him internally. He just makes it his constant practice to follow along the way things are without adding anything to life.³

Huizi's bafflement shows just how closely intertwined people's humanity and their affects are for him. Zhuangzi's reply, on the other hand, gives another twist to the distorted vision of "humanity" articulated in the text.⁴

As the *Zhuangzi* sometimes critiques and sometimes reconciles with competing discourses of the time, it inevitably builds its alternative models of human behavior around the same themes, but with a distinctive twist. In the aforementioned dialogue, Zhuangzi's clarification of what he means by having no affects demonstrates that what is actually at stake for him is whether or not affects take a strong hold on and hence harm one's person (instead of being concerned with purging one's heart of all affects).⁵ He still calls such people *ren* 人 (human being, person), but only in the nominal sense that

---

² See section 4.4 of chapter 4.
³ In Chinese, the response reads: 是非吾所謂情也。吾所謂無情者，言人之不以好惡內傷其身，常因自然而不益生也。*Zhuangzi* 5:227.
⁴ The possibility of the *Zhuangzi* offering a distorted vision of humanity is also raised in chapter 4, section 4.4, in the context of how human beings seem to be marked by their ability to let go of their humanity.
⁵ This is to say, just as making the heart tenuous should not be understood as making it "empty," not having the fixations of discriminative judgments should not be understood as making no judgments whatsoever. In a similar vein, not having (fixed) affects does not mean never letting any affects enter into one's heart.

they have the appearance (*mao* 貌) and shape (*xing* 形) of a human being.⁶ Earlier we are also told that these are characteristics that are simply given to them⁷ and enable them to congregate (*qun* 群) with others and be part of the crowd.⁸ In other words, such people live in human society without belonging to it in a way that makes easy sense to Huizi.

Such a "nonsensical"⁹ kind of existence, facilitated by the absence of tenacious affects, is a familiar notion to readers of the *Zhuangzi*, exemplified by the story of the three friends Zisanghu, Mengzifan, and Ziqinzhang. As discussed in section 5.3, even when such people befriend each other, their "bond" turns out to be so fleeting that the death of one does not even bother the others, which then shocks the disciple of Kongzi.¹⁰ Given the bonding function of affects, the text's emphasis on the mobility of affects has direct implications for issues related to human togetherness. After all, when one cultivates a noncommittal heart, it simply becomes more difficult to cement ties with other people—hence the many examples of fleeting human bonds in the *Zhuangzi*.

Certainly, as shown in section 5.3, the *Zhuangzi* does not deny the joys of human companionship and at least some human characters seem to cherish a shared sense of absurdity and humor. There might even be a peculiar human dimension to the kind of humor portrayed in the text, given that the kind of laughter that relies on a perceived incongruity is due to forming expectations about how things should unfold—a trait associated with rigidity and

---

⁶ A similar description is employed in the first episode of the Tian Zifang 田子方 chapter, in which the character after which the chapter is titled describes his master as someone who has the appearance of a human but the emptiness of Heaven (*ren mao er tian xu* 人貌而天虛). *Zhuangzi* 21:699.

⁷ As mentioned in chapter 1, section 1.4, "Heaven" connotes what is simply given.

⁸ The description of people congregating (*qun* 群; flock) together also appears in the *Xunzi* to differentiate human beings from birds and wild animals in terms of humans' ability to collaborate together to achieve certain goals. However, as stated by Kim-chong Chong, the *qun* 群 of these people in the *Zhuangzi* has no distinguishing *human* significance and can be understood as part of the more general ideal of joining "all living things" (*wanwu* 萬物; ten thousand things) including human beings. Kim-chong Chong, "Zhuangzi and Hui Shi on Qing 情," *Tsing Hua Journal of Chinese Studies*, New Series 40, no. 1 (2010): 32–33.

⁹ This description is used both in reference to Huizi's bafflement and to Stewart's theory of nonsense, which she primarily defines in terms of occupying two domains at once. See Susan Stewart, *Nonsense: Aspects of Intertextuality in Folklore and Literature* (Baltimore: Johns Hopkins University Press, 1979), 60–62. Other instances in the *Zhuangzi* of embodying different domains (such as the Heavenly and the human) and disparate life forms (such as the human and the animal) at the same time are discussed in more detail in chapter 8, section 8.2.

¹⁰ The *Zhuangzi* divorces the definition of humanity from one's ability to develop social bonds in many other dialogues and stories as well. For instance, in another chapter titled "The Great Source as Teacher" (Da zong shi 大宗師), the third-person narrator talks about the unusually imperturbable people of ancient times, described as "genuine human beings" (真人 *zhenren*), with the following words: "Their bounty may enrich ten thousand generations, but not because they love the humankind" (利澤施於萬物，不為愛人). *Zhuangzi* 6:237.

humanity in the *Zhuangzi*. Laughter then marks the moment of relief from rigid thinking.

Still, the way human companions interact with one another is not unrelated to the way they would interact with any other being. Especially if we take seriously the elements of incongruity and absurdity (or, to put it more precisely, the delight in the unexpected and the unconventional) and the pointed absence of power dynamics, then both the kind of spontaneous yet tenuous human bonding articulated in the *Zhuangzi* and the kind of enthusiastic engagement with the perspectives of various animals unfold out of the same openness to the other, however alien and unfamiliar. They all spring forth from the same kind of "cheekiness" that upends all hierarchies.

To be clear, the period that birthed the *Zhuangzi* was not without anxieties about identification with animal affects and what that could mean for the distribution of one's affective resources. A well-known passage in the *Mengzi* that portrays a conversation about how to redirect one's compassion away from animals (that are slaughtered for sacrifice) to people who might also be suffering concludes with the dictum "a gentleman stays away from the kitchen (the slaughter site)."[11] The gentleman is to avoid the kitchen, not because feeling compassion for animals is something to be frowned upon, but because their suffering is ostensibly inevitable and the primary recipient of one's affective resources is expected to be people. The economy of affects in the *Zhuangzi* also does not present compassion for animals as a moral good.[12] However, what is crucial is that there is not an anxiety around the proper distribution of one's affective resources either. Quite the contrary, the reader is made to appreciate the affective richness of animal lives without being burdened by what that might entail for the amount of care and attention one invests in human relations.

This curiosity about animal affects in the *Zhuangzi* does not lead to a sustained concern about their welfare, nor does the text present grasping the affective states of animals as a good in and of itself. After all, neither the tiger trainer's nor the monkey keeper's appreciation of the affective states of these animals results in their concluding that "perhaps these animals prefer not to live in captivity." There are limitations that come with their jobs, including

---

[11] In Chinese the line reads: 君子遠庖廚也 (*Mengzi* 1A7). A similar line appears in *Liji* 13.2/11–12 ("Yu Zao 玉藻").

[12] In fact, in an episode that is sometimes taken to be a commentary on the *Mengzi* passage, we see a positive portrayal of a butcher who is praised for his slaughtering skills (which he could only cultivate by not keeping his distance away from the kitchen). See *Zhuangzi* 3:125–130.

keeping the tigers and monkeys locked up. No one has a universal responsibility to attend to someone else's pain without considering the specific context. In fact, even in the story of the bird who dies after being exposed to human food and music, what is being criticized is the counter-productiveness of the nobleman's well-intentioned efforts (he wanted to please the bird, not kill it) rather than the fact that a bird was tormented and died.

Hence, just as with Spinoza, none of the stories in the *Zhuangzi* pick out certain activities as simply more morally righteous than others. The crucial difference is that, in the *Zhuangzi*, connecting with the affects of various animals (as well as with those of human beings with unwise demeanors) does not serve as a sign or cause of one's disempowerment. In fact, having a good handle on the affective experiences of an animal is encouraged when the situation (e.g., one's current goals or life circumstances) calls for it.

Spinoza is no stranger to reflections about animal affects. Moreover, as explored in section 6.1, Spinoza too at times places the differences in the affects of animals and humans on par with the differences in the affects of a (sober) philosopher and a drunkard. In fact, as further elucidated in chapter 7, each being for Spinoza is individuated by a different configuration of motion and rest, which makes each being unique.[13] However, that does not erase circles of similarity in nature (or, sometimes, *assumptions* of similarity between oneself and a lower other, as seen in the example of Adam). Moreover, given that adequate ideas concern common features of the world, the more adequate people's understanding becomes, the more the similarities grow between their minds (and hence also bodies). Consequently, this amplifies their rapport and agreement with each other. Strictly speaking, such a mutually enforcing feedback loop should be possible between a man and an animal—or, at least, the fundamental premises of Spinozist ontology do not forbid that—although Spinoza himself cautions against it.

It is certainly difficult to fully relieve the tension surrounding the (hu) man-animal binary in Spinoza; however, it is possible to identify common patterns behind his remarks on rapport with animals. It is clear that Spinoza associates mankind, and not beasts, with reason, and he views human companionship to be a crucial component of fostering one's mental (and thus also corporeal) powers. Still, that he exhorts mankind to distance themselves from the affects of beasts, despite leaving ample room for indulging in all

---

[13] See chapter 7, section 7.1.

sorts of passions, evinces the similarity between human and animal affects and the fragility of human bonds.

Although Spinoza does not refer to the kind of laughter we see in the *Zhuangzi* (that is, the kind that relies on delighting in incongruity and absurdity) as that which bonds mankind, he does speak of cheerfulness and blessedness, which can be cultivated primarily through interactions with one's fellow mankind. On the other end of the affective spectrum, we have melancholy, which emerges as a particular concern in Spinoza's time. That melancholy is associated with misanthropy and identifying with animals has to do with the perceived framing of the "animal question" along the lines of the suffering brought on animals by humans. Although the way Spinoza so fervently distances himself from the melancholic misanthropes and aligns himself with the "human team" may not be too helpful for the contemporary post-humanist movement (which would rather undermine the human-animal distinction altogether), reflecting on what exactly makes Spinoza uncomfortable might.

It is easy, and common practice, to overlook Spinoza's speciesist remarks as acts of whim and perhaps as argumentative oversight, but despite being written four centuries ago, these remarks actually provide us with a unique insight into our own ambivalent attitudes toward the human-nonhuman distinction today. The next section begins with an examination of the "us versus them" dichotomy that is very prominent in Spinoza's thought, together with the questions it raises for fields that critically address conceptualizations of human-animal relations.

B. The Power to Include and Exclude

Although it is clear that Spinoza's ontology allows for the crossing of human-animal boundaries, in that very possibility he locates the need to warn his readers against identifying with beasts. Spinoza's view of the issue as a matter of choosing between bonding with human beings versus with animals is crucial for contemporary readers as well, as it seems that this dichotomy continues to shape many discussions about humans' relation to nonhuman animals.[14]

---

[14] The commonality of this reductive framing of discussions about human-animal relations is precisely why a green-anarchist journal that puts particular emphasis on interactions between humans and nonhumans satirically titles itself "Species Traitor."

We are probably all familiar with hypothetical thought experiments in which one is confronted with a choice to save a human or an animal in an emergency situation (e.g., "If a house is on fire, would you first save the dog or the human?").[15] Apart from the inherent abstractness of such thought experiments in general, in the overwhelming number of instances in which humans interact with nonhuman animals, there is no such disjunctive choice to be made. Yet, like Spinoza, many people perceive bonding with animals as a potentially misanthropic choice; and like Spinoza, many tend to associate bonding with animals with sad passions. As a case in point, the hypothetical scenarios that we fabricate to help us imagine how we would balance human and animal interests are often marked by a strong sense of tragedy (e.g., in the aforementioned thought experiment, no matter what one chooses, a being has to die). In other words, such thought experiments primarily test who we think is worthier of our pity.

Animal cruelty is certainly a crucial topic to tackle, and the Benthamian question "Can they suffer?" is still relevant. However, perhaps we could also follow Haraway's lead and ask "Can they play? Or work?" and pay attention to the ways nonhuman animals increase humans' power and vitality, sometimes through their unrecognized labor and sometimes simply through their companionship.[16] Spinoza acknowledges that various animals also have lusts, appetites, and feelings of gladness. Moreover, he recognizes the positive impact that mundane pleasures have on one's development into an active and free man. Yet he misses the opportunity to mobilize these two insights to discuss the joy-generating aspects of man's interaction with animals and instead attempts to alienate animal affects from those of human beings.

Spinoza attempts to seal the borders separating mankind from animals, particularly because, as the Adam example demonstrates, these borders are very porous. Instead of exposing and celebrating this porosity, Spinoza employs an "us versus them" distinction, perhaps because it is challenging to argue for broader and interlocking circles of affinity and care when that

---

[15] For a discussion of this particular thought experiment, see Gary L. Francione, *Introduction to Animal Rights: Your Child or the Dog?* (Philadelphia: Temple University Press, 2000), 151–165.

[16] Donna J. Haraway, *When Species Meet* (Minneapolis: University of Minnesota Press, 2007), 22. This point is developed in detail by Sharp, who observes that exclusionary paradigms of humanity, which exile "dogs, plants, and robots from our sphere of primary concern," are actually cases of self-negation: "a separation of ourselves from our own power." Sharp, *Spinoza and the Politics of Renaturalization*, 218.

could mean curtailing "our" power at certain points—as demonstrated by the recent backlash to the Green New Deal.[17]

Spinoza's policing of the borders between the human and the animal does not make him a particularly appealing figure in the era of the post-humanist turn. Perhaps that is why it is not uncommon to make readjustments to Spinoza's philosophy in order to "break down the rigidity of Spinoza's conception of what does and does not 'share a common nature with us,'" as Lloyd puts it.[18] While such reimaginings of Spinoza's vision are useful in the endeavor to reformulate humans' relation with nonhuman animals, it is also essential to pay attention to a crucial gift that Spinoza's philosophy, *as it is*, offers us.

The so-called rigidity of Spinoza's conception of "us" partly has to do with the power that such borders have afforded those who are deemed "human." After all, discussions around inclusion and exclusion within a life community are inevitably inflected by who has the power to decide. Perhaps as we are inquiring into new ways of relating to one another and new ways of thinking about what constitutes "us," an exploration of more capacious concepts of power and enrichment is also needed. Such a move would shift the axis of discussion about human-animal relations away from our moral duty to acknowledge animal suffering to a recognition of the affective richness of human-nonhuman interactions.

It is obvious why an approach that blurs the human-animal binary *à la* the *Zhuangzi* would be appealing for critical animality studies. Argumentative gestures that blur the boundaries between the human and nonhuman have long been celebrated in critical animality studies and in ecological movements that are informed by Continental philosophy (such as queer ecology). If the aim is to purposefully destabilize the human-animal opposition, which is tied up with raced, gendered, and classed distinctions in the Greco-European philosophical tradition (and beyond), then one could argue that a text like the *Zhuangzi* can indeed inspire new insights into how to contest dominant theories of human-animal difference. After all, the *Zhuangzi* does invite us to examine the trappings of being at the center of the order of things and to have "the power to include." Through the tragic

---

[17] The Green New Deal is a 2019 congressional resolution that aims to transition away from a fossil-fuel-driven economy in order to address climate crisis. For an overview of the proposed set of policies and the backlash against them, see Coral Davenport and Lisa Friedman, "The Green New Deal: A Climate Proposal, Explained," *The New York Times*, February 21, 2019, https://www.nytimes.com/2019/02/21/climate/green-new-deal-questions-answers.html.

[18] Lloyd, "Spinoza's Environmental Ethics," 301.

stories of creatures like Hundun and the bird who is killed at the hands of a well-intentioned nobleman, the text offers us a glimpse into how gestures of inclusiveness coming from those who represent the norm could easily turn into acts effacing the other.

Surely, awareness of this very fact might help sharpen one's sensitivity to the alterity of different situations and beings. As discussed in the introduction, the inevitable message that the *Zhuangzi* conveys through its storytelling is that there is an incalculable aspect to every situation and being. This insight is mobilized to carry us beyond what Oliver terms "abyssal alterity"[19] and toward critical engagement with others. Such "other-directedness"—that is, gestures of thinking with those who are overlooked if not disparaged—is performed on a textual level as well. By telling stories about beings and people whose voices are often the least heard (i.e., people of humble occupations, foreign peoples, madmen, ex-convicts, trees, birds, and so on), the text demands the reader's sustained engagement with undervalued vantage points.

If, however, one wants to carry this very attitude into a direction that issues liberating solutions to conflicts surrounding humans' treatment of nonhuman animals, then what the *Zhuangzi* offers is only the gift of self-doubt, not pragmatic guideposts. After all, the *Zhuangzi*'s all-inclusive and multivocal approach, which at times manages to decenter the human through radical heteronomy and other-directedness, comes at the price of giving up its claims to authority as a text.

Part II already pointed out the difficulty of isolating themes of epistemic plurality in the *Zhuangzi* from the normatively apathetic conclusions that come with them.[20] Perhaps an equally serious challenge the *Zhuangzi* poses for scholars of human-animal studies is that its grammar of reasoning, which complicates constructions of all distinctions and rankings, including the human-animal binary, also upends many other long-held binaries, such as the one between benefit and harm.

Here lies an important caveat. Although the *Zhuangzi* is known to lend itself to different interpretations, as Perkins aptly puts it, we should still be deeply suspicious of interpretations that construct its characters in the image

---

[19] Kelly Oliver, "Animal Ethics: Toward an Ethics of Responsiveness," *Research in Phenomenology* 40 (2010): 271.

[20] See section C of the concluding portion of Part II. Also see Sonya Özbey, "On Beastly Joys and Melancholic Passions: Cross-Species Communication of Affects in Spinoza and the *Zhuangzi*," in *Dao Companion to the Philosophy of the* Zhuangzi, ed. Kim-chong Chong (New York: Springer, 2022), 748.

of ourselves: tolerant left-leaning intellectuals with a penchant for diversity.[21] Take, for instance, the opening story to the "The Signs of Fullness of Potency" (De chong fu 德充符) chapter, in which we hear the character of Kongzi praising Wang Tai, a one-footed amputee, for not being bothered even by matters of life and death and viewing "the loss of his foot as nothing more than throwing away of a clump of soil."[22] It is clear that the worldview of a character like Wang Tai is not one of kindly expanding one's circles of care to include the underprivileged. It is, instead, the arguably less palatable worldview of someone who does not see a rankable distinction between his foot and a clump of soil.

Similar drastic positions have, in fact, found some supporters within the queer ecology movement, following Timothy Morton's infamous defense of blurring even the distinction between the host and the parasite and thus confounding boundaries "at practically any level."[23] Morton's bold claims have not been received without criticism, and some critical animal theorists, such as Kari Weil, have condemned enthusiasm for such a radical disruption of boundaries as an irresponsible chase after an anarchic thrill.[24] While we are at the peak of calls to blur the boundaries between the human and the nonhuman, an honest yet non-chauvinistic appraisal of where and why we should draw the limits is still wanting. Hence, in fact, perhaps the most crucial contribution of the *Zhuangzi* to a discussion about the blurring of the human-animal boundary is its compelling us to give serious thought to a simple question: Just how far do we want to blur this boundary?

Part IV pursues this question and examines the purported price of muddying the human-animal binary, focusing on a related dichotomy, namely the one between order and disorder. Whether taken as sociopolitical goals or as fundamental assumptions about reality, themes of order (and its absence) prove to be key in weaving together normative and descriptive discourses of the humanity-animality binary. In connection with this, Part IV explores the presence or absence in Spinoza and the *Zhuangzi* of certain investments in notions of the unity and stability of human society and examines the ways these investments are intertwined with their different approaches regarding the stability of certain structures in the world.

---

[21] Perkins, *Heaven and Earth Are Not Humane*, 157.
[22] *Zhuangzi* 5:196.
[23] Timothy Morton, "Guest Column: Queer Ecology," *PMLA: Publications of the Modern Language Association of America* 125, no. 2 (2010): 275–276. 10.1632/pmla.2010.125.2.273.
[24] Kari Weil, *Thinking Animals*, xvii–xxiv.

This fundamental contrast not only lays bare the diversity that exists within various so-called ontologies of interdependence, but also reveals how assumptions about the basic structure of relations among beings—that is, the basic "fabric" of things, as Calarco puts it[25]—easily feed into investments in agenda-setting practical politics, or a lack thereof.

[25] Calarco, *Thinking Through Animals*, 11.

PART IV
THE ORDERLY AND THE CHAOTIC

[Without society, man] would have neither the capacity nor the time to plough, sow, reap, grind, cook, weave and sew for himself as well as doing many other things that are needed to sustain life—not to mention at this point the arts and sciences, which are also supremely necessary to the perfection of human nature and its happiness.

TTP 5.7

In ancient times the people knew . . . their mothers but not their fathers. They lived together with elk and deer, plowing for their food, weaving for their clothes, with no thought in their hearts of harming one another. This is the flourishing of utmost potency.

Zhuangzi 29: 988

7
From Nature's Order to Civil Order

Onto-Political Formations in Spinoza

Although the question of the human-animal divide is often explored through epistemological and sometimes affective differences, it is seldom devoid of underlying assumptions and considerations about the fundamental features of the world around us. Hence Part IV steers this study in the direction of a critical discussion of a cluster of notions that have both ontological and political stakes. More specifically, Part IV analyzes notions of personal and group identity, the body politic, and narratives about unarranged worlds (generally known as "state of nature" theories), all of which are used to justify or critique institutionalized order in Spinoza's corpus and the *Zhuangzi*. Through this multifaceted analysis, Part IV demonstrates the ways in which the ontological is political, while also highlighting that the descriptive and normative discourses of the human-animal binary can be inextricably woven together.

Much of the scholarship on Spinoza focuses on the themes of relationality and interdependence. As section 7.1 of this chapter explains, although Spinoza's philosophy provides a framework for a robust articulation of such themes, this does not change the fact that Spinoza still conceives the world as having intelligible regularities and determinate structures. Chapter 2 drew parallels between the modes of exposition employed in Spinoza's works (such as the geometric format) and the systematic arrangement of nature that ostensibly lends itself to such expository modes. As this chapter shows, Spinoza's view of reality as systematic and structured also informs his views on the relatively more micro-level issues of identity, including issues of individuation, maintaining self-sameness over time, and the lawful character of the transformations that a being can go through.

Although much of the secondary scholarship on Spinoza still treats his *Ethics* and his two political treatises separately,[1] section 7.2 explores how

---

[1] For a critique of this common interpretative approach and an examination of the metaphysical dimension of TTP, see Yitzhak Y. Melamed, "The Metaphysics of the Theological-Political Treatise,"

Spinoza's theory of individuation and maintenance of identity through time provides the ontological ground for his conception of the body politic, with human similarity and togetherness as its premise and its end. Hence, what appear to be deep currents of substance ontology reasserting themselves in Spinoza's metaphysical discussions become intertwined with his commitment to keeping familiar notions of human life and society intact. After examining the ontological positions that inform Spinoza's views on the body politic and social unity, section 7.2 moves on to examining his stated rationale for the building of civil society, such as improvement of people's material conditions and helping them seek "the true virtue and life of the mind" (TP 5.5). The latter goal, we are told, separates mankind from beasts.

The final section of the chapter, that is, section 7.3, further delves into Spinoza's mobilization of animality tropes in order to give weight to the case for the building of civil society. Through an analysis of Spinoza's depictions of transitioning from the state of nature to different kinds of civil order, the section demonstrates that animality is associated not with men in the state of nature, but with a fear-driven wretched state that mankind can "fall" into if they live in bad polities or fail to appreciate all that society has to offer. For Spinoza, such an undesirable possibility is to be averted through the contrivances of institutionalized order that are ideally built under the guidance of reason and according to the facts about the general condition of mankind.

7.1 Individuation and Identity in an Orderly World

Spinoza's philosophy has been celebrated in the last few decades for its theorizing of the interdependence of bodies (and hence also minds) with each other. This theory is especially well accentuated in his account of the operations of the imagination (which gives us information about our own bodies *as* they are affected by other bodies)[2] and in his theory of affects (which envisions bodies as impressionable openings to their surroundings and emphasizes how we identify with and imitate each other's affects).[3] Along with his emphasis on the relational and intersubjective dimensions

---

in *Spinoza's "Theological-Political Treatise": A Critical Guide*, ed. Yitzhak Y. Melamed and Michael A. Rosenthal (New York: Cambridge University Press, 2013), 128–142.

[2] For more on this point, see chapter 3, section 3.3.
[3] For more on this point, see chapter 6, section 6.2.

of one's perceptions, and his account of the circulation of affects as an interpersonal process, Spinoza also undermines atomistic models of subjectivity through his unique theory of individuation. More specifically, for Spinoza, all modes are parts of larger wholes and what is a "part" on one level can be a "whole" on another level, depending on which causal frame of reference one is using.[4] In fact, EIIp13L7 explicitly notes that the borders around an "individual" are negotiable to the extent that we could even think of the whole universe as one big individual.

Despite this flexible account of what constitutes an individual, however, the integrity and singularity of composite bodies/minds for Spinoza are still never eclipsed by the totality they are a part of. Bodies/minds enter into unions with other bodies/minds, but that does not amount to a sudden cosmological identification with the rest of nature or the disappearance of an individual's uniqueness into an undifferentiated whole. Indeed, despite its undermining of clear-cut boundaries drawn around different individuals, we still see in Spinoza's philosophy an attempt to elaborate a non-reductive ontology of difference and singularity, designed to maintain the integrity of individuals. This is because although Spinoza's account of individuation allows for a great degree of flexibility as to what counts as an individual, the *relativity* of these labels does not warrant the *arbitrariness* of certain stable and regular structures that are observed in nature.[5]

For Spinoza, although one can draw the borders around certain structures in different ways, there are still regularities characterized by a constant proportion (or ratio) of motion and rest—a notion that is certainly not peculiar to Spinoza's philosophy.[6] Spinoza, however, employs this notion (of the

---

[4] In EIId7, Spinoza states, "If a number of individuals so concur in one action that together they are all the cause of one effect, I consider them all, to that extent, as one singular thing."

[5] As Carriero also puts it, "The Plenum is not some chaotic flux. It is populated by relatively stable physical individuals: land masses, rocks, trees, dogs, and such. . . . Spinoza thinks of these stable structures as modifications of a more basic [fundamental] order: in each case, the finite thing can exist only in such an order and must be understood through the invariant principles of such an order (this is part of what Spinoza has in mind when he says that modes are 'conceived through' substance)." John Carriero, "Conatus," in *Spinoza's Ethics: A Critical Guide*, ed. Yitzhak Y. Melamed (Cambridge: Cambridge University Press, 2017), 145.

[6] In fact, a similar notion appears in the context of the conservation of movement in Descartes's *Principles of Philosophy* where the total quantity of motion and rest existing in matter remains the same. Paragraph 36 of Part II of the work reads: "God Himself, who, (being all powerful) in the beginning created matter with both movement and rest; and now maintains in the sum total of matter, by His normal participation, the same quantity of motion and rest as He placed in it at that time." As noted by Balibar, Spinoza applies the notion of the conservation of movement to each particular level of integration, where what enjoys stability becomes the proportion of motion and rest, not the total sum of it. See Étienne Balibar, *Spinoza: From Individuality to Transindividuality* [A lecture delivered in Rijnsburg on May 15, 1993] (Delft: Eburon, 1997). Spinoza retains Descartes's notion that the total

ratio of motion and rest) to articulate both the singularity and the constancy of composite entities through time. He accomplishes this through his suggestion that even if the smaller parts constituting a composite body/mind change, if the characteristic configuration of those parts does not, then the body/mind in question will still be identifiable as the same body/mind (EIIp13L4–7).[7]

Spinoza's concern with giving an account of how things keep their identity through time can be explained in terms of his desire to demonstrate that his ontology can articulate this ordinary and familiar aspect of human experience, despite its otherwise controversial conclusions.[8] Aside from explaining the singularity and self-sameness of individuals through time, Spinoza also addresses the issue of the rules of modification, particularly in the context of one being transforming into another. His aim is to provide a sensible account of how things take on different forms,[9] while also cautioning against believing in the possibility of arbitrary mutations among different beings. This is clearly expressed in EIp8s2: "Those who do not know the true causes of things confuse everything and without any conflict of mind feign that both trees and men speak, imagine that men are formed both from stones and from seed, and that any form whatever is changed into any other."[10] This peculiar caveat warning us that trees cannot speak and that men do not come from stones and seeds certainly relies on the view that certain stable structures in the world inform the range of configurations a being can assume.

---

sum of motion and rest in the universe remains unchanged, stating that "the face of the whole universe, which, although varying in infinite ways, yet remains always the same" (Ep.64).

[7] Spinoza clarifies that what he means by the stability of the ratio of motion and rest in composite bodies is the configuration whereby the constituent parts communicate their own motion to each other (although the direction and quantity of the overall motion of the body can change) (EIIp13L7).

[8] Sections 3.1 and 3.2 of chapter 3 discuss Spinoza's substance monism and its controversial implications, such as extension being part of God's nature.

[9] Note that Spinoza also uses the term "form" (*forma*) when describing different configurations of motion and rest. To be more specific, he uses "form" interchangeably with "nature" to describe a complex body, which is then equated with its "ratio" of motion and rest. See the proof to EIVp39 for an example of Spinoza's use of "form" and "ratio of motion and rest" interchangeably; see EIp8s2 for an example of an instance in which the words "nature" and "form" are used interchangeably; and see EIIp10 (together with the proof and scholium) for an example in which all three words are used interchangeably with each other.

[10] TIE 58 utilizes almost the same examples as EIp8s2: "But as we have said, the less men know Nature, the more easily they can feign many things, such as, that trees speak, that men are changed in a moment into stones and into springs, that nothing becomes something, that even Gods are changed into beasts and into men, and infinitely many other things of that kind." It is possible that Spinoza has ancient Greek mythologies in mind with these examples.

In what situations does one go through such a radical change that one loses the characteristic configuration, the ratio of motion and rest, that is one's identity? One obvious case would be a body entering into a relation of assimilation with a more powerful body, in which case we see an increase in the power of the latter body at the expense of the destruction of the weaker body (a typical case of this kind of relation would be one body eating another). Another obvious case is clinical death, which also brings with it the eventual disintegration of the body/mind.

Spinoza's views on death have generated a considerable degree of interpretive disagreement, particularly due to his theory of the "eternity of the mind," which appears in Book V of the *Ethics*. Although often discussed in relation to either everlastingness or atemporality, as Melamed demonstrates, Spinoza's notion of eternity pertains to conceiving things as they are defined through God, who is self-necessitated.[11] This also means, as Yovel points out, that the eternity of the mind is something experienced during one's lifetime (instead of something that follows one's medical death).[12] In other words, the eternity of the mind can be seen as conceiving things via reason, that is, viewing them "under a certain species of eternity" (*sub quadam specie aeternitatis*) (EIIp44c2).[13] This amounts to the generation of adequate ideas and

---

[11] Spinoza explicitly contrasts the eternity of the mind with everlastingness in EVp34s. Moreover, as Melamed notes, in EVp23s Spinoza clarifies that eternity should not be considered in relation to time. In addition, Spinoza equates eternity with necessity in EIVp62d. This serves as the textual basis for Melamed's interpretation that eternity, for Spinoza, is primarily a modal notion and, as CM 2.1 puts it, "conveys the existence of a thing whose existence necessarily follows from its own essence" (such as God). Hence, Melamed concludes that Spinoza's notion of eternity applies to that which is "self-necessitated." For further reading, see Yitzhak Y. Melamed, "Eternity in Early Modern Philosophy," in *Eternity*, 133, 148–163.

[12] Yovel reads Spinoza's view of the eternity of the mind as a form of "secular salvation," consisting not in immortality but in the realization of eternity within one's lifetime. Yirmiyahu Yovel, *Spinoza and Other Heretics*, vol. 1, *The Marrano of Reason* (Princeton, NJ: Princeton University Press, 1989), 154–168.

[13] Another common misunderstanding is that with the very discussion of the eternity of the "mind," Spinoza must be suggesting an excess of mind over body. In fact, Taylor refers to it as a fundamental incoherence in Spinoza's thought, and Bennett famously dismisses it as unsalvageable, stating that "the time has come to admit that this part of the *Ethics* has nothing to teach us and is pretty certainly worthless." See Alfred. E Taylor, "Some Incoherencies in Spinozism, Part II," *Mind* 46, no. 183 (July 1937): 281–301 (reprinted in S. Paul Kashap, ed., *Studies in Spinoza: Critical and Interpretive Essays* [Berkeley: University of California Press, 1972]); Jonathan Bennett, *A Study of Spinoza's Ethics* (Indianapolis, IN: Hackett, 1984), 372. Here I follow Lloyd's reading, which convincingly suggests that when Spinoza is talking about the eternity of the mind, he may simply be attending to the mind side of the mind-body pair. This is a move that he makes earlier in the *Ethics* in the context of his discussion of the affects when he invokes a distinction between considering an affect in relation to the mind alone versus in relation to the "mind and body together" (EIIIp9s). A similar move is also made toward the end of Book V of the *Ethics*, in EVp40s, where after an examination of the correlation between perfection and reality, Spinoza states that "there are things I have decided to show concerning the mind, *in so far as* it is considered without relation to the body's existence" (my emphasis). Finally, in EVp39, Spinoza speaks of a correlation between having a body "capable of a great many things"

hence, also, of an inannihilable active joy, which replaces painful emotions such as fear, including the fear of death.[14] In the final analysis, Spinoza clearly does not deny clinical death, neither does he argue for an excess of mental life after the death of the body.

A more challenging notion for a coherent interpretation of Spinoza's conceptualization of identity is that a body can die even when, as he adds,

> the circulation of the blood is maintained, as well as the other [signs] on account of which the body is thought to be alive. . . . For no reason compels me to maintain that the body does not die unless it is changed into a corpse. And, indeed, experience seems to urge a different conclusion. Sometimes a man undergoes such changes that I should hardly have said he was the same man. (EIVp39s)

Spinoza explains what he means with two illustrative examples, both of which suggest that he sees such a change in one's ratio as a possible, but not as a recurrent phenomenon that is repeated through one's lifetime. One example he gives is about a Spanish poet who seems to have suffered amnesia and "was left so oblivious to his past life that he did not believe the tales and tragedies he had written were his own" (EIVp39s). The other example is about a man of advanced years who "believes [infants'] nature to be so different from his own that he could not be persuaded that he was ever an infant, if he did not make this conjecture himself from others" (Ibid.). These two examples, which frame continuity in terms of whether an individual relates to his or her own past, make it obvious that Spinoza's notion of the ratio of motion and rest also serves to explain conventional notions of selfhood, according to which one enjoys enough stability to identify as the same person for extended periods of time (and, in most cases, through most of one's lifetime).

What is especially curious about the examples of the Spanish poet and the elderly man is that immediately after Spinoza gives them, he cuts the discussion short with this dismissive remark: "Rather than provide the *superstitious*

---

and having "a mind whose greatest part is eternal," emphasizing both the fact that it is the parts of the mind that are eternal (i.e., some ideas are eternal) and that his discussion of the "eternity" of the mind is about being "active" (i.e., having adequate ideas).

[14] As discussed in chapter 6, section 6.3, an affect can only be destroyed by an opposite affect. Since there is no such thing as an "active sadness," there is an enduring quality to "active joy."

with material for raising questions, I prefer to leave this discussion unfinished" (Ibid., emphasis mine). It is unclear to whom exactly Spinoza is referring with the label "superstitious." It is possible that his target is certain adherents of the Hermetic praxis, some of whom believed in reincarnation and the distinction between the soul and the body.[15] Beliefs in voluntary metamorphosis were also known to be present in seventeenth-century Europe, which might explain Spinoza's hesitance to delve further into cases of one's ratio of motion and rest changing before one's medical death. Regardless of whom Spinoza might be targeting, his focus on giving an account of how things maintain their identity through time and under different circumstances seems to be informed by his desire to distance himself from the circles that put forth a more radical view of transformation and change based on preternatural convictions about the very nature of the world.

Spinoza's formulation of both the preservation of identity through time and the orderliness of the transformations that individuals go through applies both to human subjects and, as the next section explains, to sociopolitical communities. His conceptualization of collective units as composite but unified individuals also serves as the metaphysical foundation for his body politic and gives further ontological support to his formulation of human solidarity.

7.2 Uniting as One Mind and Body

As shown in section 7.1, Spinoza's theory of individuation ultimately renders the ontological boundaries around an "individual" negotiable. However, that does not prevent Spinoza from providing an ontological ground for both the uniqueness and the perceived self-sameness of individuals. Moreover, when we look at how Spinoza actually mobilizes the ontological negotiability of what counts as an individual, we see that instead of going in the direction of disintegrating persons into a wider network of forces, relations, and assemblages (as the Deleuzian readings of Spinoza sometimes propose),[16] Spinoza simply opts for giving an ontological formulation of

---

[15] For an examination of how, beginning with the Italian Renaissance of the late fifteenth century, "Hermetic philosophy" rapidly spread throughout Europe and found many adherents, in particular during the sixteenth and the first half of the seventeenth centuries, see Roelof van den Broek and Wouter J. Hanegraaff, eds., *Gnosis and Hermeticism from Antiquity to Modern Times* (Albany: State University of New York Press, 1997).

[16] For a brilliant exploration of this particular direction, see Jane Bennett, *Vibrant Matter: A Political Ecology of Things* (Durham, NC: Duke University Press, 2010).

bigger individuals. In other words, Spinoza goes along with the politico-philosophical sensibilities of the period and mobilizes his ontology of individuation to give an account of the body politic, which he then recruits to the task of the conceptual cementation of human solidarity.

Just as Spinoza speaks of distinct forms of naturally occurring groupings, such as stones and men, in TP he also speaks of the form of a political realm and tells us that the "form of the dominion" (*imperii forma*) endows the community with its special structure and the absence of change (*mutatio*).[17] Spinoza's formulation of the kind of stability enjoyed by the political body squarely maps onto the way he envisions the stability of individual persons, which is also clearly expressed in his conception of the body politic (*civitatis corpus* or *imperii corpus*). Spinoza repeatedly speaks about how the collective forms one body and/or one mind, which relates to not only people's like-mindedness in matters of strategic interest but also their readiness to serve and guard the political body the same way they would take care of and defend themselves in the state of nature.[18] At times, Spinoza also explains the division of labor within the governing structure through body-politic metaphors, such as his referring to the king as the "mind of the commonwealth" (*mens civitatis*).[19]

Spinoza's articulation of the formation of a political structure in terms of the construction of a super-individual, combined with his theory of knowledge and affects, brings into relief a tension pointed out in chapter 3, namely, how do we talk about human beings as a group, given Spinoza's disparaging

---

[17] See TP 6.2, 7.26, 7.30, 8.7, 8.13, 8.14. Regarding Spinoza's using the term "form" (*forma*) to describe the stability of states, Moreau points out that the political use of the term "form" is more complicated. Spinoza claims in TP 6.2 that uprisings, rather than destroying the state, "change its form into another" (suggesting that change in form does not necessarily translate into destruction of the state). However, Spinoza also adds that "by means necessary to preserve a dominion, I intend such things as necessary to preserve the existing form of the dominion, without any notable change" (Ibid.). Moreau argues that the ambiguity of use is due to the fact that a political state is not a "natural" object in that context—which, on the one hand is a problematic conclusion since everything unfolds within nature in Spinoza, but on the other hand, as we have seen earlier, Spinoza occasionally does help himself by using the natural/artificial split when describing nations in contrast to individuals. See Pierre François Moreau, "The Metaphysics of Substance and the Metaphysics of Forms," in *Spinoza on Knowledge and the Human Mind: Papers Presented at the Second Jerusalem Conference (Ethica II)*, ed. Yirmiyahu Yovel and Gideon Segal (Leiden: Brill, 1994), 34.

[18] See TP 7.22. Also see TTP 3.5, EIVp18s, EIVapp.12, TP 2.16, TP 3.2, TP 3.7, and TP 3.11.

[19] TP 6.19. Spinoza also compares the council officiating before the sovereign to the external senses of the body. The series of analogies he uses reads: "The king is to be regarded as the mind of the commonwealth [*mens civitatis*], and this council as the mind's external senses [*mentis sensus externi*], or body of the commonwealth [*civitatis corpus*], through which the mind perceives the condition of the commonwealth and does what it decides is best for itself." The passage is also interesting for Spinoza's employment of what seems like mind/body dualism, where the mind controls the senses and the body.

remarks about abstract generalizations?[20] Despite the occasionally strong language Spinoza uses to express human beings' likeness to one another,[21] given his formulation of singular essences (i.e., the ratio of motion and rest that defines each individuated thing), human individuals are, strictly speaking, only similar, and not identical, to each other.[22] This similarity is often undermined given that men are subject to passions, which causes them to be "drawn in different directions" and grow "contrary to one another, while they require one another's aid" (EIVp37s2). However, as will be shown, moving from the state of nature to civil order facilitates in people an increased similarity to each other by affecting both their imaginative and rational capacities.

People have an interest in forming communities because, we are told, in the state of nature "every man lives as he pleases with his life at risk" (TP 5.2), "is every day overcome by sleep, frequently by sickness or mental infirmity, and eventually by old age" (TP 3.11), and "is permitted to regard as an enemy anyone who tries to prevent his getting his way" (TTP 16.3). Organized society provides obvious benefits, such as avoiding "injury from other people and from animals" (TTP 3.5), and also the division of labor and expertise (TTP 5.7). Hence, Spinoza also adds that "those who live barbarously, without any political organization, lead wretched and brutish lives" (TTP 5.7; translation modified).[23]

Mutual assistance is crucial not only to "support life" but also to cultivate the life of the mind (TP 2.15). After all, living in organized society, with division of labor and expertise, makes possible the arts and sciences "which are also supremely necessary to the perfection of human nature and its

---

[20] As examined in chapter 3, section 3.3, Spinoza criticizes "bad" universals, which are generalized categories that are formed solely via imagination and thus reflect its random character. Examples include different conceptions of humans as laughing animals, featherless bipeds, or rational animals (EIIp40s1).

[21] For instance, Spinoza describes the benefits of human companionship as "[when] two individuals of entirely the same nature are joined to one another, they compose an individual twice as powerful as each one" (EIVp18s; in Latin it reads: "Si enim duo exempli gratia ejusdem prorsus naturæ individua invicem junguntur, individuum componunt singulo duplo potentius"). Similarly, Spinoza offers an alternative version of the myth of the Fall in which Adam feels closer to a beast than a woman "who agrees entirely with his own nature" (*quæ cum sua natura prorsus conveniebat*) (EIVp68s).

[22] As Lee Rice puts it, two humans share a "nature not because they share an identical essence but because they share a similar essence" and "there is no higher order essence . . . which confers this state of being upon them." Lee C. Rice, "Tanquam Naturae Humane Exemplar: Spinoza on Human Nature," *Modern Schoolman* 68, no. 4 (1991): 299.

[23] Israel and Silverthorne translate "qui barbare" as those "who live primitive lives" instead of those "who live barbarously."

happiness" (TTP 5.7). The latter point—helping mankind not only survive but thrive—serves both as one of the raisons d'être of organized society and the condition of its longevity and strength. As Spinoza emphatically says, "Human life ... is characterized not just by the circulation of blood and other features common to all animals, but especially by reason, the true virtue and life of the mind" (TP 5.5). As discussed in chapter 6, due to the complexity of their minds and bodies, human beings stimulate each other in a greater variety of ways, which is good for the life of the mind.[24] Although compelling people to refrain from harming one other and promoting cooperation often requires laws that work on their passions, such as instilling hope for improved lives and fear of punishment by laws,[25] a good society is geared toward fostering the growth of reason.[26] As people become increasingly guided by reason, their agreement with one other grows, and their inclination to want for others what they want for themselves intensifies (EIVp68s).[27]

To some extent, even without the eventual enhancement of their epistemic powers, people's coming together to form a civil order can be said to be gradually making them more similar to each other because (1) according to Spinoza human beings are imitative creatures, and (2) when they form a larger super-individual—the political body—they strive for the same things, abide by the same laws, and become transformed by the same institutions (TP 3.3).

In regard to human beings' imitative nature, Balibar aptly notes that in Spinoza, inter-subjective relations easily slip into "a double process of identification: We identify ourselves with other individuals because we perceive a partial likeness" and "we project our own affections upon them (or theirs upon ourselves)."[28] To this, one should add the inclination to imitate the affects of those one deems to be similar to oneself, which then actualizes the

---

[24] For more, see chapter 6, section 6.2.
[25] TTP 5.9, EIVp37s2.
[26] In fact, stability alone can foster the growth of reason, since in a society that is "less vulnerable to fortune" people will be less prone to be vacillating between hope and fear and hence will be less prone to "superstition." On this point, see TTP 3.5.
[27] In fact, Spinoza notes that if mankind were to follow only "what true reason points them to, society would surely need no laws" (TTP 5.8).
[28] Balibar, *From Individuality to Transindividuality*, 17. Balibar notes this in relation to EIIIp27, which states that when "we imagine a thing like ourselves, toward which we have felt no affect, to be affected by an affect, we are thereby affected by a similar affect" (translation modified). The phenomenon that Balibar calls a "double process of identification" was discussed in chapter 6, section 6.2, in relation to Adam's imitation of the affects of the beast.

perceived similarity.²⁹ Spinoza's descriptions of the continuous circulation of affects through processes of identification, projection, and imitation also tell us that human sociability (and, sometimes, to Spinoza's lament, interspecies sociability)³⁰ is as much integral to their existence as their propensity to be "envious and burdensome to one another" (EIVp35s). Such imitative inclinations can lead to even greater similarities among people, as they help form the idea of "fellow citizens" who are just like oneself. These inclinations also explain why Spinoza controversially sets forth an "exemplar" of human nature in the preface to EIV, intended to guide one to individual perfection by emulation.³¹

Certainly, Spinoza does not simply rely on a model of emulation to guide human behavior. Also crucial are rules and regulations—which oblige even the less wise to act *as if* they had well-developed reason, which then actually provides them with the conditions to develop their reason. Acting under the same laws, sharing the same rules for living (*rationes vivendi*) supports what Steinberg terms a "pattern of coordinated behavior" among citizens³² that shapes the kinds of beings people develop into just as much as they shape the *ratio* themselves. This bidirectional dynamic between the citizens and the rules for living is expressed in Spinoza's observations about the patterns of human conduct upon which the rules for living are based³³ and in his declaration that "men aren't born civil, they become civil,"³⁴ which clarifies that the rules of society transform those who make and then follow them. The two kinds of law (natural³⁵ and human) are different from, but not at odds

---

²⁹ The best example of this phenomenon is Spinoza's version of the story of the Fall. In this account, Adam begins imitating the affects of the beast after deeming it similar to himself. This is discussed in detail in chapter 6, section 6.2.

³⁰ On this point, see chapter 6, section 6.2.

³¹ I owe this point to Gatens. See Moira Gatens, "The Condition of Human Nature: Spinoza's Account of the Ground of Human Action in the *Tractatus Politicus*," in *Spinoza's Political Treatise: A Critical Guide*, ed. Yitzhak Y. Melamed and Hasana Sharp (Cambridge: Cambridge University Press, 2018), 55. Spinoza himself is defensive about the gesture, noting that although the terms "good" and "bad" are simply notions that are formed through the comparison of different experiences, we still desire to "form an idea of man, as a model of human nature, which we may look to" for it may still help us pass to a state of greater perfection (EIVpref.).

³² Justin Steinberg, "Spinoza and Political Absolutism," in Melamed and Sharp, *Spinoza's Political Treatise*, 182.

³³ For instance, we all share the fear of being alone and having to acquire the necessities of life on our own (TP 6.1).

³⁴ TP 5.2. In Latin it reads: "Homines enim civiles non nascuntur, sed fiunt." I follow Curley's translation here.

³⁵ Strictly speaking, there are eternal truths that are perceived as "law" when we do not understand the causes behind them. For a discussion of this point, see Yitzhak Y. Melamed, "Eternity in Early Modern Philosophy," in *Eternity: A History*, ed. Yitzhak Y. Melamed (New York: Oxford University Press, 2016), 147–149.

with, each other.[36] The processes for making nations and fellow citizens are to be situated within the larger chain of historical developments[37]—which, if we follow the premises of Spinoza's philosophy to their coherent conclusions, unfold within nature and not against it.[38]

Although having shared institutions and rules for living yields gradual similarity and agreement among fellow citizens, a stable and strong community—i.e., a community that aids the flourishing of reason—is not simply about the uniformity of thoughts and lifestyles. The development of reason indeed brings with it agreement among mankind and causes people to desire "to maintain the principle of common life and common advantage ... [and] to live according to the common decision of the state [and to] keep common laws of the state" (EIVp73d). However, in order for reason to flourish, people must be able to cultivate doubt and voice discontent when necessary (TP 6.4). Just as Spinoza speaks of the variations that a body can undergo without changing its form, he speaks of "the quarrels and rebellions that are often stirred up in a commonwealth," which, when "settled while still preserving the structure of the commonwealth" (TP 6.2) do not lead to dissolution of a political body. In other words, a good community should be able to accommodate civil disobedience and the change that it can prompt, while keeping its integrity, so that it can foster the flourishing of reason.

Having examined the ways in which Spinoza's discussions of the body politic and human togetherness are informed by his ontological conceptualization of regularities, as well as the varying degrees of affinities and differences in the world, we can proceed to explore the associative and connotational dimensions of Spinoza's political philosophy. It is within this context that we see a consistent tendency to link aggression with animality. Spinoza mobilizes this association to give rhetorical force to his argument advocating deliberate structuring of human encounters as a key strategy to improve the material and intellectual well-being of human beings.

---

[36] That would be an instance of situating humans in nature as a "dominion within a dominion," where humans are considered to be disturbing the natural order rather than following it as everything else does (EIIIpref).

[37] Spinoza states it is only differences of language, law, and accepted customs (*mores recepta*) that separate individuals into nations (TTP 17.26; Israel and Silverthorne render "mores recepta" as "morality").

[38] Spinoza explicitly says that the state is a "natural thing" (*res naturalis*) and hence is bound by the laws of nature. TP.4.4.

7.3 Big Fish Eat Small Fish

The association between aggression and anti-social affects, on the one hand, and animality, on the other, is very clear in Spinoza's corpus, considering that the rare examples of animal life he gives consist of warring bees, jealous doves, and big fish eating small fish (Ep.19, TTP 16.2). Although Spinoza makes a point of emphasizing that the affects of beasts are different from those of humans (EIIIp57s), passive affects (especially sad passions) still seem to have a way of traveling between human beings and various animals. As discussed in chapter 6, Spinoza is troubled by the possibility of men preferring the company of beasts over that of mankind, which he presents as an act of choosing a life of subrationality and passions over the enabling companionship of human beings.

This narrative of the disjunctive choice that one shall make between humanity and animality has implications for Spinoza's political theory as well. First, in another critical address to animal sympathizers, Spinoza notes:

> Those who know how to find fault with men ... are burdensome both to themselves and to others. That is why many, from too great an impatience of mind, and a false zeal for religion, have preferred to live among beasts rather than among men. They are like boys or young men who cannot bear calmly the scolding of their parents, and take refuge in the army. (EIVapp.13; translation modified)

It is not clear whether these sad passions are the cause or the result of people's bonding with animals (perhaps both). We do not have evidence of "many" men of Spinoza's time actually exiting society to live among beasts, but there certainly was a perception of many people joining in a bitter denunciation of the society they were living in—hence Spinoza also cautioning against solitary life and venerating beasts (considering the two to be interchangeable) and reminding us that "we do derive, from the society of our fellow men, many more advantages than disadvantages" (EIVp35s).[39] In this either-or scenario of either being part of a civil order or living among beasts, the beast-loving misanthropists emerge as being under the spell of

---

[39] Note that Spinoza also associates melancholy with misanthropy and beastliness. Moreover, there was a perception of melancholy being on the rise in Spinoza's milieu. For more on these points, see chapter 6, section 6.3.

impatience and religious zealotry, which adds an element of emotional turmoil and intensity to their condition.[40] Later in the same passage they are infantilized and likened to rebellious teenagers who, out of anger for their parents, take refuge in armies and find themselves in the middle of hardships instead of enjoying the comforts of home. The depiction of the conditions that these beast-sympathizers embrace as war-like echoes Spinoza's description of the state of nature as wretched and brutish (TTP 5.7). This clearly demonstrates that Spinoza associates animality and living in the "wilderness" with violence, which then makes living in organized human societies the opposite of that.[41]

Although Spinoza consistently associates antagonism and aggression with animality, these qualities are certainly not exclusive to animals. In fact, human beings can pose greater threats to each other in the state of nature. Spinoza notes that

> insofar as men are assailed by anger, envy, or any emotion deriving from hatred, they are drawn apart and are contrary to one another and *are therefore the more to be feared, as they have more power and are more cunning and astute than other animals*. And since men are by nature especially subject to these emotions ... *men are therefore by nature enemies*. For he is my greatest enemy whom I must most fear and against whom I must most guard myself (TP 2.14; my emphasis)

Despite Spinoza's depiction of men in the state of nature as each other's natural enemies, the transition from the state of nature to civil society is still not described in terms of the acquisition of a second nature that would overwrite a belligerent "animal-nature." Quite the contrary, it involves building on people's existing inclinations, for even when they are "led more by passion than by reason," people, we are told, naturally "unite and consent to be guided as if by one mind" through some common affect, such as "a common hope or common fear" (TP 6.1).[42] In other words, although civil laws and

---

[40] Sometimes melancholy too—a condition that Spinoza associates with turning away from mankind to beasts—connoted false religious zeal in Spinoza's milieu, which is seen in sectarian attacks that portray Calvinism or Catholicism as driving one to extreme humility and melancholy. See Gowland, "The Problem of Early Modern Melancholy," 103–109.

[41] Sharp makes a similar point when she observes that *bruta*, for Spinoza, "represent bellicose and violent tendencies." See Sharp, *Spinoza and the Politics of Renaturalization*, 200.

[42] That is to say, even when people are not guided by reason, their passions do not always pull them in different directions. Passions can also pave the way toward building a civil order. This is also how

natural laws are different, the former still derives from nature *and* from the general condition of mankind.⁴³ Hence, as Armstrong aptly notes, "The passage from the state of nature to civil society is not represented in terms of a rupture or discontinuity" in Spinoza, who instead "presents the state as a stabilizing and structuring power produced from within the play of power relations operative in society."⁴⁴ This is also to say that the starting point for Spinoza's political philosophy is not individuals who are compelled by harsh conditions into forming a community through a contract.⁴⁵ Instead, his starting point is the desire to form enabling alliances so that one can grow even stronger.⁴⁶

Since, for Spinoza, one's power of thinking may increase or decrease, who belongs on the outskirts of humanity and who does not should be subject to change. Although Spinoza does not call men in the state of nature beast-like—despite their apparent antagonism toward each other—he does describe men living in bad polities as such. When describing communities that "dominate or control people by fear or subject them to the authority of another," Spinoza notes that the ultimate purpose of the state is not "to turn people from rational beings into beasts or automata, but rather to allow their minds and bodies to develop in their own ways in security and enjoy the free use of reason" (TTP 20.6). Chapter 6 analyzed Spinoza's alternative account of the Fall, which he attributes to Adam's loss of freedom after he identifies with the beast and begins imitating its affects.⁴⁷ Given the rhetorical work

---

Spinoza explains the foundation of Jewish theocracy in the TTP 2.15—that is, in terms of a group of people who fear the same enemies and love the same God.

⁴³ In fact, in TP 6.1, Spinoza also notes that it is natural for mankind to form a civil order and that this civil order can never be entirely dissolved. Also, see TP 1.7 for an approach that sees civil order as an omnipresent feature of human groupings (whether they are "barbarous" or not).

⁴⁴ Aurelia Armstrong, "Natural and Unnatural Communities: Spinoza Beyond Hobbes," *British Journal for the History of Philosophy* 17, no. 2 (2009): 279, 292–293.

⁴⁵ This separates Spinoza from someone like Hobbes for whom the state of nature is primarily defined by man's lupine tendencies and desire for self-preservation (as opposed to the desire for becoming stronger together with others). On this point, also see chapter 6, footnote 40.

⁴⁶ This has roots in Spinoza's ontology as well, given that for Spinoza the only thing that prevents something from becoming infinitely powerful is the existence of other beings (EIIIp30d). The default position is not the limitations one has but the tendency to grow more powerful unless prevented otherwise. This view is also expressed in Spinoza's employment of the notion of *conatus* (striving) to refer not only to a stubborn desire to survive, but to striving to increase one's power. For further reading on this point, see Della Rocca, *Spinoza*, 155–157, and Yitzhak Y. Melamed, "When Having *Too Much* Power Is Harmful: Spinoza on Political Luck," in Melamed and Sharp, *Spinoza's Political Treatise*, 161–162.

⁴⁷ For more on this, see chapter 6, section 6.2.

that the imagery of the beast does in Spinoza's political philosophy, the story of the Fall can also be read as an allegory for a bad polity.

In fact, in addition to hypothetical examples of communities that reduce men to beasts or automata, Spinoza gives the example of actual communities—namely, the "Turks"[48]—who allegedly exhibit "slavery, barbarism, and desolation" (*servitium, barbaries et solitudo*).[49] This characterization appears in the context of a discussion regarding communities that cause their citizens to fall prey to superstition under the cloak of religion. They, Spinoza asserts, "extinguish the light of the intellect," and "turn rational man into brutes" (TTP Pref.9). The language of deterioration and misdirection is consistently used in Spinoza's discussion of superstition, which leads people "astray,"[50] is "childish,"[51] and, once again, reduces mankind to beasts.[52] Given all these descriptions of decline stemming from superstition, it could be said that the Turks' ostensible succumbing to superstition serves an example of a contemporary "Fall" during Spinoza's time.

That there are post-lapsarian societies reducing men to a beast-like existence sheds another light on Spinoza's views on the nature and functional necessity of society. What is at stake in a well-functioning political order (that is geared toward fostering human perfection) is not the mere organization of encounters to facilitate the management of vital sources and increase efficiency in various ways. Not only "Turks" can do it, but literal beasts—such as bees, as Spinoza admits—do it.[53] As mentioned earlier, Spinoza stresses the importance of arts and sciences, as well as the ability to cultivate doubt and express discontent, to aid the flourishing of reason. The first has to do with leisure mobilized to foster reason and the second with a dynamic public discourse, which is also good for the life of the mind.[54] "Extinguishing the light of reason" through the absence of these elements and/or the presence of an environment of sanctioned credulity (or "superstition" promoted under the cloak of religion, as Spinoza would put it) is the direct opposite of what

---

[48] The term "Turks" seems to serve as a proxy for Muslims in Spinoza, which is evidenced in Spinoza's remark that Christians, Jews, Turks, and Pagans have identical lifestyles despite their desire to be different from each other (TTP pref. 9).

[49] TP 6.4. Spinoza's views on Turks (and Muslims, as the two are used interchangeably) are discussed in more detail in chapter 10, section 10.1

[50] Ep.54.

[51] Ep.21.

[52] In Ep.76, Spinoza writes: "Away with this destructive superstition, and acknowledge the faculty of reason which God gave you, and cultivate it, unless you would be counted among the beasts."

[53] KV. Part II, chapter XXIV.

[54] Spinoza also warns against too much leisure when he notes in TP 7.20 that "men who enjoy abundant leisure are prone to contemplate crime." The same sentiment is repeated in TP 10.4

a good commonwealth is supposed to achieve. Does that mean a bad polity could be even worse than the state of nature? Probably not.

Despite describing mankind as each other's natural enemies, as noted in chapter 6, Spinoza also declares that "man is a God to man" (*homo homini Deus est*) (EIVp35s).[55] Although a bad polity acting as a "false God" serves as a clear impediment to the flourishing of reason, salvation is still possible and lies in each other. The question then becomes: Does mankind's salvation simply lie in each other's company or in living within an institutionalized civil order?[56] Here we run into another form of disjunctive thinking in Spinoza's philosophy. The state of nature, for Spinoza, signifies solitude from mankind instead of, let us say, a simple gathering of people without laws and institutions.[57] In fact, although the imagery of the Garden of Eden is part of Spinoza's rhetorical arsenal, just as he imagines there to be a disjunctive choice between the company of beasts versus mankind, Spinoza's justifications for the need for organized society revolve around contrastive scenarios between living a solitary life where every man fends for himself versus living in a commonwealth (*civitas*) with all its laws and institutions.[58]

Relatedly, Spinoza does not articulate the threshold that would separate a community from an organized polity, although he does give a baseline definition of civil order when he states that the purpose of civil order (*finis status civilis*) "is nothing other than peace and security of life" (TP 5.2). An arrangement that ensures the security of life would remove one from a war-like existence, which Spinoza associates with animality.

Now, as seen earlier, Spinoza also describes the presence of factors that foster the life of the mind as that which ultimately separates mankind from beasts. However, it should be kept in mind that he also simultaneously describes a good polity as aiding "the perfection of human nature." In other words, in his descriptions of certain polities as reducing men to beasts, there is both (1) the element of conflating a "model" of human nature with that of the general nature of humankind (which then suggests that bad polities are only preventing mankind from reaching a state of greater perfection instead

---

[55] See chapter 6, section 6.3. As noted there too, Spinoza's sentiment forms a contrast with the Hobbesian dictum "man is a wolf to man."

[56] Spinoza in the TP takes monarchy, aristocracy, and democracy to constitute an exhaustive list of civil orders. His account of all three types of civil order involves descriptions of the types of institutions (e.g., supreme council, senate, and syndic) that each type of civil order requires.

[57] See, for instance, TP 2.15 where Spinoza notes about the state of nature that "it is vain for one man alone to try to guard himself against all others."

[58] See TP 6.1 for an example of such a contrastive scenario.

of making them worse than they were in the state of nature); and (2) resorting to hyperbole to express his indignation at the sight of those who fall short of what they could have been.

In the end, assuming the choice is between solitude versus living with others in an institutionalized setting that organizes our encounters (hopefully in enabling ways), then human togetherness is to be defended against the cynicism of misanthropic folks—despite people's many disappointing qualities. In the absence of the contrivances of institutionalized order that are ideally built under the guidance of reason (which enables them to further facilitate the growth of reason), fear, conflict, and hardships can take over—so much so that a polity may appear to be only a *"little different from a state of nature."*[59] Yet, not only does uniting into one body with others render one safer and prosperous, even in the post-lapsarian state; it is not any beast, but Eve who can reignite in Adam the light of reason.

---

[59] TP 5.2; my emphasis. The actual line in Latin is: "non multum ab ipso naturali statu differt."

8
Unmanaging the Personal and the Political Body in the *Zhuangzi*

Having a strong reactionary dimension, much of the *Zhuangzi*'s discussions of themes of personhood, the body politic, and institutionalized order unfold in the context of its critique of some of the prevalent discourses on the same themes. The first section of the chapter begins with an examination of the text's parallel critique of both unitary views of personhood and of the political body. The section also revisits the *Zhuangzi*'s treatment of the notion of the heart (*xin* 心), but this time from the angle of the body politic. Section 8.2 furthers the discussion by exploring the *Zhuangzi*'s tales of identity-blurring and self-fragmentation, which, whether the context is clinical death or sudden bodily and/or cognitive change, defy personal and group boundaries at the same time. This unstable and fragmentary view of personhood is certainly also informed by a cynical view of the ideological structures that organize human behavior to produce orderly, stable, and self-coherent persons and communities.

The intertwining of these ontological and political discussions about order, stability, and unity (as ontological assumptions about the world *and* as ideals for human communities) comes to full fruition in section 8.3. The section begins with an examination of some of the competing early Chinese narratives of antiquity, which are invoked to depict the envisioned order of things. Within that framework animality features as a distinct marker for the absence of moral-political arrangements. The section then analyzes the *Zhuangzi*'s views on governance and orderliness (*zhi* 治), which are varied, ranging from criticizing ideals of governance to promoting paradoxical versions of it. However, as will be shown, even the most establishmentarian layers of the text, which allow for hierarchical dynamics within a community, do not have animality as their conceptually constitutive element. This, I argue, relates to the fact that the *Zhuangzi*'s distorted vision of "order" (i.e., the "great order"; *da zhi* 大治) is not formulated in opposition to an antonym (such as *luan* 亂 [disorder, confusion, chaos]), nor is it credited for having emancipated people from a lesser existence.

8.1 From Unity to Fragmentation: Undermining the Heart of the Personal and Political Body

Although classical Chinese philosophy did not operate on the model of substance metaphysics, what might be considered rigid conceptions of personhood[1] were certainly available to early Chinese thinkers. Such discussions generally appeared in the context of creating civic-minded persons with reliable affective dispositions, commitments, and social roles; this paralleled the stated desire for building an orderly and stable community. The motif of the heart occupies a central role in such discussions, where it sometimes figures as that which, when cultivated properly, ensures the affective and behavioral stability of a person, and sometimes appears in the context of the body politic as a crucial metaphor for the sovereign unifying the political body. Consequently, the *Zhuangzi*'s undermining of the authority and unifying powers of the heart is tied not only to its criticisms of (what it portrays as) rigid conceptions of personhood but also to its critique of investments in building a society unified around a particular vision.

As shown in chapter 4, the *Zhuangzi* is rich with critical reflections on the certain limitations that come with settling on a fixed set of discriminative judgments. Making firm judgments about the world easily leads to friction between the person and the environment as things and situations change and different situations call for different value assessments. Central to that

---

[1] Throughout this section I will consciously adopt Jochim's practice of using the words "person" and "personhood" instead of the word "self." The last term carries too much philosophical baggage within Euro-American academic philosophy and comes with a whole constellation of post-Cartesian assumptions around radical notions of agency, objectification of the self and the world, and dualistic metaphysics. The words "person" and "personhood" conveniently incorporate a variety of notions relevant for our analysis, such as one's body, one's overall behavioral and cognitive attitudes, and the social dimension of one's identity. I will make use of the word "personhood" when discussing not only passages referring to one's sense of "me" [as in *wo* 我 (first person pronoun) or *ji* 己 (first person reflexive pronoun)] but also to translate *shen* 身 (body, person, also used emphatically to mean "in person"). See Chris Jochim, "Just Say No to 'No-Self,' in the Zhuangzi," in *Wandering at Ease in the* Zhuangzi, ed. Roger T. Ames (Albany: State University of New York Press, 1998), 48–50. For an analysis of issues of personhood in the *Zhuangzi*, also see Sonya Özbey, "Undermining the Person, Undermining the Establishment in the *Zhuangzi*," *Comparative and Continental Philosophy* 10, no. 2 (2018): 123–139, DOI: 10.1080/17570638.2018.1487103.

discussion is the notion of the heart (*xin* 心) and its perceived ability to absorb certain judgments and distinctions, fostering a steadfast commitment to various values when cultivated in certain ways. This is also the reason that discussions about the nature of the heart appear alongside discussions about human motivation and activity, especially in early Ru discourse. Hence, as the *Zhuangzi* decenters the authority of the heart, it also simultaneously betrays a lack of interest in fashioning persons with unified affective-cognitive processes and orderly behavioral patterns that align with the vision and values of the political body.

A good example of this double gesture is a passage that was also discussed in chapter 4, but in the context of how the *Zhuangzi* challenges the heart's sovereignty over other organs.[2] The passage is worth revisiting, but this time in order to analyze it from a sociopolitical angle:

> One hundred bones, nine orifices, six storehouses, they are together and exist here [in my body]. Which one do I take to be closest to me? Are you pleased with them all or is there one to which you are partial? Like this, do you take them all as servants and concubines? Are these servants and concubines insufficient to govern each other? Or do they take turns serving as the ruler and servants? If there is a genuine ruler existing among them, then, looking for and obtaining facts about it or not, would not add to or decrease its genuineness. (*Zhuangzi* 2:61)

The passage is arguing against viewing the psychophysiological makeup of one's person along reductive lines by pointing out the silliness of exalting only some parts of a highly diverse and heterogeneous mechanism.[3] Hence, the passage is often primarily read as a reaction against the Ru view that the heart is (or shall be made) more resolute than other organs. Although the passage clearly argues for a more pluralistic view of the person, the political undertones of the passage (in which "rulers" and "servants" take turns) are difficult to overlook.

The framing of the comparison of different organs in terms of their ruling and serving roles is a clear reference to a shared body-politic analogy in

---

[2] See section 4.2 of chapter 4.
[3] As mentioned in chapter 4, section 4.3, we indeed see argumentative moves made along these lines in other early Chinese texts, such as the *Mengzi*, where Mengzi is portrayed as saying that the heart, which he thinks has moral and reflective capacities, is the more noble (*gui* 貴) and "greater" (*da* 大) part of the person, whereas the rest are one's "petty" parts (*Mengzi* 6A14; 6A15).

early Chinese texts, where social divisions in a society are expressed using an analogy between bodily organs and the state. Aside from the common description of sensory organs as officials (*guan*官), early Chinese literature also offers us explicit analogies drawn between the human body and the political body.[4] Using the human body as a model for the government has various crucial implications, one of which is that just as a single organ of the human body cannot survive without the larger body, an individual person cannot survive in isolation from society. This view both subsumes people into an overarching political body and, at the same time, justifies the goals of bringing unity to people's various dispositions *and* to the different functionaries of the polity.[5] This unification requires being organized around a centralized authority in society, which corresponds to the heart in the body—which, as mentioned earlier, was seen as able to generate steady commitment for its choices.

Given the discursive framings of the heart as a metaphor for the ruler of the political body, the aforementioned passage seems to be written with the double aim of undermining both the goals of unifying a person's various dispositions under the authority of the heart *and* unifying various people under the authority of their rulers. Moreover, when the *Zhuangzi* says "if there is a genuine ruler existing among [the various parts of the body], then, looking for and obtaining facts about it or not, does not add to or decrease its genuineness," this not only questions the heart's capacity to rule other organs but on a sociopolitical level it undermines the obviousness of the need for a ruler. After all, that there are cultivation practices to ensure that the heart indeed rules the rest of the body shows that the heart's authority is not preestablished.[6] Similarly, the fact that one needs to argue about the necessity of following the lead of a ruler betrays the tenuousness of the ruler's rule.

---

[4] A clear example of this can be seen in the *Xunzi* (12.7), where right after a description of the bureaucratic division of labor, we are told that once people are specialized and established in their work, "they will be similar to eyes, ears, nose, and mouth in that they cannot be substituting for each other's office." *Xunzi* goes on to add that they will all work as if they were a single body (*yiti* 一體) with a ruler, and will follow his dictates the way the four limbs follow the dictates of the heart. For a broader examination of body politic metaphors in early Chinese texts, see Chun-chieh Huang, "The 'Body Politic' in Ancient China," *Acta Orientalia Vilnensia* 8, no. 2 (2007): 33–43.

[5] People's unification under the political body becomes crucial for the survival of each person, which is why, as the *Xunzi* tells us, the wise gentleman is willing to sacrifice his life for the polity, while the petty man makes preserving himself alone his priority, not knowing that abiding by "proper measure even at the risk of death, is the means to nurture one's life. . . . [Thus] if a person has his eyes only on living, such a one is sure to die" (*Xunzi* 19.1d.) I follow Hutton's translation here. See Eric L. Hutton, trans., *Xunzi: The Complete Text* (Princeton, NJ: Princeton University Press, 2016), 202.

[6] For more on this, see also chapter 4, section 4.2.

Aside from the obviousness of the ruler/heart's authority, discourses that present a polity as a unitary entity, combining various structures around the ruler/heart, also become suspect in the *Zhuangzi*. A dialogue that starts with a man from Song bragging about the chariots he received from the king of Qin ends with the character of Zhuangzi observing:

> When the king of Qin gets ill and calls his doctors, the one who pops a zit or squeezes a boil is awarded one chariot, while the one who licks the king's hemorrhoids is awarded five. The lower the thing they treat, the more chariots they receive. Might you have been licking the king's hemorrhoids for him?[7]

Zhuangzi's reply to the man from Song does not present the governing body as an entity that unifies different organs/offices into one well-integrated, harmonious whole. Instead, the governing body is equated with the king's sick body and everyone else's job is reduced to simply attending to the body's many ailments. The nastier the body part and its associated illness, the greater the reward for bringing some relief to it by squeezing and licking its inflamed bits.

The text's biting criticism of sovereign power could partly be explained by the authors' disillusionment with the political establishment of their time (although one could always choose to offer reformative solutions, as did Spinoza *and* many of the thinkers of early China). However, the text's undermining of the authority of the heart/ruler also reflects its vision of human flourishing. As mentioned earlier, the *Zhuangzi*'s overall criticism of compelling the heart to settle on a specific set of discriminative judgments (which are also responsible for rigid personality traits) parallels its criticism of subsuming people into a society ordered around a unifying vision;[8] both goals are equally limiting from a vantage point that emphasizes the plurality of values and interests.

As the *Zhuangzi* critiques its opponents for the alleged narrowness and rigidity of their visions, it also transforms the terms of these debates, so that instead of considering people as primarily members of the larger political body,

---

[7] In Chinese it reads: 秦王有病召醫，破癰潰痤者得車一乘，舐痔者得車五乘，所治愈下，得車愈多。子豈治其痔邪？何得車之多也？ *Zhuangzi* 32:1044. I follow Ziporyn's translation here. Ziporyn, *Zhuangzi: The Complete Writings*, 261.

[8] Certainly, what the *Zhuangzi* takes to be the Ru view does not entirely correspond to what the Ru actually defended. For a discussion of how the early Ru philosophy was necessarily pluralistic, see Chenyang Li, "The Confucian Ideal of Harmony," *Philosophy East and West* 56, no. 4 (2006): 583–603.

we are told that they are simply parts of the ten thousand things.[9] Similarly, instead of presenting people as performing well-defined roles and duties, we see them taking on different roles and identities.[10] This latter aspect of the text, which favors flexibility over commitment to a specific set of identities, roles, and values, intimates an attitude toward life that emphasizes its topsy-turvy ways instead of its predictability.

The next section explores this point further by revisiting the *Zhuangzi*'s treatment of death and transformation, which is discussed in more detail in the *Zhuangzi* compared to Spinoza's works. Moreover, as will be shown, in the *Zhuangzi*, issues of death and transformation are mobilized to challenge norms regarding the continuity and unity of the person. This includes questioning the idea of a person as a mere aggregate of established social roles and reevaluating the notion of the human identity in relation to animals. The two are connected, as the early Chinese views of the human-beast binary primarily revolved around the former's ability to form a social order grounded in shared notions of *yi* 義 (responsible conduct) that is defined in close relation to social divisions and performance of various roles.[11] As a result, in the *Zhuangzi*, letting go of one's attachment to various social roles goes hand in hand with letting go of one's humanity, sometimes in the literal sense of simultaneously embodying different species domains.

8.2 Transforming into a Rat's Liver or a Butterfly's Dream

Calmness in the face of death is a persistent theme in the *Zhuangzi* and is presented as a natural outcome of realizing that either there is no reason to value life over death or that death should be seen as simply part of the endless

---

[9] For a discussion of this point, see chapter 4, section 4.1. As also explained there, the distinctive feature of the *Zhuangzi* is not the gesture of simply calling people things (*wu* 物) or one of ten thousand things (*wanwu* 萬物), but the mobilization of this language to highlight the fewness of people in comparison to everything in the world and also to draw on the fundamental equality of things.

[10] This point is discussed in chapter 4, section 4.4, in the context of human flexibility and in chapter 5, section 5.3, in the context of the ways the text upends power dynamics through role reversals.

[11] For instance, the "The Rule of a King" (Wang zhi 王制) chapter of the *Xunzi* explicitly states that "water and fire have vital energy (*qi* 氣) but do not contain life (*sheng* 生). Herbs and trees contain life but have no awareness (*zhi* 知). Birds and beasts have awareness but no sense of responsible conduct (*yi* 義). People have vital energy, contain life and have awareness, but also have a sense of responsible conduct, therefore they are the most valuable creatures in the universe" (*Xunzi* 9.16a). Also see *Mozi* 15/12/1–4 for the argument that having multiple definitions of responsible conduct (*yi* 義) creates the kind of chaos (*luan* 亂) observed among the birds and beasts. Finally, see *Liji* 11.25/8–10 ("Jiao Te Sheng 郊特牲") and *Mengzi* 3A4 for explicit associations between not having a sense of responsible conduct and being like birds and beasts.

transformation of things.[12] The latter view is expressed in multiple stories, including one that involves a man named Zilai who falls fatally ill. Disregarding the wails of his wife and children who are grieving his condition, a friend of the ill man suggests that Zilai will actually be undergoing some fascinating transformations and wonders if he might turn into a rat's liver or an insect's arm. Zilai agrees with his friend about welcoming all the dramatically different experiences and life forms that will unfold after his clinical death and notes the silliness of holding onto his human form:

> Now suppose a great smith is casting metal. If the metal jumped and said "I must be made into a Mo-ye!" the smith would certainly consider it to be an inauspicious sort of metal. Now, having once stumbled onto the shape of a human, if I say "Only human! Only human!" that which fashions and transforms us will surely consider me an inauspicious sort of a person.[13]

Zilai's reaction to his friend's speculation about what might be in store for him seems to imply that human form is to a rat's liver or an insect's arm what a great sword is to other metal utensils. Regardless of whether by this implied ranking Zilai is referring to conventional values and/or his own values, in the end, he draws attention to a more fundamental similarity between raw metal and the stuff he is himself made of. Then, instead of fearing death and clinging onto the experiences afforded to him by his human form, Zilai welcomes all the different life forms that will unfold after his clinical death, regardless of how minute or lowly they might sound at first.

Similar sentiments regarding the silliness of resenting death and the loss of what one takes for granted are sometimes expressed from the perspectives of the survivors as well.[14] However, regardless of the vantage point from which they are narrated, all the stories about death in the *Zhuangzi* are set up in a

---

[12] Also see chapter 5, section 5.3, for an examination of the theme of taking death lightly in the *Zhuangzi*. Olberding points out that in a key story within the *Zhuangzi*, there is a brief moment of sorrow before one attains equanimity about death, which should be understood as having the capacity to experience a broader range of emotions in relation to death (and in general). See Amy Olberding, "Sorrow and the Sage: Grief in the *Zhuangzi*," *Dao: A Journal of Comparative Philosophy* 6 (4) (2007): 339–59

[13] *Zhuangzi* 6:267. I largely followed Ziporyn's and Graham's translations for this passage. Watson notes that Mo-ye is a famous sword of King Helü (r. 514–496 BCE) of Wu. See Ziporyn, *Zhuangzi: The Complete Writings*, 59; Graham, *Chuang Tzu*, 88; Watson, *The Complete Works of Zhuangzi*, 48.

[14] A well-known story depicts Zhuangzi's reaction to the death of his own wife: he drums and sings a song. When criticized, Zhuangzi explains that at first he was upset about his wife's death, but then he realized that human life is not that different from the sequence of seasons, in which case the death of a wife or a mother is no different from the coming of winter (*Zhuangzi* 18:613–4). Master Sanghu's friends react in a similar manner, singing a song immediately after he dies (*Zhuangzi* 6:271).

way that frames the event not simply as the death of an individual person but also the death of someone who holds a social role (a husband, father, wife, friend, and, in another example, a teacher).[15] Hence, these stories also serve as commentaries on how to relate to others and what to make of certain well-established roles and commitments. Both the dying person and the survivors manage to welcome death with joy, not simply because they loosen their grip on life in general but also because they do not cling to the perspectives of father, husband, friend, and so on.[16]

This emphasis on relationships in stories about death is not coincidental. As is well known, these fundamental human relations are well emphasized and promoted in classical Ru texts and beyond.[17] Such primary human relations serve as normative patterns for broader social relationships, as it is in the context of these routinized relationships that one is expected to cultivate proper behavioral traits. Moreover, both the continuity of these relational behavior patterns and, to some extent, the perceived unity of the deceased's personal identity are expected to be maintained after a person's clinical death; this is also the fundamental justification for mourning and memorial practices. The clearest articulation of this view is given by the *Xunzi*, which states that the goal for properly mourning the dead is to maintain the unity (*yi* 一) of the (now-deceased) person across life and death.[18] For this reason, one adorns the deceased with symbols corresponding to their status[19] and participates in certain ritual gestures as if (*ru* 如) the deceased were alive (such as putting food in the deceased's mouth) so as to re-create familiar ways of interacting with the now-dead individual.[20]

By critiquing (if not mocking) mourning practices, on top of making light of death itself, the *Zhuangzi* exhibits a lack of investment in reproducing

---

[15] For examples of such episodes, which address how to cope with the death of a loved one, see *Zhuangzi* 6:263–267, *Zhuangzi* 18:613–4, *Zhuangzi* 6: 269–271, *Zhuangzi* 3:132–134.

[16] This point is also made in Özbey, "Undermining the Person," 131.

[17] It should be added that familial relations (between the father and the son, for instance) are sometimes discussed together with ruler-subject relationships, thereby amplifying their sociopolitical significance. See *Mengzi* 3A4, *Xunzi* 9.15 and 27.31, *Mozi* 21/14/4–6.

[18] *Xunzi* 19.4.

[19] *Xunzi* 19.3.

[20] *Xunzi* 19.7a. For a comparative examination of the *Zhuangzi*'s and *Xunzi*'s approaches to death, see Chris Fraser, "Xunzi versus Zhuangzi: Two Approaches to Death in Classical Chinese Thought," *Frontiers of Philosophy in China* 8, no. 3 (2013): 410–427. Another and perhaps more well-known example is the mention of Kongzi sacrificing to the dead as if they were present (*Lunyu* 3.12). These gestures do not stem from a denial of the natural change that the deceased person has undergone but are made to reproduce the relational patterns between the deceased and the survivors, which are constitutive of one's person and identity. Citations to the *Lunyu* follow the book and section numbers adopted in D. C. Lau, trans., *The Analects* (Harmondsworth: Penguin Books, 1979).

routinized relational patterns and maintaining the cross-situational consistency of the survivors' views of themselves and of the deceased. In a double-layered gesture of letting go of one's social roles and one's humanity at the same time, neither the loss of his identity as a husband and father nor the possibility of turning into a rat's liver and an insect's arm bother Zilai. If attaining personhood and humanhood are parts of the same discourse of creating civic-minded individuals who understand themselves in relation to the larger community, then it is no surprise that Zilai lets go of his roles as a father and a husband and his humanity at the same time and celebrates all the transformations awaiting him.

Whereas Zilai only speculates on his sickbed about all the other animals that his body parts might transform into, other accounts of bodily transformation are also present in the text, as are instances of people embodying disparate life forms simultaneously. A more sudden, if not more unusual, case of bodily fragmentation is presented in the "Utmost Joy" (Zhi le 至樂) chapter, in an episode in which Uncle Zhili 支離 (Discombulated) and Uncle Huajie 滑介 (Sliding Onefoot)[21] are said to be contemplating the empty wastelands (xu 虛) of the Kunlun mountain. All of a sudden, a willow tree grows out of Huajie's left elbow. When asked whether he abhors it, he replies:

> Of course not. Why would I abhor it? To live is to borrow. What is born and born again through borrowing is but dust and dirt. Life and death are like day and night. We were both gazing at [the process of] change, and now change has caught up with me. Why would I now instead abhor it? (Zhuangzi 18:615)

Both the reference to the Kunlun mountain (the place where the Yellow Thearch [Huangdi 皇帝] ostensibly died) and the mention of the willow tree (suggesting coffins)[22] allude to death. That Huajie experiences his impending death as a sudden shooting forth of a tree from his arm and that he frames it in terms of an extension of the ongoing processes of change suggest that

---

[21] Zhuangzi 18:614–615. As Galvany notes, both names indicate physical deformities. Galvany, "Distorting the Rule of Seriousness," 50. For translations of the two names, I largely followed the Ziporyn's translation. See Ziporyn, Zhuangzi: The Complete Writings, 146.

[22] It is common to read liu 柳 (willow) as liu 瘤 (tumor). I follow Ziporyn's and Galvany's choice to not replace liu 柳 with another character and to read the story as being about a willow tree shooting out of the man's arm. Galvany supports his translation choice by noting that this type of wood was used for making coffins and catafalques, making the sudden emergence of the willow tree a harbinger of Huajie's impending death. Galvany. "Distorting the Rule of Seriousness," 50.

death is an ever-present phenomenon. What the story also suggests is a fragmented account of personhood, in which Huajie is simultaneously both alive and dead and both a man and a tree—embodying two existential and two species domains at once.

Chapters 4 and 5 discussed how the *Zhuangzi* emphasizes mobility and flexibility in one's approach to values, judgments, and roles by presenting us with characters who are able to switch from one vantage point to another, exchange social roles, and allow different affects to come and go.[23] It is safe to argue that such fluidity is enabled by (or at least goes hand in hand with) the characters' persons already being heterogenous and fragmented. At times, the characters incorporate opposites that do not culminate in one coherent and unified configuration, as seen in the example of people who combine the human and the Heavenly within themselves, embodying both domains at once.[24] At other times, two disparate (but not necessarily opposite) identities fuse together, as seen in the stories concerning the merging of human and animal identities.

Aside from stories about death (and the organic process of decay and regeneration that accompanies death), the text also includes a story about the character of Zhuangzi who dreams he is a butterfly and wonders if he is Zhuangzi who had dreamed he was a butterfly or a butterfly dreaming he was Zhuangzi. This story, which is not the only dream-related episode in the text,[25] illustrates Bergson's description of a state often realized in dreams: a fusion between two persons and two vantage points "who henceforth form only one and yet remain distinct."[26] In fact, Zhuangzi points out that a man and a butterfly are surely two separate things but then concludes that that is simply what change is about. He thus ties the topsy-turvydom of the dream world to prosaic processes of change, presenting such fusions and confusions of identity as mundane phenomena. Hence, one does not necessarily need to dream (or die) to experience the merging of identities, as in the example of Tai, who sometimes thinks he is a horse and sometimes thinks he is an ox without ever caring to decide what he "really" is.[27]

It is not that the milieu that birthed the *Zhuangzi* was lacking in discussions about certain regularities in the world, whether they pertained

---

[23] See section 4.3 of chapter 4 and section 5.3 of chapter 5.
[24] For more on this, see chapter 4, section 4.4 and chapter 5, section 5.1.
[25] For some other examples, see *Zhuangzi* 2:110, 4:175–180, 6:279–280.
[26] Wylie Sypher, ed., *Comedy: "An Essay on Comedy" by George Meredith. "Laughter" by Henri Bergson* (Baltimore: Johns Hopkins University Press, 1956), 183.
[27] *Zhuangzi* 7:293.

to preestablished groupings in the world or manmade (or, more specifically, sage-made) arrangements. As discussed in chapter 1, we see in early Chinese texts many mentions of spontaneously occurring family resemblances and hierarchical relations in the world.[28] The central focus, however, is not on settling how things stand but on shaping subjects' conduct by setting norms and standards of behavior—which are constrained by prearranged features of the world without being overdetermined by them. Often considered as preestablished features of the world are upper and lower orders,[29] groupings (*lei* 類) that recognize things as being of a similar kind,[30] and generalizable patterns of human desires and inclinations.[31] However, it is the job of sage-rulers to determine a specific, orderly scheme of distinctions so as to allot roles and duties, distribute resources, and share labor in sustainable ways.[32] Many of the received early Chinese philosophical texts, in fact, are dominated by discussions about what that system of divisions and norms should look like, so as to bring order to and govern (*zhi* 治) society and put an end to any perceived "disorder" (*luan* 亂).

These two antonymic concepts have a strong normative dimension and are understood as resulting from human activity. Used as a verb, *zhi* 治 means "to govern," "to rule," "to manage"; whereas as an adjective it refers to being orderly and often appears in relation to other normative terms such as being harmonious (*he* 和) and peaceful (*ping* 平). The semantic range of the term already gives us a glimpse into both the alleged source of "order" (efficient social norms and rule) and its alleged intrinsic value. "Disorder" (*luan* 亂), on the other hand, appears in the absence of good governance, or often, more specifically, in the absence of shared norms of propriety (*li* 禮), dutifulness (*yi* 義), and the social distinctions they help clarify.[33] The human-centered

---

[28] See chapter 1, section 1.1.

[29] Such as Heaven being above and earth being below. For a discussion of early Chinese views about hierarchical dynamics in nature, and how that becomes intertwined with views about a hierarchical social system in early Ru literature, see Donald J. Munro, *The Concept of Man in Early China* (Ann Arbor: Center for Chinese Studies, University of Michigan, 2001), 23–40.

[30] On this point, see chapter 1, section 1.1.

[31] For an overview of early Chinese pleasure theories, which involve discussions about the character and satisfaction of human desires and inclinations, see Nylan, *The Chinese Pleasure Book*.

[32] Much ink has been spilled on the extent to which Ru and/or Mohist texts lend themselves to "naturalist" or "conventionalist" interpretations. In reality, early Chinese Masters texts are abundant with textual grounds for either interpretation. My interpretative approach when reading early Chinese Masters texts is close to that of Hagen's, who applies a constructivist approach to interpret the *Xunzi* in particular and reads it to argue that there are preestablished groupings in the world but also more than one way to categorize and name them. See Kurtis Hagen, *The Philosophy of Xunzi: A Reconstruction* (Chicago: Open Court, 2007).

[33] See, for instance, *Lunyu* 8.2, *Mozi* 42/27/4, *Xunzi* 3.7 and 10.4. I owe warm thanks to Meili Wood who traced usages of "order" (more specifically "*zhi* 治") and "disorder" (*luan* 亂) in early Chinese

nature of this antonymic conceptual pair should be obvious, considering their human origin and their political overtones. Less obvious are the various ways they are interlinked with the human-animal binary.

The next section explores some of the dominant features of early Chinese narratives of the emergence of an orderly society out of an ostensibly disordered existence in distant antiquity. Although varying in the themes they emphasize, they unite in mobilizing animality tropes as a foil against which to construct their own vision of good governance. As will be shown, the *Zhuangzi* offers a diverse range of views on the issue. While some layers of the text present a nostalgic account of the unarranged past, others offer an alternative vision of governance that stays away from top-down apparatuses of active management but not from hierarchical dynamics. The former invites the readers to reimagine the nature of unarranged nature itself and the latter explores what else governance can stand for, while they both unite in not resorting to negative animality tropes to convey their message.

8.3 Muddying the Waters: Reimagining Hundun and Antiquity

Marked by social strife and competition for political power, much of the Warring States period witnessed ideological debates about how to best bring an end to "chaos" (*luan* 亂) and bring about "order" (*zhi* 治). By "using the past to serve the present," different philosophers reconstructed narratives of distant pasts and told stories of the emergence of order from disorder as a way to articulate what they thought was causing contemporary ills. Many of these narratives center on the initial absence of all social distinctions (between human beings and wild animals, fathers and sons, rulers and ministers, husbands and wives), which are then said to be established and clarified by ancient sages and their strategic acts of demarcation and exclusion.

Among the world-making acts of the ancients was securing the physical separation between human beings and wild animals, as well as introducing the bureaucratic division of labor by delegating various tasks to capable

---

literature as part of an Undergraduate Research Opportunities Program (UROP) at the University of Michigan. For a related and detailed analysis of early Chinese ideals of "order" in relation to views about norms of propriety (*li* 禮), see Masayuki Sato, "The Development of the Idea of *Li* 禮 in pre-Qin Thought," in *The Confucian Quest for Order: The Origin and Formation of the Political Thought of Xun Zi* (Leiden: Brill, 2003), 163–236.

people. However, what ultimately distinguishes the human realm from that of wild beasts is not the simple transformation of the material conditions of the people but the introduction of social relations and inculcation of a sense of proper conduct. This is why the *Mozi* describes the ancient past with no ruler as a disorderly state of existence resembling the existence of birds and wild animals (*qin shou* 禽獸), with no separation between the superior and the subordinate or between the father and the son, and no division of labor.[34] Similarly, the *Record of Rites* tells us that what separates people from birds and wild animals is that people have a proper relationship between the father and the son[35] as well as proper mourning rituals determined by ancient sage-kings to prevent disorder (*luan* 亂).[36] The *Mengzi*, which presents one of the most elaborate narratives of what could be described as the state of nature, traces the ultimate emergence of people from a beastly existence to clarification of the five relations: the kinship between fathers and sons, the proper conduct between the sovereigns and ministers, the distinction between husband and wife, the sequencing of the old and the young, and fidelity between two friends.[37] The *Xunzi* tells us that what separates human beings from wild animals are their distinctions (*bian* 辨), social divisions (*fen* 分), and, of course, their sense of responsible conduct (*yi* 義), all of which simultaneously enable people to overcome disorder and make use of animals that are otherwise stronger than they are.[38]

Despite some differences, which are due to different thinkers' projections of their own particular ideologies into antiquity, all such accounts of distant pasts associate animality with disorder; and disorder is equated with the lack of social divisions, roles, and hierarchy. Also shared among these narratives is the assumption that it is only a matter of letting go of these fundamental markers of humanity, and people will start regressing back to an animal-like existence. This is why the *Mengzi* tells us "that whereby man differs from birds and wild animals is but extremely slight. The multitude discards it, the gentleman preserves it."[39] The *Mengzi*'s articulation of the difference between the gentleman and the rest in terms of the latter's closeness to an animal-like

---

[34] *Mozi* 15–16/12/1–5.
[35] *Liji* 1.6/19–20 ("Qu Li Shang 曲禮上"). This prevents the two from having the same mate, so the proper relationship between the father and the son also translates into the proper relationship between a husband and wife, and between a mother and son.
[36] *Liji* 39.3–5/16–21("San Nian Wen 三年間").
[37] *Mengzi* 3A4.
[38] *Xunzi* 5.4.
[39] *Mengzi* 4B19.

existence shows how the trope of animality functions as the constitutive outside of humanity proper and continually haunts humanity from within, enabling one to deem some people more animal-like than others.

That the trope of animality serves to exclude some people from "humanity proper" is best exemplified by the rhetorical attempts to connect the emergence of an ordered human society to the division of human lands into various regions, distinguishing the political center with its self-described developed culture from the peripheral regions of alien peoples that are said to lack in various markers of refinement, social division, proper human relationships, and so on.[40] Some of these accounts include criminality as one of the features of the chaotic world (prior to the establishment of the necessary divisions that constitute the organized human society)[41] and then add that the emergence of an ordered society was linked to the expulsion of villainous people to the peripheral regions.

One of these stories appears in the *Zuo zhuan* 左傳, which also features Hundun, the faceless creature who, according to the *Zhuangzi*'s version of the story, dies after its friends attempt to carve a face into its head in an attempt to humanize it.[42] In the *Zuo zhuan*, however, Hundun features first as the vulgar and vicious son of the Yellow Thearch who sends him away, and later as one of the four mythical fiends (*si xiong* 四凶) who are cast out by Shun 舜 into the four distant regions where alien peoples and "savages" were also thought to live.[43] Later variations of Hundun mythology include a reference to it as a divine dog with dysfunctional orifices (that is, unseeing eyes, unhearing ears, and a non-defecating rectum), who associates with people of bad character.[44]

The first thing that strikes one about these different references to Hundun is the notable disparity in their implications. This variance probably has to with different attitudes toward the root meanings of the words *hun* and *dun*, which are "murky," "chaotic," "turbid," and "confused." In some texts these

---

[40] An elaborate articulation of these connections could be seen in the "Tribute of Yu" (Yu gong 禹貢)" chapter of the *Shang shu* 尚書 (*Ancient Documents*). See Bernhard Karlgren, "The Book of Documents," *Bulletin of the Museum of Far Eastern Antiquities* 22 (1950): 1–81, https://archive.org/details/Bulletin22 (reprinted as a separate volume by Göteborg: Elanders Boktrycher Aktiebolag, 1950), 12–18).

[41] See Lewis's examination of the theme of criminality in early Chinese flood myths. Mark Lewis, *The Flood Myths of Early China* (Albany: State University of New York Press, 2006), 49–78.

[42] The story of Hundun, as appears in the *Zhuangzi*, is discussed in chapter 5, section 5.1.

[43] Norman J. Girardot, *Myth and Meaning in Early Taoism: The Theme of Chaos (Hun-Tun)* (Berkeley: University of California Press, 1983), 129. It must be noted that *Zuo Zhuan* uses Húndùn 渾敦 for Hùndùn 混沌. The meanings of the characters 渾 and 混 are almost identical, and the variation in the second character may be due to its lack of a pre-Han seal script.

[44] I am indebted to Girardot for this point. See Girardot, *Myth and Meaning*, 188.

meanings are associated with being vicious, barbaric, and animal-like; in other texts (especially those that were later labeled as "Daoist"), they have connotations of not being determined (and hence limited) yet. The version of the Hundun story in the *Zhuangzi* could easily be a play on all these connotations that cluster around the same words, where the act of boring holes into Hundun's face refers both to the emergence of organized human society with all its limiting distinctions and discriminations, and to the well-intentioned-yet-destined-to-fail agendas people have about refining and humanizing what is deemed vulgar and subhuman. Also intimated in the *Zhuangzi* is yet another critical commentary on body-politic metaphors, where the organs carved into Hundun's face parallel the bureaucratic division of labor, which is part and parcel of institutionalized order. Accordingly, in the story offered in the *Zhuangzi*, the process of organizing an unarranged whole into clearly defined patterns of activity is presented as a counterproductive act of violence that produces suffering when it intends the opposite.

These different portrayals of the character of Hundun mirror different textual communities' attitudes toward the initial absence of distinctions in the imagined ancient times and what that antiquity represents to them as an enduring backdrop to existence. As Lewis notes, to some, tropes of primordial chaos symbolized "a constant menace of universal dissolution and chaos, should the principles that had been forged out of nondistinction ever be abandoned"; to others (such as the *Zhuangzi*), "it formed a constant reservoir of infinite potentiality."[45] In a similar vein, for those who take a critical view of the ancient state of non-distinction (however imagined), this trope of primordial chaos serves as an allegory for the present state of affairs, which appeared to many as too chaotic. The alleged relapse into chaos is explained by the abandonment of divisions essential to human society.[46] As for the association of the absence of divisions with infinite potentiality in the *Zhuangzi*, applications of such a view of human action were discussed in chapter 4 in the context of loosening the hold of fixed distinctions in order to infinitely multiply the variety of ways one could view the world and lead one's life.[47] In addition, the *Zhuangzi* also happens to portray the primordial state

---

[45] Lewis, *Flood Myths*, 24–25.

[46] This abandonment of essential social divisions is blamed on not only bad rulers and their subjects, but sometimes also on rival philosophers. See, for instance, *Mengzi* 3B9 for an association of Mo Di (Mozi) and the society collapsing back into an existence that is as chaotic as the time before Yao, Shun, and Yu managed the flood. The *Zhuangzi* also trades on this rhetorical gesture at times when it blames the Ru and the Mohists for their counterproductive attempts to bring order to a perceived chaos, which only makes things worse. See, for instance, *Zhuangzi* 14:529.

[47] See sections 4.3 and 4.4 of chapter 4.

of the world in nostalgic terms, arguing that the sages' forging a society out of a state of non-distinction simply made things worse.

A well-developed narrative of antiquity appears in the "Horse Hooves" (Mati 馬蹄) chapter of the *Zhuangzi*, which tells us that in those times people were "clothed by their own weaving, fed by their own plowing" and that "all creatures lived together, merging their territories into one another. The birds and wild animals clustered with each other, the grasses and trees grew unhampered." The text continues:

> The people lived together with the birds and wild animals, bunched together with all things. What did they know about the "gentleman" and the "petty men"? All the same in knowing nothing.... They were all the same in wanting nothing.... Then along came the sages. Limping and staggering after "humaneness" (*ren* 仁), straining on tiptoe after "responsible conduct" (*yi* 義), they filled everyone in the world with self-doubt. Mouthing and gushing over music, nitpicking and biasing over ritual, they got everyone in the world to take sides. For unless the undyed and unhewn are mutilated, what can be made into libation goblets? Unless the white jade is broken, what can be made into the ritual scepters and batons? And unless the way and its potency (*de* 德) are broken down, what can be picked through to select out "humaneness" and "responsible conduct"?[48]

Whereas the reference to the absence of a division of labor serves as a rhetorical attack with a wide target, the references to the "gentleman," "petty men," "humaneness," and "responsible conduct" all suggest that this alternative account of antiquity was possibly written as a criticism of a certain Ru view about the emergence of order out of disorder.[49] The passage clearly

---

[48] *Zhuangzi* 9:344. For this passage I largely followed Ziporyn's translation with some modifications. See Ziporyn, *Zhuangzi: The Complete Writings*, 81–82.

[49] It must be noted that a few chapters are more reconciliatory in tone. The "Being There and Giving Room" (Zai you 在宥) chapter presents laws, ritual, sense of dutiful conduct (*yi* 義) and humaneness (*ren* 仁) as things that are of low status, but yet must be depended on (*Zhuangzi* 11:405–407). The "Heaven and Earth" (Tiandi 天地) chapter portrays the gentleman (*junzi* 君子) in a positive light, except that it adds that the gentleman must gouge out his entire heart and mind (*ku xin* 刳心) to make space for the vast, ocean-like *dao* (*Zhuangzi* 12:413). The chapter also praises humaneness (*ren* 仁), defined as "cherishing others and creating benefit for all beings" (*airen li wu zhi wei ren* 愛人利物之謂仁) (*Zhuangzi* 12:413). The "Heaven's Way" (Tian dao 天道) chapter suggests that notions of non-contending action (*wuwei* 無為), as well as being tenuous (*xu* 虛) and still (*jing* 靜), *only* applies to sovereigns and sages, not the subjects. The chapter also serves as the only place in which an elaborately hierarchical view of society is articulated (a passage reads: "The ruler precedes, the subjects follow. The father precedes, the sons follow. The elder brother precedes, the younger brothers follow" [*Zhuangzi* 13:474]). Finally, it is worth noting that early Ru accounts of distant pasts are not monolith either. For instance, as Ing observes, the "Liyun 禮運" chapter of the *Liji* offers a narrative

undercuts the virtues and structures of the human world by presenting the introduction of culturally valued artifacts and norms as an act of mutilating the raw condition of existence.[50] More significantly, however, while the passage maintains the association between animality and the absence of material and normative markers of human civilization, it does not associate either of these with a subpar existence. On the contrary, antiquity is characterized by the unconstrained flourishing and mingling of human beings, wild animals, and grasses and trees (as opposed to crops).[51] Contrary to, let us say, the *Mengzi*'s, *Xunzi*'s, or *Han Feizi*'s accounts,[52] animals in this unarranged past were not pressing upon human beings, and people were content with not dividing up their territories, their labor, and fellow human beings into morally significant categories.

The *Zhuangzi* offers similar alternative accounts of antiquity multiple times in the text, each with an emphasis on a different aspect of antiquity. Some explicitly blame Yao and Shun among other ancient sage-rulers, along with their self-proclaimed intellectual heirs such as the Ru and the Mohists, for bringing disorder in their attempts to govern the world and rectify people's behaviors.[53] Some call for abolishing sages and their norms to bring an end to the disorder they created.[54] Other passages draw explicit parallels

---

of a time when people treated everyone as family and took care of each other. However, they later lost their way, necessitating the establishment of a ritual tradition to help regain a semblance of the order they had lost. For an account of a view of rituals that emphasizes not only their function means of (re)constructing an ordered world but also acknowledges the likelihood of failure, see Michael David Kaulana Ing, *The Dysfunction of Ritual in Early Confucianism* (Oxford: Oxford University Press, 2012).

[50] My reading here follows that of Ziporyn. See Ziporyn, *Zhuangzi: The Complete Writings*, 82 n.6.

[51] This forms a direct contrast with *Mengzi* 3A4, which draws a parallel between agricultural activity and humans' emancipation from a beastly existence.

[52] *Mengzi* 3A4, 3B9, *Xunzi* 9.16a, *Han Feizi* 19.49:1085. Citations to the Han Feizi provide the book, chapter, and page numbers from CHEN Qiyou 陳奇猷, *Han Feizi, with New Collations and Commentary* 韓非子新校注, 2 vols. (Shanghai: Shanghai guji chu ban she 上海古籍儲版社, 2000).

[53] More specifically, a passage from the "Being There and Giving Room" (Zai you 在宥) chapter blames the Yellow Thearch, Yao, and Shun for meddling with people's hearts by preaching virtues such as humaneness and dutiful conduct. According to this narrative, this development is later followed by the emergence of the Ru and the followers of Mozi in a later period. Both the Ru and the Mohists are described as making people suspect and condemn each other (*Zhuangzi* 11:381–386). Another passage from the "Repairing the Inborn Nature" (Shan xing 繕性) chapter blames Yellow Thearch, along with Tang and Yu, for leading the world into decline in their attempts to administer it (*Zhuangzi* 16:551–552). Finally, a different passage from the Gengsang Chu 庚桑楚 chapter blames Yao and Shun for planting the roots of disorder (*Zhuangzi* 23:771).

[54] The chapter titled "Breaking into Trunks" (Qu qie 胠篋) is especially aggressive in tone and calls for gagging the mouths of Yang Zhu and Mo Di and burning musical instruments cherished by the Ru (*Zhuangzi* 10:362). Also in the "Being There and Giving Room" (Zai you 在宥) chapter, we are told to "abolish sageness and abandon knowledge, and the world will have 'great order'" (*jue sheng qi zhi er tianxia dazhi* 絕聖棄知而天下大治) (*Zhuangzi* 11:386).

between antiquity and non-contending action[55] and speak wistfully about returning to the state of "muddy and murky," which is a translation of *hun hun dun dun* (渾渾沌沌)[56]—the characters that make up the name of the creature Hundun.

Describing the primordial state of existence as *hun hun dun dun* is a simple and obvious gesture of recounting the narrative of antiquity in terms that are outside the usual *zhi* 治/ *luan* 亂 (order/disorder) pair. This shows that the *Zhuangzi*'s various accounts of primordial times are not merely biting criticisms of rival accounts but at times also offer positive visions for a distant past. The root, the origin, or the *hun hun dun dun* is a state prior to a world that establishes and pits distinctions against one another—approval and disapproval (*shi* 是/*fei* 非), order and chaos, the gentlemen and the masses, the center and the periphery, the refined and the base, the human and the beastly, and so on.[57] The muddy and murky origin is not necessarily an undifferentiated and homogenous mass, as the *Zhuangzi*'s depictions of antiquity can testify, but it is nonetheless devoid of hierarchy and ranked interests of different groups. According to this vision of contentment and all-inclusive bounty, wild plants flourish where crops could have been planted, and beasts live alongside people, resulting not in chaos but in a "great order" (*da zhi* 大治),[58] which, just like *hun hun dun dun*, is prior to the state in which "order" is differentiated from and ranked higher than "disorder." *Hun hun dun dun* is neither orderly nor chaotic; it simply refers to the unarranged and indeterminate state of the world, which has a spontaneously egalitarian ethos that crosses rank, regional, and species barriers.

The primordial state of the world described by the *Zhuangzi* is not devoid of various affinities and resemblances among living beings. However, recognizing the presence of various affinities is still different from engaging in deliberate acts of segregating and positioning things within a grand scheme of order. If we recall that the primordial, unarranged state of the world—regardless of whether it is depicted in a negative or positive light— is to be viewed as a permanent background condition to human existence, when the *Zhuangzi* speaks of returning to the origin, to the root, or to *hun hun dun dun*, it is not necessarily calling for a literal return to such a state

---

[55] *Zhuangzi* 12:410.
[56] *Zhuangzi* 11:398.
[57] A similar description of the ancient folks as being beyond all distinctions appears in the more well-known "The Discourse that Levels Things" (Qi wu lun 齊物論) chapter. See *Zhuangzi* 2:80.
[58] *Zhuangzi* 11:386.

in the world (as "we" are all already living in the aftermath of the activities of order-bearing sages), but is rather asking us to tap into the potentiality it represents.[59] The enabling aspect of returning to that potentiality is obvious: it involves not being bound by ideologies that sort and rank things to achieve a specific vision of human flourishing. The alternative is multiplying the range of ways one can live, flourish, and view the world. The price this exacts is not chaos, as in an upheaval, but the absence of deliberate control and direction, theoretical apparatuses of right and wrong, and commitments to building a "human" or "humane" (ren 仁) realm defined in exclusionary terms.

As the Zhuangzi reworks tropes about Hundun and the rhetoric around antiquity, it refrains from attributing sagacious heroism to indulging in clarifying various affinities and resemblances among living beings. However, it is worth noting that just as the connotational range of "Hundun" is wide—in the Zhuangzi as well, in fact[60]—so is the text's approach toward acts of order-building. At this juncture a few points need to be addressed concerning the layers of the Zhuangzi that discuss sagacious governance, encompassing normative notions of propriety and hierarchical rankings in society. The purpose of highlighting these layers is not merely to partake in interpretive gestures of comprehensiveness, but to draw attention to a particular point they happen to reveal.

In regard to instances of commending sagacious governance (shengzhi 聖治; sagely order), the mechanics underlying such governance is paradoxical in nature, emphasizing the absence of the desire to govern, the lack of interventionist impulses, and sometimes opposition to imperialist urges.[61] The sage-sovereign's "non-rule," however formulated, relies on the presumption that when they are left to their own devices, people do not act in odious ways to begin with. Quite the contrary, in ways parallel to the rise of a great order (da zhi 大治) that is conceptually and chronologically prior to ideologies

---

[59] This is presented in chapter 4, section 4.3 in the context of a discussion about the notion of pivoting from one dao to another, without limiting ourselves to any single dao.

[60] In the "Heaven and Earth" (Tiandi 天地) chapter, one of the incarnations of Kongzi praises the arts of Mr. Hundun (Hundun shi zhi shu 渾沌氏之術) while separating the bogus (jia 假) version of it from the actual one. The latter, he clarifies, is not simply about ordering the internal (zhi qi nei 治其內), but also the external (zhi qi wai 治其外), so that one can wander through the everyday world (you shisu zhi jian 遊世俗之間). Kongzi's comment reads as a refusal to submit to a withdrawalist ideology that prioritizes an inward focus at the expense of engaging with external affairs. In this context, the trope of Hundun is used to evoke a sense of a balanced approach. See Zhuangzi 12:438–443.

[61] For the latter point, see the episode in the Tian Zifang 田子方 chapter, which features an old fisherman who accepts the role of the ruler of a small community (and rules without intervening in the usual course of things), but flees when he is asked to spread his rule to all under heaven. Zhuangzi 21:717–720.

of order and disorder, they act in proto-virtuous ways because they are not taught codes of conduct that impel or dissuade them to act in certain ways.

Regardless of the various approaches to governance within different parts of the *Zhuangzi*, even in the more reconciliatory layers of the text, in which sagacious governance is promoted in some form, we do not see any anxiety around pulling people out of an imagined state of beastliness. In fact, at times there is an intriguing sense of ease around the perceived animality of such peoples. The "Heaven and Earth" (Tiandi 天地) chapter presents a graphic example of this when we are told that the rule of the ancient sage-sovereign Shun amounted to nothing more than remedial measures and that under the rule of a (real) sage,

> the worthy are not esteemed and the able are not employed. Those above are the upper branches of a tree, and the ordinary people are like wild deer below. They are upright and proper without knowing it is "responsible conduct," love and care for another without knowing it is "humaneness," true without knowing it is "loyalty," reliable without knowing it is "trustworthiness."[62]

The early Chinese literature is not without analogies that liken people to a group of animals, but it is more common for ordinary people to be described as horses or sheep and for leaders to be described as the charioteers or shepherds taking care of them and guiding them.[63] Here the ruling class is likened to the upper branches of a tree, which do nothing other than be there (and perhaps provide shade).[64] People, on the other hand, are not likened to domestic animals but to wild ones. No one is labeled "worthy" or taught normative judgments and because of that everything is in a balance without requiring ideological contrivances. No one is being lifted up and saved from an animal-like existence, and instead people simply remain "wild" like the deer.

---

[62] *Zhuangzi* 12:451. For this passage I largely follow Ziporyn's translation. Ziporyn, *Zhuangzi: The Complete Writings*, 106.

[63] Sterckx, *The Animal and the Daemon*, 151. It should also be noted that the "Horse Hooves" (Mati 馬蹄) chapter of the *Zhuangzi* draws a parallel between violating the nature of horses when trying to domesticate them and of people when trying to govern them. See *Zhuangzi* 9:338–345.

[64] That would suggest a parallel between the description of the sagacious governance here and Zhuangzi's description of the big but "useless" tree in the opening chapter of the work, which also does nothing other than provide shade. For more, see chapter 1, section 1.2.

In spite of this theme of ruling via non-rule, the very presence of a sage-sovereign, if not a wider ruling entity, still suggests the presence of a hierarchical dynamic. After all, the aforementioned passage itself mentions an "above" (the upper branches of a tree), which is contrasted with the subjects (who are like wild deer) below. Sometimes these hierarchical clusters take on a more elaborate form, which involves the introduction of ministers who, unlike the ruler, do not practice *wuwei* 無為 [non-contending action]).[65] Furthermore, in one instance, hierarchical relations are established between the father and son, as well as husband and wife.[66] This brings us to the interesting part about these politically and socially more establishmentarian layers. What is remarkable about them is not simply that they form a contrast with the rest of the text that explicitly mocks and undermines hierarchies. As explained in chapter 1, such inner contradictions are not particularly scandalous for a composite text that also was not compiled according to modern philosophical norms of systematic coherence.[67] Instead, what perhaps makes such layers of the *Zhuangzi* with pro-hierarchy attitudes interesting is the intertextual tensions they form with the aforementioned depictions of hierarchical arrangements seen in other Masters texts. More specifically, even when the *Zhuangzi* commends various forms of hierarchies, at no point are they articulated around the human-animal, or the related central-peripheral or refined-uncouth divisions.

It is safe to argue that this is because instances of sagacious order are not formulated around interfering and coercive action,[68] or glorification of certain virtues, such as humaneness (*ren* 仁) and responsible conduct (*yi* 義).[69]

---

[65] See *Zhuangzi* 11:408.

[66] *Zhuangzi* 13:474. It is also worth noting that it is not uncommon to see in early Chinese texts a parallel between the relation between the ruler and minister, on one hand, and the relation between husband and wife, on the other hand. The latter dynamic is revisited in chapter 9, section 9.2.

[67] Moreover, as also discussed in chapter 1, section 1.2, the text at times makes a deliberate point of not settling on either side of a debate.

[68] See *Zhuangzi* 12:410 for an articulation of rulership (*jun* 君) formulated around non-contending action (*wuwei* 無為). Similarly, in a chapter titled "Heavenly Way" (Tian dao 天道), we are told that thearchs, kings, and sages (帝王聖 *di wang sheng*) engage in non-contending action (*wuwei* 無為). See *Zhuangzi* 13:462. The former episode also associates sovereignty with the Heavenly (as opposed to the human). The latter, on the other hand, suggests a harmonious trinity among Heaven, Earth, and good rulers. Both these approaches are different from the one that deliberately muddies the distinction between the Heavenly and the human altogether (which was discussed in chapter 4, section 4.4).

[69] The associations in early Chinese texts between animality and the absence of these virtues are discussed in chapter 1, section 1.1. and are revisited in Part V, chapter 9, in the context of the text's portrayal of frontier peoples. At most, we see a conciliatory stance toward such virtues in the *Zhuangzi*. For instance, the chapter titled "Being There and Giving Room" (Zai you 在宥) frames models (*fa* 法), humaneness (*ren* 仁), responsible conduct (*yi* 義), and rites (*li* 禮) as contrivances that are not ideal and yet also inevitable (*Zhuangzi* 11:405–406). In the "Heavenly Way" (Tian dao 天道) chapter, models (*fa* 法) and rites (*li* 禮) are described as (inessential) branches (as opposed

As such, these layers of the *Zhuangzi* with pro-hierarchy attitudes serve to underscore the specific threads of thought that establish and fortify the human-animal binary. These include the (1) presence or absence of forced action (that rely on established patterns of thinking and values), and (2) the performance of norms that elaborate and fortify social distinctions, such as *yi* 義 (responsible conduct, duty).

At the same time, such layers offer us relatively more conventional narratives of leadership and community management—sometimes incorporating hierarchical distinctions as well—but notably without employing negative animality tropes. While this shows that even the relatively wide range of positions expressed in the received *Zhuangzi* have their limits, we are also dared to imagine political governance without the discursive acts of shaming people out of an allegedly beastly existence. Most important of all, we are invited to conjure up new imaginations of an existence akin to that of birds and wild animals, and to contemplate it without fear or contempt.

---

to roots) of governance (*zhi zhi mo* 治之 末), which the ancients did study without making them primary (*Mo xuezhe, guren you zhi, er fei suoyi xian ye*末學者， 古人有之，而非所以先也。). See *Zhuangzi* 13:472, 474. Finally, in the chapter titled "The Turning of Heavens" (Tian yun 天運), we are told that humaneness (*ren* 仁) and responsible conduct (*yi*義) were only the temporary lodging "huts" of former kings "suitable for an overnight stay but not for long-term dwelling" (*ren yi, xianwang zhi qu lu ye, zhi keyi yi su er by keyi jiu chu*仁義，先王之蘧廬也，止可以一宿而不可以久處). See *Zhuangzi* 14:519.

Conclusion

The State of the World: The Topsy-Turvy and the Ship-Shape

When we compare Spinoza's and the *Zhuangzi*'s views on personhood and group identity, the obvious differences between the two can be largely explained by Spinoza's confidence in preestablished and intelligible regularities in the world, contrasting with the *Zhuangzi*'s emphasis on all the capricious surprises life has to offer. Also relevant is the fact that the negotiability of the borders that separate things and groups is closely tied to the level of investment in hierarchically ranked affinities within the world.

None of these observations are without implications for the sociopolitical visions of Spinoza and the *Zhuangzi*. The *Zhuangzi*'s lack of investment in grand visions of human unity and recipes for sociopolitical order is obvious. As for Spinoza, although he too grants that the borders around individual and group identities are somewhat negotiable, in the end he puts this negotiability in the service of his vision for the body politic, owing to his conviction that mankind can better uplift each other in ways that no other beings can.

The way one views organized society and apparatuses of governmentality is also inevitably intertwined with how one imagines existence without them. Section B revisits Spinoza's and the *Zhuangzi*'s narratives of the nature of unarranged worlds. It contrasts the relatively gloomy and sunny visions of humanity expressed in the two comparanda. The section observes that this sharp contrast has largely to do with whether one imagines proprietary sensibilities, which pit one's interests against another's, to predate or result from the rise of organized societies. Finally, in both Spinoza and the *Zhuangzi*, animality is associated with the absence of contrivances that organize people's lives and create "excess," such as the arts and sciences or rites and social roles. In the end, the utopian version seen in the *Zhuangzi* is perhaps as uplifting of a vision as it is threatening for those who benefit from the prevailing systems of control and hierarchy.

A. Tales of Identity and Disintegration

Contrary to early Ru discussions about the integration of different affective inclinations and role identifications into a unitary personhood, the *Zhuangzi* offers us tales of identity blurring and fragmentation that results from combining, in one's person, disparate domains that do not culminate in a unity. Such tales certainly intimate a different ontological approach to issues of personhood and personal identity—one that emphasizes self-heterogeneity and the absence of self-coherence, as evidenced by some of the stories of extreme transformation that defy personal and group boundaries at the same time.

If we recall Spinoza's views on issues of identity and selfhood, he too could be said to be presenting us with a heterogenous view of the subject, except that for him the different elements that make up a composite body/mind are incorporated into a unified configuration. In other words, what we see in Spinoza is an account of personhood that combines various elements without compromising self-coherence. Given Spinoza's emphasis on the enduring stability of persons (and other entities) over time and the lawful transformations they undergo, one wonders to what extent Spinoza's view of death differs from that of someone like Zilai in the *Zhuangzi*, who eagerly anticipates undergoing transformations into different life forms. Of course, as a philosopher who aimed to give an exhaustive account of human beings' place in the world, Spinoza also discusses death and liberating ways of thinking about death. However, whereas Zilai's carefree attitude toward death is due to his overall embracing of the changes that everything goes through, a Spinozist free man's calmness in the face of death is due to his understanding of his mind/body in relation to features of the world that are necessary by their essence.

Regardless of how one interprets Spinoza's theory of the eternity of the mind, it is clear that one's calmness in the face of death is not explained in terms of one's awareness that everything is changing anyway. A graphic observation that Kupperman makes can be employed here to clarify the contrast: "It is sometimes said that every time someone opens a water tap, it is likely that one molecule of Julius Caesar's body flows out."[1] It is especially due to this kind of view that the *Zhuangzi*'s Zilai has such a carefree disposition as he lies on his deathbed. Certainly, a Spinozist Caesar would recognize the

---

[1] Joel J. Kupperman, "Not in So Many Words: Chuang Tzu's Strategies of Communication," *Philosophy East and West* 39, no. 3 (1989): 315. Kupperman adds that "had Julius Caesar had a clear sense of this, it might have changed his life." (Kupperman, "Not in So Many words," 315).

interconnectedness of the whole universe of which he is part, but that would still not lead to a sudden "liquefying" of his person, which would entail losing oneself in the never-ceasing and unpredictable processes of change and transformation. It is the necessary and unchanging features of God or Nature that comfort the Spinozist free man, not his embrace of the inevitability of contingency. Moreover, Spinoza would certainly not view the possibility of a man turning into an insect's arm as a lateral development. This is evident from his assertions that human bodies (and hence also minds) excel above all others,[2] as well as his emphatic statement to Blyenbergh that men do not simply "die and perish after the manner of beasts."[3] Even in one's encounter with death, Spinoza upholds the distinction between mankind and animals.

The difference between Spinoza and the *Zhuangzi* here may be modest, but it demonstrates the former's emphasis on necessary truths about the world (which is also conceived to have various regularities) and the possibility of having epistemic access to those truths. In contrast to this view, the *Zhuangzi* trivializes what seem like capricious transformations and traces them to natural processes of change. This approach undermines one's perception of regularity and stability in the world. In addition, the *Zhuangzi* does not rank things against one another—whether in life or in death. It is therefore no coincidence that Zilai's calmness in the face of death is presented as an instance of navigating the unpredictable transformations of nature, which in the end can turn him into an insect's arm or a rat's liver.

Needless to say, the *Zhuangzi* also allows for the kind of "superstitious" beliefs and arbitrary transformations that frustrate Spinoza, such as imagining trees to speak like humans or men to be formed from stones and seeds.[4] Certainly, Spinoza lived during a period in which polymath philosophers vied to lay out the most convincing account of the preestablished order in nature, perceived as awaiting discovery and comprehension by human beings. The *Zhuangzi*, on the other hand, was written in an intellectual milieu when

---

[2] This point is discussed in chapter 3, section 3.4 and is revisited in the concluding section of Part II.

[3] Ep.21.

[4] See, for instance, the dream sequence discussed in chapter 4, section 4.1, which involves a tree talking to a carpenter. As noted in the same section, the *Zhuangzi* also undermines the difference between dreaming and being awake in the "The Discourse that Levels Things (Qi wu lun 齊物論) chapter. Another instance of a nonhuman speaking like a human (and not in a dream) can be seen in the "External Things" (Wai wu 外物) chapter, which features a dialogue between a fish and the character of Zhuangzi. *Zhuangzi* 26:917. Also see *Zhuangzi* 27:942 for a discussion of myriad things being seeds of one another (*wanwu jie zhong ye* 萬物皆種也), giving place to one another, which is described as the Heavenly equality (*tian jun* 天均). See *Zhuangzi* 2:76.

the difference between the fantastic and the virtual was not unambiguous.[5] Given the *Zhuangzi*'s emphasis on the marvels of the world, which had no preestablished code that needed to be cracked by the human mind, it is perhaps not as jolting to see a man celebrating the possibility of being turned into different types of animals.

After examining both the ontology Spinoza lays out in the *Ethics* and his political program, it is safe to assert that Spinoza's formulation of how composite beings enjoy singularity, integrity, and identity over time aligns with his vision of human communities. According to this vision, communities can incorporate a diversity of opinions without necessarily losing the stability or equilibrium that characterizes the collective body. Of course, Spinoza's investment in building stable and sustainable human communities is rooted in his more fundamental investment in human companionship, which, he asserts, helps mankind reach higher levels of understanding and happiness. His penning of two political treatises, addressing issues of religious and political authority, as well as different forms of governance, is similarly informed by his commitment to human togetherness and by his view that there are simply better and worse ways of living one's life. That by itself justifies the effort to organize one's day-to-day encounters so as to enter into enabling alliances, which Spinoza imagines along human-centered lines because of the presence of hierarchically ranked affinities in the world.

When we look at the Zhuangzian approach to the issue, we also see an interplay between two visions. On an ontological level, there is the conviction that the boundaries that delineate things are highly negotiable. On a political level, attempts to structure the world for the purpose of establishing a sociocultural order are criticized for trying to fix what is not broken. This certainly has to do with the text's generally skeptical attitude toward gaining mastery of a situation when we are all at the mercy of forces that we cannot grasp, let alone control and manipulate. However, this is also largely why the text refrains from providing a blueprint for any sort of sociopolitical organization.

While refraining from forging universal and definitive correlations between specific onto-epistemological and political attitudes, it is nonetheless safe to assert that the *Zhuangzi*'s overall undermining of pan-contextual and

---

[5] The same period also offers us classics like "The Classic of Mountains and Seas" (Shan hai jing 山海經), which combines verifiable data with the fantastic. See Strassberg's lively and accessible study and translation of this work. Richard E. Strassberg, *A Chinese Bestiary: Strange Creatures from the Guideways through Mountains and Seas* (Berkeley: University of California Press, 2008).

pan-historical knowledge claims about the world is intertwined with its critique of grand narratives promoting order and unity (which also rely on exclusionary visions of human society). However, this critique is also tied to the absence of a commitment to a distinct and agenda-laden political stance. The crucial question to ponder at this point is whether one can be engaged, like Spinoza, with institutional politics and political thinking at the policy level, and yet, like the *Zhuangzi*, also avoid ranking some ways and forms of living as indubitably better than others.

B. In the Absence of Civil Order

The *Zhuangzi*'s undermining of the human-animal distinction is partly informed by its indifference toward categories of *zhi* 治 (to order, govern) and *luan* 亂 (disorder), which are already entangled in ideologies that claim to emancipate people from an allegedly animal-like existence. Instead of weaponizing comparisons between human beings and birds and wild beasts to depict a chaotic existence resulting from the absence of appropriate social structures, the *Zhuangzi* offers a narrative in which people live together with birds and wild animals, without a division of labor, social distinctions, or culturally valued artifacts and norms (in other words, without material and normative markers of human civilization). This imagery of ancient antiquity does not point to a subpar existence, but rather to an unconstrained flourishing of all beings without the bias of ranked interests.

The *Zhuangzi*'s depiction of antiquity is not a scenario Spinoza considers. Mankind in Spinoza's imagination of the state of nature is solitary and each man needs to protect himself from other people and animals (TTP 3.5). Although Spinoza is credited for giving an optimistic account of mankind in the state of nature, that is so only in comparison to someone like Hobbes. In the end, even with all the sociability Spinoza attributes to mankind, people still seem to have a pronounced sense of "self versus others" even in the state of nature, which informs the ways they act in odious ways in the state of nature and beyond. Of course, in Spinoza's version of the state of nature, just like in the *Zhuangzi*'s version of antiquity, there is no "wrong" or "sin" (TP 2.18–19). Yet, for instance, Spinoza still imagines people to have a notion of "mine" even in the state of nature in the absence of a legal concept of "property" (TP 7.19), which is one of the features of the human condition that a good state takes into consideration (TP 10.8). That people are said to have a sense of ownership even in the state of nature—as imagined by Spinoza, where solitude is the default situation and social roles and distinctions are absent—suggests the presence of a preestablished core of self-identity that pits one's interests against another's as much as it facilitates formation of tribalistic alliances.[6]

It not that the *Zhuangzi*'s version of antiquity is an undifferentiated mass *sans* boundaries; there are identifiable things and groupings. However, perhaps boundaries, including personal boundaries, come in degrees[7] and there is a distinction between having a sense of your own vantage point on the world and having a sense of exclusive ownership of a part of the world. What is clear is that in the *Zhuangzi*, one's personal identity is tied up with social roles and duties, and that with ossified behavioral patterns come rigid notions of identity. Since early Chinese views of the human-beast binary also primarily revolved around the former's ability to form social divisions and perform various roles, in the *Zhuangzi*, letting go of one's attachment to such social roles is tied to letting go of one's humanity. This is sometimes depicted quite literally, as individuals may simultaneously embody different domains of species.

Such an option is not entirely available to Spinoza, who grounds individuation and self-sameness over time (traits that are integral to notions of personal identity) in relations of motion and rest.[8] There *is* negotiability of boundaries around different individuals, in the sense that what counts as an "individual thing" is informed by our explanatory interests, where "if a number of individuals so concur in one action that together they are all cause of one effect, [we] consider them all, to that extent, as one singular thing" (EII2d7). As shown, Spinoza mobilizes this negotiability to articulate his vision of human solidarity around the notion of body politic instead

---

[6] In TP 7.18 we are told that "all men are so constituted by nature that each wants to be identified with his own kind and to be distinguished by lineage from others." Sometimes this tribalism is made possible by antagonistic behavior. See, for instance, TP 3.9, which notes: "It is without doubt a natural thing for men to conspire together either by reason of a common fear or through desire to avenge a common injury."

[7] In fact, Perkins argues that both in the *Daodejing* and the *Zhuangzi* we see that the "rigidity" that comes with being a thing (*wu* 物) is a matter of degree. That is, one can be more or less fixed as a thing. See Perkins, "What Is a Thing (*wu* 物)?," 66–67). There is a psycho-phenomenological dimension to this view in the sense that the evaluations that are attached to things generate increased levels of affective investment in them. This investment, as one might say, enhances the presence of these things in our lives, entangles us with them, and contributes to anchoring us in rigid modes of thinking.

[8] The thinness of Spinoza's account of human personal identity is noted by Thiel. See Udo Thiel, "Personal Identity," in *The Cambridge History of Seventeenth-Century Philosophy*, vol. 1, ed. Daniel Garber and Michael Ayers (Cambridge: Cambridge University Press, 1998), 879–880.

of disintegrating individuals and groups. Hence, although his ontology does not necessitate investment in a notion of human togetherness, it is, in the end, mobilized to ground it. This is crucial given that Spinoza is nowadays celebrated for having an ontology that allegedly allows us to reimagine post-humanist futures,[9] when his true ingenuity lies in his ability to argue for human togetherness without appealing to any God-given gifts and responsibilities.

What is equally crucial is the dark vision of humanity that lurks underneath Spinoza's salvationary rhetoric about the need for mankind to come together to elevate each other. Part of Spinoza's pessimism stems from the fact that his discussions about mankind blend supposedly preestablished features of human beings with historically grounded ones—and sometimes in a way that verges on conflating the two. As mentioned earlier, Spinoza in his political works aims to look at men as they are instead of how they should be. In fact, doing otherwise, he adds, would border on "on fantasy or could be put into effect in Utopia or in that golden age of the poets where there would naturally be no need of such" (TP 1.1). That he presents mankind as in need of being restrained and regulated is, to some extent, explainable by his looking at men's features after they had already been amplified or transformed by various social structures. After all, there is a circularity inherent in narratives about the state of nature in the sense that they are fictions that are shaped by the present—and which, in turn, further shape the present itself.

When Spinoza declares that "men are by nature enemies, and even when they are joined and bound together by laws they still retain their nature" (TP 8.12), it behooves us to ask the extent to which this eternal antagonism he sees in mankind might be, in fact, the effect of a system that is geared toward protecting the interests of the minority in power. After all, Spinoza himself acknowledges the corrupting influence of power (TP 7.27). More significantly, he admits that "the wealthier men become, the more natural it is for them to take measures to protect themselves" (TP 7.16). Then the obvious question to ask at this point is this: To what extent is the fear of social disorder simply the fear of the poor on the part of the economic and ruling elite, who perhaps tend to view the rest in their own image and take defensive

---

[9] The parts of Spinoza's *Ethics* that emphasize relationality have been appropriated especially by Deleuze to imagine new paradigms of action that go beyond group affiliations (and beyond Spinoza's own human-centered formulations of empowered ways of acting and thinking). See Deleuze, *Spinoza*, 122–130.

measures accordingly?[10] Relatedly, when Spinoza observes that due to men's competitive antagonism, governments have a way of gradually falling "into the hands of a few men" (TP 8.12), to what extent is that race for hoarding more power and opportunity the result of a system that is already built on a logic of scarcity—which ironically ends up being the engine that generates the scarcity?[11]

The *Zhuangzi*'s narrative of antiquity can be seen as a vision that is as soothing as it is threatening for some—especially for those few who arrogate themselves to the position of managing the many. When institutional structures and norms are knocked down, perhaps what lies behind is not directionless want and distress, but self-sufficient people who do just fine without the regulatory acumen of political leaders and ideological pathfinders. Considering that ordinary folks feed the ruling elite, so that the few can have enough leisure to manage the labor of the many,[12] the *Zhuangzi*'s vision of folks being "clothed by their own weaving, fed by their own plowing" is not simply about evoking a nostalgic vision of simpler times but also (deliberately or inadvertently) diffusing power from top to bottom.

Of course, with the division of labor gone, so is the "excess" that serves as a marker of people's difference from beasts. For the early Ru (which the *Zhuangzi* is critiquing in its narrative of antiquity), it is teachings (about social distinctions, roles, and duty) that separate people from beasts. For Spinoza, it is arts and sciences. Hence, it is no coincidence that in the *Zhuangzi*'s idyllic vision of antiquity "people lived together with the birds and wild animals, bunched together with all things." This sunny alternative of how people's

---

[10] This point is developed by Rebecca Solnit who argues that historical responses to disasters show that when the usual order is suspended and people are left to their own devices, most people behave in altruistic ways. The mayhem that follows natural disasters is largely shaped by elite panic and the fear of looting and property crime, which then cause responses to shift from rescue missions to preemptive criminalization of poorer communities. Rebecca Solnit, *A Paradise Built in Hell: The Extraordinary Communities That Arise in Disaster* (New York: Penguin, 2010).

[11] This problem is as perennial as it is contemporary. For a brief look at the history of socially created scarcity, see Charles M. A. Clark, "Wealth and Poverty: On the Social Creation of Scarcity," *Journal of Economic Issues* 36, no. 2 (2002), 415–421.

[12] The topic of the division of labor and its alleged role in the emancipation of people from a beastly existence is already treated in chapter 8, but as a reminder that highlights how the idea of the division of labor so conveniently serves the interest of courtly powers, see *Mengzi* 3A4. In this passage we are told that "some labor with their minds, some labor with their strengths. Those who labor with their minds bring order to those who labor with their strength, and those who labor with their strength are ordered by those who labor with their minds. Those who are put in order by others feed people, and those who order people are fed by others." The translation is from Robert Eno, *Mencius: An Online Teaching Translation*, May 2016, https://scholarworks.iu.edu/dspace/bitstream/handle/2022/23421/Mengzi.pdf?sequence=2&isAllowed=y.

lives would look in an unarranged world is perhaps as much about imagining what else being animal-like can stand for as it is about questioning the benefit of the contrivances that are promoted as making people's lives more refined and evolved.

In the preface to the Fourth Book of the *Ethics*, Spinoza acknowledges the desire to form the idea of a man that "we" may look up to as a model of human nature. After all, if one has a model to look up to, then one can better know the means to better oneself. The same is perhaps also true of the models we entertain when we imagine distant pasts. Narratives about what "we" used to be are also always about what else "we" could be. When we have an image of unarranged nature as an existence red in tooth and claw (even when the empirical evidence suggests a more complex picture),[13] that inevitably justifies a model of community that is built on taking defensive measures to restrain people's allegedly antagonistic tendencies. What is more, when the imagery of animality is invoked to paint a vivid picture of the threats awaiting humanity should they lose their direction, then maintaining existing apparatuses of governmentality becomes not only a matter of the preservation of welfare but also of identity. If, as Spinoza claims, we are imitative creatures who are shaped by our interactions with others and also by the models we set for ourselves, then our beliefs about what we are make us in that image.

Part V continues to explore depictions of people in or out of the state of nature, but this time with an attention toward social groups that are gendered, "raced," classed, and/or disabled. Also examined are possible links between the way different social groupings are depicted, on the one hand, and portrayals of animality, on the other. As will be shown, the links between social groupings and the human-animal binary are not always straightforward. Attention to not only the presence but also the absence of such links reveals that although animality tropes often end up clustering around those that are farther away from the (often male) civic ideal in a community, such cases do not exhaust the conceptual entanglements that attend depictions of social difference. While this does not undo the conceptual comingling of human and animal realities, it does reveal further sites of exploration for human-animal studies.

---

[13] On this point, see Marc Bekoff, *The Emotional Lives of Animals: A Leading Scientist Explores Animal Joy, Sorrow, and Empathy—and Why They Matter* (Novato, CA: New World Library, 2007), 85–109. Also see Willett, *Interspecies Ethics*, 60–63.

PART V
HUMANS' ANIMALITY
Textual Traces and Absences

Down south in Yue, there is a place called the Land of Established Potency. The people there are simple and unadorned, having few private concerns and desires . . . not knowing what duty is required of them nor what propriety calls for. Heedless and wild, they go their reckless ways. . . . My wish is that you leave your land, renounce your customs, and with the Way as your helper, proceed there.

Zhuangzi 20:670

It follows finally that anyone who neither knows the biblical histories nor knows anything by the natural light of reason, though not actually impious or obstinate, is however inhuman and almost brutish, and has no gift from God.

TTP 5.16

9
Rethinking Animal Imagery in the *Zhuangzi*

The observation that conceptions of animality are often tied to those of humanity is frequently mentioned in critical animality studies, which owes its long-running endurance to the intersectional dimension of the field. This intersectionality is further reinforced by the fact that much work on critical race theory, gender studies, and disability studies easily opens into questions of animality. Of course, even though many traditions and texts draw on animal imageries to make sense of human realities, it should not be assumed that identical patterns of intersectionality are present across different texts and discourses.

The final part of this study traces depictions of peoples of foreign lands and of humble backgrounds, as well as of disabled and gendered people, in the *Zhuangzi* and Spinoza and their respective intellectual contexts, with an eye toward the invocation of animality tropes in such depictions. The point in tracing possible associations of animality in depictions of these groups is not to lend support to a ready-made conclusion (e.g., the human-animal boundary informs all social distinctions), but to hopefully (1) understand the precise reach of the human-animal binary in constructing and undoing difference, and (2) to further understand the rhetorical work that animal imageries do when they are employed to make sense of human realities.

This chapter traces depictions of peoples of foreign lands or humble backgrounds, as well as those deemed or rendered "disabled" or subjected to gendered distinctions, in the *Zhuangzi* and its intellectual context. The objective is to examine potential connections between these depictions and the concept of animality. Section 9.1 takes up the prevalent reading of the *Zhuangzi* as a subversive and defiant text that ostensibly overturns the hierarchies between the "civilized" and the "barbarian" (imagined to map onto "Zhou versus non-Zhou" identities) as well as between the ruling elite and people of humble backgrounds. Also examined are the text's positive portrayals of individuals with "disability." Section 9.1 contends that while exploring the subversive dimensions of the *Zhuangzi*'s approach to marginalized social groups, it is crucial to precisely identify what the text is presumably subverting. With this goal in mind, the section contests the assumption that early Chinese masters of philosophy had coherent and unified attitudes toward "barbarians" or people with "disability" (which are also terms with questionable suitability for early Chinese texts). In fact, the extant textual evidence suggests a heightened preoccupation with one's professional background, perhaps even more so than preoccupations about one's regional origin. Also noteworthy is that having an "intact" body might not be the default assumption in an era when war wounds and harsh corporeal punishments (which included amputation) were not uncommon.

In the end, as the chapter demonstrates, the overarching area of concern in assessing one's closeness to the male civic ideal seems to be one's behavioral traits and whether they conform to ideals of humanness proper. It is this concern that inflects approaches about one's regional background, one's profession, as well as one's criminal background—thereby also shaping the *Zhuangzi*'s subversive gestures regarding such approaches.

Finally, aside from the actual target of the *Zhuangzi*'s subversive gestures, the very character and the likely purpose of the so-called subversive gestures of the text matter. I argue that while the *Zhuangzi* introduces significant twists into common narratives by romanticizing foreign and distant lands or by trivializing social mobility, it is likely that the text primarily aims to offer escapist and at times hopeful visions of finding contentment in unlikely circumstances to its primary audience—that is, lower-level elite men of service (*shi* 士), whose opportunities for serving in the court were perhaps greater than before and yet were still unwarranted given the tumultuous nature of the times.[1]

Being mindful of the text's primary audience also helps explain the text's scarce and at times male-centered treatment of gender relations, which is analyzed in section 9.2. While our examination of depictions of women in the *Zhuangzi* serves as a reminder of the limits of the interpretational approach that presents the *Zhuangzi* as a counter-discourse that challenges *all* authoritative norms, it also offers a glimpse into where the intellectual investments of the authors and compilers lay.

---

[1] On this point, see chapter 1, section 1.1.

9.1 The *Zhuangzi* on Distant Lands, Humble Professions, and Unruly Minds

It is not uncommon to read into early Chinese textual traditions coherent attitudes toward frontier peoples, as evinced by the blanket translation of different ethnonyms as "barbarian."[2] However, it is difficult to extract from early Chinese texts a cohesive and static attitude toward peoples of the frontier regions especially considering that alliances and territorial boundaries were constantly shifting.[3] Moreover, as Nylan adds, the difficulty of communication and frequent migrations should make us "anticipate more micro-identities" instead of a unified attitude on the part of elite folks of central regions toward the people of outlying lands en masse.[4]

Certainly, the textual tradition is not lacking in disparaging remarks toward various peoples of frontier regions. A recurrent tendency is to employ animal pejoratives when making self-serving observations about the alleged absence of social distinctions or propriety and etiquette (*li* 禮) in regions that were, at the time, marked as different and/or far away. Clear examples of this rhetorical move include the *Guoyu*'s 國語 (Discourses of the States) remark about the uncouth table manners of the people of the Rong 戎 and Di 狄 tribes, likening them to "birds and wild animals."[5] The very same people are sometimes described with more specific animality tropes, such as the characterization of them as acting like "wolves and jackals" that "cannot be satisfied" in the *Zuozhuan*.[6] The latter remark seems to be about these people's perceived character failures, which are, in the end, tied to their alleged lack

---

[2] In some instances, but not all, descriptions of foreign peoples are pejorative and the term "barbarian" comes close to capturing these connotations. Even then, the use of the term "barbarian" as a broad label encompassing all frontier peoples implies the existence of a uniform attitude toward diverse communities, which may not necessarily be the case. Having noted this, I must acknowledge that I too used the term "barbarian" in a blanket fashion to describe all the frontier peoples in an earlier piece. See Özbey, "Undermining the Person," 132. For a critical examination of this term in relation to ancient Chinese ethnonyms that are used for designating foreign peoples, see Nicola Di Cosmo, *Ancient China and Its Enemies: The Rise of Nomadic Power in East Asian History* (New York: Cambridge University Press, 2004), 95–101.

[3] See chapter 1, section 1.1.

[4] Nylan gives the example of the emergence of micro-identities even within the same "culture," such as the bifurcation of the Qin into the "old Qin (*Gu* Qin 古秦)" and the "new people (*xinmin* 新民)" during the Zhanguo period due to frequent migrations. See Michael Nylan, "Talk about 'Barbarians' in Antiquity," 590.

[5] *Guoyu* 2:58 ("Zhou Yu Zong 周語中"). References to the Guoyu are to the chapter and page numbers in Xu Yuangao 徐元誥, *Guoyu jijie* 國語集解 (Discourses of the States, with Collected Explanations) (Beijing 北京: Zhonghua shuju 中華書局, 2002).

[6] *Zuozhuan* Min 1.2(2), 1:228–229. It is Guan Zhong 管仲 who is reported in the *Zuozhuan* to be describing Rong and Di peoples as jackals and wolves.

of norms of propriety that are expected to shape affective and behavioral traits. Another marker of acting animal-like is the absence of clearly defined distinctions among people, which makes *Lüshi Chunqiu* describe people of the four frontier regions, who allegedly have no rulers, as living like "deer, birds and wild animals." This, we are explained, amounts to a lifestyle where the young give orders to the old, the strong are considered the worthy, and the haughty and violent are revered.[7]

What ultimately makes them the targets of such remarks is their overall conduct, which is attributed to their upbringing. Perhaps the clearest articulation of this view is presented in the *Xunzi*, where we are told that "the children of Han, Yue, Yi and Mo peoples are all born making the same sounds, but when grown up they have different customs because teaching makes them thus."[8] In other words, the variations among people from different regions do not stem from inherent biophysical traits but rather from their adoption of different mores and customs. Such a view could easily be carried into a full-blown relativistic approach to human cultures, where one region's way of life is no better than others. However, that is not the direction that someone like Xunzi, a Ru traditionalist with a staunch allegiance to traditions of early Zhou, ever takes.

Chapter 1 noted that a shared contention among early Chinese masters concerned the comprehensiveness of their teachings, which they contrasted with narrow-mindedness and partiality.[9] An articulation of this line of reasoning would be to associate local customs (*su* 俗) with provincial attitudes while presenting one's ideology to be all-encompassing and valid across regions.[10] For Ru thinkers, that sometimes translated into an attitude that framed interaction with people of frontier regions in terms of a unilateral transformation by teaching.[11] Hence, on the one hand, we see a sense of ease

---

[7] *Lüshi Chunqiu* 20/1.3 (translation modified). The directional reference has to do with the fact that in many early Chinese texts, the Man 蠻, Yi 夷, Di 狄, and Rong 戎 peoples are associated with the four cardinal directions (*si fang* 四方). *Lüshi Chunqiu*'s description of these people as living like deer forms a contrast with the *Zhuangzi*'s description of people who live under the rule of a "real sage" as deer-like (see chapter 8, section 8.3).

[8] *Xunzi* 1.2. Note that Han 邗, Yue 越, Yi 夷 and Mo 貉 are all names of frontier regions. I consulted Eric Hutton's translation for this passage. See Hutton, *Xunzi*, 1.

[9] See chapter 1, section 1.1.

[10] Lewis makes this point in *The Construction of Space*, 199–202.

[11] See Brindley, *Ancient China and the Yue*, 177. Jan Assmann notes that in early civilizations it was not the case that there was an "elite culture as opposed to lower class culture," but that the elite were simply "the bearer of culture itself." This seems to also apply to central elite authors' views of "non-Zhou" regions (however defined depending on the interstate politics of the specific time), where "culture" should be taken as *wen* 文 (pattern, style, culture), which is intertwined with rites (*li* 禮) of Zhou. See Jan Assmann, *Cultural Memory and Early Civilization: Writing, Remembrance,*

about one's background, which drives tales of radical mobility that feature people of far-off lands ascending to govern the central heartland, such as the thearch Shun 舜 of Eastern Yi (Dong-Yi 東夷) or king Wen 文 of Western Yi (Xi-Yi 西夷). On the other hand, we are told that despite coming from different regions, these rulers actually operated according to a shared framework that surpassed regional particularities. Take, for instance, what the *Mengzi* writes about Shun and Wen:

> Their territories were separated by more than a thousand *li*, and their eras were separated by over a thousand years. But their wills prevailed alike through the central states: as perfectly matched as the two halves of a tally. As former sage and later sage they aligned to a single measure (*Mengzi* 4B1).[12]

The two men came from two different regions and lived in different times, yet they ruled alike, because, after all, they were both proficient in the patterns of a cultural universe that transcended local interests, customs, and values.

As noted earlier, within the early Chinese textual tradition, what counts as different or distant from the Zhou culture changes depending on the period and interstate relations. This can be seen in the examples of the Chu 楚 and Qin 秦 polities (the boundaries of which were also constantly changing), who were formidable contenders for power and were often straddling the line between "similar to" and "different from" Zhou culture.[13] Moreover, even with the polities that were portrayed as radically different and at times as downright barbaric, their perceived inferiority was not always used to justify civilizing efforts but instead to draw a parallel between their affairs and those of central polities. Take, for instance, Mozi's reply when he is told of a tribe south of Chu that allegedly had a custom of devouring the firstborn son. The interlocutor continues:

---

and Political Imagination (Cambridge: Cambridge University Press, 2011), 130 (cited in Nylan, "Talk about 'Barbarians' in Antiquity," 600n42).

[12] The translation is adapted from Eno, *Mencius*.

[13] See Yuri Pines, "'The One That Pervades the All' in Ancient Chinese Political Thought: The Origins of the 'The Great Unity' Paradigm," *T'oung Pao*, Second Series 86, Fasc. 4/5 (2000): 298n46. Pines notes that in the case of Qin their exclusion from the Zhou culture was at times a case of self-proclaimed difference. Yuri Pines, "Changing Views of 'Tianxia' in Pre-imperial Discourse," *Oriens Extremus* 43 (2002): 111–112.

If he tastes delicious, he will be offered to their ruler, and if the ruler is pleased the father will be rewarded. Isn't this a wicked custom? Mozi says: Even the customs of central territories are like this. How is killing the father and rewarding the son different from eating the son and rewarding the father?[14] If humaneness and dutifulness (*ren yi* 仁義) are not practiced, how can we condemn the Yi 夷 for eating their sons?[15]

Although Mozi's reply does not overturn his interlocutor's prejudices against the peoples he is vilifying, by mobilizing their alleged vice to criticize the ills of "central" regions, he at least avoids indulging in self-righteous fantasies about distant lands to validate the superiority of one's own.

Similar to its contemporaries, the *Zhuangzi*'s portrayal of frontier peoples is diverse and nuanced as well. As pointed out by previous studies, there is indeed a critical and satirical aspect to the *Zhuangzi*'s portrayal of peoples of outlying lands;[16] however, it is still not the case that all the stories of alien peoples in the *Zhuangzi* could be interpreted in terms of an overturning of a straightforward Zhou versus non-Zhou or even civilized-barbarian dichotomy, given that the broader textual tradition presents us with a rather shifting spectrum of identities.[17] Take, for instance, the well-known story of a man from Song 宋 who goes to Yue 越 to sell them ceremonial hats, only to find out that they did not care for hats and were happy cutting their hair short and tattooing their bodies.[18] It is a story that exposes the silliness of imposing one's own values and standards of properness on other people—a

---

[14] Fraser notes that "killing the father and rewarding the son" might be a reference to the practice of compensating families for the loss of their father in a military campaign. See Chris Fraser, trans., *The Essential Mozi: Ethical, Political, and Dialectical Writings* (Oxford: Oxford University Press, 2020), 254n199.

[15] *Mozi* 89/49/28–30. Yi 夷, generally, refers to communities living in "central" territories' eastern frontiers.

[16] Alexus McLeod, *The Dao of Madness: Mental Illness and Self-Cultivation in Early Chinese Philosophy and Medicine* (Oxford: Oxford University Press, 2021), 145. I am grateful to McLeod for allowing me to read this study in manuscript form before its publication. Also see Yuri Pines, "Beasts or Humans: Pre-Imperial Origins of Sino-Barbarian Dichotomy," in *Mongols, Turks and Others: Eurasian Nomads and the Sedentary World*, ed. Reuven Amitai and Michal Biran (Leiden: Brill, 2005), 77. Pines adds that despite their ease about ridiculing the pretensions of the central regions, the authors of the *Zhuangzi* still seem to have found little interest in the lives of frontier peoples (Pines, "Beasts or Humans," 77).

[17] For a recent study that demonstrates the inconsistencies in early Chinese texts' treatments of Yue peoples, see Brindley, *Ancient China and the Yue*.

[18] *Zhuangzi* 1:35. I follow Brindley's translation of *duan fa* 斷髮 as "shearing the hair" or "cutting the hair short" (instead of "shaving the head," which is the common translation, even though it is not the literal translation of *duan fa* 斷髮, nor were Yue peoples known for shaving their heads. See Brindley, *Ancient China and the Yue*, 129, 143–149).

common theme in the *Zhuangzi*.[19] In addition to this, the story also disrupts patronizing narratives about peoples of the southern frontier, without, I will argue, being necessarily concerned about overturning a Zhou versus non-Zhou or civilized-barbarian duality.

The man from Song (Song *ren* 宋人) was a popular comedic trope in early Chinese texts, commonly seen to be doing something foolish. Despite being one of the "central" polities, Song folks were associated with the customs of the old Shang 商 court, which hardly makes them the ideal representatives of the Zhou tradition. They were also a common butt of jokes, which does little to position the *Zhuangzi* episode as an example of satiric criticism speaking truth to power. As for "Yue," the word is an ethnonym ascribed to diverse groups of peoples living in the South.[20] Among their distinguishing markers was the combination of sheared hair and tattooed bodies,[21] which perhaps is why the tattoos of these people are mentioned in the *Zhuangzi* episode even though being tattooed does not prevent one from wearing hats.[22] As the episode in the *Zhuangzi* punches down on Song folks, it does uplift another group, Yue peoples, about whom the (elite) thinkers of the period had ambiguous attitudes at best, negative attitudes at worst. The episode still has a subversive aspect to it, which has to do with its shifting from the vantage point of the man of Song to that of Yue peoples, allowing the narrative to unfold from the latter's viewpoint. The reader, in the end, is compelled to conclude that it is not that they "lack" hats, it is that they have no use for them.

Yue peoples also feature as the subject of a more developed and evocative passage in the *Zhuangzi*, which, once again, disrupts a common narrative angle in a nuanced manner. The passage features a nobleman from Lu 魯, which happens to be the hometown of Kongzi and a stronghold of Ru values. The nobleman complains that no matter how hard he tries to follow the way of the former kings, he cannot seem to avoid trouble. The official

---

[19] Other (and sometimes more extreme) examples include the episode about the character of Hundun (discussed in chapter 5, section 5.1 and chapter 8, section 8.3), the nobleman and the bird (discussed in chapter 5, section 5.1), and Kongzi and the swimmer (discussed in chapter 4, section 4.4)

[20] As Brindley notes: "Despite the separation of the polities of Wu and Yue, and despite the historic rivalry between them, the history of the state of Wu is also usually considered to be a history of Yue peoples." Sometimes we also see the term Bai Yue 百越 (numerous Yue) as a shorthand for various groups associated with the Yue. See Brindley, *Ancient China and the Yue*, 86–87, 92.

[21] As Sterckx notes, southern peoples would often clothe themselves in animal hides or imitate animal patterns, such as reptile patterns, when they were tattooing their bodies (*wen shen* 文身; inscribing the body) in order to avoid being wounded by alligators and water spirits. Sterckx, *The Animal and the Daemon*, 189.

[22] I owe this point to Brindley. Brindley, *Ancient China and the Yue*, 151.

listening to him diagnoses what his problem is and suggests an interesting solution:

> Your technique to dispel misfortune is too shallow. The thick-coated fox and the elegantly patterned leopard (*fenghu wenbao* 豐狐文豹) dwell in the mountain forest and lie hidden in cliffside caves. At night, they go about, and during the day they stay put—how cautious they are.... And yet they are unable to avoid the misfortune of falling into a trap or a net. Is it due to some fault of theirs? It is their hides which bring upon them such disaster. And is not the land of Lu your hide? I wish you to strip away your form and cast away your hide, to cleanse your heart and to cast away your desires, and to wander in the open wilderness where no one goes.[23] Down south in Yue, there is a place called the Land of Established Potency (*jian de zhi guo* 建德之國). The people there are simple and unadorned (*yu er pu* 愚而朴), having few private concerns and desires, knowing how to work but not how to hoard, giving without seeking any for return, not knowing what accords with duty (*yi* 義) nor what conforms with propriety (*li* 禮). Heedless and wild, they move about recklessly (*changkuang wang xing* 猖狂妄行).... My wish is that you leave your land, renounce your customs (*su* 俗), and with the Way as your helper, proceed there.[24]

The passage holds many interlinked layers. The parallel drawn between various animals possessing conspicuous and prized hides and the nobleman being in charge of the affairs of a visible land like Lu, adorned with the traditions of Zhou, carries an intriguing suggestion. It implies that just like the hides of a fox or a leopard, the life that the nobleman leads feels natural to him as he is born into it, akin to how a leopard is born with its patterns (*wen* 文). This reading is supported by the fact that later the nobleman's interlocutors refer to his way as "custom (*su* 俗)," a term typically used to describe the local practices and manners that individuals simply inherit. There is, nonetheless, a key difference between his ways and a leopard's hide: he is able to change his. He can relinquish his position, discard the elegant patterns of the tradition with which he adorns his conduct, and journey

---

[23] In Chinese the line reads: 吾願君刳形去皮，洒心去欲，而遊於無人之野。
[24] *Zhuangzi* 20:670.

to the land of peoples whose way of life remains untouched by notions of duty or propriety.²⁵

The descriptions of the simplicity and obliviousness of these peoples of a distant land also echo depictions of people of distant antiquity in the text, evoking a dreamy imagery of their way of life. As seen in chapter 8, idyllic narratives of antiquity involve people living together with birds and wild beasts, without any notion of duty (*yi* 義) or propriety (*li* 禮). These depictions can be seen as a parody of tales of humans' emancipation from an animal-like existence, achieved through the establishment of societal norms such as duty, propriety, and the accompanying social distinctions they imply and foster.²⁶ The passage above uses the same rhetorical strategy to use the distant to take a fresh look at the familiar, except that instead of, let us say, mobilizing alien people's alleged cannibalism to shame the cruel ways of central territories (like Mozi does), the official in the *Zhuangzi* story suggests that the nobleman find peace and security in the faraway land of Yue.

Casting away the "customs" of Zhou, which make his land and his position conspicuous, and journeying instead to a distant land would certainly help the nobleman avoid the trappings of political games. Although the land he is encouraged to travel to is not unpeopled, it is not where a nobleman like him goes, unless, of course, he is exiled there. The nobleman, in a way, is encouraged to undertake a self-exile, which is a possibility that is also suggested in the broader textual tradition. Indeed, the trope of a weary or thwarted elite withdrawing from civil society is a familiar trope in early Chinese literature. Some such examples involve journeying to distant lands, which goes hand in hand with casting away their duties and responsibilities, and sometimes feigning madness (*yang kuang* 佯狂).²⁷ Here it should be recalled that in the aforementioned passage in the *Zhuangzi*, being *kuang* 狂 (mad, frenzied, wild, violent) is a state that is ascribed to people of Yue, which should already tell us something about the semantic content of the word. As McLeod demonstrates, the state of *kuang* 狂 primarily refers to actions that are done without the restraints of social norms and was associated with "living outside of respectable social boundaries."²⁸ Considering that Yue

---

²⁵ Ironically, Yue peoples also happen to literally pattern their bodies (*wen shen* 文身 tattooing of the body; lit: patterning of the body) with animal patterns (see footnote 21 on this point), however, in their cases, their patterns enable them to gain greater invisibility in their own abode instead of causing them to stand out.
²⁶ *Zhuangzi*'s descriptions of distant antiquity are analyzed in chapter 8, section 8.3.
²⁷ Brindley, 148, 146. For a more detailed discussion of the notion of feigning madness, see McLeod, *The Dao of Madness*, 107–131, 136–137.
²⁸ McLeod, *The Dao of Madness*, 13.

peoples are described as ignorant of norms of propriety, the description of them as *kuang* 狂 is apt, except that the *Zhuangzi* presents this as a positive.

The nobleman is urged to travel to Yue not with the goal to reform them but to be one of them. In doing so, he would be crossing over into alien lands, into being wild and mad, and into a life unburdened with the binding norms of propriety or dutifulness. The ignorance or flouting of such norms has implications for the heart as well, as can be seen in the advice for the nobleman to cleanse his heart (*xi xin* 洒心). Chapter 4 has discussed the notion of recalibrating the heart (*xin zhai* 心齋) and making its distinctions tenuous (*xu* 虛), both of which connote a sense of not overcommitting to certain values and thereby gaining the ability to adapt to different situations with ease.[29] Although such an affective-cognitive state is associated with enabling modes of action in the *Zhuangzi*, the people who carry the markers of this state are sometimes described (or self-described) as *kuang* 狂.[30] While being described as *kuang* 狂 could be said to be part of their empowerment (as it helps them cast away responsibilities, if anything), it could also be seen as an accurate description of their unrestrained behavior and noncommittal heart. Although in the aforementioned story the interlinks between foreign lands, being wild and mad, and casting away propriety and dutifulness are clear, obviously one does not need to journey to distant lands to act outside of social norms. Neither are people of the central regions exempt from charges of flouting social norms and being less than the civic ideal, however defined. In fact, tropes of human excellence are sometimes contrasted with much wider groups of people, without specific regional focus—which aligns with the diversity of characters the *Zhuangzi* employs as subversive role models.

A well-known example of derogatory remarks targeting a wider group of people, regardless of geographic location, is Xunzi's attacks on what he describes as "petty people" (*xiao ren* 小人), who are often contrasted with the male civic ideal, the gentleman (*junzi* 君子). Criticized for a wide array of flaws including having a weak sense of propriety and dutifulness (*li yi* 禮義), such people are sometimes even described as having the heart of a tiger and wolf and the conduct of wild animals.[31] Similarly, *Mengzi* describes the lives of people who have food and clothes, yet are devoid of instructions and

---

[29] See chapter 4, section 4.3.

[30] Tenuousness (*xu* 虛) of the heart and being *kuang* 狂 seem to be linked to each other through their shared association with the theme of wandering (*you* 遊). The intertwine between the three notions is suggested in McLeod, *The Dao of Madness*, 157–158, 168.

[31] *Xunzi* 2.1. Also see *Xunzi* 13.7.

teachings (*jiao* 教), as getting close to the lives of birds and wild animals (3A4); and he asserts that the people who fail to preserve their hearts through humaneness and propriety (*yi ren cunxin, yi li cunxin* 以仁存心，以禮存心) do not differ from birds and wild animals (4B28).

Common folks who do not transgress social norms are not entirely exempted from animality tropes either, given the analogies drawn between the administrative success of the rulers and the herding of animals, or even the domestication of animals.[32] Although the primary purpose of such figurative parallels is to draw attention to the sovereign's duty to care for his people,[33] it can also be argued, along with the *Zhuangzi*, that these parallels reveal that the prevailing discourses of governance have a disciplinary orientation, despite being packaged and presented as edifying and nurturing.[34]

The sheer variety of the ways in which a commoner of the central regions could be described in less than positive terms makes clear that the external influences on a person's behavioral and affective development are not limited to regional factors. In fact, an equally important (and more frequently discussed) source of influence on a man's self-cultivation efforts and his social status is his occupation. Take, for instance, this passage from the *Xunzi*:

> If people accumulate experience in weeding and plowing, they become farmers.
>
> If they accumulate experience in chopping and carving, they become craftsmen.
>
> If they accumulate experience in selling and vending, they become merchants.
>
> If they accumulate experience in propriety and dutifulness, they become gentlemen.

---

[32] Examples of these kinds of analogies can be seen in the *Mengzi*'s calling the ruler the shepherd of people (1A6) and using a shepherd's flock as an analogue for the people (2B4); and the *Xunzi*'s drawing a direct analogy between how to manage a set of horses frightened by the carriage and how to manage people frightened by their government (*Xunzi* 9.4). This point is made by Sterckx as well in the *Animal and the Daemon*, 151.

[33] This is apparent from the fact that treating people as if they are animals is generally not viewed in positive terms. See, for instance, *Mengzi* 5B6, 4B3, 7A37, in which treating people as if they are animals (more specifically, as if they are horses, dogs, livestock, or pigs) is considered to be a despicable thing (4B3, 5B6, 7A37). What is being highlighted in shepherding analogies is the ruler's "care" for his people—which, of course, still has condescending overtones.

[34] As noted earlier, the chapter titled "Horse Hooves" (Mati 馬蹄) opens with an episode on horse training and how the process harms the horses, which later is followed by a reflection on the harms of the arts of governance (*zhi* 治). See *Zhuangzi* 9:338–345.

The sons of craftsmen all continue their fathers' work, and the people of a country are comfortably accustomed to the clothing of that area—if they reside in Chu they follow the ways of Chu, if they reside in Yue, they follow the ways of Yue, and if they reside in refinement, they follow the ways of refinement.³⁵ This is not because of their Heavenly-given inborn nature, but rather because accumulation and polishing have made them so (*ji mi shiran ye* 積靡使然也). (*Xunzi* 8:11)³⁶

The parallel drawn between being profession-bound and being region-bound is not accidental as both situations connote limitation and narrow-mindedness.³⁷ Just as the gentleman transcends regional differences by following the norms and values of a tradition that ostensibly has pan-regional validity, his occupational aspirations preclude jobs that require narrow expertise. Instead, a gentleman is expected to play a leading role in his community and ideally is in a position where he manages and organizes others' labor instead of engaging in menial labor himself.

Occupational limitations could ideally be transcended if one were to "polish" himself in ways that promote social mobility. However, in a stratified community (which is what is promoted in the vast majority of early Chinese texts) *some* people will always be laboring in fields and markets, although they might not always be from the *same* lineage of people.³⁸ This stratified

---

³⁵ A more literal translation of this line would say, "If they reside in Xia, they follow the ways of Xia" (in Chinese it reads *ju xia er xia* 居夏而夏), referring not to a place, but to traditions of the Xia 夏 dynasty. I follow Brindley's translation of it as "refinement." See Brindley, *Ancient China and the Yue*, 126. Moreover, in *Xunzi* 4.8, a similar parallel is drawn between Yue people being content with Yue, Chu people being content with Chu, and the gentleman being content with *ya* 雅 (refinement). Both Knoblock and Wang Yinzhi take the two characters to be interchangeable in certain contexts. See Knoblock, *Xunzi* vol.1, 289n56.

³⁶ For this passage I closely followed Hutton's translation with minor modifications. See Hutton, *Xunzi*, 66.

³⁷ For more examples followed by a discussion of what Lewis terms the contrast between "partiality" and "totality" in early Chinese literature (focusing on ideas about customs and professions), see Lewis, *Construction of Space*, 192–212. Aside from the familiar theme of comprehensiveness versus narrow-mindedness, in the context of this particular passage from the *Xunzi*, there seems to be an element of inertia in both cases as well, considering that specializing in a line of work that is passed down across generational lines is likened to following the customs of one's region, both of which are then contrasted with making an effort to polish oneself.

³⁸ While it is true that especially in early Ru texts the semantic scope of the term "gentleman" (*junzi* 君子) is expanded to encompass people with good character and values, it still does not imply that the ideal became readily attainable for everyone. For more on (1) the semantic range and evolution of the term, and (2) the social and occupational constraints affecting the *junzi* ideal, see Erica Brindley, "'Why Use an Ox-Cleaver to Carve a Chicken?' The Sociology of the Junzi Ideal in the Lunyu," *Philosophy East and West* 59, no. 1 (January 2009): 47–70, and Yuri Pines, "Confucius's Elitism: The Concepts of *Junzi* and *Xiaoren* Revisited," in *A Concise Companion to Confucius*, ed. Paul R. Goldin (Chichester: Wiley Blackwell, 2017), 164–184.

but mobile vision of society is sometimes conveyed through stories of former ministers and even rulers who rose from rags to riches, thanks to their meritorious conduct that can be discerned by a sagacious sovereign.[39] While praising the sage-ruler's ability to recognize talent even in the least likely places, these narratives also promote the upward mobility of folks who are not born into hereditary privilege.

Considering the negative associations commonly linked with humble professions, as well as the narratives of social advancement requiring the discerning gaze of an astute ruler, it is important to acknowledge that the subversive vision often attributed to the *Zhuangzi* finds clearer and more consistent expression in its portrayals of individuals engaged in humble occupations, in contrast to its uncertain and intermittent treatment of those residing in frontier regions.

As noted earlier, the *Zhuangzi* often diffuses epistemic centers of power by offering readers stories that feature role reversals, where the master becomes disciple, or by presenting us with objectionable masters.[40] A large bulk of these unexpected sources of wisdom are people of humble professions who end up inspiring insight in people in positions of power. The satirical dimension of such stories has been noted.[41] While mounting a challenge to norms concerning who shall engage in knowledge production, as well as also possibly mocking the very idea of role models, such satiric fantasies also offer a novel vision of what one's life and values could be.

The *Zhuangzi* brings about this shift in perspective by offering stories that feature, let us say, a swimmer who lectures a stunned Kongzi about adapting to the way of the water[42] or, in another case, a bell-stand maker who explains to an impressed nobleman how he manages to find the right tree that has the bell-stand already concealed in it.[43] Such stories inevitably prompt the readers to imagine an erudite master or a nobleman in a humbling light, while also offering a vision of a fulfilling life that need not be bettered by climbing up any social ladder.

---

[39] Well-known examples include the legendary ruler Shun, who worked in the fields before the ruler Yao selected him as his successor; and Yi Yin, who was a talented cook before he rose to the position of minister.

[40] See chapter 1, section 1.2 and also chapter 5, section 5.2.

[41] D'Ambrosio and Moeller read the *Zhuangzi* to be offering a parody of role models in such stories and thereby satirizing the very attitude of looking up to exemplary figures. See Moeller and D'Ambrosio, *Genuine Pretending*, 155.

[42] *Zhuangzi* 19:654–656. This example is also discussed in chapter 4, section 4.4.

[43] *Zhuangzi* 19:657.

Although it is the setting of such dialogues (which feature a low-ranking person lecturing a superior) that has garnered attention in the secondary literature, what is equally crucial is the ending of such dialogues—or, to put it more accurately, the absence of a certain kind of ending. To be more precise, at the end of such conversations, the practitioners of humble professions do not ask to be someone's disciple or hope to be offered a governmental position. Moreover, even if the person is already serving in the court of a noblemen, as in the case of the bell-stand maker, their servitude becomes a distant thought when they go about their trade. As the bell-stand maker explains, his preparation process involves fasting for seven days just so that he does not care about rewards, ranks, or punishments, nor even about his own person. By the time he is about to go into the forest to select his tree, he explains, "the ruler and the court do not exist [for me]."[44]

While the subversive aspect of such stories is obvious, their less acknowledged dimension is the comfort they possibly provide to people who are themselves part of an elite stratum of society. As explained in chapter 1, the audience of the *Zhuangzi* is most likely members of the lower-level elite, whose opportunities for serving in the court were greater than before unpredictability of their times.[45] Instead of trying to make a case for the eligibility of petty aristocrats (*shi* 士) for leading roles in society, the and yet were still not guaranteed given the *Zhuangzi* offers stories of contentment that feature people with the lowest social status. Such a move steers the conversation away from cultivating one's understanding of the norms of propriety and the arts of governance (which is not a realistic prospect for many people to begin with) to finding contentment in arrangements that are even below the *shi* status. The inclusion of stories about individuals from humble ranks in the *Zhuangzi* aligns with narratives that present dwelling in a place like Yue as an uplifting prospect. In both instances, arrangements that would conventionally be considered below the *shi* status are presented in a very favorable light, undermining the weight of the societal norms that govern elite life. Given the ever-changing landscape of power that must have shaped these men's lives,

---

[44] *Zhuangzi* 19:657. These insights are also raised by Graziani in the context of an analysis of a more well-known story that involves a butcher. I take the bell-stand maker story to share similar features with the story of the butcher, in the sense that in both cases we see people of humble occupations finding fulfillment in a mundane job, inspiring insight in someone who is in a position of authority (and doing so without expecting favors or promotion), and finally also serving someone in a position of power without being invested in that role. See Romain Graziani, "When Princes Awake in Kitchens: Zhuangzi's Rewriting of a Culinary Myth," in *Of Tripod and Palate: Food, Politics, and Religion in Traditional China*, ed. Roel Sterckx (New York: Palgrave Macmillan, 2005), 62–74.

[45] See chapter 1, section 1.1.

coupled with the heavily stratified nature of society (which is built on the very premise that only a select few will occupy the top echelons), finding contentment in unlikely circumstances might have offered a hopeful vision in a hopeless time.

Aside from buoyant portrayals of people of distant lands, wannabe or actual *kuang* 狂 (wild, mad) people, and people of low public standing or humble occupations, the *Zhuangzi* also presents its readers with an unusually large cast of people with congenital or punishment-induced deformities. Here a preemptive caveat is necessary. While it is tempting to read the *Zhuangzi* as an ancient Chinese example of a "disability discourse" for this very reason,[46] we should also keep in mind that physical "disability" might not have meant the same thing for early Chinese thinkers and that what counted as a "usual" body, especially in the Warring States period, might not be the same as an "intact" body. As Milburn points out, many people in the late Zhou era would have lived with the debilitating effects of accidental injury, disease, poor nutrition, and of course, in the case of men, battle wounds.[47] Added to these were the scars of penal mutilation, which Milburn adds, were associated with the exactions of military discipline.[48] Hence, an undamaged physical appearance in men was not necessarily the default expectation. Neither were mutilated or deformed men necessarily deemed unemployable.[49]

What makes the *Zhuangzi*'s account of its own deformed characters stand out is that many occupy the intersection of having a low social status *and* having a congenitally improbable body. Take, for instance, the character named Outspread the Disjointed (Zhili Shu zhe 支離疏者). We are told that this man's "chin was buried into his navel, his shoulders were higher than the crown of his head, his ponytail was pointing at the sky, his five internal organs were all on top, his thigh bones took the place of his ribs."[50] However, none of these prevent Outspread the Disjointed from sewing and washing

---

[46] See, for instance, Michael J. Stoltzfus and Darla Y. Schumm, "Beyond Models: Some Tentative Daoist Contributions to Disability Studies," *Disability Studies Quarterly* 31, no. 1 (Winter 2011).

[47] Olivia Milburn, 2007, "Marked Out for Greatness? Perceptions of Deformity and Physical Impairment in Ancient China," *Monumenta Serica* 55, no. 1: 4–6, DOI: 10.1179/mon.2007.55.1.001.

[48] Milburn, "Marked Out for Greatness?" 4.

[49] In fact, as Milburn further points out, the *Han Shu* 漢書 details a program to employ mutilated individuals in specific ways, where those who had their noses cut off guard the borders, those who are castrated guard women's quarters, those who had their ears cut off were to guard the hunting places, and so on. Milburn, "Marked Out for Greatness?," 6. Although we cannot know for sure whether such a program was actually carried out in real life, it still offers us a glimpse into the kind of discourses that revolved around mutilated individuals.

[50] *Zhuangzi* 4:185. A very similar description is also used for a man named Ziyu after he suddenly falls ill (*Zhuangzi* 6:264).

for a living, which earns him enough to feed ten people. Moreover, the condition of his body helps him preserve what is already a satisfying life. When the authorities call for troops, he is exempted from military duty, saving him down the line from battle wounds, if not death. Hence, we are told, his disjointed body helps him live out his natural lifespan without it being cut short. While resonating with the theme of the use of the useless,[51] the story also invites us to question what is fortunate and what is not instead of invoking pity for Outspread the Disjointed.

Some of the other disfigured characters in the *Zhuangzi* are amputees who are mutilated as a result of punishment, which adds an element of agency to their condition. This sometimes invites the scorn of others, which, in the end, is turned against them. As such, stories depicting mutilated former transgressors of norms are mobilized to erect yet another critique of discourses that dictate rights and wrongs. This move can be seen in the example of a story that features a character called Toeless of Uncle Mountain (Shushan Wuzhi 叔山無趾), who is chastised by the character of Kongzi for his former criminal behavior. Disappointed, Toeless tells Kongzi: "There is nothing that Heaven doesn't cover, nothing that Earth doesn't support" (*Tian wu bu fu, di wu bu zai* 天無不覆，地無不載) and notes that he had expected Kongzi to be a master that is like Heaven and Earth.[52] Later when he relays the story to Lao Dan (Laozi), he notes that Heaven has punished Kongzi (*Tian xing zhi* 天刑之), which is why he cannot see the acceptable and the unacceptable as a single thread (*yi ke buke wei yiguan* 以可不可為一貫).[53] In saying so, Toeless turns the table on Kongzi, portraying him as someone who has been punished due to his narrow-mindedness. The result of Kongzi's punishment is not a mutilated body but a mindset that fails to recognize that dyadic norms require each other to be intelligible.[54]

---

[51] See chapter 1, section 1.2, for a discussion about the motif of the big but useless tree in the *Zhuangzi*, which is mobilized to comment on the (conventional) "uselessness" of the text of the *Zhuangzi* itself (which, in the end, proves to have many other overlooked uses). The same section also touches on the early Chinese literary tradition of using botanical metaphors to talk about the cultivation of people and draws a parallel between the *Zhuangzi*'s choice of focusing on anomalous trees (as opposed to "neat" rice plants, bamboo shoots, or grass) and its telling of stories of unconventional people.

[52] *Zhuangzi* 5:208.

[53] *Zhuangzi* 5:211.

[54] For other examples of stories featuring mutilated ex-convicts, see the chapter titled "The Signs of Fullness of Potency" (De chong fu 德充符). The chapter opens with a story that portrays Kongzi as an open-minded figure who is quick to praise a one-footed amputee for seeing beyond dualities, including life and death. This enables the man to view "the loss of his foot as nothing more than casting away a clump of soil" (*Zhuangzi* 5:196).

Having seen many examples of stories in the *Zhuangzi* that give voice to the ignored, if not the looked down upon, we are now in a position to make a few observations about their shared features. In these stories, we certainly see an emphasis on finding fulfillment in unlikely spaces and divorcing self-empowerment from one's closeness to courtly power. Some stories are colored with a satiric tinge that trades in transgressive thematic material, which is then tied to the broader theme of detachment from circles of power. Of course, there is still another low-ranking social group that we have not discussed. Does the theme of finding fulfillment in life without wielding power apply to women as well? Second, does the text consistently upend gender hierarchy as well, as it does with some other social hierarchies?

The answer to the first question is yes, and to the latter is no. Before we even move on to fleshing out these answers in the next section, it should be noted that women characters in the received *Zhuangzi* are awfully scarce. It can here be pointed out that the text was most likely (or at least *primarily*) written by and for a male audience. However, it is also equally unlikely that many of its readers would be from Yue or would be animals (!). Moreover, as will be shown, the content of the few episodes featuring women or gendered dynamics do not always challenge established norms either. While this shows the limits of the *Zhuangzi*'s so-called subversive attitude toward the underdogs of the world, it also invites us to remember and reconsider the possible aims and interests of the text in exploring animal and many other perspectives.

9.2 Women in the *Zhuangzi*

The representation of women in early Chinese philosophical literature has received considerable attention especially in the last few decades. An observation that is, by now, uncontroversial concerns the likely gap between the ritual code for gender roles (as they are laid out in prescriptive writings) and the daily social reality of elite women. In relation to Zhou rituals in general, Falkenhausen reminds us that "we should think of ancient Chinese ritual as a set of tools for regularizing the infinite variety of daily social reality" instead of faithful records of the lifestyles of elite families across different polities.[55]

---

[55] Lothar von Falkenhausen, *Chinese Society in the Age of Confucius (1000–250 BC): The Archeological Evidence* (Los Angeles: Cotsen Institute of Archeology Press at UCLA, 2006), 126.

Aside from differences on the local and family level, historical writings on the lives of palace and gentry women also portray a more complicated picture, where elite women seek good education, sometimes engage in occupations outside of the home, and, in general, actively negotiate the power structures within which they act.[56] If, however, one grants that early Chinese Masters texts and Classics give us at least some idea of the sensibilities around the ideal patterning of people's behavior (which is, in the end, to be negotiated by individuals who adapt these patterns to actual situations), then it is safe to assert that women are prescribed to be in subordinate roles.[57]

The importance of the difference between men's and women's social roles is stressed by early Chinese masters of philosophy so much that it is, at times, exalted to the status of being one of the fundamental social distinctions that deliver humans from a state of primordial bestiality.[58] It is for this reason that the *Xunzi* identifies the differentiation between male and female as a distinguishing characteristic that sets human beings apart from birds and wild animals. Similarly, the *Liji* describes the absence of gender distinctions as "the way of wild birds and beasts," and the *Guanzi* sees the state of men and women not being kept separate as reverting to animal behavior.[59] As Raphals points out, *nan-nü zhi bie* 男女之別 ("separation of men and women," or

---

[56] On this note, see Michael Nylan, "Golden Spindles and Axes: Elite Women in the Achaemenid and Han Empires," in Chenyang Li, *The Sage and the Second Sex*, 199–222, and Lisa Raphals, "Gendered Virtue Reconsidered: Notes from the Warring States and Han," in Chenyang Li, *The Sage and the Second Sex*, 223–247.

[57] See, for example, *Mengzi* 3B2 and *Xunzi* 12.3. Even this seemingly simple statement regarding women's ritually subordinate status invites interpretational challenges of its own, such as the fact that especially in early Ru literature, all people (*ren* 人) are said to have the same capacity for reaching the *junzi* 君子 (gentleman) ideal. Raphals addresses this tension by noting the difference between "capacity" and "opportunity"; whereas Brindley observes that although even the *junzi* ideal was not necessarily off-limits to women, it also was not encouraged. Munro, on the other hand, reframes the discussion by highlighting the rhetorical nature of the claims about the uniformity of people's capacities. He notes that they were most likely made with the primary purpose of undermining hereditary privilege and thus opening the path to greater social mobility for the *shi* 士 (men of service). Hall and Ames offer perhaps the most cynical reading and suggest that the majority of early Chinese masters simply meant "men" by "people" (*ren* 人). Ames's reading, of course, is not without textual evidence. See, for instance, *Mengzi* 5A1 for a clear example of an androcentric usage of *ren* 人. See Raphals, "Gendered Virtue Reconsidered," 225; Brindley, *Ancient China and the Yue*, 54; Donald J. Munro, *The Concept of Man in Early China* (Ann Arbor: University of Michigan Center for Chinese Studies, 2001), 2; David L. Hall and Roger T. Ames, *Thinking from the Han: Self, Truth, and Transcendence in Chinese and Western Culture* (Albany: State University of New York Press, 1998), 294n18.

[58] One could speculate that the emphasis placed on the gender distinction by early Chinese masters of philosophy perhaps further evinces the gap between prescription and actual reality. After all, they perhaps would not be so alarmed at confusion of gender roles if it were not perceived to be a very possible, if not actual, scenario.

[59] *Xunzi* 5.4; *Liji* 11.25/9–10 ("Jiao Te Sheng 郊特牲"); *Guanzi* 21.65:1193 ("Li Zheng Jiu Bai Jie 立政九敗解").

"differentiation between male and female") was presented as "an essential ingredient of civilization and the defining feature of human society" and that they ascribed "the incorrect mingling of the sexes to the pre-human behaviour of animals, to the practices of primitive society before the influence of the sage-kings, and to states in decline and on the verge of disaster."[60]

This symbolic tie between gendered distinctions and people's emancipation from an animal-like existence seems to be acknowledged by an episode in the *Zhuangzi*. The episode, more broadly, serves as a critique of the conceptual boundaries that demarcate not only distinct things but also different phases of life from one another. It opens with a description of a spirit ritualist, who is said to predict people's deaths and misfortunes. Huzi confronts this spirit ritualist and manipulates his predictions by embodying different aspects and phases of life, showing the futility of being invested in the borders separating life from death, which overwhelms and scares away the ritualist.[61] When Liezi hears what happened between Huzi and the spirit ritualist, he, we are told, "understood that he had not yet begun [his] learning, and returned home.... He cooked for his wife, fed the pigs as if he were feeding people. He showed no preferences in affairs, and from being a cut and polished gem he returned back to simplicity" (*Zhuangzi* 7:312). Liezi's recognition of the contingency of all the distinctions and boundaries that people take for granted is accompanied by his reversing of gender roles, which is then mentioned alongside his feeding the pigs as if they are people. If maintaining one distinction (between men and women) is symbolically tied to maintaining the other (between humans and beasts), then it is understandable that Liezi ends up upending both distinctions at the same time.

Aside from the women who feature as background characters in stories with male protagonists,[62] the *Zhuangzi* also features a certain female sage as the lead character in a story.[63] Furthermore, in another episode, it offers a

---

[60] Lisa Raphals, *Sharing the Light: Representations of Women and Virtue in Early China* (Albany: State University of New York Press, 1998), 195.

[61] As Puett observes, the episode serves as criticism of spirit ritualists' (*shen wu* 神巫) attempt to control things, which differentiates the *Zhuangzi*'s approach toward spirit ritualists from that of the *Neiye* 內業 (Inner Enterprise) chapter of the *Guanzi*. Puett concludes that the goal for the *Zhuangzi* is not having direct control over things but going along with them. For further reading, see Puett, *To Become a God*, 115, 125–127, 130–133. For a discussion of how to understand and translate *wu* 巫 (ritualist or shaman), see Michael James Winkelman, "Chinese Wu, Ritualists and Shamans: An Ethnological Analysis," *Religions* 14, no. 7 (2023): 852, https://doi.org/10.3390/rel14070852.

[62] See also the story of Zilai who suddenly falls ill, which includes a brief mention of a wailing wife and children. The episode is discussed in chapter 8, section 8.2. We also see Zhuangzi's deceased wife mentioned in *Zhuangzi* 18:613–614.

[63] *Zhuangzi* 6:257–261

fresh retelling of a known tale, inviting the readers to view the story from the vantage point of its infamous female protagonist. The latter example concerns the story of Lady Li. As Ivanhoe notes, Lady Li, a woman who was considered to be beautiful yet dangerous, was from the Rong戎 tribe and was given as a hostage to Duke Xian to be his concubine.[64] As the story goes, she later estranges the nobleman from his wife and causes his legitimate heir to commit suicide, and eventually makes it so that her own son succeeds to the throne.[65] When the story is retold in the *Zhuangzi*, its focus shifts from the courtly dramas she was involved in to her initial capture. In the *Zhuangzi*, we see Lady Li crying until her clothes were wet with tears (2:109). However, she later reconsiders her judgment of the situation after she fills her stomach with meat dishes and sees the comfort of the nobleman's bed—which perhaps informs us about the relatively poor conditions of her previous life more than anything, considering that all it takes for her to be impressed is a meat roast and a cushy bed.

Lady Li's reconsideration of her situation is presented in a longer series of arguments about how one can give a positive twist to even the most dreadful-looking situations, including one's own death. Apart from taking the perspective of a Rong person, the story distances itself from the trope of parvenu-aristocratic women who stir up trouble behind the scenes by their manipulative use of sexuality and deceit. In the *Zhuangzi*, Lady Li is presented as a person with her own preferences (which did not include being kidnapped by a nobleman), and as someone who managed to deal with her own subjugation by relabeling her situation differently—which is a crucial skill that is employed by a variety of sagely figures throughout the text.

The same chapter of the received *Zhuangzi* also makes a provocative remark about whether the subjugation of a concubine is necessary or obvious. If we revisit a passage that should be familiar by now, situated within the context of critiquing the hierarchical ranking of various organs (with the heart being considered the ruler), the *Zhuangzi* asks:

> One hundred bones, nine orifices, six storehouses, they are together and exist here [in my body]. Which one do I take to be closest to me? . . . Like

---

[64] Philip J. Ivanhoe and Bryan W. Van Norden, eds., *Readings in Classical Chinese Philosophy* (Indianapolis, IN: Hackett, 2003), 218n28..

[65] Robin R. Wang, *Images of Women in Chinese Thought and Culture: Writings from the Pre-Qin Period through the Song Dynasty* (Indianapolis, IN: Hackett, 2003), 120n2. A brief account of the courtly dramas involving Lady Li is also given by Han Feizi, who states that she was manipulated by a minister into having the crown prince killed. *Han Feizi* 5.17:321.

this, do you take them all as servants and concubines? Are these servants and concubines insufficient to govern each other? Or do they take turns serving as the ruler and servants? If there is a genuine ruler existing among them, then, looking for and obtaining facts about it or not, would not add to or decrease its genuineness. (*Zhuangzi* 2:61)[66]

As noted in chapter 4, the passage suggests that if the ruler among these organs were so obvious, then we would not be producing arguments about it to begin with.[67] The same could also be said about the actual sovereign (and power holders) of a country, given the body politic dimension of the passage.[68] In a similar vein, if the subordinate status of concubines (and servants) was so obvious, then perhaps social hierarchy would need to be defended so ardently by many masters of philosophy—hence the passage asking why those who are rendered subordinate (more specifically, servants and concubines) cannot govern each other and take turns being the ruler.

Now, if the *Zhuangzi*, as a text, were to offer an unbroken thread of thought that unswervingly criticized distinctions and rankings in general (and the limitations that come with them), then perhaps it would also offer a consistently subversive attitude toward gendered hierarchies. However, we do not get either one of these from the *Zhuangzi*. As discussed in Part IV, there are layers of the text that speak of sagacious governance (*sheng zhi* 聖治; sagacious order) instead of undermining power structures altogether.[69] Although, as mentioned earlier, the mechanics behind such governance is paradoxical in nature (that is, pointing toward an absence of the desire to govern, and an absence of interventionist impulses), they still allow room for hierarchical rankings in society. It was observed then that at no point are hierarchical distinctions articulated around the mission to emancipate people from a perceived beastly existence, which places the *Zhuangzi*'s account of ideal governance at odds with the accounts of many other Masters texts. In fact, at times there is an intriguing sense of ease around the perceived animality of the peoples in such a community, as seen in the episode that likens them to wild deer.[70] However, that does not stop these pro-"governance" layers from endorsing gendered distinctions:

---

[66] The passage is first discussed in chapter 4. Its political overtones are discussed in chapter 8.
[67] See chapter 4, section 4.2.
[68] For more on this, see chapter 8, section 8.1.
[69] See chapter 8, section 8.3.
[70] *Zhuangzi* 12:451. The episode is discussed in chapter 8, section 8.3.

The ruler precedes, the subjects follow. The father precedes, the sons follow. The elder brother precedes, the younger brothers follow. The elder precedes, the younger follows. The male precedes, the female follows. The husband precedes, the wife follows. The honored and the lowly, precedence and following are the workings of heaven and earth, and thus the sage obtains his model from them (*gu shengren qu xiang yan* 故聖人取象焉).[71]

The difference between the ruler and his subjects is a given. One could also argue that differences between the younger and the older are simply unavoidable. Can one say the same for the distinction between men and women, between husband and wife? The authors of the passage seem to think so.

In regard to gendered distinctions in early Chinese philosophical discourse, Raphals entertains the possibility that "views on human perfectibility and self-cultivation may have spanned social class, but not gender"; whereas Brindley points out that the practical restrictions affecting people of lower social and ritual ranks seem especially severe for women.[72] That would partly explain the casual reference to women's subordinate status in the *Zhuangzi*'s politically and socially more establishmentarian layers. Of course, this complicitous attitude toward women's subordinate status features in only one passage (rather than many) within the received text, but that is only because, as noted earlier, women and the topic of the distinction between men and women rarely arise throughout the transmitted text.

In the end, what we see in the received *Zhuangzi* is the lack of a consistent and persistent concern to upend gendered distinctions, which forms a sharp contrast with the way occupational differences and regional differences are treated in the text. Hence, despite all of its contrarian dimensions, and its ability to imagine Lady Li's life from her own vantage point and to ask whether concubines and servants need a ruler, the *Zhuangzi*, in one crucial moment, comes closer to other Masters texts in allowing, in its own peculiar way, more social mobility for people (or men?) of humble professions or frontier regions than for women.

Getting a sense of the political attitudes that accompany representations of various groups in the *Zhuangzi* is not an easy undertaking, given that not only details about its authors but also details about its intended audience and

---

[71] *Zhuangzi* 13:474.
[72] Lisa Raphals, "A Woman Who Understood the Rites," in *Confucius and the Analects: New Essays*, ed. Bryan W. Van Norden (Oxford: Oxford University Press, 2002), 285. Brindley, *Ancient China and the Yue*, 54–55.

the target of some of its criticisms are not always clear. Moreover, perhaps not all of its satirical stories are written with a polemical thrust, as it is entirely possible that some of them were composed to provide comfort about a bleak present that cannot be changed or a possible future that might not seem hopeful. If we grant that there might also be a calming dimension to sanguine tales about distant lands (to which a *shi* 士 [men of service; well-bred men] might be exiled), or about people finding fulfillment in menial jobs or with mutilated bodies (which are situations that even a *shi* perhaps might fear), then perhaps there was simply less of an interest in offering uplifting reimaginations of women's lives.

In the end, just as the *Zhuangzi* entertains animal vantage points to question the centrality of one's humanity and personhood, it also mobilizes menial folks' perspectives to undercut the weight of one's social status, imagines distant lands in utopian terms to loosen the grip of one's "central" roots, and pictures mutilated ex-cons in empowering positions to trivialize the intactness of one's body and one's integrity (in the eyes of scornful moralizers). The same subversive attitude does not consistently extend to one's status as a man perhaps because it is also a status that is viewed as a given *and* one that allows one to move up and down the social hierarchy in ways that perhaps the status of a woman does not.

10
Animalized Others in Spinoza's "Imagination"

One of the recurrent themes in this study has proved to be the tension between what Spinoza could have said and what he ended up saying.[1] This tension is perhaps even more palpable when it comes to Spinoza's remarks about gendered, classed, "raced," and disabled groups. A good portion of Spinoza's comments on women, ordinary folks of humble origins, foreign peoples (mostly "Turks"), and the intellectually lacking appear in his political works. It is in this particular context that Spinoza's writings more consistently conform to exclusionary social norms and attitudes.

Spinoza explains in his TP that he intends to conceive "men" as they are, instead of how they should be in a utopian scenario, so that his political theory can have practical application (TP 1.1.). Still, different and competing perspectives on "what men are" and on the capabilities of marginalized social groups were certainly present at the time, not to mention that Spinoza's views about women strike one as being particularly and knowingly hostile.

Furthermore, Spinoza's programmatic political philosophy still has its roots in his onto-epistemological views expressed in the *Ethics*, which is not devoid of biased remarks on different and disadvantaged social groups either.[2] This makes it all the more problematic to try to neatly separate Spinoza's political philosophy from his metaphysics or epistemology—especially when such a separation is carried out to explain away Spinoza's contemptuous remarks toward certain social groups.

Despite the temptation to write off Spinoza's remarks on women or ordinary folks as accidental slip-ups, there is a clear and interconnected pattern to the way he disparages them all. Spinoza's negative remarks on women, foreign peoples, ordinary folks, and the intellectually atypical neatly map onto

---

[1] The discrepancy between what Spinoza could have said and what he ended up saying is pointed out in chapter 3, section 3.4, and then is revisited in the conclusion portion of Part II.

[2] On these points, see chapter 3, section 3.3 and chapter 6, section 6.1.

each other for the way he construes them as being governed by passions, as having inferior abilities to seek what is to their own advantage, or as lacking agency in general—in other words, for the way they are all portrayed as lacking in reason.[3] This also explains why animality tropes are deployed in relation to all of them, considering the way animality is likewise associated in Spinoza's thinking with passions, absence of agency, and, in general, irrationality.[4]

10.1 On "Turks" and Common People

Spinoza uses the imagery of animality consistently to draw comparisons between different types of social orders, occasionally accompanied by examples of societies he deems barbaric. One significant thread running through these instances is Spinoza's linking of animality with irrationality. To illustrate the connection, let us examine an example from one of his earlier works, in which the extent of one's distance from reason correlates with one's proximity to beastliness. Spinoza in his recapitulation of Descartes's *a posteriori* proof of God states that

> there are some who deny that they have any idea of God, and yet, as they declare, they worship and love him. And though you were to set before them the definition of God and the attributes of God, you will meet with no more success than if you were to labor to teach a man blind from birth the differences of colors as we see them. However, except to consider them as a strange type of creature halfway between man and beast, we should pay small heed to their words.[5]

Assuming the term "God" meant the same thing for Spinoza when he was penning his *Principles of Cartesian Philosophy* as it did in his later works, one's failure to grasp God's existence and its attributes could be read along the lines of one's lacking adequate ideas of reason, which then makes one closer to a beast. A similar sentiment is expressed in Spinoza's *Theologico-Political*

---

[3] For the connection between adequate understanding and agency, see chapter 3, section 3.3. This connection is revisited in chapter 6, sections 6.2 and 6.3, which also discuss the affective aspect of reason in Spinoza.

[4] For discussions of Spinoza's associations of animality with irrationality, passions, and the absence of agency, see chapter 3, section 3.3 and chapter 6, sections 6.2 and 6.3.

[5] *Principles of Cartesian Philosophy*, Book I, Proposition 6, scholium.

Treatise, where Spinoza says that "it follows finally that anyone who neither knows the biblical histories nor knows anything by the natural light of reason, though not actually impious or obstinate, is however inhuman and almost brutish, and has no gift from God" (TTP 5.16).

Failure to live according to the guidance of reason also has implications for agency and "freedom."[6] This is why in TTP 20.6 Spinoza notes that the ultimate purpose of the state is not "to dominate or control people by fear or subject them to the authority of another" and "to turn people from rational beings into beasts or automata, but rather to allow their minds and bodies to develop in their own ways in security and enjoy the free use of reason."[7]

Since one's power of thinking, and, accordingly, one's activity or passivity, could increase or decrease, who belongs to the outskirts of humanity and who does not should be subject to change. What does not change in these analogies is what the beastliness represents: irrationality. A clear statement of this association is made again in TP 5.5 when Spinoza writes:

> [W]hen we say that the best state is one where men pass their lives in harmony, I am speaking of human life, which is characterized not just by the circulation of the blood and other features common to all animals, but especially by reason, the true virtue and life of the mind.

In regard to societies that rob people of their agency and hence their humanity, Spinoza, at times, gives the example of Turks (*Turci*). He uses this term to refer to the Ottomans, which in turn serves as a proxy for Muslims. In particular, he states that they "fill the minds of every individual with so many prejudices that they leave no room for sound reason, let alone for doubt" (TTP Pref.6).[8] Spinoza does not detail the source or precise reason behind this impression, although it was not uncommon for seventeenth-century European thinkers to describe the outsiders inside—the Ottomans—as tyrannical. As Çırakman shows, this impression largely had to do with the perceived absoluteness of the monarch in the Ottoman system, which was

---

[6] For a discussion of Spinoza's understanding of human freedom in a deterministic universe, see chapter 3, sections 3.2 and 3.3.

[7] A similar statement is also made in TTP Pref. 9 about the misuses of religion that "turn rational men into brutes since they completely prevent each person from using his own free judgment and distinguishing truth from falsehood."

[8] A similar description appears in Ep.76, where the Mahomedan Church is said to deceive people and control their minds.

not counterbalanced by a nobility class.⁹ While this implied a sense of unity, endurance, and stability, it also connoted oppression and domination of its subjects.¹⁰ A similar reasoning can be seen in Spinoza's remark in TP 6.4:

> For no state has stood so long without any notable change as that of the Turks, and, conversely, none have proved so short-lived as popular or democratic states, nor have any been so liable to frequent rebellion. But if slavery, barbarism, and desolation are to be called peace, there can be nothing more wretched for mankind than peace.

That Spinoza did not observe any notable change in a society that was already four centuries old by then is perhaps not surprising, since he does not appear to be a man of nuance when it comes to foreign peoples—as could be evidenced by his conflation of Brazilians and Ethiopians within the same paragraph (Ep.17). Although it is easy (and thus perhaps also lazy) to chalk off these remarks as Spinoza being a man of his time, his time was also replete with travelogues detailing, with an air of fairness, the many and diverse habits of different peoples.¹¹

In an oft-cited episode Spinoza generalizes his opinion of Turks/Ottomans/Muslims to a broader set of ethnic and religious groups when he states that Christians, Jews, Turks, and gentiles (or "pagans"; *ethnici*) have identical lifestyles despite their desire to look different from each other (TTP Pref. 9). This is sometimes taken as a marker of an egalitarian attitude toward people of different creeds,¹² when, in reality, Spinoza makes that comparison in the context of a perceived gap between how Christian societies should look (considering, he notes, it is a "religion of peace") and how they turn out in reality.¹³ In other words, he is simply using a group of perceived others

---

⁹ Spinoza too is opposed to feudal nobles (TP 7.20), but not to noblemen of royal descent (Ibid.). Moreover, he thinks that in monarchies the powers of the ruler should be counterbalanced by the powers of a large council with rotating members (TP 6.15–16). In contrast, he considers the Ottoman sovereignty to be the rule of one man and one man alone (TP 6.4).

¹⁰ Aslı Çırakman, *From the "Terror of the World" to the "Sick Man of Europe": European Images of Ottoman Empire and Society from the Sixteenth Century to the Nineteenth* (New York: Peter Lang, 2002), 67, 215–216.

¹¹ Çırakman, *From the "Terror of the World" to the "Sick Man of Europe,"* 36–38.

¹² See, for instance, Curley, *Collected Works of Spinoza*, vol. 2, 663.

¹³ The entire passage reads: "I have often been amazed to find that people who are proud to profess the Christian religion, that is [a religion of] love, joy, peace, moderation and good will to all men, opposing each other with extraordinary animosity and giving daily expression to the bitterest mutual hatred. So much so that it has become easier to recognize an individual's faith by the latter features than the former. It has been the case for a long time that one can hardly know whether anyone is a Christian, Turk, Jew or gentile, other than that he has a certain appearance and dresses in a certain

as a foil against which to criticize the shortcomings of Christian European societies—which was not an uncommon rhetorical move in early modern writing.[14]

Spinoza occasionally launches even more generalized attacks against much wider groups of people especially in his TTP.[15] More specially, Spinoza complains that the common people (*vulgus*) submit to prejudices that "turn rational men into brutes" (TTP Pref.9), which is rooted in their wretched affective state where they are straddled between hopes and fears (TTP Pref.15). Spinoza uses *vulgus* (common people, masses, mob) interchangeably with *plebis* (people, mob) (TTP 4.10); and though *vulgus* does not amount to the entirety of humankind (*humanum genus*) (TTP 5.17), it still does refer to the overwhelming majority (TTP 5.14). Furthermore, *vulgus* or *plebis* is contrasted with the "learned" (*doctus*) (TTP 7.9, 13.9), which is not surprising given that, at the time, the majority of the population was still illiterate.[16] Spinoza admits that the common people simply have no time to examine proofs or study different languages to better understand the Scripture (TTP 7.20). Insofar as this predicament is applicable to many historical periods, Spinoza's downcast and weary assessment of the critical thinking skills of the masses (TTP 6.5) takes on a more enduring significance.

---

way or attends one or another church and upholds a certain belief or pays allegiance to one magistrate rather than another. Otherwise their lives are identical in each case."

[14] Zachary Lockman, *Contending Visions of the Middle East: The History and Politics of Orientalism*, 2nd ed. (Cambridge: Cambridge University Press, 2009), 43.

[15] Melamed points out that Spinoza's TTP stands out for its harsh tone against common folks (*vulgus*) and that Spinoza softens his tone in his TP, noting that in the latter work he refers to the general populace with the more neutral sounding term "multitude" (*multitudo*) instead of with *vulgus*. See Melamed, "When Having Too Much Power Is Harmful: Spinoza on Political Luck," 163. Although it is certainly possible that Spinoza's authorial voice evolved between the preparations of the two works (the uncompleted TP is a later work and there is roughly a decade between the two), it should also be noted that the two works try to accomplish different goals (which Melamed also notes; see Melamed, "When Having *Too Much* Power Is Harmful," 163), which impose different rhetorical tones and moods. Whereas in the TTP Spinoza takes aim at the clergy and attempts to expose the corruption of the church and its reciprocal impact on the people, in the TP he largely compares different types of regimes and constitutions and thus adopts a more judicial language. The *multitudo* in the TP often simply refers to the many, the populace, as opposed to the ruling few; and, as Shirley also notes, usage of the term *multitudo* was common in seventeenth-century judicial writings in general (Spinoza, *Complete Works*, trans. Shirley, 687n22).

[16] Richard Tuck estimates that around 1600 "about 60 to 70 percent of the male population of Europe was illiterate" and that the numbers could be as high as 90 percent for the female population; while Houston notes a relative expansion of literacy for the middling ranks in the Dutch Republic (and beyond) by the end of seventeenth century. See Tuck, "The Institutional Setting," 11; and R. A. Houston, *Literacy in Early Modern Europe: Culture and Education 1500–1800*, 2nd ed. (London: Routledge, 2002), 141.

Spinoza, at times, also speaks ill of humanity in its entirety—so much so that he, ironically, verges on misanthropy.¹⁷ He notes that it is "rare" that "men live by the guidance of reason" (EIVP35s) and that both people's conditional *and* essential features are to be blamed, which he expresses by saying that "it is therefore clear that men are prone to hatred and envy, and this is accentuated by their upbringing" (EIIIP56). On one occasion Spinoza also criticizes those who despise the common people and points to mankind's essential similarity with the following words:

> Yet perhaps our suggestions will be received with ridicule by those who restrict to the common people (*plebs*) the faults that are inherent in all mortals, saying, "There is no moderation in the mob (*vulgus*); they terrorize unless they are frightened," and, "A commoner is either a humble servant or an arrogant master, there is no truth or judgment in it," and the like. But all men share in one and the same nature; it is power and culture that mislead us. (TP 7.27; translation modified)¹⁸

Apart from the fact that Spinoza himself declares elsewhere that "the mob (*vulgus*) is terrifying, if unafraid" (EIVP54s), this statement is also interesting for its resorting to a universalizing (and dark) description of human nature. In fact, in the same paragraph Spinoza later adds: "All men have the same nature (*natura omnibus eadem est*). All . . . terrorize unless they are frightened (*terrent, nisi paveant*)" (TP 7.27). With these reminders Spinoza takes a quality that he himself sometimes attributes to the populace and generalizes it to everyone while emphasizing the role upbringing plays in the way people think and behave.

Since upbringing makes a difference in people's mental and corporeal development, a good polity structures people's lives in ways that help them thrive. However, according to Spinoza, common people happen to be too stubborn to change for the better (TTP Pref. 15), which is perhaps why he time and time again reminds us that providing the conditions that

---

¹⁷ For a discussion of Spinoza's criticism of "misanthropists," see chapter 6, section 6.3. For Spinoza, however, a misanthropist is characterized not only by his disdain for humanity, but also by his love of beasts.

¹⁸ As noted earlier, Spinoza also makes generalized attacks against the masses (*vulgus* in particular) in the TTP. Hence, it is also possible that the target of this criticism is Spinoza's own earlier writings. This depends on whether one explains Spinoza's change of tone in terms of a change of attitude or a change of purposive and thematic context (on this point, also see footnote 15). I owe thanks to the anonymous reviewer for the observation that Spinoza might be criticizing his (former) self in this passage.

are suitable for the development of reason in the long run often requires the utilization of people's sad passions (TTP 19.12, EIVp54s, TP 7.27). The problem is that disciplining people through their sad passions is a tool that Spinoza criticizes for reducing people to beasts (TTP 20.6). However, as noted in chapter 7, obliging the masses to behave *as if* they are guided by reason by working on their sad passions can pave the way for them to reach a state where they understand and not simply obey the laws (which are, in the end, directed to their own good) (TTP 16.10).[19] Although that does not make Spinoza's reasoning less paternalistic, it does offer a less elitist vision of ideal society, in the sense that Spinoza at least does not argue for structuring the society in ways that rely on deliberately keeping masses uninformed and in their place. In fact, the ideal regime, for Spinoza, is democracy for the way it allows people to "remain equal as they had been previously, in the state of nature" (TP 16.11). However, as will be discussed in the next section, it turns out that not everyone is equal in the state of nature either.

10.2 On Women, the Infantile, and the Sub-rational

Perhaps the most insidious aspect of Spinoza's political philosophy rears its ugly head during a discussion of his own model of democracy, which is not a particularly inclusive one. In the TP, where Spinoza compares different sorts of regimes and elaborates on the kinds of constitutions that are most fit for them, he explains that when it comes to democracy his purpose is to discuss the kind "wherein all without exception who owe allegiance only to their country's laws and are in other respects in control of their own right and lead respectable lives have the right to vote in the supreme council and undertake offices of state." Spinoza further elaborates on the meaning of this statement:

> I say expressly, "who owe allegiance only to their country's laws" so as to exclude foreigners, who are deemed to be subject to another government. In addition to owing allegiance to the laws of the state, I added, "and are in other matters in control of their own right" so as to exclude women and servants who are under the control of their husbands and masters, and also children and wards as long as they are under the control of parents and guardians. Lastly, I said, "who lead respectable lives" so as to exclude

---

[19] See chapter 7, section 7.2.

especially those who are in bad repute for their crimes or for a dishonorable way of life. (TP 11.3)

The passage offers a lot to unpack, but one consistent theme appears to be agency and the ability to make good decisions for oneself. Since "when each man most seeks his own advantage for himself, then men are most useful to one another" (EIVp35c2), those who are under the control of an authority cannot freely seek what is to their own advantage and thus cannot also decide what is useful for the community. It is not clear whether by "foreigners" (*peregrini*) Spinoza also has in mind those who were born abroad but later settled in the Dutch Republic (though *peregrinus* connotes traveling, aside from being foreign). It is also not clear whether those who have a bad reputation for their crimes or lead "dishonorable" lives can rectify their social standing and regain the right to vote. Likewise, *servus*, depending on the context, could mean "servant," but also "serf" or "slave"; but either way, they are described as being under the control of their masters and it is unclear whether that control is taken to be permanent. In regard to children, we know for certain their non-voting status is temporary. How about women?

Among all the groups who are excluded from political participation (foreigners, dishonorable folks, servants, children, and women), only the last is taken up in the next paragraph for a further discussion about whether their servitude is by convention or by nature. Is it because Spinoza indeed viewed all the other instances to be actually or potentially temporary situations while regarding women's servitude as an eternal given? Or is it because Spinoza simply could not ignore all the contemporaneous discussions on women's status in society and was prompted to offer his opinion on the issue? Perhaps it is both.

As Stuurman points out, the evidence of public debates, lectures, and the literary field shows that the topic of the equality of the sexes was taken seriously by learned circles.[20] Aside from the fact that since the Renaissance women had entered the literary circles, the advent of the "Cartesian moment" (with its emphasis on reason being equal in everyone), as well as travelogues documenting women engaging in heavy manual labor in various parts of the world, opened up new grounds for debates over gender equality.[21]

---

[20] Siep Stuurman, "The Deconstruction of Gender: Seventeenth-Century Feminism and Modern Equality," in *Women, Gender and Enlightenment*, ed. Sarah Knott and Barbara Taylor (New York: Palgrave Macmillan, 2017), 384.

[21] For the status of Cartesianism in the seventeenth-century Dutch Republic, see chapter 2, section 2.1. A recurrent argument used by advocates of gender equality was that the mind (or soul) has no

Public defenses of greater female participation in society and women's natural talents gained their initial momentum in Italian and French salon culture, though they did not remain limited to it. In fact, a famous mid-century polemical exchange took place between the internationally renowned Dutch thinker Anna Maria van Schurman and André Rivet, which was first published in Latin in the Dutch Republic in 1641. The discussion, like others that came before it, touches on the topic of women's native abilities and the extent to which their inferior social status was due to the lack of opportunities for them to engage in higher studies.[22]

In his discussion of his exclusion of women from his model of democracy, Spinoza anticipates these questions and offers an answer:

> Perhaps someone will ask whether it is by nature or by convention that women are subject to the authority of men. For if this has come about simply by convention, there is no reason compelling us to exclude women from government. But if we look simply to experience, we shall see that this situation arises from their weakness. For nowhere is there an instance of men and women's ruling together; wherever in the world men and women are to be found, we find men ruling and women's being ruled and both sexes thus living in harmony. Against this, it is said of the Amazons who once held rule that they did not suffer men to stay in their native land, rearing females only and killing the males whom they had borne. Now if women were naturally the equal of men and were equally endowed with strength of mind and ability-qualities wherein human power and consequently human right consists—then surely so many and such a wide variety of nations would have yielded some instances where *both* sexes ruled on equal terms and other instances where *men* were ruled by women, being so brought up as to be inferior in ability. But as such instances are nowhere to be found, one is fully entitled to assert that women do not naturally possess equal right with men and that they necessarily give way to men. Thus it is not

---

sex. This idea can be traced not only to Cartesian mind-body relations but also to Platonic philosophy and its Christian elaborations. Not all proponents of gender equality identified as Cartesian, however. Anna Maria van Schurman, for instance, was a strict Calvinist who (at least for a period) sided with Voetius against the Dutch Cartesians. For more, see Desmond M. Clarke, trans., *The Equality of the Sexes: Three Feminist Texts of the Seventeenth Century* (Oxford: Oxford University Press, 2013), 1–53, and Stuurman, "The Deconstruction of Gender."

[22] See Clarke, *The Equality of the Sexes*, 94–111.

possible for both sexes to have equal rule, and far less so that men should be ruled by women. (TP 11.4; my emphasis).

The Amazon example was a popular one among authors who championed gender equality, except that the lesson they drew from it is vastly different from that of Spinoza. Marinella, for instance, argues that "man cannot live without women, though women, such as the Amazons, have ruled and governed not just cities but entire provinces without men"; Gournay celebrates the fighting spirit of Amazons, citing Seneca who speaks of Amazons terrorizing the Greeks; a few decades later Poulain gives the example of Amazons, noting that men are there for the sake of women.[23] Spinoza, obviously, disagrees. His remark that if there were a society ruled by women, men would be "brought up (*educarentur*) to be inferior in ability" aligns with his overall approach of challenging the nature-culture dichotomy.[24] However, whereas Spinoza acknowledges the correlation between being brought up to be inferior and actually being inferior in the hypothetical case of men, he does not apply the same logic to women.

Strictly speaking, there is no nature-history dichotomy in Spinoza. This means various relations of oppression can all be explained by appealing to the laws of motion without assuming the existence of any kind of mental forces that could transcend and act on the physical world.[25] The absence of a nature-history dichotomy means that the interactions of bodies are explainable by appealing to the laws of bodies alone. What it does *not* mean is that we can simply draw trans-historical conclusions about the capacities of certain bodies by looking at the history of their interactions with other bodies. Yet, this is exactly the approach Spinoza takes when from the limited observation that there have not been societies where women rule men, he arrives at the conclusion that women are necessarily inferior to men.

Spinoza's arguments for women's inferiority are especially curious because, according to him, one's capabilities are never fixed and they develop as the body and the mind become more powerful and active (EIIP13–14).

---

[23] Stuurman, "The Deconstruction of Gender," 373; Clarke, *The Equality of the Sexes*, 67, 149. Marinella and Gournay were also cited by van Schurman and her opponent Rivet. As Stuurman observes, this pattern of citation suggests that "early-modern feminist writings are more than isolated utterances. They constitute a tradition, a feminist 'counter-canon.'" Stuurman, "The Deconstruction of Gender," 375.

[24] It is worth recalling that Spinoza rejects the idea of human societies existing as a separate "dominion within a dominion" (EIIIpref.), emphasizing their inseparability from the laws of nature.

[25] As explained in chapter 3, section 3.1, according to Spinoza, to every idea, that is, to every mental state, corresponds a physical state, and vice versa.

This is also captured in the famous phrase "no one has yet determined what the body can do" (EIIIp2s). Moreover, Spinoza also states that subjugated individuals regain the control of their own right as soon as hope and fear are removed (TP 2.10), which could easily be applied to the condition of women who are rendered dependent on their husbands and fathers. By excluding women from democratic citizenship, Spinoza forever denies them the power to change their own conditions; but then, according to Spinoza's own distorted reasoning, they can never be the masters of their own destinies anyway, as they are necessarily subservient to men.

Aside from the eternal conclusion Spinoza arrives at about the social status of women, the implication that women do not have the agency required to participate in society the way men do is an especially menacing one. As chapter 3 has shown, in the context of a discussion of Spinoza's remarks about the paradox of Buridan's ass, the absence of agency clearly implies mental debility (for Spinoza and his contemporaries) and is associated with anyone who is "less than a man": "madmen (*vesani*)," "fools (*stulti*)," and children.[26] A similar repertoire of dupes also makes an appearance in EIIIp2s, when Spinoza speaks of an infant seeking milk, an angry child seeking revenge, and a timid man seeking escape. Expanding upon this, he adds a drunkard, a deranged person (*delirans*), and a gossiping woman (*garrula*) to the collection. This latter list also appears in the context of a discussion about folks who have a false sense of agency (believing they have "free will" in the Cartesian sense), because they lack understanding of the true workings of nature. That is why, Spinoza elaborates, they are all either acting under the influence of passions or are simply "delirious" (Ep.58). At other times, women are portrayed in Spinoza's works as they are shedding unnecessary tears (either due to superstition or undue compassion for animals)[27] or as they are trying manipulate men with sexual gifts (EIVp71s).

Notably, as others have pointed out, the passage in the TP where women are said to be necessarily subservient to men forms a sharp contrast with the story of the Fall (as told by Spinoza).[28] To briefly recall the outline of the story, in Spinoza's version of the Fall, the first man loses his freedom after he starts imitating the affects of beasts and associating with them instead of turning his attention to the woman "who agrees entirely with his own nature" to the extent that "there could be nothing in nature more to his advantage

---

[26] See chapter 3, section 3.3.
[27] See TTP Pref.3 and EIVp37s1.
[28] See chapter 6, section 6.2 for a detail examination of Spinoza's take on the Fall.

than woman" (EIVp68s). Although, as Barbone points out, Spinoza's assertion that the natures of two people perfectly agree with one another is an exaggeration given the singularity of each mode,[29] this is not the only place Spinoza resorts to such an expression. As mentioned in chapter 6, Spinoza occasionally resorts to exaggerated descriptions when emphasizing humans beings' similarity with each other.[30] Spinoza's use of the same exaggerated description of two individuals agreeing with each other (to the extent that they are identical) to characterize Adam and Eve's relation, followed by the statement that they are most "advantageous" for each other, shows that Spinoza was at least able to think of women as being able to live according to the guidance of reason and to seek their own advantage, which then makes them advantageous for their human companions (recalling EIVp35c2).

The point of the story, of course, is not to promote gender equality but to promote human companionship, which, Spinoza thinks, could be threatened by some feeling "too close" to beasts. With regard to Spinoza's statement about Adam's equality with Eve, Beth Lord and Genevieve Lloyd argue that in his *Political Treatise* Spinoza might be simply talking about the actual reality of men-women relationships whereas in the ideal human community things are otherwise.[31] Although Spinoza was certainly able to imagine men and women as equals, it is difficult to explain away his statement about women's inferiority in TP 11.4 with an ideal-actual discrepancy in women's conditions, because, first, Spinoza makes a point of presenting women's inferiority as a trans-historical fact, and second, it would be a mistake to view the Garden of Eden as an ideal society, as there is no "society" there. Adam and Eve are the only two humans in Eden, which also means that Adam cannot associate with male humans even if he wants to.[32] In an attempt to give a more charitable reading, it could perhaps still be pointed out, along with Sharp, that in Spinoza's version of the story it is not the woman who provokes irrationality in Adam by imitating the affects of the beast, but it is Adam who

---

[29] Steven Barbone, "What Counts as an Individual for Spinoza?," in *Spinoza: Metaphysical Themes*, ed. Olli Koistinen and John Biro (Oxford: Oxford University Press, 2002), 101. Grey entertains another possibility, namely that for Spinoza "humans do share a species nature that no nonhuman shares but that individual humans may express this nature to a greater or lesser degree." John Grey, "'Use Them at Our Pleasure': Spinoza on Animal Ethics," 375–376.

[30] See section 6.2 of chapter 6.

[31] Genevieve Lloyd, *Part of Nature: Self-Knowledge in Spinoza's Ethics* (Ithaca, NY: Cornell University Press, 1994); Beth Lord, "'Disempowered by Nature': Spinoza on the Political Capabilities of Women," *British Journal for the History of Philosophy* 19, no. 6 (2011): 1085–1106.

[32] Moreover, there is also no male rivalry to win the favors of Eve. As will be shown in the following pages, Spinoza also views women as potential threats to male rationality and fraternity.

himself identifies and associates with the beast.[33] The fact that the beast's affects do not pass through Eve to Adam forms a contrast with the traditional version of the story where Adam is deceived due to Eve's rapport with the snake. However, Spinoza's choice to tell the story through Adam alone also suggests that this is a tale about men's/humans' losing their freedom, and Spinoza takes Adam, and not Eve, as the prototype of the "(hu)man."

If these series of observations regarding Spinoza's depiction of women and discussions surrounding gender differences were not troubling enough, women also appear as agents of disturbance to (hu)man solidarity in Spinoza's works. Spinoza's investment in human solidarity, which is expressed both in his *Ethics* and in his two political treatises, has been mentioned before.[34] Human companionship is a necessary component of reaching higher levels of understanding and happiness, which is why, Spinoza states, "it is especially useful to men to form associations, to bind themselves by those bonds most apt to make one people of them" (EIVApx12). Spinoza at times expresses a fear that this solidarity could be disrupted if (1) people let their passions divide them (EIVP34, EIV37s1), or (2) if they feel strong connections with beings other than humans (EIVP37s1). As I will finally demonstrate in this chapter, in both cases, women, or those with "womanish" qualities, often figure as agents of disturbance to (hu)man solidarity.

The latter group was discussed in chapter 6 in the context of people feeling "womanish compassion" toward animals (EIVp37s1), which, Spinoza fears, could take the form of preferring animal companionship over humans (EIVp35s, EIVapp13). It is not just overly compassionate women who misdirect their affective energy away from mankind to beasts, but also satirists, melancholics, and zealots (EIVp35s, EIVapp13), which is a list that also connotes an excess of sad passions.[35] The same expression of "womanish compassion" (*muliebris misericordia*) also makes an appearance in EIIP49s where it is contrasted with living under the guidance of reason (which is what unites humanity). A similar expression, namely, "womanish tears" (*lacrimae muliebres*), appears again in the context of Spinoza's general criticism of people whose beliefs about God are steeped in superstition and lack all reason (TTP pref.3).

---

[33] Sharp, "Eve's Perfection," 575.
[34] See chapter 6, section 6.2 and chapter 7, section 7.2.
[35] For more on this, also see chapter 6, section 6.3.

Spinoza's association of women with undesirable passions and his description of allegedly unnecessary displays of empathy through tears as "womanish" are not trivial. The absence of a reason-affect distinction in Spinoza's philosophy has often been discussed in relation to the way it undermines phallogocentric theories of knowledge that heavily rely on a gendered reason-emotion dichotomy.[36] It is true that Spinoza's philosophy does allow us to think of human action without divorcing rationality from the affective aspect of one's existence. As discussed in chapter 6, passive affects, for Spinoza, are not eliminable by adequate ideas but by the active affects that accompany those adequate ideas, which means that the goal of adequate understanding is not to eliminate one's affects but to transform them.[37] However, Spinoza's elimination of the reason-affect dichotomy certainly does not bring with it an elimination of a male-female dichotomy.[38] It is simply that, instead of associating women with affects and men with reason, he associates certain undesirable affects (such as teary compassion and superstition) with femininity, which comfortably positions him alongside the gender-biased philosophical tradition. This certainly does not render useless the attempts to undermine logocentric thought patterns by drawing attention to the affective side of reason à la Spinoza. It simply points to the complexity of discourses of gendered epistemology and affectivity.

Apart from harboring silly emotions, including compassion for beasts, women can also disrupt (hu)man "fraternity" not because of anything they themselves do but because men are not able to control their own lust and compete among themselves to win the favors of women. Spinoza takes the problem of male rivalry (and incontinence) so seriously as to use it as yet another argument against women's participation in the political life:

> And if, furthermore, we consider human emotions, men generally love women from mere lust, assessing their ability and their wisdom by their beauty and also resenting any favors which the women they love show to

---

[36] For a collection of influential essays that explore the resources Spinoza's philosophy offers for critical gender theory, see Gatens, *Feminist Interpretations of Benedict Spinoza*.

[37] As discussed in section 6.2 of chapter 6 as well, Spinoza thinks of affects in terms of changes in one's power and activity, which are directly correlated with the degree of adequate knowledge one has.

[38] Here it is also difficult not to share Lloyd's concern that celebrating Spinoza's affirmation of affects as an act of valuing the "feminine" side of reason runs the danger of perpetuating these symbolic alignments. Genevieve Lloyd, *The Man of Reason: "Male" and "Female" in Western Philosophy* (London: Routledge, 1993), xii.

others and so on, soon we shall see that rule by men and women on equal terms is bound to involve much damage to peace. (TP 11.4)

As Gatens notes, women's exclusion from politics on the basis of men's passions is odd particularly because men have all sorts of passions that are to be regulated by laws if not transformed via reason; but when it comes to their lust for women, the only solution, for Spinoza, becomes simply excluding half the human population (that is, women, and not the sexually weak men who do not appear to be masters of their own passions) from the political realm.[39]

In regard to Spinoza's views on women, particularly in the *Political Treatise*, Gullan-Wuhr notes that when Spinoza was denying women political participation he was perhaps "seduced by the need, at a time of violent European upheaval, to show himself as a useful political pragmatist."[40] Certainly, arguing that women are eternally submissive creatures is not the only way to prove oneself to be a political pragmatist, nor are sexist remarks in Spinoza's corpus limited to one passage of the TP. However, it is plausible that there were indeed some additional motivations (that are unknown to us) behind Spinoza's explicitly hostile remarks in the TP. After all, Spinoza was capable of seeing Eve as an equal companion of Adam, albeit in the odd setting of the Garden of Eden; but, as Sharp states alluding to Spinoza's referencing of Ovid, although Spinoza saw the better course, he yet chose the worse.[41]

Going back to an earlier observation about what Spinoza could have said and what he ended up saying in regard to certain social groups (given that the option of taking a less exclusionary route *was* available to him), another explanation that also aligns with Spinoza's own reasoning would be that his troubling comments with regard to women (or "Turks" or "madmen") show the power of imagination. As discussed in chapter 3, according to Spinoza, the imagination can never be completely left behind no matter how many adequate ideas one forms.[42] In a way, Spinoza's own

---

[39] Gatens, *Imaginary Bodies*, 134.
[40] Margaret Gullan-Wuhr, "Spinoza and the Equality of Women," *Theoria* 68 (2008): 110
[41] Sharp, "Eve's Perfection," 579.
[42] As shown in chapter 3, section 3.3, "imagination" in Spinozist epistemology refers to a kind of knowledge that solely relies on haphazard experiential learning from which, depending on one's causal history, one could draw wildly different associations among different things. Imagination thus presents us with a world where certain groupings simply appear before our eyes as "conclusions without premises" (EIIp28d) together with associations that rely on haphazard exposure (including exposure to imageries that circulate in collective life). Operations of the imagination can be brought under the scrutiny of reason and can be reworked, but one cannot leave the imagination behind.

remarks inadvertently demonstrate that certain inadequate ideas can gain more power than other ideas due to all the neighboring ideas supporting them (EIVp1s).

Regardless of how we explain Spinoza's exclusionary remarks, they should be closely studied and not ignored. As Gatens points out along with Le Dœuff, the opinions of the "great philosophers" on women have, for so long, been dismissed as merely "anecdotal" remarks with no relevance to their "serious" philosophical ideas whatsoever. However, such an approach ignores the unconscious dimension of our cultural heritage altogether,[43] not to mention that it decides for us what is a "serious" issue to be discussed and what is not. Moreover, these unfortunate remarks and imageries that appear in the works of the "fathers" of philosophy are often also tied to more general thought patterns within these texts. Spinoza's humanism hinges on (hu)mans' difference from beasts, and this distinction brings forth a hierarchical portrayal of humanity. It is difficult to separate the two patterns of thinking from each other and view the examples about women resorting to irrational behavior (pitying, gossiping, trying to manipulate men with sexual gifts) as mere accidents. It is their allegedly deficient rationality that justifies the exclusion of women from politics, a quality that also features in Spinoza's description of fear-based communities as being beastly and barbaric. Although a human-animal distinction is not necessarily bound to bring with itself a misogynistic or xenophobic attitude, in Spinoza's case imageries of beasts, women, Turks, infants, and madmen do all clearly cluster around themes of sub-rationality, passions, and the absence of agency.

The way these imageries feed into each other in Spinoza's thought must not be overlooked, particularly because another insight Spinoza has taught us is to take imagination seriously. Just as every body is in an interdependent relation with all the surrounding bodies, every idea is embedded in a larger system of ideas that nourish and sustain it. Similarly, just as we do not sense the movement of all the microorganisms moving about in our bodies, we are also not conscious of all the micro-ideas that feed into our thought patterns.[44] One could be aware of how stereotypes or habitual ideas emerge in general, but that knowledge by itself does not relegate them into

---

[43] Gatens, *Imaginary Bodies*, xi–xii
[44] Sharp draws a similar analogy between micro-movements within one's body and mind in "The Force of Ideas in Spinoza," 744.

non-existence. The alternative thought patterns we see and even approve should still be supported by a larger network of the ideas, experiences, and affects accompanying them, so they will not be brushed aside as unworthy of at least an earnest exploration. Otherwise, like Ovid, we can see and approve the better course, but yet keep following the worse.

Conclusion
Our Kind

Whether the struggles and oppressions of different beings and social groups are demonstrably interlinked or not, such connections are not always readily apparent, even in works that are known to be cognizant of relations of power and the inequities they generate. As section A elucidates, this is especially true of the *Zhuangzi*, in which the link between animality tropes and social difference is not readily apparent. Neither is the text's attitude toward marginalized groups always consistent.

Spinoza exhibits a higher degree of coherence on these fronts, in the sense that he is consistent in the disparaging ways he utilizes animality tropes to describe social groups that deviate from the norm. Providing an exhaustive list of the factors that might have led to the variations in discursive practices between the two comparanda is an unattainable task. However, we can still enhance our understanding by examining the rhetorical associations surrounding animality and subhumanity that were prevalent in their respective environments, as well as by considering what we know or can reasonably surmise about the authors and their habitus.

Finally, as Section B argues, while both comparanda exhibit dismissive and complicitous, if not hostile, attitudes toward women, they also offer us tools to mobilize their own insights to offer a critique of their writings in their own terms and to take their ideas in further and forward-looking directions.

A. Those "We" Uplift or Leave Behind

If and when tropes of animality are used as foils against which positive conceptions of humanity proper are articulated, then it is only natural to see animal pejoratives being used to describe people who are perceived as falling short of ideals of human perfection. Whether such ideals revolve around performances of propriety or the kind of agency that comes with greater understanding, the path to human perfection ends up being more accessible to some than to others for historical, political, and sociological reasons. As a result, animality tropes often end up clustering around those that are farther way from the (often male) civic ideal in a community: foreigners, commoners, women, and so on. However, especially as chapter 9 has evinced, the exclusionary logic of human perfection is not always straightforward.

A recurrent thread in early Chinese philosophy is the association of the absence of a distinction between men and women with being animal-like. However, women themselves are not portrayed as being closer to animal life and all its imagined vices. Given that humanity proper is associated with enacting social distinctions and, at times, with more particular demonstrations of proper conduct, the absence of these behavioral components—which amounts to being uncouth if not wild—is not viewed in connection with women (who can defy social distinctions as much as men). Instead, it is often linked to communities with different customs, common folks who do not "know their place," and those perceived as lacking refinement and propriety in some register. This dynamic does not grant women greater social mobility, of course, given that their prescribed role involves following men instead of leading them.[1]

Views about women's subservient role in society make an appearance in the *Zhuangzi* as well. And although subversive views about the separation of men and women are also present in the text, overall we do not see a strong investment in the issue. If the received *Zhuangzi* is representative of the views of the textual community that composed and compiled the larger text that was later edited and trimmed down, then the scant portrayal of women characters speaks to the mechanisms of habitus that make it easier (and perhaps more convenient) to upend some roles more than the others.

Bias toward women emerges as part of a larger hegemonic construction in Spinoza's works, which overall do little to undermine the exclusionary assumptions ingrained in the notions of "we" and "us." As Spinoza safeguards human solidarity against a descent into an animal-like existence, the "us" that he wants to protect and uplift is imagined to be male, culturally familiar (sometimes even Christian—or, at least, non-Muslim), not affected by certain cognitive differences and debilities, and so on. Among Spinoza's disparaging views toward different groups, his negative opinion of women strikes

---

[1] It is worth noting that we also see warnings for wives whose husbands are not following norms of propriety, such as Xunzi's advice for wives of such men to be "fearful and self-vigilant" (*kongju er zi song* 恐懼而自竦) instead of simply following the lead of such men. *Xunzi* 12.3.

one as especially well articulated (although had TP been completed, perhaps he would also have added another passage on criminals or foreigners). Of course, differently than the *Zhuangzi*, Spinoza inherited a tradition that associates emotions with women. Although we do not see an affect-reason dichotomy in Spinoza's philosophy, he does consistently associate women with sad passions—sometimes along with children, madmen, drunk folks, and so on. That he describes compassion for animals as "womanish" also relates to his broader view of women as agents of disruption to (hu)man fraternity, which makes their equal participation in society not just improbable but also dangerous.

Overall, when we look at how the views on animals articulated in the two comparanda relate to attitudes toward social differences, we see a clear pattern of exclusionary language in Spinoza toward all those who are associated with what animality stands for: irrationality, absence of agency, excess of sad passions. The fact of the matter is, due to his lack of sustained interest in animal lives and perspectives in their own right, Spinoza also uses assumptions of human difference to devise the human-animal binary.[2] This certainly generates a curious loop in Spinoza's oeuvre in which animals are imagined around human vices while the human populations he disparages are imagined to be animal-like.

The key element that connects the *Zhuangzi*'s approach toward animals and its approach to social distinctions is its critique of distinction-making in general. The *Zhuangzi*'s penchant for entertaining animal vantage points in their own right is also undeniably tied to its broader interest in seeing things from the viewpoint of the different and the neglected. Finally, the text's critique of ideologies that present their norms to be emancipating people from an animal-like existence also seems to inform most of its representations of undervalued groups in society. Still, despite our aesthetic yearning for smooth interpretations, it must be admitted that the connection between social distinctions and the human-animal distinction is not always straightforward in the text. This perhaps suggests a heightened interest in entertaining animal perspectives for the intellectual stimulation and amusement they provide. In other words, the authors and compilers of the *Zhuangzi* might not have had a sustained investment in exploring the interrelations between

---

[2] This is particularly why Hasana Sharp observes that Spinoza sometimes seems to be imagining animals as uncivilized anti-men. Sharp, *Spinoza and the Politics of Renaturalization*, 18. This is also discussed in chapter 7, section 7.3.

ranking different human groups and using animality tropes to facilitate that. This does not necessarily repudiate the view that discursive representations of different undervalued groups have a way of being intertwined in implicit or explicit ways. However, it does show that our endeavors to hear overlooked voices can sometimes take place within isolated social and intellectual bubbles—which inherently hinders the emergence of voices of certain groups, even when their struggles and triumphs are interlinked with our own.

B. The Limits of What "We" Can Imagine "Us" to Be

The layers of the *Zhuangzi* and Spinoza's oeuvre that comment on different social groups are worthy of attention for the way they further reveal the functions and reach of animality tropes. Likewise significant is their capacity to expose the intricate challenges that arise when we recruit "non-canonical" texts to the task of helping us reimagine humans' place in the world in more equitable and inclusive terms. Considering that the vast majority of the philosophical literature (regardless of how broadly we define it) is riddled with biases toward nonhuman, dehumanized, or subhuman others, the question facing us concerns how to do history of philosophy in ways that respect the integrity of a text while also staying true to the very purpose of doing philosophy to begin with: fostering collective self-understanding and imagining new futures.

It is safe to claim at this point that Spinoza's philosophy is built on a dual vision. On the one hand, it views all of life as governed by the common laws of nature. On the other hand, it employs an exclusionary logic when suggesting we organize people's "imaginative" experiences, so as to help them enter into enabling alliances. Of course, pointing to the imaginative roots of certain thought patterns—where the "imagination" is understood in Spinozist terms—does not render them less weighty, although it does highlight the reimaginable quality of such patterns.

Conjuring up new conceptions of the human includes recognizing the human-animal binary not only as a "zoological designation" but also as a "discursive resource." This recognition should make us vigilant about the ways certain populations are coded as dependent, subrational, irrational, savage, or mad due to their deviation from a specific conception of "man" favored to represent the "human."[3] Not only can these categories have a way of spilling into each other in mutually reinforcing ways[4] but they can, in the end, even determine whose lives "matter."

All of this might sound exhortative but so is Spinoza's ethical and political program devised to aid "man's salvation."[5] If we disarticulate Spinoza's parochial and yet universalizing vision for "our" salvation from a divisive "us versus them" approach,[6] then the recognition of humanity in all its forms becomes a program of collective self-empowerment and self-enrichment instead of a reallocation of power from one group to another.

For those of us who aspire to challenge the "us versus them" approach in human-animal relations, perhaps the foremost dilemma lies in the balance between affirming the humanity of marginalized groups, who have been unjustly dehumanized, while simultaneously avoiding the perils of propagating human superiority over animals or denying the continuity between humans and animals.[7] Also challenging is articulating humans' continuity with animals without defining the latter only in terms of lack and deficit.[8] Views of animals—which is a vast group of organisms—as less complex versions of humans arise because the criteria for the measurement of animal aptitudes tend to be based on human intelligence and human language[9]—which are also rarely inclusive

---

[3] The wording of the distinction between "zoological designation" and "discursive resource" belongs to Wolfe. Cary Wolfe, *Before the Law: Humans and Other Animals in a Biopolitical Frame* (Chicago: University of Chicago Press, 2012), 10.

[4] This can be seen in the oppressive ways that diagnoses—and often overdiagnoses—of mental illness have historically played out for marginalized communities, further complicating their liberation struggles. On this point, see Paul Doyen, The Overdiagnosis of Bipolar Disorder Within Marginalized Communities: A Call to Action. *Columbia Social Work Review*, 19, no. 1 (2021), 80–99. https://doi.org/10.52214/cswr.v19i1.7388.

[5] On this point, see chapter 2, section 2.2.

[6] As addressed in section B of the conclusion to Part IV, this approach is largely founded on the logic of scarcity, where the interests of individuals are placed in opposition to each other. Also see section B of the conclusion to Part III for a discussion of how exclusionary conceptions of "us" partly stems from the power that such borders have afforded those who are deemed "human."

[7] I owe this insight to Taylor. See Sunaura Taylor, *Beasts of Burden: Animal and Disability Liberation* (New York: New Press, 2017), 110.

[8] As a criticism of the still-prevalent preoccupation with finding the "big" difference that sets humans apart from the rest, primatologist Frans de Waal uses an iceberg metaphor according to which "there is a vast mass of cognitive, emotional, and behavioral similarities between us and our primate kin. But there is also a tip containing a few dozen differences" and that instead of trying to come to grips with the whole iceberg, many are "happy to stare at the tip." De Waal, *Are We Smart Enough to Know How Smart Animals Are?*, 125.

[9] Take, for instance, the "mirror self-recognition test" used to measure self-awareness, which privileges vision when it is not even the most prominent sense for many animals. Sunaura Taylor insightfully describes this situation as a catch-22 for animals "who are deemed intelligent only when they remind us of ourselves, and yet, if they *do* remind us of ourselves, we often dismiss the evidence with accusations of anthropomorphism. Taylor, *Beasts of Burden*, 78–79. De Waal notes that instead of testing animals on skills that humans are particularly good at, we could develop species-appropriate tests to measure the many abilities that they need to survive in their environment, which,

of all humans.[10] Monovalent depictions of animal (and hence human) life are not only self-serving but also verge on solipsism, telling us little about other beings' own peculiar pleasures, understandings, and struggles.[11]

On the other end of the spectrum we have the complete alienation of animals' pleasures and pains for being too different from "our" experiences, which Spinoza also performs when he simultaneously warns his fellow men that beasts' nature is simply too different from "ours" for them to be appropriate targets of our compassion (EIVp37s1).[12] At the end of the day, animals' capacities and behaviors are either measured against human touchstones or deemed too alien for humans to even understand (often both).[13]

Needless to say, both ends of the spectrum happen to serve human interests by either verifying their status as the apex of intellectual and emotional complexity or by relieving them of the emotional burden surrounding animal suffering. As many have noted, a similar dynamic is operative in the treatment of marginalized groups in society as well, where a group is viewed as both a lacking version of the white man while also being too radically different from him to be the proper subject of consideration.[14] The absurdity of arguing that a group is both quite similar to but also very different from "us" is difficult to overlook and is indicative of the sway of self-interest in the production of knowledge.

---

in the end, is an exercise in transforming the linear *scala naturae* model into one that resembles "a bush with many branches." De Waal, *Are We Smart Enough to Know How Smart Animals Are?*, 22.

[10] Aside from cultural differences inflecting people's performances in tests that are devised to test cognitive capacity, Salomon also makes note of neurotypicalism, which privileges reasoning that relies heavily on the brain's vermis (which is crucial in developing an abstract concept of the world) and fails to account for the strengths of people with autism who "see each entity as a separate reality, resulting in greater awareness of the details of the world-around-them." Daniel Salomon, "From Marginal Cases to Linked Oppressions: Reframing the Conflict between the Autistic Pride and Animal Rights Movements," *Journal for Critical Animal Studies* 8, no. 1/2 (2010): 48–49. Grandin has famously argued that many nonhuman animals also have this same capability. Temple Grandin and Catherine Johnson, *Animals in Translation: Using the Mysteries of Autism to Decode Animal Behavior* (Orlando, FL: Harcourt, 2006), 6–7.

[11] As Frans de Waal notes, there are many types of cognitive adaptations that humans do not have or need and that "a single environment offers hundreds of realities peculiar to each species." On the topic of whether one can enter into the inner lives of others (human or not), he takes a middle way between being stuck in one's own perceptual box versus being able to perfectly dwell in another's inner world. To illustrate his point, he references Thomas Nagel's "What Is It Like to Be a Bat?" essay and makes a distinction between "how a human would feel as a bat" versus "how a bat feels like a bat," choosing the former as a more viable path. See de Waal, *Are We Smart Enough to Know How Smart Animals Are?*, 8–9, 12, 22.

[12] This point is discussed in detail in chapter 6, section 6.1.

[13] To give a simple example, what makes animal testing so common is the conviction that certain animals are very similar to humans and thus make great subjects for the study of certain drugs. However, this similarity could also mean that they could suffer in ways that are similar to the way a human would suffer under the same circumstances, which then necessitates arguments used to demonstrate that they are also very much different from humans.

[14] Historically, the paradoxical perspective of perceiving others as both remarkably similar to and also very different from "us" has materialized in medical testing conducted on marginalized groups

Perhaps as a byproduct of not having a distinct agenda to guard human interests (regardless of how narrowly or broadly "human" is defined) against certain threats, the *Zhuangzi* does not exhibit a hard-hitting "us versus them" attitude toward various groups (whether they are animalized or not). On the contrary, its critique of norm-imposing ideologies translates into an openness toward many groups that are farther away from circles of power. This has sometimes fed into a tendency to interpret the *Zhuangzi* along the lines of radical political engagement, as can be seen in attempts to interpret the text, along with the *Laozi*, as a proto-anarchist work.[15]

It is undeniable that the *Zhuangzi* has a defiant streak and an aversion toward coercive authority, making it a compelling source for discussing ways to condemn dominant forms of power. However, the work also presents us with plenty of figures who navigate society with success (and sometimes in close proximity to people in positions of power), as well as those who prioritize maintaining a low profile in order to have an easygoing life. Other times, owning one's subjection and finding a way to enjoy it is being praised, as seen in the example of Lady Li. In other words, although the underdogs of society are often portrayed in an empowering light in the *Zhuangzi*, there is no call to actively improve the structural inequalities that created those underdogs to begin with. Hence, perhaps the work's true treasure lies not in its possible adaptability to a radical political agenda, but in the ways it makes readers question the distinction between the place of power and the place of resistance.

Remarkably, with all its iconoclastic and defiant aspects, the *Zhuangzi* also presents us with an example of a hierarchist attitude that subdues women. This should perhaps serve as a reminder that there is no pure domain of resistance that is uncontaminated with power and that could simply see and hear "us" all

---

in society. This practice was premised on a similar contradiction that some people (be they Romanis, Jews, or gay folks) make excellent subjects for medical experimentation, because, well, they are human; but they are not worthy of any form of empathy or concern, because they are, in fact, subhuman. The parallel between the "self-servingly exclusionary" treatments of marginalized human groups and animals has been noted by Adorno, who famously wrote: "The possibility of pogroms is decided in the moment when the gaze of a fatally-wounded animal falls on a human being" who then expels its gaze because, after all, "it's only an animal." See Theodor Adorno, *Minima Moralia*, trans. E.F.N. Jephcott (New York: Schocken Books, 1978), 68.

[15] See John A. Rapp, *Daoism and Anarchism: Critiques of State Autonomy in Ancient and Modern China* (Continuum: New York City, 2012); John J. Clarke, "Taoist Politics: An Other Way?," in *Border Crossings: Toward a Comparative Political Theory*, ed. Fred Dallmayr (Lanham, MD: Lexington Books, 1999), 253–276. These attempts have faced criticisms, with some pointing to the vagueness of what is meant by an "anarchist" theory, which refers to a diverse group of political theories that at best share certain family resemblances. Others lay out some of the shared assumptions among several anarchist theories (such as a particular understanding of individuality and autonomy) and demonstrate that they are actually absent in what goes by the name classical "Daoist" texts (which includes the *Zhuangzi* and the *Laozi*). See Alex Feldt, "Governing through the Dao: A Non-Anarchistic

when the "us" is never a *fait accompli* to begin with. Remarkably, the heterogeneity of "us" is actually one of the recurrent insights raised in the text, which, after all, does have a penchant for giving the spotlight to various figures that are excluded from dominant centers of power: people of humble professions, alien peoples, ex-convicts, and all kinds of beasts that threaten the centrality and coherence of what is sold as common values. In other words, the *Zhuangzi* overall does a great job of showing how to effectively mobilize storytelling to give attention to the sheer multiplicity of lives that are excluded from ideals of human perfection, if not humanity altogether. Despite all this, women's subservient status is still casually sanctioned in an episode, which perhaps invites a critical reflection on the status of the narrator.

We know that the "subaltern cannot speak."[16] It is indeed difficult to get voices from the margin (and should they be able voice their stories, are they still in the margin?). Still, multiplying not simply the voices that a narrator attends to but also the voices that do the narrating is bound to lead to some degree of epistemic enrichment. After all, the *Zhuangzi* acknowledges the role that one's standpoint plays in one's judgments, as articulated in a dialogue between the character of Zhuangzi and Huizi that concludes with Zhuangzi admitting that he knows what he knows from where he stands, above the Hao River.[17]

In the end, what the *Zhuangzi* offers is endless movement between different vantage points while acknowledging that we cannot fully know the needs, the preferences, and, in general, the inner lives of others. But perhaps the real question is who else is doing the wondering, wandering, and getting to narrate the stories of themselves, let alone of others? If multivocality is to be sustained as a tool to help one step out of one's own perceptual box (for self-enrichment, if not for emancipatory reasons), then perhaps the praxis of hearing the "preferably unheard" has to move beyond an imaginative exercise to candid encounters.[18]

Interpretation of the Laozi," *Dao* 9 (2010): 323–337; Roger Ames, "Is Political Taoism Anarchism?," *Journal of Chinese Philosophy* 10 (1983): 24–47.

[16] In her possibly most frequently cited work, Spivak examines the political and ideological structures of knowledge dissemination that obstruct marginalized voices. The essay famously suggests that even when the marginalized speak, they have no choice but to resort to using hegemonic vocabulary in order to be heard. Gayatri Chakravorty Spivak, "Can the Subaltern Speak?," in *Can the Subaltern Speak? Reflections on the History of an Idea*, ed. Rosalind C. Morris (New York: Columbia University Press, 2010), 21–78. Spivak's essay sent ripples out into not only post-colonial theory, critical race theory, feminist theory, and disability studies but also into critical animality studies that has a stake in considerations of what counts as a "voice." On this point, see Taylor, *Beasts of Burden*, 63.

[17] The passage in question is also discussed in chapter 5, section 5.1.

[18] The phrase "preferably unheard" is employed by Arundhati Roy, who notes that "there's really no such thing as the 'voiceless.' There are only the deliberately silenced, or the preferably unheard." Cited in Taylor, *Beasts of Burden*, 62.

Epilogue

Looking at There and Then to Reflect on Here and Now

Any philosophical study inevitably reveals its author's understanding of philosophical thinking itself. This author believes that philosophical thinking is about opening up an inquiry to many more angles in order to multiply our questions and to inspect and expand the boundaries of our terms and concepts, including (gasp) the boundaries of the concept of philosophy itself.[1] One can go about this expansive praxis of intellectual inquiry in many ways, which include studying texts that belong to different historical contexts and different philosophical traditions.

When engaging with texts from distant and different pasts, it is tempting to seek out works that seem to harbor an alternative wisdom that might help cure our many modern ills. If one is also tracing the source of these ills to a

---

[1] One's choice of texts always already reveals what one thinks should count as philosophy—something we philosophers tend to disagree on not only in the context of intercultural philosophy but also when it comes to the intra-cultural, yet equally pesky, analytic-continental divide. The issue regarding how to delimit the concept of philosophy is a decidedly irresolvable one because, as Russell has famously put it, any definition of philosophy always already embodies a philosophic attitude. Cited in Sarah A. Mattice, *Metaphor and Metaphilosophy: Philosophy as Combat, Play, and Aesthetic Experience* (Lanham, MD: Lexington Books, 2014), 1. Mattice, in the same work, also addresses philosophers' disagreement about what counts as philosophy and suggests having "enough of a 'family resemblance' to be able to share certain aims or goals in our activities" as the basis for the usage of the label "philosophy." See Mattice, *Metaphor and Metaphilosophy*, 17n4. It should also be noted that not only do different philosophers hold different understandings of what philosophy is at any given time; different eras also have different dominant conceptions of "philosophy." More specifically, the same early moderns who conflated Spinoza's philosophy with Chinese philosophy still called the latter "philosophy," as evinced by the title of Malebranche's work *Dialogue between a Christian Philosopher and a Chinese Philosopher on the Existence and Nature of God* (see the introduction, section C of this study for a brief discussion of Malebranche's work). Defoort problematizes the usage of the label "philosophy" for early Chinese texts, considering that the label has been applied that way only in retrospect and that early Chinese texts are too rich to be bound by the limitations that come with modern academic disciplines today. However, in the end, Defoort convincingly argues that the discussion on the legitimacy of the term "Chinese philosophy" "has been overtaken by the historical clock" as the institutional existence of "Chinese philosophy in China" (and increasingly in the United States) cannot be undone. Carine Defoort, "Is There Such a Thing as Chinese Philosophy? Arguments of an Implicit Debate," Eight East-West Philosophers' Conference, *Philosophy East and West* 51, no. 3 (July 2001): 394, 409. Also see Carine Defoort, "Is 'Chinese Philosophy' a Proper Name? A Response to Rein Raud," *Philosophy East and West* 56, no. 4 (October 2006): 629.

few but fundamental views about the world and our position within it, then it becomes especially enticing to search for works with different metaphysical features. Leonard Lawlor has recently observed that interest in philosophies of "immanence" has been a major theoretical trend defining the continental tradition.[2] A similar observation could be made about other subdisciplines that engage with the history of philosophy, such as comparative philosophy and the streams of environmental philosophy that harvest insights from "non-canonical" philosophical texts that are also labeled "monistic."[3] This is not a coincidence but rather the result of an influential trend that associates different metaphysical outlooks with different attitudes toward difference, multiplicity, and the "others" of a society. Such an approach has yielded inspiring interpretations and hopeful approaches to texts from different historical contexts. However, a crucial insight the *Zhuangzi* has taught us is that any interpretive choice necessarily forecloses other interpretive possibilities.

A principal methodological commitment of this study was to avoid allowing the alleged or actual metaphysical features of a text to inflect, if not predetermine, the arc of the reading. In the same vein, this book refrained from speculating about the paradigm shifts that Spinoza's corpus or the *Zhuangzi* could inspire in us, remedying our anthropocentrism and all the ills associated with it. Instead, it looked into the "messier picture" and put under a microscope their expressions of discontinuity between human beings and the nonhuman world, and their many moments of ambiguity, if not contradiction, in regard to the human-animal binary. From the perspective of a discipline that is known to be uncomfortable with ambiguities and contradictions, these features of Spinoza and the *Zhuangzi* might be characterized as flaws. However, by exploring the moments of familiarity and foreignness harbored in such "flaws," we can hope to learn something about our own confusing, contradictory, and ambiguous thought patterns about ourselves and our place in the world.

For instance, Spinoza's reaction against the "melancholic" folks who despise men and admire beasts draws attention to the reactionary misanthropy that is sometimes ingrained in movements concerned with animal welfare. At the same time, his framing of human-animal relations in terms of an "us versus them" binary highlights the difficulty of coming around to

---

[2] Leonard Lawlor, *Early Twentieth-Century Continental Philosophy* (Bloomington: Indiana University Press, 2011), viii.

[3] See the introduction of this study (section B in particular) for a discussion of the problems with using these labels (immanentist and monistic) for the *Zhuangzi* and even for Spinoza.

our interconnectedness when one group has so much power and say over the fate of all others. Surely, in the long run, the struggles and joys of different living beings are intimately connected with each other. However, when one party attains so much short-term gain through the suffering of others, then no wonder calls to share the world with other species in more equitable terms are perceived as misanthropy, even when there is no argument being made against the importance of human welfare.

Our analysis has also shown that Spinoza's alarmist remarks about the human-animal difference and his emphasis on the need to prioritize "our" welfare are not mere expressions of didactic pathos on his part. The human-centered language that Spinoza uses has some roots in his ontology—or, at least, his ontology allows for the articulation of certain beings' greater similarity with and use for each other. What ultimately creates interpretive tensions for Spinoza scholars is his occasional use of taxonomic categorizations ("man," "horse") in finalizing and, at times, in boundary-policing ways. Certainly, Spinoza's ontology allows for more radical articulations of difference and similarity, but it still does matter that that is not the route he chooses.

Throughout this study we pointed to the tensions between what Spinoza could have said and what he ends up saying. In the end, perhaps the biggest lesson one can learn from Spinoza's works and the tensions they harbor is the fact that allegedly having this or that type of ontological feature (e.g., monism or immanence) alone does not bring with it liberatory attitudes toward groups and communities that are on the fringes or outside of humanity proper. This is not to bring up the age-old and misguided theory-versus-practice binary or to ask whether "books can cause revolutions." Instead, it is to draw attention to a related lesson that Spinoza teaches us, which is the need for vigilant effort to work on the tropes, associations, and narratives that populate our collective imagination.[4] This crucial effort includes reflecting on the narratives about care for animals and how this care is often presented as a misdirection and sometimes as an excess of sentimentality (packaged together with disparaging feminization of affective proximity to animals).[5] Only then we can reimagine human and animal realities, with

---

[4] This point is developed and defended in detail in Moira Gatens and Genevieve Lloyd, *Collective Imaginings: Spinoza, Past and Present* (London: Routledge, 2002).

[5] This manner of thinking is not unique to Spinoza or even to early modern European discourse. It is actually seen in contemporary animal rights discourse as well. For a criticism of Singer and Regan's infamous warning that the animal rights cause could be jeopardized by "womanish" sentiments that trivialize it, see Josephine Donovan, "Animal Rights and Feminist Theory," *Signs* 15, no. 2 (Winter 1990): 350–375.

all their conceptual and affective entanglements. In the end, this is what Spinoza's onto-epistemological program asks us to do as well; that is, it asks us to pay attention to different levels of our thinking and being.

A unique benefit of a comparative analysis of different texts is the ease with which it allows us to bring to the fore the idiosyncratic features of each. The orderly (and order-focused) and didactic tone of Spinoza's works were pronounced in this study, partly because they were juxtaposed next to the *Zhuangzi*. In the *Zhuangzi* we see a persistent emphasis on change and transformation instead of stability and predictability. As shown, the text's undermining of assumptions about the predictability of life in general goes hand in hand with its criticism teachings that instruct how to bring an order to a chaotic land and unify its diverse people. It is partly in reaction to such ideologies and attitudes that the *Zhuangzi* throws familiar knowledge claims into question and even empties the category of "human" of its unifying function.

The *Zhuangzi*'s lack of investment in cementing human beings together around a specific vision allows for expressions of unconventional visions of the good life and human flourishing. These visions could include immersing oneself in the lifestyles of alien lands, mimicking behaviors of nonhuman beings and even experiencing moments of sudden identification with the rest of the cosmos so much so that one could be looking forward to being turned into a rat's liver or an insect's arm. The *Zhuangzi*'s consideration of the perspectives of different creatures as being on par with each other is directly tied to the text's recognition of the limitations of pan-contextual knowledge claims. This recognition also leads to its casual attitude toward different life paths. The *Zhuangzi* often also casts doubt on what one can definitively know and say about a subject. Instead, it emphasizes the ability to exploit the contingent character of discriminatory judgments and to relabel conventionally unappealing situations in positive ways.

As uplifting as all this sounds, the focus on affirming anything that comes one's way could yield some startling results. For one thing, the emphasis on finding contentment in all things as they are necessarily problematizes efforts to improve one's surroundings. When this attitude is pushed to its limits, one is to find contentment in one's and others' subjugation[6] or, let us say, welcome

---

[6] The point about being comfortable with one's or another's subjugation is explored in section A of the conclusion to Part III (in the context of a discussion about an episode that involves a monkey trainer) and in chapter 9, section 9.2 (in the context of an analysis of an episode that features a certain Lady Li).

what many might view as a profound loss as one of the wonders of life.[7] This leaves us with decidedly difficult questions concerning the costs and returns of endorsing a definitive agenda for social change—if we grant that such an undertaking necessitates having a vision for the needs and wants of others and involves drawing up guiding hierarchies between different forms and ways of living.

Finally, in regard to the *Zhuangzi*'s occasional pronouncement of a human-animal difference, the text reflects a familiar view about human beings' unique ability to rise above their conditions and to form a meta-perspective on reality. However, there is also the obvious fact that humans constitute the only audience for the text, which, at times, informs the tone and spirit of the work (as well as any philosophical work, in general). This compels us to face the *aporia* that characterizes many works that aim to decenter human perspectives in some fashion. That is, trying to expose the futility of human concerns and endeavors by crafting a philosophical masterpiece about it suggests anything but nonchalance about humanity and all that it entails.[8]

---

[7] For an example of a man who views his terminal illness as a prelude to experiencing exciting transformations, see chapter 8, section 8.2.

[8] I am indebted to Richard A. Lee, Jr. for this point.

References

Adams, Carol J., and Lori Gruen. "Groundwork." In *Ecofeminism: Feminist Intersections with Other Animals and The Earth*. Edited by Carol J. Adams and Lori Gruen, 7–36. New York: Bloomsbury, 2014.

Adorno, Theodor. *Minima Moralia*. Translated by E. F. N. Jephcott. New York: Schocken Books, 1978.

Agamben, Giorgio. *The Open: Man and Animal*. Stanford, CA: Stanford University Press, 2004.

Allan, Sarah. *The Way of Water and Sprouts of Virtue*. Albany: State University of New York Press, 1997.

Ames, Roger T. "Is Political Taoism Anarchism?" *Journal of Chinese Philosophy* 10 (1983): 24–47.

Angle, Stephen C. *Growing Moral: A Confucian Guide to Life*. Oxford: Oxford University Press, 2022.

Armstrong, Aurelia. "Autonomy and the Relational Individual: Spinoza and Feminism." In Gatens, *Feminist Interpretations of Benedict Spinoza*, 43–64.

Armstrong, Aurelia. "Natural and Unnatural Communities: Spinoza Beyond Hobbes." *British Journal for the History of Philosophy* 17, no. 2 (2009): 279–305.

Assmann, Jan. *Cultural Memory and Early Civilization: Writing, Remembrance, and Political Imagination*. Cambridge: Cambridge University Press, 2011.

Balibar, Étienne. *Spinoza: From Individuality to Transindividuality* [A lecture delivered in Rijnsburg on May 15, 1993]. Delft: Eburon, 1997.

Barbone, Steven. "What Counts as an Individual for Spinoza?" In *Spinoza: Metaphysical Themes*. Edited by Olli Koistinen and John Biro, 89–112. Oxford: Oxford University Press, 2002.

Baxter, William H., and Laurent Sagart. *Old Chinese: A New Reconstruction*. Oxford: Oxford University Press, 2014.

Bayle, Pierre. *Dictionnaire Critique et Historique*. Amsterdam: Par la Compagnie des Libraries, 1734.

Behnke, Elizabeth A. "From Merleau-Ponty's Concept of Nature to an Interspecies Practice of Peace." In *Animal Others: On Ethics, Ontology, and Animal Life*. Edited by H. Peter Steeves, 93–116. Albany: State University of New York Press, 1999.

Bekoff, Marc. *The Emotional Lives of Animals: A Leading Scientist Explores Animal Joy, Sorrow, and Empathy—and Why They Matter*. Novato, CA: New World Library, 2007.

Bell, Jeremy. "Taming Horses and Desires: Plato's Politics of Care." In *Plato's Animals: Gadflies, Horses, Swans, and Other Philosophical Beasts*. Edited by Jeremy Bell and Michael Naas, 115–130. Bloomington: Indiana University Press, 2015.

Bennett, Jane. *Vibrant Matter: A Political Ecology of Things*. Durham, NC: Duke University Press, 2010.

Bennett, Jonathan. *A Study of Spinoza's Ethics*. Indianapolis, IN: Hackett, 1984.

Blair, Ann. "Natural Philosophy." In Park and Daston, *The Cambridge History of* Science, 365–406.

Boggs, Colleen Glenney. *Animalia Americana: Animal Representations and Biopolitical Subjectivity.* New York: Columbia University Press, 2013.

Boltz, William G. "The Composite Nature of Early Chinese Texts." In *Text and Ritual in Early China.* Edited by Martin Kern, 50–78. Seattle: University of Washington Press, 2005.

Bove, Laurent. "Hilaritas and Acquiescentia in se ipso." In *Ethica IV: Spinoza on Reason and the "Free Man."* Edited by Yirmiyahu Yovel and Gideon Segal, 209–226. New York: Little Room Press, 2004.

Brindley, Erica Fox. *Ancient China and the Yue: Perceptions and Identities on the Southern Frontier, c. 400 BCE–50 CE.* Cambridge: Cambridge University Press, 2015.

Brindley, Erica Fox. "'Why Use an Ox-Cleaver to Carve a Chicken?' The Sociology of the Junzi Ideal in the Lunyu." *Philosophy East and West* 59, no. 1 (January 2009): 47–70.

Brown, Joshua R., and Alexus McLeod. *Transcendence and Non-Naturalism in Early Chinese Thought.* London: Bloomsbury, 2021.

Brown, Miranda. "Neither 'Primitives' nor 'Others,' but Somehow Not Quite Like Us: The Fortunes of Psychic Unity and Essentialism in Chinese Studies." *Journal of the Economic and Social History of the Orient* 49, no. 2 (2006): 219–252.

Brown, Miranda, and Uffe Bergeton. "'Seeing' Like a Sage: Three Takes on Identity and Perception in Early China." *Journal of Chinese Philosophy* 35, no. 4 (2008): 641–662.

Bryne, Laura. "The Geometrical Method in Spinoza's *Ethics*." *Poetics Today* 28, no. 3 (2007): 443–474.

Butler, Judith. *Gender Trouble: Feminism and the Subversion of Identity.* New York: Routledge, 2006.

Calarco, Matthew. *Thinking through Animals: Identity, Difference, Indistinction.* Stanford, CA: Stanford University Press, 2015.

Callicott, J. Baird. *Earth's Insights: A Multicultural Survey of Ecological Ethics from the Mediterranean Basin to the Australian Outback.* Berkeley: University of California Press, 1997.

Callicott, J. Baird, and Roger T. Ames, eds. *Nature in Asian Traditions of Thought: Essays in Environmental Philosophy.* Albany: State University of New York Press, 1989.

Carriero, John. "Conatus." In *Spinoza's* Ethics: *A Critical Guide.* Edited by Yitzhak Y. Melamed, 142–168. Cambridge: Cambridge University Press, 2017.

Chakrabarty, Dipesh. *Provincializing Europe: Postcolonial Thought and Historical Difference.* Princeton, NJ: Princeton University Press, 2007.

Chan, Alan Kam-Leung. "A Matter of Taste: *Qi* (Vital Energy) and the Tending of the Heart (*Xin*) in *Mencius* 2A2." In *Mencius: Contexts and Interpretations.* Edited by Alan Kam-Leung Chan, 42–71. Honolulu: University of ai'i Press, 2002).

Chan, Shirley. "Identifying Daoist Humor: Reading the *Liezi*." In *Humour in Chinese Life and Letters: Classical and Traditional Approaches.* Edited by Jocelyn Chey and Jessica Milner Davis, 73–88. Hong Kong: Hong Kong University Press, 2011.

CHEN, Guying 陳鼓應, *Lao-Zhuang Xin Lun* 老莊新論 [New theories on Laozi and Zhuangzi]. Beijing 北京: Commercial Press 商務印書館, 2008.

Chen, Ning. "The Etymology of *Sheng* (Sage) and Its Confucian Conception in Early China." *Journal of Chinese Philosophy* 27, no. 4 (December 2000): 409–427.

CHEN, Qiyou 陳奇猷, *Han Feizi, with New Collations and Commentary* 韓非子新校注. 2 vols. Shanghai: Shanghai guji chu ban she 上海古籍儲版社, 2000.

Chong, Kim-chong. "Zhuangzi and Hui Shi on Qing 情." *Tsing Hua Journal of Chinese Studies*, New Series 40, no. 1 (2010): 21–45.
Chong, Kim-chong. *Zhuangzi's Critique of the Confucians: Blinded by the Human*. Albany: State University of New York Press, 2016.
Çırakman, Aslı. *From the "Terror of the World" to the "Sick Man of Europe": European Images of Ottoman Empire and Society from the Sixteenth Century to the Nineteenth*. New York: Peter Lang, 2002.
Clark, Charles M. A. "Wealth and Poverty: On the Social Creation of Scarcity." *Journal of Economic Issues* 36, no. 2 (2002): 415–421.
Clarke, Desmond M., trans. *The Equality of the Sexes: Three Feminist Texts of the Seventeenth Century*. Oxford: Oxford University Press, 2013.
Clarke, John J. "Taoist Politics: An Other Way?" In *Border Crossings: Toward a Comparative Political Theory*. Edited by Fred Dallmayr, 253–275. Lanham, MD: Lexington Books, 1999, 253–276.
Clemens, Justin. "Spinoza's Ass." In *Spinoza Now*. Edited by Dimitris Vardoulakis, 65–95. Minneapolis: University of Minnesota Press, 2011.
Copenhaver, Brian. "The Occultist Tradition and Its Critics." In *The Cambridge History of Seventeenth-Century Philosophy*. Edited by Garber and Ayers. vol. 1, 454–512.
Csikszentmihalyi, Mark. *Material Virtue: Ethics and the Body in Early China*. Leiden: Brill, 2004.
Cuomo, Chris J., and Lori Gruen. "On Puppies and Pussies: Animals, Intimacy, and Moral Distance." In *Daring to Be Good: Essays in Feminist Ethico-Politics*. Edited by Bat-Ami Bar On and Ann Ferguson, 129–142. New York: Routledge, 1998.
Dahlbeck, Moa De Lucia. *Spinoza, Ecology and International Law: Radical Naturalism in the Face of the Anthropocene*. London: Routledge, 2019.
D'Ambrosio, Paul J. "Non-humans in the *Zhuangzi*: Animalism and Anti-anthropocentrism," *Asian Philosophy* 32, no. 1 (2022): 1–18. DOI: 10.1080/09552367.2021.1934218.
D'Ambrosio, Paul J. "Rethinking Environmental Issues in Daoist Context: Why Daoism Is and Is Not Environmentalism." *Environmental Ethics* 35, no. 4 (2013): 407–417.
Davenport, Coral and Lisa Friedman, "The Green New Deal: A Climate Proposal, Explained," The New York Times, February 21, 2019, https://www.nytimes.com/2019/02/21/climate/green-new-deal-questions-answers.html.
De Dijn, Herman. *Spinoza: The Way to Wisdom*. West Lafayette, IN: Purdue University Press, 1996.
Defoort, Carine. "Instruction Dialogues in the *Zhuangzi*: An 'Anthropological' Reading." *Dao* 11, no. 4 (2012): 459–478.
Defoort, Carine. "Is 'Chinese Philosophy' a Proper Name? A Response to Rein Raud." *Philosophy East and West* 56, no. 4 (October 2006): 625–660.
Defoort, Carine. "Is There Such a Thing as Chinese Philosophy? Arguments of an Implicit Debate." Eight East-West Philosophers' Conference. *Philosophy East and West* 51, no. 3 (July 2001): 393–413.
Deleuze, Gilles. *Expressionism in Philosophy: Spinoza*. Translated by Martin Joughin. New York: Zone Books, 1990.
Deleuze, Gilles. *Spinoza: Practical Philosophy*. Translated by Robert Hurley. San Francisco: City Lights, 1988.
Deleuze, Gilles, and Felix Guattari. "1730: Becoming Intense, Becoming Animal, Becoming Imperceptible." In *A Thousand Plateaus: Capitalism and Schizophrenia*.

Translated by Brian Massumi, 232–309. Minneapolis: University of Minnesota Press, 1987.

Della Rocca, Michael. *Spinoza*. New York: Routledge, 2008.

DeMello, Margo. *Animals and Society: An Introduction to Human-Animal Studies*. New York: Columbia University Press, 2012.

Denecke, Wiebke. *The Dynamics of Masters Literature: Early Chinese Thought from Confucius to Han Feizi*. Cambridge, MA: Harvard University Asia Center, 2011.

Derrida, Jacques. *The Animal That Therefore I Am*. Edited by Marie-Louise Mallet and translated by David Wills. New York: Fordham University Press, 2008.

Descartes, René. *The Philosophical Writings of Descartes: Volume 1*. Translated by John Cottingham, Robert Stoothoff, and Dugald Murdoch. Cambridge: Cambridge University Press, 1985.

Descartes, René. *The Philosophical Writings of Descartes: Volume 2*. Translated by John Cottingham, Robert Stoothoff, and Dugald Murdoch. Cambridge: Cambridge University Press, 1985.

Detienne, Marcel. "Back to the Village: A Tropism of Hellenists?" *History of Religions* 43, no. 2 (2001): 99–113.

Devall, Bill, and George Sessions. *Deep Ecology: Living as if Nature Mattered*. Salt Lake City: Peregrine Smith Books, 1985.

de Waal, Frans. *Are We Smart Enough to Know How Smart Animals Are?* New York: W. W. Norton, 2016.

Di Cosmo, Nicola. *Ancient China and Its Enemies: The Rise of Nomadic Power in East Asian History*. New York: Cambridge University Press, 2004.

Doyen, Paul, The Overdiagnosis of Bipolar Disorder Within Marginalized Communities: A Call to Action. *Columbia Social Work Review*, 19, no. 1 (2021): 80–99. https://doi.org/10.52214/cswr.v19i1.7388.

Fang Dongmei 方東美. *Zhongguo ren sheng zhe xue* 中國人生哲學 [The Chinese philosophy of life]. Taipei台北市: Li Ming Cultural Enterprise Co. Ltd 黎明文化事業股份有限公司, 1980.

Donovan, Josephine. "Animal Rights and Feminist Theory." *Signs* 15, no. 2 (Winter 1990): 350–375.

Douglas, Alexander X. *Spinoza and Dutch Cartesianism: Philosophy and Theology*. Oxford: Oxford University Press, 2015.

Durrant, Stephen W., Wai-yee Li, and David Schaberg, trans. *Zuo Tradition/Zuozhuan* 左傳: *Commentary on the "Spring and Autumn Annals."* Seattle: Washington University Press, 2016.

Eloff, Aragorn. "Do Anarchists Dream of Emancipated Sheep? Contemporary Anarchism, Animal Liberation and the Implications of New Philosophy." In *Anarchism and Animal Liberation: Essays on Complementary Elements of Total Liberation*. Edited by Anthony J. Nocella II, Richard J. White, and Erika Cudworth, 194–211. Jefferson, NC: McFarland, 2015.

Eno, Robert. *The Confucian Creation of Heaven: Philosophy and the Defense of Ritual Mastery*. Albany: State University of New York Press, 1990.

Eno, Robert. "Cook Ding's Dao and the Limits of Philosophy." In *Essays on Skepticism, Relativism and Ethics in the Zhuangzi*. Edited by Paul Kjellberg and Philip J. Ivanhoe, 127–151. Albany: State University of New York Press, 1996.

Eno, Robert. *Mencius: An Online Teaching Translation*, May 2016. https://scholarworks.iu.edu/dspace/bitstream/handle/2022/23421/Mengzi.pdf?sequence=2&isAllowed=y.

Fanon, Frantz. *Black Skin, White Masks*. Rev. ed. Translated by Richard Philcox. New York: Grove Press, 2008.

Feldt, Alex. "Governing through the Dao: A Non-Anarchistic Interpretation of the Laozi." *Dao* 9 (2010): 323–337.

Foucault, Michel. *History of Madness*. Edited by Jean Khalfa. New York: Routledge, 2006.

Foucault, Michel. "Truth and Power." In *Power*. Edited by J. B. Faubion, 111–133. Vol. 3 of *Essential Works of Foucault 1954–1984*, edited by Paul Rabinow. New York: New Press, 2000.

Francione, Gary L. *Introduction to Animal Rights: Your Child or the Dog?* Philadelphia: Temple University Press, 2000.

Fraenkel, Carlos, Dario Perinetti, and Justin E. H. Smith, eds. *The Rationalists: Between Tradition and Innovation*. Dordrecht: Springer, 2011.

Fraser, Chris. "Distinctions, Judgment, and Reasoning in Classical Chinese Thought." *History and Philosophy of Logic* 34, no. 1 (2013): 1–24.

Fraser, Chris. trans. *The Essential Mozi: Ethical, Political, and Dialectical Writings*. Oxford: Oxford University Press, 2020.

Fraser, Chris. "Psychological Emptiness in the *Zhuangzi*." *Asian Philosophy* 18, no. 2 (2008): 123–47.

Fraser, Chris. "Wandering the Way: A Eudaimonistic Approach to the *Zhuāngzǐ*." *Dao* 13, no. 4 (2014): 541–565.

Fraser, Chris. "Xunzi versus Zhuangzi: Two Approaches to Death in Classical Chinese Thought," *Frontiers of Philosophy in China* 8, no. 3 (2013): 410–427.

Fried, Daniel. "A Never-Stable Word: Zhuangzi's 'Zhiyan' 卮言 and 'Tipping-vessel' Irrigation." *Early China* 31 (2007): 145–170.

Galvany, Albert. "Discussing Usefulness: Trees as Metaphor in the *Zhuangzi*." *Monumenta Serica*, 57, no. 1 (2009), 71–97.

Galvany, Albert. "Distorting the Rule of Seriousness: Laughter, Death, and Friendship in the *Zhuangzi*." *Dao* 8, no. 1 (2009): 49–59.

Garber, Daniel. "Descartes, the Aristotelians and the Revolution That Did Not Happen in 1637." *The Monist* 71, no. 4 (October 1, 1988): 471–486.

Garber, Daniel, and Michael Ayers, eds. *The Cambridge History of Seventeenth Century Philosophy*. Vol. 1. Cambridge: Cambridge University Press, 2003.

Gatens, Moira. "The Condition of Human Nature: Spinoza's Account of the Ground of Human Action in the *Tractatus Politicus*." In Melamed and Sharp, *Spinoza's Political Treatise*, 47–60.

Gatens, Moira, ed. *Feminist Interpretations of Benedict Spinoza*. University Park: Pennsylvania State University Press, 2009.

Gatens, Moira. *Imaginary Bodies: Ethics, Power, and Corporeality*. London: Routledge, 1996.

Gatens, Moira, and Genevieve Lloyd. *Collective Imaginings: Spinoza, Past and Present*. London: Routledge, 2002.

Geaney, Jane. "Grounding "Language" in the Senses: What the Eyes and Ears Reveal about Ming 名 (names) in Early Chinese Texts." *Philosophy East and West* 60, no. 2 (2010): 251–293.

Geaney, Jane. *Language as Bodily Practice in Early China: A Chinese Grammatology*. Albany: State University of New York Press, 2018.

Geaney, Jane. *On the Epistemology of the Senses in Early Chinese Thought*. Honolulu: University of Hawai'i Press, 2002.

Girardot, Norman J. *Myth and Meaning in Early Taoism: The Theme of Chaos (Hun-Tun)*. Berkeley: University of California Press, 1983.

Goldin, Paul R. *The Art of Chinese Philosophy: Eight Classical Texts and How to Read Them*. Princeton, NJ: Princeton University Press, 2020.

Goldin, Paul R. "Non-Deductive Argumentation in Early Chinese Philosophy." In *Between History and Philosophy: Anecdotes in Early China*. Edited by Paul van Els and Sarah A. Queen, 41–62. Albany: State University of New York Press, 2017.

Gowland, Angus. "The Problem of Early Modern Melancholy." *Past & Present*, no. 191 (May 2006): 77–120.

Graham, A. C. *Disputers of the Tao: Philosophical Argument in Ancient China*. Chicago: Open Court, 1989.

Graham, A. C., trans. *Chuang Tzu: The Inner Chapters*. London: George Allen and Unwin, 2001.

Grandin, Temple, and Catherine Johnson. *Animals in Translation: Using the Mysteries of Autism to Decode Animal Behavior*. Orlando, FL: Harcourt, 2006.

Graziani, Romain. *Fiction and Philosophy in the Zhuangzi: An Introduction to Early Chinese Taoist Thought*. London: Bloomsbury, 2020.

Graziani, Romain. "When Princes Awake in Kitchens: Zhuangzi's Rewriting of a Culinary Myth." In *Of Tripod and Palate: Food, Politics, and Religion in Traditional China*. Edited by Roel Sterckx, 62–74. New York: Palgrave Macmillan, 2005.

Grey, John. "'Use Them at Our Pleasure': Spinoza on Animal Ethics." *History of Philosophy Quarterly* 30, no. 4 (October 2013): 367–388.

Grim, John, and Mary Evelyn Tucker. *Ecology and Religion*. Washington, DC: Island Press, 2014.

Guerrini, Anita. "The Ethics of Animal Experimentation in Seventeenth-Century England." *Journal of the History of Ideas* 50, no. 3 (1989): 391–407.

Gullan-Whur, Margaret. "Spinoza and the Equality of Women." *Theoria* 68 (2008): 91–111.

GUO Qingfan 郭慶藩. Zhuangzi Jishi 莊子集釋 [Collected explanations of the Zhuangzi]. Beijing 北京: Zhonghua Shuju 中華書局, 2012.

Hagen, Kurtis. *The Philosophy of Xunzi: A Reconstruction*. Chicago: Open Court, 2007.

Hall, David L. *Eros and Irony: A Prelude to Philosophical Anarchism*. Albany: State University of New York Press, 1982.

Hall, David L., and Roger T. Ames. *Thinking from the Han: Self, Truth, and Transcendence in Chinese and Western Culture*. Albany: State University of New York Press, 1998.

Hampe, Michael. "Explaining and Describing: Panpsychism and Deep Ecology." In *Contemporary Perspectives on Early Modern Philosophy: Nature and Norms in Thought*. Edited by Martin Lenz and Anik Waldow, 179–202. Heidelberg: Springer, 2013.

Hansen, Chad. *A Daoist Theory of Chinese Thought: A Philosophical Interpretation*. Oxford: Oxford University Press, 2000.

Haraway, Donna J. *When Species Meet*. Minneapolis: University of Minnesota Press, 2007.

Harbsmeier, Christoph. "Authorial Presence in Some Pre-Buddhist Chinese Texts." In *De l'un au multiple. Traductions du Chinois vers les langues Europennes*. Edited by Viviane Alleton and Michael Lackner, 221–254. Paris: Fondation Maison des Sciences de l'Homme, 1999.

Harel, Naama. "The Animal Voice behind the Animal Fable." *Journal for Critical Animal Studies* 7, no. 2 (2009): 9–21.

Harel, Naama. "Constructing the Nonhuman as Human: Scientific Fallacy, Literary Device." In *Restoring the Mystery of the Rainbow: Literature's Refraction of Science*. 2 vols. Edited by Valeria Tinkler-Villani and C. C. Barefoot, 897–911. Leiden: Brill, 2011.
Harper, Donald, trans. *Early Chinese Medical Literature: The Mawangdui Medical Manuscripts*. London: Kegan Paul International, 1998.
Hobbes, Thomas. *On the Citizen*. Edited and translated by Richard Tuck and Michael Silverthorne. Cambridge: Cambridge University Press, 1998 [1642].
Houston, R. A. *Literacy in Early Modern Europe: Culture and Education 1500–1800*. 2nd ed. London: Routledge, 2002.
Howell, Philip. "The Trouble with Liminanimals." *Parallax* 25, no. 4 (2019): 395–411.
Chun-chieh Huang. "The 'Body Politic' in Ancient China." *Acta Orientalia Vilnensia* 8, no. 2 (2007): 33–43.
Huang Hui 黄晖. *Lunheng jiaoshi* 論衡校釋 [The explanations and annotations of the Discursive Weighing]. Beijing北京: Zhonghua Shuju 中華書局, 2011.
Husserl, Edmund. *Cartesian Meditations: An Introduction to Phenomenology*. Translated by Dorion Cairns. Leiden: Martinus Nijhoff, 1977.
Hutton, Eric L. "柏拉图论'仁'" [On Confucian "benevolence" in the philosophy of Plato]. Translated by 刘旻娇 Liu Minjiao. 伦理学术 *Academia Ethica* 4, edited by 邓安庆 Deng Anqing (June 2018): 29–45.
Hutton, Eric L., trans. *Xunzi: The Complete Text*. Princeton, NJ: Princeton University Press, 2016.
Ing, Michael David Kaulana. *The Dysfunction of Ritual in Early Confucianism*. Oxford: Oxford University Press, 2012.
Ing, Michael David Kaulana. *The Invulnerability of Integrity in Early Confucian Thought*. Oxford: Oxford University Press, 2017.
Ip, Po-Keung. "Taoism and the Foundations of Environmental Ethics." *Environmental Ethics* 5, no. 4 (January 1983): 335–343.
Israel, Jonathan I. *Enlightenment Contested: Philosophy, Modernity, and the Emancipation of Man 1670–1752*. Oxford: Oxford University Press, 2006.
Irigaray, Luce. *Speculum of the Other Woman*. Translated by Gillian Gill. Ithaca, NY: Cornell University Press, 1985.
Irigaray, Luce. *This Sex Which Is Not One*. Translated by Catherine Porter and Carolyn Burke. Ithaca, NY: Cornell University Press, 1985.
Ivanhoe, Philip J., and Bryan W. Van Norden, eds. *Readings in Classical Chinese Philosophy*. Indianapolis, IN: Hackett, 2003.
Jaspers, Karl. *The Origin and Goal of History*. Translated by Michael Bullock. New Haven, CT: Yale University Press, 1953.
Jochim, Chris. "Just Say No to 'No-Self' in the Zhuangzi." In *Wandering at Ease in the Zhuangzi*. Edited by Roger T. Ames, 35–74. Albany: State University of New York Press, 1998.
Johnson, Mark. "Introduction: Metaphor in the Philosophical Tradition." In *Philosophical Perspectives on Metaphor*. Edited by Mark Johnson, 3–47. Minneapolis: University of Minnesota Press, 1981.
Joy, Lynn S. "Scientific Explanation from Formal Causes to Laws of Nature." In *The Cambridge History of Science*. Edited by Park and Daston, 70–105.
Karlgren, Bernhard. "The Book of Documents." *Bulletin of the Museum of Far Eastern Antiquities* 22 (1950): 1–81. https://archive.org/details/Bulletin22 (reprinted as a separate volume by Göteborg: Elanders Boktrycher Aktiebolag (1950)).

Kashap, S. Paul, ed. *Studies in Spinoza: Critical and Interpretive Essays*. Berkeley: University of California Press, 1972.

Kim, David. "What is Asian American Philosophy?" In *Philosophy in Multiple Voices*. Edited by George Yancy, 219–271. Lanham, MD: Rowman and Littlefield, 2007.

Kirkland, Russell. "'Responsible Non-Action' in a Natural World: Perspectives from the *Neiye*, *Zhuangzi*, and *Daodejing*." In *Daoism and Ecology: Ways within a Cosmic Landscape*. Edited by N. J. Girardot, James Miller, and Liu Xiaogan, 283–304. Cambridge, MA: Harvard University Press, 2001.

Kisner, Matthew J., and Andrew Youpa, eds. *Essays on Spinoza's Ethical Theory*. Oxford: Oxford University Press, 2014.

Klein, Esther Sunkyung. "Were There 'Inner Chapters' in the Warring States? A New Examination of Evidence about the *Zhuangzi*," *T'oung Pao* 96, fasc. 4/5 (2011): 299–369.

Klein, Esther Sunkyung. "Early Chinese Textual Culture and the *Zhuangzi* Anthology: An Alternative Model for Autorship." *Dao Companion to the Philosophy of the* Zhuangzi. Edited by Kim- chong Chong, 13–42. New York: Springer, 2022.

John Knoblock, trans.. *Xunzi: A Translation and Study of the Complete Works*. 3 vols. Stanford, CA: Stanford University Press, 1988–94.

Knoblock, John, and Jeffrey Riegel, trans. *The Annals of Lü Buwei*. Stanford, CA: Stanford University Press, 2000.

Korhonen, Tua. "Anthropomorphism and the Aesopic Animal Fables." In *Animals and their Relation to Gods, Humans and Things in the Ancient World*. Edited by Raija Mattila, Sanae Ito, and Sebastian Fink, 211–231. New York: Springer, 2019.

Kupperman, Joel J. "Not in So Many Words: Chuang Tzu's Strategies of Communication." *Philosophy East and West* 39, no. 3 (1989): 311–317.

Lakoff, George, and Mark Johnson. *Metaphors We Live By*. Chicago: University of Chicago Press, 2003.

Lau, D. C., trans. *The Analects*. Harmondsworth: Penguin Books, 1979.

Lau, D. C., and Fanzheng Cheng, eds. *A Concordance to the Liji*. Hong Kong: Commercial Press, 1992.

Lawlor, Leonard. *Early Twentieth-Century Continental Philosophy*. Bloomington: Indiana University Press, 2011.

Lécrivain, André. "Spinoza and Cartesian Mechanics." In *Spinoza and the Sciences*. Edited by Marjorie Grene and Debra Nails, 15–60. Dordrecht: D. Reidel, 1986.

Levinovitz, Alan. "The *Zhuangzi* and *You* (遊): Defining An Ideal without Contradiction." *Dao* 11, no. 4 (2012): 479–496.

Lewis, Mark Edward. *The Construction of Space in Early China*. Albany: State University of New York Press, 2006.

Lewis, Mark Edward. *The Flood Myths of Early China*. Albany: State University of New York Press, 2006.

Lewis, Mark Edward. *Writing and Authority in Early China*. Albany: State University of New York Press, 1999.

Li, Chenyang. "The Confucian Ideal of Harmony." *Philosophy East and West* 56, no. 4 (2006): 583–603.

Li, Chenyang, ed. *The Sage and the Second Sex: Confucianism, Ethics, and Gender*. Chicago: Open Court, 2000.

Lincoln, Bruce. *Apples and Oranges: Explorations In, On, and With Comparison*. Chicago: University of Chicago Press, 2018.

Littlejohn, Ronnie. "Kongzi in the Zhuangzi." In *Experimental Essays on Zhuangzi*. Edited by Victor H. Mair, 177–194. Dunedin: Three Pines Press, 2010).

Liu Chengji. *Wuxiang Meixue* 物象美學 [The image of aesthetics]. Zhengzhou: Zhengzhou Daxue Chubanshe, 2002.

Liu, Xiaogan 劉笑敢. *Laozi gujin* 老子古今 [Laozi past and present]. Beijing: Zhongguo Shehui Kexue Chubanshe, 2006.

LIU Zhao 劉釗. *Guodian Chujian Jiaoshi* 郭店楚簡校釋 [An interpretation with corrections on the Guodian Chu Slips]. Fuzhou 福州: Fujian Renmin Chubanshe 福建人民出版社, 2003.

Lloyd, Genevieve. *The Man of Reason: "Male" and "Female" in Western Philosophy*. London: Routledge, 1993.

Lloyd, Genevieve. *Routledge Philosophy Guidebook to Spinoza and the* Ethics. London: Routledge, 1996.

Lloyd, Genevieve. *Part of Nature: Self-Knowledge in Spinoza's* Ethics. Ithaca, NY: Cornell University Press, 1994.

Lloyd, Genevieve. "Spinoza's Environmental Ethics." *Inquiry* 23, no. 3 (1980): 293–311.

Lockman, Zachary. *Contending Visions of the Middle East: The History and Politics of Orientalism*. 2nd ed. Cambridge: Cambridge University Press, 2009.

Lord, Beth. "'Disempowered by Nature': Spinoza on the Political Capabilities of Women." *British Journal for the History of Philosophy* 19, no. 6 (2011): 1085–1106.

Lynn, Richard John. "Birds and Beasts in the Zhuangzi, Fables Interpreted by Guo Xiang and Cheng Xuanying." *Religions* 10 (2019): 445. https://doi.org/10.3390/rel10070445.

Macherey, Pierre. *Introduction à l'éthique de Spinoza. La Seconde partie: la réalité mentale*. Paris: Presses Universitaires de France, 1997.

Maeder, Erik W. "Some Observations on the Composition of the 'Core Chapters' of the *Mozi*." *Early China* 17 (1992): 27–82.

Mair, Victor H., trans. *Wandering on the Way: Early Taoist Tales and Parables of Chuang Tzu*. Honolulu: University of Hawai'i Press, 2000.

Makeham, John. *Name and Actuality in Early Chinese Thought*. Albany: State University of New York Press, 1994.

Malebranche, Nicolas. *Dialogue between a Christian Philosopher and a Chinese Philosopher on the Existence and Nature of God*. Translated by Dominick A. Iorio. Lanham, MD: University Press of America, 1980.

Malinowski-Charles, Syliane. *Affects et Conscience chez Spinoza: L'automatisme dans le progrès éthique*. Hildesheim: Georg Olms Verlag, 2004.

Marshall, Eugene. "Man is a God to Man: How Human Beings Can Be Adequate Causes." In Kisner and Youpa, *Essays on Spinoza's Ethical Theory*, 160–177.

Marsili, Filippo. *Heaven is Empty: A Cross-Cultural Approach to "Religion" and Empire in Ancient China*. Albany: State University of New York Press, 2018.

Mattice, Sarah A. *Metaphor and Metaphilosophy: Philosophy as Combat, Play, and Aesthetic Experience*. Lanham, MD: Lexington Books, 2014.

McLeod, Alexus. *The Dao of Madness: Mental Illness and Self-Cultivation in Early Chinese Philosophy and Medicine*. Oxford: Oxford University Press, 2021.

Melamed, Yitzhak Y. "Charitable Interpretations and the Political Domestication of Spinoza, or, Benedict in the Land of the Secular Imagination." In *Philosophy and Its History: Aims and Methods in the Study of Early Modern Philosophy*. Edited by Mogens Laerke, Justin E. H. Smith, and Eric Schliesser, 258–277. Oxford University Press, 2013.

Melamed, Yitzhak Y. "Eternity in Early Modern Philosophy." In *Eternity: A History*. Edited by Yitzhak Y. Melamed, 129–167. New York: Oxford University Press, 2016).
Melamed, Yitzhak Y. "The Metaphysics of the Theological-Political Treatise." In *Spinoza's "Theological-Political Treatise": A Critical Guide*. Edited by Yitzhak Y. Melamed and Michael A. Rosenthal, 128–142. New York: Cambridge University Press, 2013.
Melamed, Yitzhak Y. "Spinoza, Althusser, and the Question of Humanism." *Crisis and Critique* 8, no. 1 (2021): 170–177.
Melamed, Yitzhak Y. "Spinoza's Anti-Humanism: An Outline." In Fraenkel, Perinetti, and Smith, *The Rationalists: Between Tradition and Innovation*, 147–166.
Melamed, Yitzhak Y. "Spinoza's 'Atheism': God and Nature in the Ethics and the TTP." In *Spinoza: Reason, Religion, Politics: The Relation Between the* Ethics *and the* Tractatus Theologico-Politicus. Edited by Daniel Garber. Oxford: Oxford University Press, forthcoming.
Melamed, Yitzhak Y . "Spinoza's Metaphysics of Thought: Parallelisms and the Multifaceted Structure of Ideas," *Philosophy and Phenomenological Research* 86, no. 3 (May 2013): 636–683.
Melamed, Yitzhak Y. *Spinoza's Metaphysics: Substance and Thought*. Oxford: Oxford University Press, 2013.
Melamed, Yitzhak Y. "When Having *Too Much* Power is Harmful: Spinoza on Political Luck." In Melamed and Sharp, *Spinoza's Political Treatise*, 161–174.
Melamed, Yitzhak Y., and Hasana Sharp, eds. *Spinoza's Political Treatise: A Critical Guide*. Cambridge: Cambridge University Press, 2018.
Milburn, Olivia. "Marked Out for Greatness? Perceptions of Deformity and Physical Impairment in Ancient China." *Monumenta Serica* 55, no. 1 (2007): 1–22. DOI: 10.1179/mon.2007.55.1.001.
Moeller, Hans-Georg. "Chinese Language Philosophy and Correlativism." *Bulletin of the Museum of Far Eastern Antiquities* 72 (2000): 91–109.
Moeller, Hans-Georg, "Humor and Its Philosophical Significance in the *Zhuangzi*." *Dao Companion to the Philosophy of the* Zhuangzi. Edited by Kim- chong Chong, 287–303. New York: Springer, 2022.
Moeller, Hans-Georg, and Paul J. D'Ambrosio. *Genuine Pretending: On the Philosophy of the Zhuangzi*. New York: Columbia University Press, 2017.
Moreau, Pierre François. "The Metaphysics of Substance and the Metaphysics of Forms." In *Spinoza on Knowledge and the Human Mind: Papers Presented at the Second Jerusalem Conference (Ethica II)*. Edited by Yirmiyahu Yovel and Gideon Segal, 27–35. Leiden: Brill, 1994.
Morton, Timothy. "Guest Column: Queer Ecology." *PMLA: Publications of the Modern Language Association of America* 125, no. 2 (2010): 273–282. 10.1632/pmla.2010.125.2.273
Mozi Yinde 墨子引得. (*A Concordance to Mo Tzu*), Harvard-Yenching Institute Sinological Index Series, Supplement no. 21. Cambridge MA: Harvard University Press, 1956.
Munro, Donald J. *The Concept of Man in Early China*. Ann Arbor: Center for Chinese Studies, University of Michigan, 2001.
Munro, Donald J. "When Science Is in Defense of Value-Linked Facts." *Philosophy East and West* 69, no. 3 (2019): 900–917.
Nadler, Steven. "The Lives of Others: Spinoza on Benevolence as a Rational Virtue." In Kisner and Youpa, *Essays on Spinoza's Ethical Theory*, 41–56.

Nadler, Steven. *Spinoza's* Ethics: *An Introduction*. Cambridge: Cambridge University Press, 2006.
Naess, Arne. "Identification as a Source of Deep Ecological Attitudes." In *Deep Ecology*. Edited by M. Tobias, 256–270. San Diego: Avant Books, 1985.
Naess, Arne. "The Shallow and the Deep, Long-Range Ecology Movements: A Summary." In Sessions, *Deep Ecology for the Twenty-First Century*, 151–155.
Nelson, Eric Sean. "The Human and the Inhuman: Ethics and Religion in the *Zhuangzi*." *Journal of Chinese Philosophy* 41, no. 5 (2014): 723–739.
Nelson, Eric Sean. "Responding with *Dao*: Early Daoist Ethics and the Environment." *Philosophy East and West* 59, no. 3 (July 2009): 294–316.
Noske, Barbara. "Speciesism, Anthropocentrism, and Non-Western Cultures." *Anthrozoös* 10, no. 4 (1997): 183–190.
Nussbaum, Martha C. *Love's Knowledge: Essays on Philosophy and Literature*. New York: Oxford University Press, 1992.
Nylan, Michael. "Academic Silos, or 'What I Wish Philosophers Knew About Early History in China.'" In *The Bloomsbury Handbook of Chinese Research Methodologies*. Edited by TAN Sor-Hoon, 91–114. London: Bloomsbury, 2016.
Nylan, Michael. *The Chinese Pleasure Book*. New York: Zone Books, 2018.
Nylan, Michael. "Golden Spindles and Axes: Elite Women in the Achaemenid and Han Empires." In Li, *The Sage and the Second Sex*, 199–222.
Nylan, Michael. "Humans as Animals and Things in Pre-Buddhist China." *Religions* 10, no. 6 (2019): 360. https://doi.org/10.3390/rel10060360.
Nylan, Michael. "Talk about 'Barbarians' in Antiquity." *Philosophy East and West* 62, no. 4 (October 2012): 580–601.
Olberding, Amy. "Sorrow and the Sage: Grief in the *Zhuangzi*." *Dao: A Journal of Comparative Philosophy* 6 (4) (2007): 339–359.
Oliver, Kelly. "Animal Ethics: Toward an Ethics of Responsiveness." *Research in Phenomenology* 40 (2010): 267–280.
Osler, Margaret J. *Reconfiguring the World: Nature, God, and Human Understanding from the Middle Ages to Early Modern Europe*. Baltimore: John Hopkins University Press, 2010.
Özbey, Sonya. "Undermining the Person, Undermining the Establishment in the *Zhuangzi*." *Comparative and Continental Philosophy* 10, no. 2 (2018): 123–139. DOI: 10.1080/17570638.2018.1487103.
Özbey, Sonya. "The Plasticity of the Human and Inscribing History within Biology: A Response to Donald J. Munro." *Philosophy East and West* 69, no. 3 (2019): 918–926.
Özbey, Sonya. "On Beastly Joys and Melancholic Passions: Cross-Species Communication of Affects in Spinoza and the *Zhuangzi*." *Dao Companion to the Philosophy of the Zhuangzi*. Edited by Kim-chong Chong, 733–750. New York: Springer, 2022.
PANG Pu庞 朴. *Zhu Bo "Wu Xing" Pian Jiao Zhu Ji Yan Jiu* 竹帛五行篇校注研究. Taibei 臺北: Wanjuan Lou 萬卷樓, 2000.
Park, Katharine, and Lorraine Daston, eds. *The Cambridge History of Science*. Vol. 3, *Early Modern Science*. New York: Cambridge University Press, 2016.
PARK, So Jeong. "On Sound: Reconstructing a Zhuangzian Perspective of Music." *Humanities* 5, no. 1 (2016): 3. DOI:10.3390/h5010003.
Parkes, Graham. "Zhuangzi and Nietzsche on the Human and Nature." Special Issue: East Asian and Comparative Approaches to the Environment. *Environmental Philosophy* 10, no. 1, (Spring 2013): 1–24.

Perkins, Franklin. "Following Nature with Mengzi or Zhuangzi." *International Philosophical Quarterly* 45, no. 3, issue 179 (2005): 327–340.

Perkins, Franklin. *Heaven and Earth Are Not Humane: The Problem of Evil in Classical Chinese Philosophy*. Bloomington: Indiana University Press, 2014.

Perkins, Franklin. "Motivation and the Heart in the *Xing Zi Ming Chu*." *Dao* 8 (2009):117–131.

Perkins, Franklin. "Of Fish and Men: Species Difference and the Strangeness of Being Human in the Zhuangzi." In *Zhuangzi and the Happy Fish*. Edited by Roger T. Ames and Takahiro Nakajima, 182–205. Honolulu: University of Hawai'i Press, 2017.

Perkins, Franklin. "What Is a Thing (*wu* 物)? The Problem of Individuation in Early Chinese Metaphysics." In *Chinese Metaphysics and Its Problems*. Edited by Chenyang Li and Franklin Perkins, 54–68. Cambridge: Cambridge University Press, 2018.

Perkins, Franklin. "The *Zhuangzi* and the Division Between Heaven and Human." In *Dao Companion to the Philosophy of the* Zhuangzi. Edited by Kim-chong Chong, 119–134. New York: Springer, 2022.

Pines, Yuri. "Beasts or Humans: Pre-Imperial Origins of Sino-Barbarian Dichotomy." In *Mongols, Turks and Others: Eurasian Nomads and the Sedentary World*. Edited by Reuven Amitai and Michal Biran, 59–102. Leiden: Brill, 2005.

Pines, Yuri. "Changing Views of 'Tianxia' in Pre-Imperial Discourse." *Oriens Extremus* 43 (2002): 101–116.

Pines, Yuri. "Confucius's Elitism: The Concepts of *Junzi* and *Xiaoren* Revisited." In *A Concise Companion to Confucius*. Edited by Paul R. Goldin, 164–184. Chichester: Wiley Blackwell, 2017.

Pines, Yuri. "'The One That Pervades the All' in Ancient Chinese Political Thought: The Origins of 'The Great Unity' Paradigm." *T'oung Pao*, Second Series 86, Fasc. 4/5 (2000): 280–324.

Puett, Michael J. *To Become a God, Cosmology, Sacrifice, and Self-Divinization in Early China*. Cambridge, MA: Harvard University Press, 2004.

Queen, Sarah A., and John S. Major, trans. *Luxuriant Gems of the Spring and Autumn*. New York: Columbia University, 2016.

Raphals, Lisa. "Craft Analogies in Chinese and Greek Argumentation." In *Literature, Religion, and East/West Comparison: Essays in Honor of Anthony C. Yu*. Edited by Eric Ziolkowski, 181–201. Newark: University of Delaware Press, 2005.

Raphals, Lisa. "Gendered Virtue Reconsidered: Notes from the Warring States and Han." In Li, *The Sage and the Second Sex*, 223–247.

Raphals, Lisa. *Sharing the Light: Representations of Women and Virtue in Early China*. Albany: State University of New York Press, 1998.

Raphals, Lisa. "Skilled Feelings in Chinese and Greek Heart-Mind-Body Metaphors." *Dao* 20 (2021): 69–91.

Raphals, Lisa. "A Woman Who Understood the Rites." In *Confucius and the Analects: New Essays*. Edited by Bryan W. Van Norden, 275–302. Oxford: Oxford University Press, 2002.

Rapp, John A. *Daoism and Anarchism: Critiques of State Autonomy in Ancient and Modern China*. New York: Continuum, 2012.

Rice, Lee C. "Tanquam Naturae Humanae Exemplar: Spinoza on Human Nature." *Modern Schoolman* 68, no. 4 (1991): 291–303.

Riskin, Jessica. *The Restless Clock: A History of the Centuries-Long Argument over What Makes Living Things Tick*. Chicago: University of Chicago Press, 2018.

Robins, Dan. "It Goes Beyond Skill." In *Ethics in Early China: An Anthology*. Edited by Chris Fraser, Dan Robins, and Timothy O'Leary, 105–123. Hong Kong: Hong Kong University Press, 2011.

Robins, Dan. "The Warring States Concept of *Xing*." *Dao* 10 (2011): 31–51.

Rorty. Amelie Oksenberg. "Experiments in Philosophic Genre: Descartes' 'Meditations.'" *Critical Inquiry* 9, no. 3 (March 1983): 545–564.

Rorty. Amelie Oksenberg. "Spinoza on the Pathos of Idolatrous Love and the Hilarity of True Love." In Gatens, *Feminist Interpretations of Benedict Spinoza*, 65–86.

Rossello, Diego. "Hobbes and the Wolf-Man: Melancholy and Animality in Modern Sovereignty." *New Literary History* 43, no. 2 (Spring 2012): 255–279.

Russell, Bertrand. *A History of Western Philosophy*. New York: Simon and Schuster/Touchstone, 1967.

Salomon, Daniel. "From Marginal Cases to Linked Oppressions: Reframing the Conflict between the Autistic Pride and Animal Rights Movements." *Journal for Critical Animal Studies* 8, no. 1/2 (2010): 47–72.

Sato, Masayuki. "The Development of the Idea of *Li* 裡 in pre-Qin Thought." In *The Confucian Quest for Order: The Origin and Formation of the Political Thought of Xun Zi*, 163–236. Leiden: Brill, 2003.

Savan, David. "Spinoza and Language." *Philosophical Review* 67, no. 2 (1958): 212–225.

Schäfer, Dagmar, Martina Siebert, and Roel Sterckx. "Knowing Animals in China's History: An Introduction." In *Animals through Chinese History: Earliest Times to 1911*. Edited by Roel Sterckx, Martina Siebert, and Dagmar Schäfer, 1–19. Cambridge: Cambridge University Press, 2019.

Schmaltz, Tad. M. *Early Modern Cartesianisms: Dutch and French Constructions*. New York: Oxford University Press, 2017.

Schmaltz, Tad. *The Metaphysics of the Material World: Suarez, Descartes, Spinoza*. New York: Oxford University Press, 2019.

Schneider, Daniel. "Spinoza's Epistemological Methodism." *Journal of the History of Philosophy* 54, no. 4 (October 2016): 573–599.

Schopenhauer, Arthur. *The World as Will and Idea: 3 Volumes in 1*. Translated by R. B. Haldane and J. Kemp. Scotts Valley: CreateSpace Independent Publishing Platform, 2016.

Scruton, Roger. *Spinoza*. Oxford: Oxford University Press, 1986.

Sessions, George, ed. *Deep Ecology for the Twenty-First Century: Readings on the Philosophy and Practice of the New Environmentalism*. Boston: Shambhala, 1995.

Sessions, George, ed. "Ecocentrism and the Anthropocentric Detour." In Sessions, *Deep Ecology for the Twenty-First Century*, 290–310.

Shapin, Steven. "The Man of Science." In Park and Daston, *The Cambridge History of Science*, 179–191.

Sharp, Hasana. "Animal Affects: Spinoza and the Frontiers of the Human." *Journal for Critical Animal Studies* 9, no. 1–2 (2011): 48–68.

Sharp, Hasana. "Eve's Perfection: Spinoza on Sexual (In)Equality." *Journal of the History of Philosophy* 50, no. 4 (2012): 559–580.

Sharp, Hasana. "The Force of Ideas in Spinoza," *Political Theory* 35, no. 6 (2007): 732–755.

Sharp, Hasana. "'Nemo non videt': Intuitive Knowledge and the Question of Spinoza's Elitism." In Fraenkel, Perinetti, and Smith, *The Rationalists: Between Tradition and Innovation*, 101–122.

Sharp, Hasana. *Spinoza and the Politics of Renaturalization*. Chicago: University of Chicago Press, 2011.

Shaviro, Steven. "Consequences of Panpsychism." In *The Nonhuman Turn*. Edited by Richard Grusin, 19–44. Minneapolis: University of Minnesota Press, 2015.

Slingerland, Edward. *Effortless Action: Wu-Wei as Conceptual Metaphor and Spiritual Ideal in Early China*. New York: Oxford University Press, 2003.

Slingerland, Edward. *Mind and Body in Early China: Beyond Orientalism and the Myth of Holism*. New York: Oxford University Press, 2019.

Smith, Steven B. *Spinoza, Liberalism, and the Question of Jewish Identity*. New Haven, CT: Yale University Press, 1997.

Soldatenko, Gabriel. "A Contribution toward the Decolonization of Philosophy: Asserting the Coloniality of Power in the Study of Non-Western Philosophical Traditions." *Comparative and Continental Philosophy* 7, no. 2 (December 2015): 138–156.

Solnit, Rebecca. *A Paradise Built in Hell: The Extraordinary Communities That Arise in Disaster*. New York: Penguin, 2010.

Spinoza, Benedictus de. *The Collected Works of Spinoza*. Vol.1. Translated by Edwin Curley. Princeton, NJ: Princeton University Press, 1985.

Spinoza, Benedictus de. *Spinoza: Complete Works*. Edited by Michael L. Morgan and translated by Samuel Shirley. Indianapolis, IN: Hackett, 2002.

Spinoza, Benedictus de. *The Principles of Cartesian Philosophy*. Translated by Samuel Shirley. Indianapolis, IN: Hackett, 1961.

Spinoza, Benedictus de. *Theological-Political Treatise*. Edited by Jonathan Israel and translated by Michael Silverthorne and Jonathan Israel. Cambridge: Cambridge University Press, 2007.

Spivak, Gayatri Chakravorty. "Can the Subaltern Speak?" In *Can the Subaltern Speak? Reflections on the History of an Idea*. Edited by Rosalind C. Morris, 21–78. New York: Columbia University Press, 2010.

Stalnaker, Aaron. "Mastery, Authority, and Hierarchy in the 'Inner Chapters' of the Zhuāngzǐ." *Soundings: An Interdisciplinary Journal* 95, no. 3 (2012): 255–283.

Stalnaker, Aaron. *Overcoming Our Evil: Human Nature and Spiritual Exercises in Xunzi and Augustine*. Washington, DC: Georgetown University Press, 2006.

Stanford Encyclopedia of Philosophy. "Influence of Social Origins on Mohist Thought." https://plato.stanford.edu/entries/mohism/social.html.

Steenbakkers, Piet. *Spinoza's Ethica, From Manuscript to Print: Studies on Text, Form and Related Topics*. Assen: Van Gorcum, 1994.

Steinberg, Justin. "Spinoza and Political Absolutism." In Melamed and Sharp, *Spinoza's Political Treatise*, 175–189.

Steinberg, Justin. *Spinoza's Political Psychology: The Taming of Fortune and Fear*. Cambridge: Cambridge University Press, 2018.

Sterckx, Roel. *The Animal and the Daemon in Early China*. Albany: State University of New York Press, 2002.

Sterckx, Roel. *Chinese Thought: From Confucius to Cook Ding*. London: Pelican Books, 2019.

Stewart, Susan. *Nonsense: Aspects of Intertextuality in Folklore and Literature*. Baltimore: John Hopkins University Press, 1979.

Stoltzfus, Michael J., and Darla Y Schumm. "Beyond Models: Some Tentative Daoist Contributions to Disability Studies." *Disability Studies Quarterly* 31, no. 1 (Winter 2011): 103–122.

Strassberg, Richard E. *A Chinese Bestiary: Strange Creatures from the Guideways through Mountains and Seas*. Berkeley: University of California Press, 2008.
Sturgeon, Donald. Chinese Text Project (2011). https://ctext.org/xiao-jing/government-of-the-sages.
Stuurman, Siep. "The Deconstruction of Gender: Seventeenth-Century Feminism and Modern Equality." In *Women, Gender and Enlightenment*. Edited by Sarah Knott and Barbara Taylor, 371–388. New York: Palgrave Macmillan, 2005.
Sypher, Wylie, ed. *Comedy: "An Essay on Comedy" by George Meredith. "Laughter" by Henri Bergson*. Baltimore: Johns Hopkins University Press, 1956.
Taylor, Alfred. E. "Some Incoherencies in Spinozism, Part II." *Mind* 46, no. 183 (July 1937): 281–301.
Taylor, Sunaura. *Beasts of Burden: Animal and Disability Liberation*. New York: New Press, 2017.
Thiel, Udo. "Personal Identity." In *The Cambridge History of Seventeenth-Century Philosophy*. Edited by Garber and Ayers. Vol.1, 868–912.
Todorov, Tzvetan. "Literary Genres." In *Current Trends in Linguistics*. Vol. 12, *Linguistics and Adjacent Arts and Sciences, Part 3*. Edited by T. A. Sebeok, 957–962. The Hague: Mouton, 1974.
Tuck, Richard. "The Institutional Setting." In Garber and Ayers, *The Cambridge History of Seventeenth Century Philosophy*. Vol. 1, 7–32.
Valmisa, Mercedes. *Adapting: A Chinese Philosophy of Action*. New York: Oxford University Press, 2021.
Van Bunge, Wiep. *From Stevin to Spinoza: An Essay on Philosophy in the Seventeenth-Century Dutch Republic*. Leiden: Brill, 2001.
Van den Broek, Roelof, and Wouter J. Hanegraaff, eds. *Gnosis and Hermeticism from Antiquity to Modern Times*. Albany: State University of New York Press, 1997.
Vassányi, Miklós. *Anima Mundi: The Rise of the World Soul Theory in Modern German Philosophy*. Dordrecht: Springer, 2011.
Virág, Curie. *The Emotions in Early Chinese Philosophy*. New York: Oxford University Press, 2017.
Von Falkenhausen, Lothar. *Chinese Society in the Age of Confucius (1000–250 BC): The Archeological Evidence*. Los Angeles: Cotsen Institute of Archeology Press at UCLA, 2006.
WANG Bo 王博. *Zhuangzi zhexue* 莊子哲學 [The philosophy of Zhuangzi]. Beijing 北京: Peking University Publishing北京大學出版, 2004.
Wang, Robin R. *Images of Women in Chinese Thought and Culture: Writings from the Pre-Qin Period through the Song Dynasty*. Indianapolis, IN: Hackett, 2003.
WANG, Youru. *Linguistic Strategies in Daoist Zhuangzi and Chan Buddhism: The Other Way of Speaking*. New York: Routledge, 2014.
Watson, Burton, trans. *The Complete Works of Zhuangzi*. New York: Columbia University Press, 2013.
Weil, Kari. *Thinking Animals: Why Animal Studies Now?* New York: Columbia University Press, 2012.
Weishu tongkao 偽書通考 [Comprehensive investigation of forged writings]. Compiled by Zhang Xincheng張心澂. Shanghai, Commercial Press, 1939.
Weitzenfeld, Adam, and Melanie Joy. "An Overview of Anthropocentrism, Humanism, and Speciesism." In *Defining Critical Animal Studies: An Intersectional Social Justice*

Approach for Liberation. Edited by Anthony J. Nocella II, John Sorenson, Kim Socha, and Atsuko Matsuoka, 3–27. New York: Peter Lang, 2014.
Weststeijn, Thijs. "Spinoza sinicus: An Asian Paragraph in the History of the Radical Enlightenment." *Journal of the History of Ideas* 68, no. 4 (2007): 537–561.
Wetlesen, Jon. *The Sage and the Way: Spinoza's Ethics of Freedom*. Assen: Van Gorcum, 1979.
White, Lynn. "The Historical Roots of Our Ecologic Crisis." *Science*, New Series 155, no. 3767 (March 1967): 1203–1207.
Willett, Cynthia. *Interspecies Ethics*. New York: Columbia University Press, 2014.
Williams, Bernard. *Shame and Necessity*. Berkeley: University of California Press, 1993.
Wilson, Margaret D. "'For They Do Not Agree in Nature with Us.'" In *New Essays on the Rationalists*. Edited by Rocco J. Gennaro and Charles Huenemann, 336–352. New York: Oxford University Press, 1999.
Winkelman, Michael James. 2023. "Chinese Wu, Ritualists and Shamans: An Ethnological Analysis." *Religions* 14, no. 7: 852. https://doi.org/10.3390/rel14070852.
Wolfe, Cary. *Animal Rites: American Culture, the Discourse of Species, and Posthumanist Theory*. Chicago: University of Chicago Press, 2003.
Wolfe, Cary. *Before the Law: Humans and Other Animals in a Biopolitical Frame*. Chicago: University of Chicago Press, 2012.
Wolloch, Nathaniel. "Christiaan Huygens's Attitude toward Animals." *Journal of the History of Ideas* 61, no. 3 (July 2000): 415–432.
Xu Yuangao 徐元誥. *Guoyu jijie* 國語集解 [Discourses of the states, with collected explanations]. Beijing 北京: Zhonghua shuju 中華書局, 2002.
Yearley, Lee H. "Daoist Presentation and Persuasion: Wandering among Zhuangzi's Kinds of Language." *Journal of Religious Ethics* 33, no. 3 (September 2005): 503–535.
Yearley, Lee H. *Mencius and Aquinas: Theories of Virtue and Conceptions of Courage*. Albany: State University of New York Press, 1990.
Yearley, Lee H. "Zhuangzi's Understanding of Skillfulness and the Ultimate Spiritual State." In *Essays on Skepticism, Relativism, and Ethics in the Zhuangzi*. Edited by Paul Kjellberg and Philip J. Ivanhoe, 152–182. Albany: State University of New York Press, 1996.
Young, Iris Marion. *Justice and the Politics of Difference*. Princeton, NJ: Princeton University Press, 2011.
Yovel, Yirmiyahu. "Incomplete Rationality in Spinoza's *Ethics*: Three Basic Forms." In *Ethica IV: Spinoza on Reason and the "Free Man."* Edited by Yirmiyahu Yovel and Gideon Segal, 15–35. New York: Little Room Press, 2004.
Yovel, Yirmiyahu. *Spinoza and Other Heretics*. Vol. 1, *The Marrano of Reason*. Princeton, NJ: Princeton University Press, 1989.
Zhang, Qianfan. "The Idea of Human Dignity in Classical Chinese Philosophy: A Reconstruction of Confucianism." *Journal of Chinese Philosophy* 27, no. 3 (2000): 299–330.
Zhou, Boqun. "Mechanical Metaphors in Early Chinese Thought." PhD diss., University of Chicago, 2019.
Ziporyn, Brook. *Ironies of Oneness and Difference: Coherence in Early Chinese Thought; Prolegomena to the Study of Li*. Albany: State University of New York Press, 2012.
Ziporyn, Brook. "Zhuangzi as a Philosopher," hackettpublishing.com. https://hackettpublishing.com/zhuangziphil (accessed July 27, 2022).
Ziporyn, Brook, trans. *Zhuangzi: The Complete Writings*. Indianapolis, IN: Hackett, 2020.
Ziporyn, Brook, trans. *Zhuangzi: The Essential Writings with Selections from Traditional Commentaries*. Indianapolis, IN: Hackett, 2009.

Index

For the benefit of digital users, indexed terms that span two pages (e.g., 52–53) may, on occasion, appear on only one of those pages.

Page numbers followed by n. indicate footnotes.

accommodationism, 63n.65
Adam: Spinoza's version of the story of the Fall, 161–67, 168, 197n.29, 201–2, 272–73
Adams, Carol J., 3n.7
adequate understanding, 88–98, 121–23, 164–70, 275
Adorno, Theodor, 284–85n.14
Aesop, 35–36
affects
    animal, 129–84, 192n.14
    Spinoza's theory of, 188–89, 196–97, 199, 275
Agamben, Giorgio, 2–3
agency, 16, 66–67, 78, 81–82, 103
    Spinoza's views on issues of, 88–93, 262–63
    the *Zhuangzi*'s views on issues of, 103–9
alien or foreign peoples, 26, 36–37, 218
    Spinoza's remarks on, 262–63
    the *Zhuangzi*'s depictions of, 182, 241–55
Allan, Sarah, 41n.61
Althusser, Louis, 87n.15
Amazons, 270–71
Ames, Roger T., 6n.14, 256n.57, 285–86n.15
Analects (*Lunyu*, 論語), 24n.7, 33n.36, 212n.20, 215–16n.33
ancient Greeks, 66, 99n.3, 190n.10, *see also* Plato, Aristotle
Angle, Stephen C., 147n.46
animal cruelty, 180
animal experimentation, 159n.7, 284n.13
animal fables, 35–37
animal rights, 289n.5

animal soul, 85
animality studies. *See* critical animality studies
"The Annals of Lü Buwei" (*Lüshi Chunqiu*, 呂氏春秋), 26–27n.17, 29n.24
anthropocentrism, 8–9, 12n.31, 157–61
anthropomorphic God, 84–88
anti-humanism, 87n.15, 119n.1
antiquity, 216–26, 231–35
Aquinas, Thomas, 50n.14
aristocrats, petty (*shi*, 士), 23–24, 240, 252–53
Aristotelianism, 50–51, 85
Aristotle, 40n.60, 50n.14
Armstrong, Aurelia, 6n.13, 200–1
Asian philosophy, 5–7
ass(es)
    Buridan's ass, 88–93, 119, 272
    what distinguishes a man from an ass, 88–93
Assmann, Jan, 242–43n.11
atheism, 10–12, 52–54, 83n.4
autism, 284n.10
automata, 66–67
axial age, 24n.8

"bad" universals, 91, 160n.11, 195n.20
Bai Yue (百越, numerous Yue), 245n.20
Balibar, Étienne, 189–90n.6, 196–97
barbarians, 114n.54, 239–40, 241, 244–45
Baxter, William H., 135n.7
Bayle, Pierre, 10–11, 11n.27, 49n.11, 54n.33
beast-machine approach, 81–82, 85, 159–60
bees, 202–3
Behnke, Elizabeth A., 123

Bekoff, Marc, 235n.13
Bell, Jeremy, 66n.74
Bennett, Jane, 193n.16
Bennett, Jonathan, 96n.39, 191–92n.13
Bentham, Jeremy, 1
Bergeton, Uffe, 147n.44
bian (辯, debate), 107–8
birds and wild animals (*qin shou*, 禽獸), 28–30, 36, 134, 150–51n.58, 182, 210n.11, 216–18, 220, 231, 234–35, 241–42, 247, 248–49, 256–57
black Africans, 3
Blair, Ann, 49–50
body-mind question, 4, 82–84, 105–6n.21, 194n.19
body politic metaphors, 17, 64, 194, 206, 207–8, 218–19, 232–33, 258–59
Boggs, Glenney, 2n.3
Boltz, William G., 33–34n.37
Book of Odes (*Shi Jing*, 詩經), 36
botanical metaphors, 40–42, 43–44, 72–73
Bove, Laurent, 167n.30
Brazilians, 265
Bredenburg, Johannes, 53–54n.31
bridling analogies, 64, 66
Brindley, Erica Fox, 110n.38, 114n.54, 242–43n.11, 244nn.17–18, 245n.20, 245n.22, 250n.35, 250n.38, 256n.57
Brown, Joshua R., 7–8n.16
Brown, Miranda, 147n.44
Bryne, Laura, 64n.67
Buddhism, 5–6, 10–11
  Buddhist notions of emptiness and ineffability 71n.5
Buridan's ass, 88–93, 119, 272
Burton, Robert, 169n.35
Butler, Judith, 3n.5

Calarco, Matthew, 10n.25, 183–84
Callicott, J. Baird, 4n.8, 6n.14, 99n.1
Calvinism, 51–52, 63n.65, 200n.40
Carriero, John, 189n.5
Cartesianism, 46–47, 49–52, 54n.33, 85, 269–70
Catholicism, 200n.40
Chakrabarty, Dipesh, 48n.5
Chan, Alan Kam-Leung, 143n.30

Chan, Shirley, 114n.53
chaos
  disorder (*luan*, 亂), 205–6, 210n.11, 214–16, 222, 231
Chen Guying, 34n.40
Chinese philosophy, 5n.10, 9–10, 206, 287n.1, *see also* Masters texts
  attitudes toward gender distinctions, 255–57, 260, 280
  attitudes toward foreign people, 241–55
  attitudes toward harmony with nature, 12
  descriptions of human distinctiveness, 104
  descriptions of the body politic, 206, 207–8, 218–19, 258–59
  early Chinese pleasure theories, 142–43, 215n.31
  early Chinese texts, 139–40, 141, 147–48, 206–8, 214–15, 215n.32, 225n.66, 241, 244–45, 250n.37, 255–57, 260, 280, 287n.1
  early Chinese theories of language, 39–40
  ming 名/*shi* 實 pairings, 139–40
Chong, Kim-chong, 34n.40, 176n.8
Christians and Christianity, 9n.22, 53n.23, 202n.48, 265–66
Chu (楚), polity of, 243, 250
Chunqiu fanlu (春秋繁露), 40–41
Chunqiu Zuozhuan (春秋左傳, *Zuo's Commentary on Spring and Autumn Annals*), 143n.30, 218, 241–42
civil order
  absence of, 231–35
Çırakman, Aslı, 264–65
Clark, Charles M.A., 234n.11
Clarke, Desmond M., 269–70n.21
Clemens, Justin, 88n.17
comedy
  bonding through banter and laughter, 149–55
  Equalizing Joke (*Qi Xie*, 齊諧), 154–55
  man from Song (*Song ren*, 宋人) trope, 245
  parody, 32, 34, 72, 247, 251n.41
  satire, 77, 116, 152, 168–70

common notions, 91–92, 165n.25
common people, 262–68
companionship
   bonding through banter and laughter, 149–55
   cementing and loosening of human bonds, 173–79
   misanthropic melancholy, 167–72, 178–79
comparative philosophy, 5n.10, 10–14, 69–78
compassion toward animals, 55, 157, 168, 177, 272, 274–75, 280–81, 284
Compendium Grammatices Linguae Hebraeae (Hebrew Grammar) (Spinoza), 56–57, 60, 67n.79
complexity, Spinoza's ladder of, 94–98
Confucius. *see* Kongzi
congenital deformities, people with, 253–54
criminality, 218
critical animality studies, 1–18, 239, 286n.16, *see also* human-animal studies (HAS)
critical mimesis, 10–14
cross-cultural philosophy, 1–18
Csikszentmihalyi, Mark, 83n.6, 142n.27, 143n.29, 145, 147
Cuomo, Chris J., 70n.2, 122n.4
Curley, Edwin, 94n.31, 197n.34, 265n.12

da zhi (大治, great order), 205–6, 222, 223–24
Dadai Liji (大戴禮記, *Records of Rites compiled by Elder Dai*), 141n.25
Dahlbeck, Moa De Lucia, 13n.32
D'Ambrosio, Paul J., 13n.32, 99n.2, 148n.48, 152n.64, 251n.41
dao (道, way, ways, teachings), 103, 110–12, 132, 142
   finding the pivot of all *daos*, 109–12, 122, 132
Daodejing (道德經) (*Laozi*, 老子), 24–25, 24n.7, 32n.33, 99n.1, 232n.7
Daoism, 5–6, 8–9, 99n.1, 218–19, 285–86n.15
Davenport, Carol, 181n.17

De Dijn, Herman, 58n.45, 67n.79, 165n.23
de la Barre, Poulain, 4–5
de Waal, Frans, 38n.53, 283–84nn.8–9, 284n.11
death and transformation
   Spinoza's treatment of, 191–93
   Zhuangzi's reaction to the death of his wife, 211n.14
   the *Zhuangzi*'s treatment of, 210–16
debate (*bian*, 辯), 107–8
deer, 132–33, 185, 224–25, 241–42
Defoort, Carine, 25n.10, 114n.55, 148–49n.52, 287n.1
Deleuze, Gilles, 5–6, 96n.41, 161n.12, 165, 193–94, 233n.9
Della Rocca, Michael, 85–86, 201n.46
DeMello, Margo, 1n.1
demonology, 169n.35
Denecke, Wiebke, 149–50
Derrida, Jacques, 2–3, 4n.8
Descartes, René, 4, 49–51, 53–55, 85n.10, 86n.12, 88n.16, 94n.31, 189–90n.6
Detienne, Marcel, 14n.37
Devall, Bill, 6n.14
Di Cosmo, Nicola, 241n.2
Di (狄) peoples, 146n.42, 241–42
disability
   disability studies, 239, 286n.16
   Spinoza's depictions of, 88–89, 90, 262–63
   the *Zhuangzi*'s depictions of, 253–54
disorder or chaos (*luan*, 亂), 205–6, 210n.11, 214–16, 222, 231
distant lands, descriptions of, 241–55
divine potter metaphor, 64n.68
Donovan, Josephine, 289n.5
Doyen, Paul, 283n.4
dualism, 2–5
   mind-body, 4, 16–17, 105–6n.21, 194n.19
   ontological, 8
Dutch Republic (United Provinces of the Netherlands), 46–47, 48, 49–50, 51, 53, 55, 64, 266n.16, 269–70
dutifulness or responsible conduct (*yi*, 義), 107, 133n.1, 210, 215, 217, 225–26

early Chinese texts, 287n.1, *see also specific works*
  discussions of the body politic, 207–8
  discussions of the division of labor, 26–27, 33–34, 208n.4, 216–18, 234n.12
  discussions of foreign people, 241–55
  discussions of the heart, 104–5, 107–8, 147, 206–9
  discussions of sagacious people, 147–48
  discussions of social divisions, 214–15, 216–18, 225n.66
  gender distinctions, 255–57, 260, 280
  Masters texts (*zishu*, 子書), 23–24, 33–34, 39n.59
  ming 名/*shi* 實 pairings, 139–40
  pleasure theories, 142–43, 215n.31
  Ru texts, 104, 147, 206–7, 209n.8, 215n.29, 215n.32, 234–35, 250n.38
  theories of language, 39–40
Ecology
  deep ecologists, 5–6
  deep ecology movement, 6n.14, 54n.36, 87
  ecological self, 5–6, 87
  environmental philosophy, 5–6, 99–100
  Green New Deal, 180–81
  green politics, 99–100
  queer ecology, 181–82, 183
Elements (Euclid), 60–61
elitism, 94n.30, 250–51
Eloff, Aragorn, 123n.6
Eno, Robert, 33n.36, 101n.7, 138–39n.19, 234n.12, 243n.12
environmental philosophy, 5–6, 99–100
epistemology, 56–68, 88–98, 161–67
Equalizing Joke (*Qi Xie*, 齊諧), 154–55
equine analogy, 66, 224n.63, *see also* bridling analogies
eternity of the mind, 191
Ethica (*Ethics, E*) (Spinoza), 6n.12, 16, 53–54n.31
  aversion toward broad generalizations, 121, 125. *see also* "bad" universals
  on body-mind question, 82–84
  circulation among learned men, 53
  critical reception, 54
  descriptions of common people, 267
  descriptions of women, 269, 271–74, 276–77
  eliminating the anthropomorphic God and the theomorphic man, 84–88
  on individuation and identity, 188–93, 194–98, 232–33
  ladder of complexity, 94–98
  literary approach, 58–62, 64
  on man as God to man, 203
  on refraining from slaughtering animals, 54–55
  relation to Spinoza's other works, 67n.79
  Spinoza's version of the story of the Fall, 161–67, 168, 197n.29, 201–2, 272–73
Ethiopians, 265
Euclid, 60–61
Eve: Spinoza's version of the story of the Fall, 161–67, 168, 197n.29, 201–2, 272–73
experiential gestalt, 66
experimentation, animal, 159n.7, 284n.13

fables, 32–45
Fall: Spinoza's version of the story of the, 161–67, 168, 197n.29, 201–2, 272–73
familial relations, 212n.17
Fang, Dongmei, 8n.17
Fanon, Frantz, 2n.4
fantastic divine creatures, 36
Feldt, Alex, 285–86n.15
figurative language, 61–68, 73–74. *see also* metaphors
fish
  happy, 134–38
  wandering with, 132–39
  what distinguishes people from turtles and, 112–17
flying stone: Spinoza's comparison between mankind and, 86–87, 118–20
foreign or alien peoples, 26, 36–37, 218
  Spinoza's remarks on, 262–63
  the *Zhuangzi*'s depictions of, 182, 241–55
Foucault, Michel, 90n.21, 112n.48
Francione, Gary L., 180n.15
Fraser, Chris, 23–24n.5, 107n.27, 110n.37, 144, 212n.20, 244n.14

fraternal cheer, 167–72
free will
    Spinoza's denial of, 51–54, 73, 88–93
Fried, Daniel, 39n.57
Friedman, Lisa, 181n.17
friendship, 149–55, 160–61, *see also* companionship
frontier peoples, 241–55. *see also* alien or foreign peoples

Galen, 50n.14
Galenic symptomatology, 169n.35
Galvany, Albert, 41n.61, 41n.62, 151n.61, 152n.62, 153n.66, 213n.21, 213n.22
Garber, Daniel, 50n.12
Gassendi, 53
Gatens, Moira, 8n.18, 197n.31, 275n.36, 276, 277, 289n.4
Geaney, Jane, 39nn.58–59, 139–40n.20
gender equality, 4–5, 269–70, 271, 273–74, *see also* women
Genesis, 64n.66
    Spinoza's version of the story of the Fall, 161–67, 168, 197n.29, 201–2, 272–73
genuine human beings (真人, *zhenren*), 176n.10
geometric format, 52, 60–62, 65n.71, 74–75n.15, 187
Girardot, Norman J., 218n.44
goblet speech (*zhi yan*, 卮言), 38–39, 42–43, 107n.27
God
    anthropomorphic, 84–88
    Spinoza's definition of, 82–84
Goldin, Paul R., 15n.38, 33–34, 135n.7
governance, 22, 25–26, 28n.21, 40–41, 43–44, 71, 216, 230, 249, 252–53
    absence of civil order, 231–35
    order, to put in good order, to govern (*zhi*, 治), 205–6, 214–16, 222, 231
    via non-rule, 223–24
    sagacious (*sheng zhi*, 聖治), 223–24, 224n.64, 259
Gowland, Angus, 168–69, 200n.40
Graham, A. C., 23–24n.5, 30n.28, 143n.30, 211n.13

Grandin, Temple, 284n.10
Graziani, Romain, 70, 252n.44
Great Ape Project, 124n.9
great order (*da zhi*, 大治), 205–6, 222, 223–24
Greco-European traditions, 30n.26, 71n.5, 99n.3, 181–82
Greco-Roman traditions, 3–4
Green New Deal, 180–81
green politics, 99–100
Grey, John, 95n.34, 273n.29
Grim, John, 6n.14
group identity, 14, 187, 228–31
Gruen, Lori, 3n.7, 70n.2, 122n.4
Guan Zhong (管仲), 241n.6
Guanzi (管子), 40–41, 105n.19, 256–57
Guattari, Felix, 5–6, 96n.41
Guerrini, Anita, 51n.17, 159n.7
Gullan-Whur, Margaret, 8n.19, 276
Guo Xiang (郭象), 39n.57, 43, 104n.15, 150–51, 154
Guoyu (國語, *Discourses of the States*), 241–42

Hagen, Kurtis, 215n.32
Hall, David L., 9n.22, 256n.57
Hampe, Michael, 54n.36
Han Feizi (韓非子), 24n.7, 41n.62, 220–21, 258n.65
Han Shu (漢書), 253n.49
Hanegraaff, Wouter J., 193n.15
Hansen, Chad, 110–11
Haraway, Donna, 180
Harbsmeier, Christoph, 33n.35
Harel, Naama, 37, 38n.54
heart (*xin*, 心), 44n.68, 206–9
    passages from the *Zhuangzi* on, 103–9, 142–44, 206–10
Heaven (*tian*, 天) (term), 101
    All under Heaven (*tianxia*, 天下)(term), 25–26
Hebrew Grammar (Compendium Grammatices Linguae Hebraeae) (Spinoza), 56–57, 60, 67n.79
Hermetic philosophy, 193n.15
Hippocrates, 50n.14
Hobbes, Thomas, 49n.11, 53, 89n.18, 170n.40, 201n.45

Holland, 49n.11, *see also* Dutch Republic (United Provinces of the Netherlands)
horses, 29, 36, 64, 66, 140, 224, 249nn.32–34, *see also* equine analogy, bridling analogies
Houston, R. A., 266n.16
Howell, Philip, 22n.4
Huainanzi (淮南子), 107n.25
Huang, Chun-chieh, 208n.4
Huangdi Neijing (黃帝內經, *Yellow Emperor's Classic of Internal Medicine*), 105n.19
human-animal intimacy, 168
human-animal studies (HAS), 1n.1, 26, *see also* critical animality studies
human-centered thinking
  people as the heart of Heaven and Earth, 100, 107, 112–13
  Spinoza's eliminating the anthropomorphic God and the theomorphic man, 84–88
  Spinoza's speciesism, 178–79
human companionship
  benefits of, 195n.21
  bonding through banter and laughter, 149–55
  cementing and loosening of human bonds, 173–79
  misanthropic melancholy, 167–72
human distinctiveness
  complex bodies, 92–93, 94–98
  portrayals of exceptionality, 100
  Spinoza's portrayals, 79, 81–98, 118–27, 156–61, 180–81
  "us versus them" approach, 156–57, 168, 179–84, 282–86, 288–89
  the *Zhuangzi* portrayals, 79, 81, 99–117, 118–27, 181–82
humility, 123–27
humor
  Equalizing Joke (Qi Xie, 齊諧), 154–55
  man from Song (Song ren, 宋人) trope, 245
  parody, 32, 34, 72, 247, 251n.41
  satire, 77, 116, 152, 168–70
hun hun dun dun (渾渾沌沌, muddy and murky), 221–23

Hundun, 181–82, 245n.19
  later depictions of, 218–19
  the *Zhuangzi*'s depictions of, 137–38, 216–26
Husserl, Edmund, 163n.16
Hutton, Eric L., 99n.3, 208n.5, 250n.36

identity
  group, 228–31
  micro-identities, 241n.4
  Spinoza's views on issues of, 188–98, 228–31
  the *Zhuangzi*'s views on issues of, 206–16, 228–31
imagination, 62n.60, 90–92, 96, 163–64, 282–86
immanentism, 6–7, 9–10, 82–83, 287–88, 289–90
individuation, Spinoza's theory of, 188–98
Ing, Michael David Kaulana, 106n.23, 220–21n.49
intellectual disability
  Spinoza's remarks on, 90, 262–63
  the *Zhuangzi*'s depictions of, 253–54
intersectional critiques
  of dualistic thinking, 2–5
  of oppression, 2–3
intimacy, human-animal, 168
Ip, Po-Keung, 6n.14
Irigaray, Luce, 3n.6, 12n.30
Israel, Jonathan, 7n.15, 63n.63, 195n.23, 198n.37
Italian Renaissance, 193n.15
Ivanhoe, Philip J., 257–58

Jaspers, Karl, 24n.8
Jews, 200–1n.42, 202n.48, 265–66
Jochim, Chris, 206n.1
Johnson, Mark, 40n.60
Joy, Lynn S., 49n.8
Joy, Melanie, 3n.7
joyful passions, 164–65, 171
Judeo-Islamo-Christian traditions, 3–4, 53n.23

Kabbalah, 53n.23
Karlgren, Bernhard, 218n.40
Kim, David, 5n.10

King Wen (文), 242–43
Kirkland, Russell, 8–9
Klein, Esther Sunkyung, 22n.3, 34n.38, 39n.56
Knoblock, John, 250n.35
Kongzi (孔子, Master Kong), 21–22, 33–34, 38, 70, 113–14, 133–34, 140, 141–42, 144, 148, 151, 182–83, 251, 254
Korte Verhandeling van God, de Mensch en deszelfs Welstand (Short Treatise on God, Man, and His Well-Being, KV) (Spinoza), 53–54n.31, 56–57, 60–61, 64n.68, 92n.25
kuang (狂, wild, mad) people, 247–48, 253
Kupperman, Joel J., 228–29
KV. see *Korte Verhandeling van God, de Mensch en deszelfs Welstand (Short Treatise on God, Man, and His Well-Being)* (Spinoza)

La Fontaine, 35–36
labor, division of
  early Chinese descriptions of, 26–27, 33–34, 208n.4, 216–18, 234n.12
  portrayals in the *Zhuangzi*, 218–21, 231, 234–35
  Spinoza's descriptions of, 194–96, 234–35
Lady Ju, 148n.51
Lady Li, 257–58, 260, 285
Lakoff, George, 40n.60
language. *see also* metaphors
  arbitrary nature of words, 61n.59
  early Chinese theories of, 39–40
  figurative, 61–68
Laozi (老子) (*Daodejing*, 道德經), 24–25, 24n.7, 32n.33, 99n.1, 232n.7, 285
laughter, 149–55, 169–70, 176–77
Lawlor, Leonard, 287–88
Lécrivain, André, 93n.29
Lee, Richard A., Jr., 159n.6, 169n.36, 291n.8
Leibniz, Gottfried Wilhelm, 53n.26
leisure, 202n.54, 234
Levinovitz, Alan, 148–49n.52
Lewis, Mark Edward, 24n.9, 25n.11, 33–34, 218n.41, 219–20, 242n.10

li (禮, propriety), absence of, 215–16, 241–42, 246–49, 280
Li Chenyang, 209n.8
Liezi (列子), 99n.1, 107n.25, 114n.53
Liji (禮記, *Record of Rites*), 26–27n.17, 28–29, 216–17
  gender distinctions, 256–57
  metaphors, 40–41
  portrayals of human distinctiveness, 100n.6, 107nn.25–26
  tiger imagery, 141n.25
Lincoln, Bruce, 13n.35, 15n.39
Littlejohn, Ronnie, 34n.39
Liu, Chengji, 36
Liu, Zhao, 112n.47
Lloyd, Genevieve, 8n.19, 95n.33, 96n.40, 123n.5, 181, 191–92n.13, 273–74, 275n.38, 289n.4
Locke, John, 49n.11
logic of scarcity, 17, 233–34
Lord, Beth, 273–74
Lu (魯), 245–46
luan (disorder or chaos, 亂), 205–6, 210n.11, 214–16, 222, 231
lun (論, discourse), 107–8
Lunheng (論衡, *Discursive Weighing*), 141n.25
Lunyu (論語, *Analects*), 24n.7, 33n.36, 212n.20, 215–16n.33
Lüshi Chunqiu (呂氏春秋, "The Annals of Lü Buwei"), 26–27n.17, 29n.24, 107n.26, 241–42
lycanthropy, 169n.35
Lynn, Richard John, 37n.51

Macherey, Pierre, 84n.7
Maeder, Erik W., 33–34n.37
Maimonides, 162n.14
Makeham, John, 28n.21, 39n.58, 139–40n.20
Malebranche, Nicholas, 10–11, 85n.10, 287n.1
Malinowski-Charles, Syliane, 165n.24
man from Song (Song *ren*, 宋人) trope, 245
Man (蠻) peoples, 242n.7
Marshall, Eugene, 171n.41
Marsili, Filippo, 7–8n.16

Marx, Karl, 87n.15
Masters texts (*zishu* 子書), 23–25, 33–34, 39n.59, *see also specific works*
mathematical thought, 61n.56
Mattice, Sarah A., 287n.1
Mawangdui medical texts, 134n.3
McLeod, Alexus, 7–8n.16, 244n.16, 247–48, 248n.30
mechanical metaphors, 72n.7
Meijer (Meyer), Lodewijk, 52–53, 61n.55, 61n.58
Melamed, Yitzhak Y., 4n.8, 5n.11, 8n.19, 9n.24, 53n.23, 54n.32, 83nn.4–6, 87n.15, 119n.1, 187–88n.1, 191, 197n.35, 201n.46, 266n.15
melancholy, misanthropic, 167–72, 178–79, 199–200nn.39–40
men of service (*shi*, 士), 23–24, 240, 252–53
Mengzi (孟子), 9–10, 24n.7, 26–27n.17, 44, 133–34, 147n.47, 219n.46, 234n.12, 249nn.32–33, 256n.57
  descriptions of antiquity, 216–17, 219n.46, 220–21
  descriptions of the body politic, 210n.11
  descriptions of the division of labor, 234n.12
  descriptions of familial relations, 212n.17
  descriptions of what separates human beings from animals, 217–18
  descriptions of governance, 249nn.32–33
  descriptions of the heart, 104–5, 207n.3
  descriptions of human distinctiveness, 104
  descriptions of nature, 216–17
  descriptions of *qi*, heart, and affects, 143n.30, 144n.32
  descriptions of Shun and Wen, 242–43
  descriptions of unruly people, 248–49
  "a gentleman stays away from the kitchen" (phrase), 177
metaphors
  body politic, 17, 64, 194, 206, 207–8, 218–19, 232–33, 258–59
  botanical, 40–42, 43–44, 72–73
  divine potter, 64n.68
  goblet speech (*zhi yan*, 卮言), 38–39

  mechanical, 72n.7
  Spinoza's use of, 64–65, 72–73
  for turning or pivoting, 72n.7, 109–11
  the *Zhuangzi*'s use of, 22–23, 38–40, 41–43, 44, 72–73, 109–11
metaphysics, 6–7, 54n.33
methodology
  comparative, 10–14, 69–78
  issues of methodology in Spinoza, 56–68
  issues of methodology in relation to the *Zhuangzi*, 32–45
Milburn, Olivia, 253
mimetic analysis, 12n.30
mind, eternity of, 191
ming (名, names/titles), 28n.21
ming jia (名家, School of Names), 39n.58
mirror self-recognition test, 283–84n.9
misanthropy, 267
  misanthropic melancholy in Spinoza, 167–72, 178–79, 199–200nn.39–40
  reactionary, 288–89
misogyny, 3, 8–9, 277
Mo (貉) peoples, 242
Mo-ye, 211
Moeller, Hans-Georg, 39n.58, 148n.48, 152n.64, 153n.67, 251n.41
Mohism, 23–24n.5, 39n.58, 215n.32, 219n.46, 221–22. *see also Mozi* (墨子)
monism, 5–10, 11–12, 92–93, 190n.8, 287–88, 289–90
monkeys, 36n.44, 132–33, 139–40, 290n.6
More, Henry, 49–50
Moreau, Pierre François, 194n.17
Morgan, Michael L., 61n.58
Morocco, 61n.59
Morton, Timothy, 183
Moses, 53n.24
Mozi (墨子), 24n.7, 26–27n.17, 28–29, 219n.46, *see also* Mohism
  on the ancient past as disorderly, 216–17
  on the body politic, 210n.11
  on death and transformation, 215–16n.33
  descriptions of frontier peoples, 243–44
  on familial relations, 212n.17
  on human distinctiveness, 109n.34
  markers of sagacity, 147n.47

muddy and murky (*hun hun dun dun,* 渾渾沌沌), 221–23
Munro, Donald J., 27n.20, 215n.29, 256n.57
music
    animals responding to, 31n.30
    in the *Zhuangzi,* 146n.43, 151n.61
Muslims, 202n.48, 264–66
mutilated people, 253, 254

Nadler, Steven, 46n.1, 171n.42
Naess, Arne, 11n.29, 87n.15
Nagel, Thomas, 38n.53, 284n.11
names/titles (*ming,* 名), 28n.21
natural philosophy, 46–47, 48–49
naturalism, 215n.32
nature, 99–100
    ancient Chinese attitudes toward, 12
    harmony with, 12
    Spinoza's equation of God with Nature, 82–84
necessitarianism, 86
Nelson, Eric Sean, 119n.1, 123n.7
Neo-Confucianism, 10–11
neurotypicalism, 284n.10
non-dualistic thinking, 9n.22
Nussbaum, Martha C., 70n.2, 75n.17, 116n.64
Nylan, Michael, 13n.35, 14n.37, 24n.9, 28n.21, 31n.30, 110n.38, 150–51n.58, 215n.31, 241, 256n.56

objectionable masters, 114n.55
occupations, 241–55
Olberding, Amy, 211n.12
Oldenburg, Henry, 94
Oliver, Kelly, 182
ontology
    Spinoza's, 82–84, 188–98, 228–31
    in the *Zhuangzi,* 101–3, 210–16, 228–31
oppression, 2–7, 18, 141n.25, 264–65, 271
order and disorder, 185–235
    absence of civil order, 231–35
    chaos (*luan,* 亂), 205–6, 210n.11, 214–16, 222, 231
    civil order, 187–204
    governance and order (*zhi,* 治), 205–6, 214–16, 222, 231
    great order (*da zhi,* 大治), 205–6, 222, 223–24
    individuation and identity in an orderly world, 188–93
    muddy and murky (*hun hun dun dun,* 渾渾沌沌), 221–23
    sagely order (*sheng zhi,* 聖治), 223–24, 259
others
    animalized, 241–55, 262–78
    Spinoza's remarks on foreign peoples, 263–68
    "us versus them" approach, 156–57, 168, 179–84, 282–86, 288–89
    the *Zhuangzi's* descriptions of foreign peoples, 241–55
Ottomans, 264–66
Outspread the Disjointed (Zhili Shu zhe, 支離疏者) character, 253–54
Ovid, 164n.20
Özbey, Sonya, 27n.20, 182n.20, 206n.1, 212n.16, 241n.2

pagans, 202n.48, 265–66
Pang Pu, 105n.20
panpsychism, 54
Park, So Jeong, 146n.43
Parkes, Graham, 13n.32
parody, 32, 34, 72, 247, 251n.41
Perkins, Franklin, 9n.23, 44, 99n.2, 101–2, 104n.15, 112–13, 138–39n.19, 143n.29, 144n.34, 150n.55, 182–83, 232n.7
person (*shen,* 身), 206n.1
personhood, 27, 30–31, 205, 206, 212–14, 227, 228, 261
petty people (*xiao ren,* 小人), 248–49
philosophy, 287n.1, *see also specific works*
    Asian, 5–7
    Chinese. *see* Chinese philosophy
    comparative, 5n.10, 10–14, 69–78
    cross-cultural, 1–18
    environmental, 5–6, 99–100
    "Monistic," 5–10
    non-canonical, 287–88
    seeking true philosophy in Spinoza, 56–68, 76n.19
physical disability, 253–54

Pines, Yuri, 26n.13, 243n.13, 244n.16, 250n.38
plants. *see also* trees
  botanical metaphors, 40–42, 43–44, 72–73
  references in the *Zhuangzi*, 36
Plato, 66n.74
  Platonic dialogues, 32–33
  Platonic philosophy, 269–70n.21
pleasure, 133
  early Chinese pleasure theories, 142–43, 215n.31
  likes and dislikes, 16–17, 29n.25, 35–36, 131–32, 134, 137, 139, 142–44, 157, 175
  localized, 167n.29
  mundane, 180
  pleasures and pains, 136–37, 140, 142–44, 283–84
Principles. see Renati Descartes principia philosophiae (The Principles of René Descartes's Philosophy) (Spinoza)
Principles of Philosophy (Descartes), 189–90n.6
professions, 48–49, 241–55, 285–86
propriety (*li*, 禮), absence of, 215–16, 241–42, 246–49, 280
Puett, Michael J., 100n.6, 257n.61

qi (氣), 142–44, 145–46
Qin (秦), polity of, 241n.4, 243
Qin Shi Huang, 141n.25
qin shou (禽獸, birds and wild animals), 28–29, 36
Que Gu Shi Qi (卻穀食氣), 134n.3
queer ecology, 181–82, 183
quietism, 71n.5

Raphals, Lisa, 105n.19, 256–57, 256nn.56–57
Rapp, John A., 285–86n.15
"reality hurts" (phrase), 165n.22
Record of Rites, see Liji (禮記)
ren (人, human being or person), 27–28, 30–31, 175–76, 256n.57
ren (仁, humaneness, humane), 220, 222–23, 225–26
ren yi (仁義, humaneness and dutifulness), 133n.1, 137n.14, 244

Renati Descartes principia philosophiae (The Principles of René Descartes' Philosophy, Principles) (Spinoza), 52, 57n.43, 60–62, 67n.79, 79
resourcism, anthropocentric, 12n.31
Rice, Lee, 195n.22
Riskin, Jessica, 50–51, 85n.11
rites and rituals, 147n.46, *see also li* (禮, propriety)
Rivet, André, 269–70
Robber Zhi, 148n.51
Robins, Dan, 30n.28, 111n.42, 114n.56
Rong (戎) peoples, 146n.42, 241–42, 257–58
Rorty, Amélie Oksenberg, 58, 165n.22
Rossello, Diego, 169n.35
Roy, Arundhati, 286n.18
Ru texts, 234–35. *see also specific texts*
  descriptions of the heart, 104–5, 107nn.25–26, 147, 206–7, 208nn.4–5
  descriptions of human distinctiveness, 104
  descriptions of peoples of frontier regions, 242–44
  as pluralistic, 209n.8
Russell, Bertrand, 49n.11, 287n.1

sad passion(s), 89n.20, 164–65, 166–67, 169, 171, 180, 199–200, 267–68
  excess of, 274, 281
  Spinoza's association of women with, 6n.13, 274, 280–81
sagacious people (*shengren*, 聖人), 147–48
Sagart, Laurent, 135n.7
sagely order (*sheng zhi*, 聖治), 223–24, 259
salvation, 79, 203
  secular, 191n.12
  seeking, 48–68, 73–74, 170–71, 267
satire, 77, 116, 152, 168–70
Sato, Masayuki, 215–16n.33
Savan, David, 62n.60
scarcity, logic of, 17, 233–34
scars of penal mutilation, people with, 253–54
Schäfer, Dagmar, 145–46
Scharfstein, Ben-Ami, 15n.38
Schmaltz, Tad M., 4–5, 50nn.12–13, 51nn.18–19

Schneider, Daniel, 59n.49
Scholasticism, 49–51, 85
School of Names (*ming jia*, 名家), 39n.58
Schopenhauer, Arthur, 152n.64
Schumm, Darla Y., 253n.46
scientific revolution, 48
Scruton, Roger, 46n.1
self-hatred, 156–57, 168–69
selfhood
  ecological self, 5–6, 87
  Spinoza's views on issues of, 228–31
Seneca, 271
Sessions, George, 6n.14, 11n.29
Shan hai jing (山海經, *The Classic of Mountains and Seas*), 230n.5
Shang shu (尚書, *Ancient Documents*), 218n.40
Shapin, Steven, 47n.4, 49n.6
Sharp, Hasana, 8n.19, 84n.7, 94n.30, 97, 162n.14, 164n.20, 168nn.31–32, 169n.36, 180n.16, 200n.41, 276, 277n.44, 281n.2
Shaviro, Steven, 54n.36
sheep, 51n.16, 61n.59, 224
shen (身, body, person), 206n.1
shen wu (神巫, spirit ritualists), 257
sheng zhi (聖治, sagely order, sagely governance, sagacious governance), 223–24, 259
shengren (聖人, sagacious people), 147–48
shi (士, men of service, petty aristocrats), 23–24, 240, 252–53
Shirley, Samuel, 63n.63, 266n.15
Shun (舜), 30–31n.29, 242–43, 251n.39
Siebert, Martina, 145–46
Silverthorne, Michael, 63n.63, 195n.23, 198n.37
Slingerland, Edward, 104n.18
Smith, Steven B., 94n.30
social bonds
  bonding through banter and laughter, 149–55
  cementing and loosening of human bonds, 173–79
  power to include and exclude, 179–84
social difference(s), 239–61, 262–78, 279–86

social divisions
  early Chinese descriptions of, 26–27, 207–8, 210, 214–15, 216–18, 219n.46
  portrayals in the *Zhuangzi*, 218–21, 225–26, 231, 234–35, 241–55
Soldatenko, Gabriel, 5n.10
solidarity, 173–84
  human solidarity, 17, 97, 125–27, 131, 156, 170
Solnit, Rebecca, 234n.10
Song *ren* (宋人, man from Song) trope, 245
soul, animal, 85
Spinoza, Benedict de
  animal affects, 129, 156–72, 173–84
  anthropocentrism, 8–9, 157–61
  atheism, 10–12, 53n.23, 54n.32, 83n.4
  audience, 56–68, 89–90
  aversion toward broad generalizations, 121. *see also* "bad" universals
  comparison between mankind and Buridan's ass, 88–93, 118–20
  comparison between mankind and a flying stone, 86–87, 118–20
  comparison between mankind and a worm in the blood, 94–98, 118–20
  comparison with the *Zhuangzi*, 1–18, 69–78, 118–27, 173–84, 227–35, 279–86
  Compendium Grammatices Linguae Hebraeae (Hebrew Grammar), 56–57, 60, 67n.79
  conflation of Brazilians and Ethiopians, 265
  denial of free will, 51–54, 73, 88–93
  elimination of the anthropomorphic God and the theomorphic man, 84–88
  epistemological views, 56–68, 88–98, 161–67
  Ethica (*Ethics, E*), 6n.12, 16, 53–55, 56–62, 64, 67n.79, 73n.9, 81, 82–98, 121, 125, 129, 157–67, 188–93, 195–200, 203, 232–33, 262, 267, 269, 271–74, 276–77
  figurative language, 61–68, 73–74
  geometric format, 60–62, 65n.71, 74–75n.15, 187
  Hebrew name, 5n.11

Spinoza, Benedict de (*cont.*)
  "Imagination," 62n.60, 90–92, 96, 163–64, 276–78, 282–86
  immanentism, 9–10, 82–83
  Korte Verhandeling van God, de Mensch en deszelfs Welstand (Short Treatise on God, Man, and His Well-Being, KV), 53–54n.31, 56–57, 60–61, 92n.25
  The Letters (Epistolae, Ep), 53nn.28–30, 57n.43, 59, 62n.60, 64n.68, 86–87, 90n.22, 92–93, 92n.26, 94, 96n.39, 199, 264n.8, 265, 272
  literary approach, 56–68
  metaphors, 64–65, 72–73
  methodology, 56–68
  misanthropy, 167–72, 178–79, 199–200nn.39–40, 267, 281, 288–89
  monism, 9–10, 11–12, 92–93, 190n.8, 289–90
  necessitarianism, 86
  ontology, 82–84, 188–98, 228–31
  portrayal of human distinctiveness, 79, 81–98, 118–27
  remarks on cementing and loosening of human bonds, 178–79
  remarks on common people, 263–68
  remarks on division of labor, 66, 194–96, 234–35
  remarks on foreign peoples, 263–68
  remarks on intellectual disability, 90, 262–63
  remarks on making use of beasts as we please, 157–58
  remarks on personhood and identity, 188–98, 228–31
  remarks on the power to include and exclude, 179–84
  remarks on Turks, 202, 262, 263–68
  remarks on women, 6n.13, 8–9, 47n.4, 62n.62, 65n.72, 161–62, 262–63, 268–78, 279, 280–81
  Renati Descartes principia philosophiae (The Principles of René Descartes' Philosophy, Principles), 52, 57n.43, 60–62, 67n.79, 79
  story of the Fall, 161–67, 168, 197n.29, 201–2, 272–73
  theory of affects, 188–89, 196–97, 199
  theory of the eternity of the mind, 191
  theory of individuation, 188–98, 232–33
  Tractatus de Intellectus Emendatione (Treatise on the Emendation of the Intellect, TIE), 46, 56–59, 60–61, 64–65, 67n.79, 74–75, 92n.25, 125, 171, 190n.10
  Tractatus Politicus (TP), 56–57, 60–62, 65, 67n.79, 166n.28, 194–96, 198, 200–1, 203, 231–32, 233–34, 262–65, 267–69, 271–74, 276
  Tractatus Theologico-Politicus (Theological-Political Treatise, TTP), 52–53, 55–57, 60–65, 67n.79, 84–85, 166n.28, 169n.37, 185, 187–88n.1, 195–96, 199–200, 200–1n.42, 201–2, 231–32, 237, 263–66, 267–68, 274
  "us versus them" distinction, 156–57, 168, 179–84, 283, 288–89
spirit ritualists (*shen wu*, 神巫), 257
Spivak, Gayatri Chakravorty, 286n.16
staged conversations, 32–45, 60–61
staged reflection, 58
Stalnaker, Aaron, 13n.35, 14n.36, 148
Steenbakkers, Piet, 53n.26, 53–54n.31, 55n.39, 61nn.55–56
Steinberg, Justin, 63n.63, 67n.79, 76–77, 197–98
Sterckx, Roel, 30nn.26–27, 31n.30, 107n.25, 114n.54, 137–38, 145–46, 245n.21, 249n.32
stewardship, Christian, 158
Stewart, Susan, 176n.9
Stoltzfus, Michael J., 253n.46
stone, flying: Spinoza's comparison between mankind and, 86–87, 118–20
storytelling, 16, 70, 116, 182, 285–86
Strassberg, Richard E., 230n.5
Stuurman, Siep, 269–70, 271n.23
Sunzi Bingfa (孫子兵法), 105n.19
superstition, 55, 66n.75, 74–75n.15, 129, 157, 171, 192–93, 202–3, 229–30, 272, 274–75

Taylor, Alfred E., 191–92n.13
Taylor, Sunaura, 283n.7, 286n.16

teleology, 84–85
theocracy, Jewish, 200–1n.42
theology, Christian, 9n.22
theomorphic man, 84–88
Thiel, Udo, 232n.8
Thirty Years War, 48
TIE. *see* Tractatus de Intellectus Emendatione *(Treatise on the Emendation of the Intellect)* (Spinoza)
tiger imagery, 28–29, 36n.46, 140–41, 248–49
titillation, 167n.29
Todorov, Tzvetan, 75n.16
Toeless of Uncle Mountain (Shushan Wuzhi, 叔山無趾) character, 254
TP. *see* Tractatus Politicus *(TP)* (Spinoza)
Tractatus de Intellectus Emendatione (Treatise on the Emendation of the Intellect, TIE) (Spinoza), 46, 56–59, 60–62, 64–65, 67n.79, 74–75, 92n.25, 190n.10
  on salvation, 171
  staged reflection, 58
  tool-making analogies, 58n.47, 64n.68, 125
Tractatus Politicus (TP) (Spinoza), 56–57, 60–62, 65, 67n.79, 166n.28
  definition of the best state, 264
  definition of civil order, 203
  descriptions of the body politic, 194–95, 196, 198
  descriptions of common people, 267
  descriptions of mankind, 200–1, 233–34, 262
  descriptions of the state of nature, 195–96, 203n.57, 231–32
  descriptions of Turks, 264–65
  descriptions of women, 268–69, 271–74, 276
  list of civil orders, 203n.56
Tractatus Theologico-Politicus (Theological-Political Treatise, TTP) (Spinoza), 52–53, 55–57, 60–65, 67n.79, 84–85, 166n.28, 185
  animal imagery, 263–64
  descriptions of common people, 266, 267–68

  descriptions of good and bad polities, 201–2, 264
  descriptions of Jewish theocracy, 200–1n.42
  descriptions of misanthropic melancholy, 169n.37
  descriptions of the state of nature, 195–96, 231–32
  descriptions of Turks, 202, 264–66
  descriptions of women, 274
  metaphysical dimension, 187–88n.1
trees
  comparisons between humans and, 118–20
  imagery of, 41–42, 182, 189n.5, 220–21, 254n.51
  useless, 224n.64
TTP. see Tractatus Theologico-Politicus (Theological-Political Treatise) (Spinoza)
Tuck, Richard, 49n.6, 53, 266n.16
Tucker, Mary Evelyn, 6n.14
Turks, 202, 262, 263–68
turtles and fish, what distinguishes people from, 112–17

United Provinces of the Netherlands (Dutch Republic), 46–47, 48, 49–50, 51, 53, 55, 64, 266n.16, 269–70
universals, "bad," 91, 160n.11, 195n.20
"us versus them" approach, 156–57, 168, 179–84, 282–86, 288–89

Valmisa, Mercedes, 113n.50
van Bunge, Wiep, 53–54n.31
van den Broek, Roelof, 193n.15
van Schurman, Anna Maria, 269–70
Vassányi, Miklós, 54n.35
Virág, Curie, 174n.1

Wang, Youru, 71n.5
Wang Bo, 34n.40
Wang Yinzhi, 250n.35
Warring States (Zhanguo, 戰國) era, 22, 23, 142n.27, 216, 241, 253
Watson, Burton, 211n.13
way *(dao,* 道), 103, 110–12, 132, 142
  finding the pivot of all *daos*, 109–12, 122, 132

Weil, Kari, 2n.2, 124n.8, 183
Weishu tongkao (偽書通考) *(Comprehensive Investigation of Forged Writings)*, 33n.36
Weitzenfeld, Adam, 3n.7
weltseele (world-soul) theories, 54
Weststeijn, Thijs, 11n.26
Wetlesen, Jon, 94n.30
White, Lynn, 4n.8
Willett, Cynthia, 154n.70, 235n.13
Williams, Bernard, 99–100
Wilson, Margaret D., 8n.19, 95–96, 160, 166n.27
Wilson, Trenton, 110n.38
Winkelman, Michael James, 257n.61
"wolf-child" phenomenon, 163–64
Wolfe, Cary, 3n.7, 124n.9, 283n.3
Wolloch, Nathaniel, 85n.10
women
　Amazons, 270–71
　authors in early modern Europe, 269–70
　in early Chinese texts, 255–57, 260, 280
　misogyny, 3, 8–9, 277
　Spinoza's remarks on, 6n.13, 8–9, 47n.4, 62n.62, 65n.72, 161–62, 262–63, 268–78
　Spinoza's version of the story of the Fall, 161–67, 168, 197n.29, 201–2, 272–73
　Xunzi's advice for wives, 280n.1
　the *Zhuangzi*'s depictions of, 211n.14, 255–61, 279, 280–81, 285
world-soul *(weltseele)* theories, 54
worm in the blood, 94–98, 118–20, 157n.1
Wuxing (五行, *Five Forms of Conduct*), 104–5

xian (仙), 134n.4
xiao ren (小人, petty people), 248–49
xin (心, heart), 44n.68
　in early Chinese texts, 104–5, 107, 206–9
　passages from the *Zhuangzi* (莊子) on, 103–9, 142–44, 206–10
Xing Zi Ming Chu (性自命出, *Inborn Inclinations Derive from [Heavenly] Decree)*, 105n.19, 112n.47, 143nn.29–30

Xunzi (荀子), 24n.7, 26–27n.17, 28–30, 32n.33, 133n.1
　advice for wives, 280n.1
　descriptions of antiquity, 220–21
　descriptions of the body politic, 208nn.4–5
　descriptions of death and transformation, 212
　descriptions of familial relations, 212n.17
　descriptions of foreign peoples, 242, 250
　descriptions of the heart (*xin*, 心), 104–5, 106–7
　descriptions of human distinctiveness, 100n.6
　descriptions of occupations, 249–50
　descriptions of people frightened by their government, 249n.32
　descriptions of petty people, 248–49
　descriptions of what separates human beings from animals, 216–17
　descriptions of gender distinctions, 256–57, 256n.57
　tiger imagery, 141n.25

Yan Hui (顏回), 21, 141–44, 148
Yao (堯), 221–22, 251n.39
Yearley, Lee H., 14n.36, 71n.4, 140n.21
yi (義, dutifulness, responsible conduct), 107, 133n.1, 210, 215, 217, 225–26
Yi (夷) peoples, 242, 242n.7
Young, Iris Marion, 3n.7
Yovel, Yirmiyahu, 92n.27, 191n.12
Yue (越) peoples
　Bai Yue (百越, numerous Yue), 245n.20
　descriptions of, 35n.43, 237, 242, 244–48, 250, 252–53

Zhang Qianfan, 100n.5
Zhang Xincheng (張心澂), 33n.36
Zhanguo (戰國, Warring States) era, 22, 23, 142n.27, 216, 241n.4, 253
zhi (治, governance and order, to put in good order), 205–6, 214–16, 222, 231
zhi yan (卮言, goblet speech), 38–39, 42–43, 107n.27
Zhou (周) era, 243, 253, 255–56

INDEX   323

Zhuangzi (莊子)
  animal affects, 129, 131–55, 173–84
  audience, 23–24, 240, 252–53, 255, 260–61, 291
  aversion toward broad generalizations, 115, 121
  comparison with Spinoza, 1–18, 69–78, 118–27, 173–84, 227–35, 279–86
  critique of normative discourses, 31, 36–37, 109n.32, 111–12, 111n.42, 116, 137–38, 173–74, 210, 211–13, 214–16, 220–22, 231, 234, 247–49, 252–53, 254, 285, 290
  Da sheng (達生, "Grasping Vitality") chapter, 113
  Da zong shi (大宗師, "The Great Source as Teacher") chapter, 21–22, 111–12, 116n.63, 126, 151–52, 176n.10
  De chong fu (德充符, "The Signs of Fullness of Potency") chapter, 182–83, 254n.54
  depictions of antiquity, 216–26, 231–35
  depictions of death and transformation, 210–16
  depictions of foreign peoples, humble professions, disability, and madness, 182, 241–55
  depictions of women, 255–61, 279, 280–81, 285–86
  discussions of governance and orderliness (*zhi*, 治), 205–6, 214–16, 222, 231
  discussions of music, 146n.43
  discussions of personhood and group identity, 206–10, 227
  discussions of social divisions, 218–21, 225–26, 231, 234–35, 241–55
  disfigured characters, 253–54
  on finding the pivot of all *dao*s, 109–12, 122, 132
  Gengsang Chu (庚桑楚) chapter, 221n.53
  "happy fish" passage, 134–38
  Keyi (刻意, "The Graven Intentions") chapter, 144n.31
  Mati (馬蹄, "Horse Hooves") chapter, 109n.32, 220–21, 224n.63, 249n.34
  metaphors, 22–23, 38–40, 41–43, 44, 72–73, 109–11
  Outspread the Disjointed (Zhili Shuzhe, 支離疏者) character, 253–54
  passages on the heart (*xin*, 心), 103–9, 142–44, 206–10
  passages that compare the tastes and preferences of humans and animals, 132–39
  Qi wu lun (齊物論, "The Discourse that Levels Things") chapter, 120n.2, 143n.30, 222n.57, 229n.4
  Qiu Shui (秋水, "Autumn Waters") chapter, 101n.8, 109n.33
  Qu qie (胠篋, "Breaking into trunks") chapter, 221n.54
  Rang wang (讓王, "Yielding Sovereignty") chapter, 152n.65
  references to aquatic life, 36, 37–38
  references to birds, 36, 134, 150–51n.58, 182, 220, 231, 234–35, 247
  references to deer, 132–33, 185, 224–25
  references to fabulous animals, 31n.30, 36
  references to fish, 112–17, 132–39
  references to horses, 140, 249n.34
  references to insects, 36
  references to land animals, 36
  references to monkeys, 36n.44, 132–33, 139–40, 290n.6
  references to plants, 36
  references to tigers, 36n.46, 140–41
  references to trees, 41–42, 118–20, 182, 224n.64, 254n.51
  Ren jian shi (人間世, "In the Human World") chapter, 102, 110n.38, 140–41
  Shan xing (繕性, "Repairing the inborn nature") chapter, 221n.53
  stories, fables, anecdotes, staged conversations, 32–45
  story of Hundun, 137–38, 216–26
  Tian dao (天道, "Heavenly way") chapter, 116n.62, 220–21n.49, 225–26nn.68–69
  Tian Zifang (田子方) chapter, 176n.6, 223n.61
  Tiandi (天地, "Heaven and Earth") chapter, 220–21n.49, 223n.60, 224
  Tianxia (天下, "All under Heaven") chapter, 71n.5, 111n.41

Zhuangzi (莊子) (cont.)
   Tianyun (天運, "The turning of the Heavens") chapter, 116n.62, 225–26n.69
   Toeless of Uncle Mountain (Shushan Wuzhi, 叔山無趾) character, 254
   Wai Wu (外物, "External Things") chapter, 36n.44, 229n.4
   Xu wugui (徐無鬼, "Ghostless Xu") chapter, 150
   Yu Yan (寓言, "Imputed Words" or "Lodging Place Speech") chapter, 34n.41
   Zai you (在宥, "Being There and Giving Room") chapter, 111n.41, 220–21n.49, 221nn.53–54, 225–26n.69
Zhi bei you (知北游, "Knowing that Wanders in the North") chapter, 142n.28
Zhi le (至樂, "Utmost Joy") chapter, 133–34
Ziporyn, Brook, 7–8n.16, 27, 110n.37, 116n.63, 129n.1, 135–36n.8, 136n.10, 140n.23, 154n.71, 209n.7, 211n.13, 213n.21, 213n.22, 221n.50, 224n.62
zishu (子書, Masters texts), 23–24, 33–34, 39n.59, *see also specific works*
Zuo Zhuan. see Chunqiu Zuozhuan